FEB 1 8 2022

W9-ADU-463

the nineties

Also by CHUCK KLOSTERMAN

Fiction

Downtown Owl

The Visible Man

Raised in Captivity

Nonfiction

Fargo Rock City:
A Heavy Metal Odyssey in Rural North Dakota

Sex, Drugs, and Cocoa Puffs:
A Low Culture Manifesto

Killing Yourself to Live:
85% of a True Story

Chuck Klosterman IV:
A Decade of Curious People and Dangerous Ideas

Eating the Dinosaur

I Wear the Black Hat:
Grappling with Villains (Real and Imagined)

But What If We're Wrong?
Thinking about the Present As If It Were the Past

Chuck Klosterman X:
A Highly Specific, Defiantly Incomplete History
of the Early 21st Century

the nineties

CHUCK KLOSTERMAN

Penguin Press
New York
2022

Glenview Public Library
1930 Glenview Road
Glenview, Illinois 60025

PENGUIN PRESS
An imprint of Penguin Random House LLC
penguinrandomhouse.com

Copyright © 2022 by Charles Klosterman
Penguin supports copyright. Copyright fuels creativity, encourages diverse
voices, promotes free speech, and creates a vibrant culture. Thank you for buying an authorized edition of this book and for complying with copyright laws by
not reproducing, scanning, or distributing any part of it in any form without
permission. You are supporting writers and allowing Penguin to continue to
publish books for every reader.

"The Modern Things"
Words and Music by Björk Guðmundsdóttir and Graham Massey.
Copyright © 1995 by Jora Ehf and Universal Music Publishing Ltd.
All Rights for Jora Ehf Administered by Kobalt Songs Music Publishing.
All Rights for Universal Music Publishing Ltd. in the United States and Canada
Administered by Universal - PolyGram International Publishing, Inc.
All Rights Reserved. Used by Permission.
Reprinted by Permission of Hal Leonard LLC.

LIBRARY OF CONGRESS CATALOGING-IN-PUBLICATION DATA

Names: Klosterman, Chuck, 1972– author.
Title: The nineties : a book / Chuck Klosterman.
Other titles: 90's
Description: New York : Penguin Press, 2022. | Includes bibliographical
    references and index.
Identifiers: LCCN 2021014971 (print) | LCCN 2021014972 (ebook) |
    ISBN 9780735217959 (hardcover) | ISBN 9780735217973 (ebook)
Subjects: LCSH: Popular culture—United States—History—20th century. |
    United States—Civilization—1970– | United States—Social life and
    customs—1971– | United States—Intellectual life—20th century.
Classification: LCC E169.12 .K556 2022 (print) | LCC E169.12 (ebook) |
    DDC 306.0973/09049—dc23
LC record available at https://lccn.loc.gov/2021014971
LC ebook record available at https://lccn.loc.gov/2021014972

Printed in the United States of America
1st Printing

Book design by Daniel Lagin

For Melissa, Silas, and Hope,
and in memory of
Jimmy Meiers (1989–2020) and J. Thomas Kidd (1953–2020)

All the modern things

Like cars and such

Have always existed

They've just been waiting in a mountain

For the right moment

—Björk, "The Modern Things" (1995)

Contents

the nineties

THE NINETIES BEGAN ON JANUARY 1 OF 1990, EXCEPT FOR THE FACT THAT of course they did not. Decades are about cultural perception, and culture can't read a clock. The 1950s started in the 1940s. The sixties began when John Kennedy demanded we go to the moon in '62 and ended with the shootings at Kent State in May of 1970. The seventies were conceived the morning after Altamont in 1969 and expired during the opening credits of *American Gigolo*, which means there were five months when the sixties and the seventies were happening at the same time. It felt like the eighties might live forever when the Berlin Wall fell in November of '89, but that was actually the onset of the euthanasia (though it took another two years for the patient to die).

When writing about recent history, the inclination is to claim whatever we think about the past is secretly backward. "Most Americans regard the Seventies as an eminently forgettable decade," historian Bruce J. Schulman writes in his book *The Seventies*. "This impression could hardly be more wrong." In the opening sentence of *The Fifties*, journalist David Halberstam notes how the 1950s are inevitably recalled as a series of black-and-white photographs, in contrast to how the sixties were captured as moving images in living color. This, he argued, perpetuates the illusionary memory of the fifties being "slower, almost languid." There's always a disconnect between the world we seem to remember and the world that actually was. What's complicated about the 1990s is that the central illusion is memory itself.

The boilerplate portrait of the American nineties makes the whole era look like a low-risk grunge cartoon. That portrait is imperfect. It is not, however, wildly incorrect. The decade was heavily mediated and assertively self-conscious, but not skewed and misshapen by the internet and social media. Its trajectory can be traced with accuracy. Almost every meaningful moment of the nineties was captured on videotape, along with thousands upon thousands of trivial moments that meant nothing at all. The record is relatively complete. But that deluge of data remained, at the time, ephemeral and unavailable. It was still a present-tense existence. For much of the decade, *Seinfeld* was the most popular, most transformative live-action show on television. It altered the language and shifted comedic sensibilities, and almost every random episode was witnessed by more people than the 2019 finale of *Game of Thrones*. Yet if you missed an episode of *Seinfeld*, you simply missed it. You had to wait until it was re-aired the following summer, when you could try to manually record it on VHS videotape. If you missed it again, the only option was to go to a public archive in Los Angeles or Manhattan and request a special viewing on eight-millimeter videotape. But of course, this limitation was not something people worried about, because caring that much about any TV show was not a normal thing to do. And even if you did, you would pretend you did not, because this was the nineties. You would be more likely to claim that you didn't own a television.

That, more than any person or event, informed the experience of nineties life: an adversarial relationship with the unseemliness of trying too hard. Every generation melodramatically assumes it will somehow be the last, and there was some of that in the nineties, too—but not as much as in the decade that came before and far less than in the decades that would come after. It was perhaps the last period in American history when personal and political engagement was still viewed as optional. Many of the polarizing issues that dominate contemporary discourse were already in play, but ensconced as thought experiments in academic circles. It was, in retrospect, a remarkably easy time to be alive. There were still nuclear weapons, but there was not going to be a nuclear war. The internet was coming, but reluctantly, and there was no reason to believe it would be anything but awesome. The United States experienced a prolonged period of economic growth without the protracted complications of a hot or cold war, making it possible to focus on one's own subsistence as if the rest of society were barely there. Concerns and anxieties were omnipresent, but the stakes were vague: Teenagers were allegedly obsessed with *angst*, and the explanation as to why was pondered constantly without any sufficient answer. It didn't even seem like those asking the question particularly cared what the explanation was, or at least not until twelve kids were massacred by their classmates at a Colorado high school in 1999. But by then it was too late, and the question seemed less important than the problem, and the problem had just become what was now considered normal.

It's impossible to claim that all people living through a period of history incontrovertibly share any qualities across the board. It's also difficult to dissect a decade that was still operating as a monoculture without habitually dwelling on the details of dominance (when I write "it was a remarkably easy time to be alive," I only refer to those for whom it was, and for whom it usually is). Nothing can ever be everything to everyone. But it's hard to exaggerate the pervasion of self-constructed, self-aware apathy that would come to delineate the caricature of a time period that already feels forgotten, mostly because those who embodied it would feel embarrassed to insist it was important. The fashions of the 1980s did not gradually fade. The fashions of the 1980s collapsed, and—almost immediately—the zeitgeist they'd elevated appeared garish and gross. There was a longing for the 1970s, but not in the way people of the seventies had longed for the fifties. It was not nostalgia for a time that was more wholesome. It was nostalgia for a time when you could relax and care less. In the nineties, doing nothing on purpose was a valid option, and a specific brand of cool became more important than

3

almost anything else. The key to that coolness was disinterest in conventional success. The nineties were not an age for the aspirant. The worst thing you could be was a sellout, and not because selling out involved money. Selling out meant you needed to be popular, and any explicit desire for approval was enough to prove you were terrible.

The paradox is that the indoctrination of these attitudes had little impact on how the decade actually unspooled. The nineties ethos was deeply internalized but sporadically applied. The number of midlevel celebrities increased, as did the public appetite for personality-driven news. Unemployment peaked in '92 but decreased thereafter. The economy boomed, much more than it had during the wealth-obsessed administration of Ronald Reagan. Banking deregulations untethered the financial superstructure from frugal orthodoxy, most notably the 1999 repeal of legislation separating commercial banking from investment banking. Income disparity enlarged. Many of the goals now associated with the eighties did not really come into fruition until the nineties. Despite an overabundance of historical information, the collective memory of the decade tends to be simplified and minimized, dictated more by the texture of the time than by anything that transpired.

And yet: The texture is what mattered. The *feeling* of the era, and what that feeling supposedly signified, isolates the nineties from both its distant past and its immediate future. It was a period of ambivalence, defined by an overwhelming assumption that life, and particularly American life, was underwhelming. That was the thinking at the time.

It is not the thinking now.

Now the 1990s seem like a period when the world was starting to go crazy, but not so crazy that it was unmanageable or irreparable. It was the end of the twentieth century, but also the end to an age when we controlled technology more than technology controlled us. People played by the old rules, despite a growing recognition that those rules were flawed. It was a good time that happened long ago, although not nearly as long ago as it seems.

1 Fighting the Battle of Who Could Care Less

SOUTH AFRICAN REVOLUTIONARY NELSON MANDELA WAS ARRESTED AND imprisoned in 1962, ostensibly for compelling workers to strike and violating minor South African travel laws. This is both true and false, since no one really believes anyone was legitimately sentenced to twenty-eight years in prison for impersonating a chauffeur. Mandela's true crime was a desire for a classless society, punctuated by his tireless, multipronged advocacy for the end of South African apartheid, the institutionalized racial oppression that was South African law for over forty years. Negotiations to lift apartheid began in the spring of 1990, roughly three months after Mandela's personal liberation from prison on February 11. His release was broadcast live on worldwide television, and he delivered a speech to more than 100,000 people in a Johannesburg soccer stadium two days later. Mandela was awarded the Nobel Peace Prize in 1993; the year after that, he was named South Africa's first Black president, a position he held for five years. This transformation, for much of the planet, continues to be viewed as the most momentous global event of the nineties. It means less, however, to the sizable number of North American bozos who remain certain that Mandela died in prison during the 1980s.

The erroneous belief that Mandela died in the eighties (as opposed to

December of 2013, the month of his actual demise) has spawned an entire category of conspiracy theory now known as the Mandela Effect. First named by paranormal researcher Fiona Broome in 2009, the Mandela Effect is a collective delusion in which large swaths of the populace misremember a catalog of indiscriminate memories in the same way. Most of the time, the skewed recollections dwell on pop cultural ephemera—the precise spellings of minor consumer products, iconic lines of dialogue that are both famous and incorrect, and the popularity of a children's movie starring the comedian Sinbad that does not exist. The most unhinged explanation for this phenomenon involves quantum mechanics and the possibility of alternative realities; the most rational explanation is that most of these memories were generated by people of the early nineties, a period when the obsession with popular culture exponentially increased without the aid of a mechanism that remembered everything automatically.

The subsistence and mass identification of phenomena like the Mandela Effect could only come to fruition in the Internet Age. Without the internet, there would be no universal platform to academically discuss a concept so daft, nor would there be any way to efficiently and convincingly disprove so many disparate memory errors. Yet the *content* of the Mandela Effect—the objects and ideas that people misremember—is almost entirely tied to the era just before the internet became common. It was harder to prove what was true. It was harder to disprove what was false. As a society, we've elected to ignore that many people of the nineties—many *modern* people, many of whom are still very much alive—were exceedingly comfortable not knowing anything for certain. Today, paraphrasing the established historical record or questioning empirical data is seen as an ideological, anti-intellectual choice. But until the very late nineties, it was often the only choice available.

It's hard to explain the soft differences between life in the 2020s and life in the 1990s to any person who did not experience both of those periods as an adult—far more difficult than explaining the day-to-day difference between life in 1960 and life in 1990. For the most part, the dissonance between the sixties and the nineties involves how things were designed, man-ufactured, and packaged. A teenager in 1960 would purchase physical music on a circular polyvinyl record; the 1990 version of that teenager would pur-chase physical music on a circular polycarbonate disc. The cost of a record in 1960 was around $3, which accurately translated to $13.25 in 1990 dollars. That evolution is easy to comprehend, unlike the profound structural disso-nance between consumer life in 1990 and consumer life in 2020. A person native to the twenty-first century can't really reconcile why anyone would pay $13.25 for twelve fixed songs that could only be played on specific high-end electronics serving no other function; the majority of all recorded music can now be instantly accessed anywhere for less than $10 a month. For those who experienced both paradigms firsthand, the explanation for why the former did not seem idiotic is both simple and abstract: *That's just how it was. That's just what you did.* For those who missed that era entirely, the difference is so maddening that it barely justifies consideration. This is not like the differ-ence between driving a car and riding a horse. It's like the difference between building a fire and huddling in the dark, waiting for the sun to rise.

Imagine a group of friends sitting around a tavern table in 1993. If Nel-son Mandela's name came up in conversation, it's not just that there would be no expedient way to verify whether he was alive or dead; the very necessity of such verification was not considered essential. If the conversation was casual and nothing was at stake, an anecdotal memory was more than suffi-cient. If most people at the table believed Mandela was deceased, that was a viable consensus. If two of the people erroneously recalled seeing his state funeral on late-night television, the fusion of their false memories would calcify into a shared actuality. By the end of the night, everyone at the table might feel like they'd watched the same imaginary event. This process of cognitive reinforcement and mental confabulation is how the mind works. False memories have existed since the first human tried to remember any-thing for the first time. What makes the 1990s unique is the massive amount of information to potentially misremember, amplified by the nonexistence of a cybernated depository where that information could be indexed. Not only were there more television networks than ever before, but also an unprecedented increase in the sheer minutes devoted to programming (the long-standing practice of TV stations "signing off" at midnight or two a.m.—usually accompanied by a recording of the national anthem—had been completely abandoned by the decade's end). Most live video footage was not permanently saved, often taped over to reduce costs (some of the only material that remains from this period was recorded by one private citizen—Marion Stokes, a Philadelphia woman who compulsively recorded and stored over 40,000 VHS tapes of news broadcasts between the years of 1979 and 2012, eventually donating the collection to the Vanderbilt Television News Archive). The nineties were a golden age for metropolitan newspapers and glossy magazines, yet most copies were destroyed or recycled within a month and never converted to digital files. It was a decade of seeing absolutely everything before never seeing it again.

It's popular (and maybe reasonable) to claim that the labeling of any generation* is stupid and almost always wrong, but it does serve one essential function: It allows people to express prejudice toward large chunks of the populace without any risk. You can't be sexist or racist or classist if the only enemy is someone's date of birth. Younger generations despise older generations for

---

*Transparency requires me to admit a few things here, if only to aid those primarily reading this book in order to locate its biases: I was born in 1972. I'm a white heterosexual cis male. I was economically upper-lower-class in 1990, middle-middle-class in 1999, and lower-upper-class as I type this sentence. My experience across the nineties was comically in line with the media caricature of Generation X, almost as if I were a character from a Netflix movie set in 1994 but written and directed by a person born in 2001 who'd only learned about history by watching Primus videos. There are multiple photographs of me where I'm wearing a baseball hat backward in public, sometimes with a cardigan sweater. I didn't vote in the 1996 election, but I did have an "I Voted" sticker affixed to the chamber of a plastic water bong. For twenty-five years, the idea of anyone self-identifying as a "brand" struck me as the most repulsive concept imaginable, though the acidity of my repulsion was neutralized by the degree to which I found the entire concept hilarious. I am comfortable with my service as a demographic cliché. It's one of the few things in my life I got right.

creating a world they must inhabit unwillingly, an impossible accusation to rebuff. Older generations despise new generations for multiple reasons, although most are assorted iterations of two: They perceive the updated versions of themselves as either softer or lazier (or both). These categorizations tend to be accurate. But that's positive. That's progress. If a society improves, the experience of growing up in that society should be less taxing and more comfortable; if technology advances and efficiency increases, emerging generations should rationally expect to work less. If new kids aren't soft and lazy, something has gone wrong.

It would be absurd to claim that Generation X was the apex of American progress. One wouldn't make that claim even if it were somehow justified, as doing so would undermine everything Generation X purported to represent. It is, by almost any barometer, the least significant of the canonical demographics. Yet one accolade can be applied with conviction: Among the generations that have yet to go extinct, Generation X remains the least annoying. This is mostly due to size. Those born between 1966 and 1981 comprise around 65 million Americans, less than the generation that came before and less than the generation that came after (Baby Boomers and Millennials are both over 70 million apiece). All things being equal, there are simply fewer Gen Xers to exemplify their version of annoyance. But all things are never equal. For reasons both explicable and debatable, Xers complained less pedantically than the demographic they followed and less vehemently than the demographic that came next. Which is not to say they *never* complained, because they absolutely did—the vacuous center of Gen X culture was a knee-jerk distaste for Boomer ideology and a fear of invisible market forces that infiltrated everything. These amorphous oppressors were bemoaned at length. But those complaints were the exception. The enforced ennui and alienation of Gen X had one social upside: Self-righteous outrage was not considered cool, in an era when coolness counted for almost everything. Solipsism was preferable to narcissism. The idea of policing morality or blaming strangers for the condition of one's own existence was perceived as overbearing and uncouth. If you weren't happy, the preferred stance was to simply shrug and accept that you were unhappy. Ambiguous disappointment wasn't that bad.

There's a curious metric calculated in the annual World Values Survey* called "Happiness Inequality." This is not a literal measure of how happy people are, but of how much variance there is in the way people view their own happiness in comparison to the happiness of others. It's graded on a curve. People around the world are asked to rate their level of happiness on a scale of 1 to 10 (with 10 being the best life possible), and the average answer within any nation becomes the equivalent of 5. A given country's "Happiness Inequality" measures the distance most individual responses fall from whatever is considered typical within that particular society. In the United States, this distance is usually just above or just below 1.8, with one key exception: the stretch from 1992 to 1998. In 1995, the difference was actually greater than 2, which had never happened before and hasn't happened since. The mid-nineties signify a statistical peak in social disaffection, when it was unusually common to assume one's own happiness was disconnected from the happiness of other people. Such data would suggest that this must have been a period of pervasive emotional loneliness, but I must admit that it didn't seem that way at the time. Or did it, and my disaffection stopped me from noticing?

Here's the one thing we know for sure: Generation X is classified as "Generation X" because of the book *Generation X*. The causation is remarkably direct. Published in spring of 1991, *Generation X: Tales for an Accelerated Culture* is a puzzling book to consume outside of its era. It's a short novel (192 pages) with little plot, built around three twentysomething characters

---

*This is a global research project that investigates what people value and believe, with a focus on how happy or unhappy they consider themselves.

in the Coachella Valley* conversing about who they are and what they aspire to be. The margins of the pages are sprinkled with glossary buzzwords presented as dictionary definitions (the most memorable one is probably *McJob*, a term coined by sociologist Amitai Etzioni to connote boring, low-paying occupations devoid of prestige or potential). *Generation X* was written by Canadian author Douglas Coupland, twenty-nine years old at the time of its release. Originally imagined as a work of nonfiction, the book's language oscillates between wry humor and desperate pessimism ("I began to wonder if sex was really just an excuse to look deeply into another human being's eyes"). The impact was more cultural than literary. It can safely be assumed that the 60+ million people born in the sixties and seventies would be classified as something else entirely if Coupland had assigned his novel a different name.

"I've never even considered that," Coupland says now. "I didn't have any alternative titles at the time. The book was actually supposed to come out eighteen months earlier than it did. I turned in the manuscript to the publisher and didn't hear back for three months. A guy named Jim Fitzgerald, who was working at St. Martin's Press at the time, finally told me, 'They don't want to publish the book.' I asked, 'Why is that?' He said it was because it was fiction, and they wanted something more like the *Preppy Handbook*.† I said, 'Well, that's not what it is.' A month later, they said they would publish it anyway. But they published it grudgingly."

Fitzgerald, who later became a literary agent and is now deceased, recalled the origin story differently (though the basic facts are the same). Here's how he described the book's publication in a deleted scene from the 1998 Paul Devlin documentary *SlamNation*:

---

*The fact that Coachella would eventually host an annual music festival serving as a touchstone of Millennial culture is a coincidence.

†*The Official Preppy Handbook* was a hugely popular 1980 work of satire pretending to explain how a person could dress and act like an affluent member of elite WASP society.

Yeah, I worked on *Generation X*. I created *Generation X* . . . [Coupland] wanted to do a nonfiction book and write about how things were different between his generation and people considered Baby Boomers. Now, I don't believe in generations at all. I think everybody is the same age. But he was going to do this nonfiction book filled with charts and graphs and cartoons. So later he calls me and says the book is not working and he wants to do a novel. I say, "Fuck you, man. You can't just go from nonfiction to a novel." He says, "Just give me a chance." So he sends it to me and I kind of like it. But I made a compromise with him. I said, "Okay, look: We'll do it as a novel, but we'll make it look like a textbook. We'll make it look like a survival manual for twenty-year-olds." We still didn't have a title, so we went back and forth a bunch and I finally just said, "Come on, let's do it with what we were originally thinking, which was *Generation X*." So we just did that.

Prior to '91, the term "Generation X" had randomly appeared in a variety of places without an immutable definition. There was a 1965 British sociology book with the same title, and the book's title eventually became the name of a late-seventies punk band fronted by Billy Idol. Coupland himself had written an article for *Vancouver* magazine in 1987 with the headline "Generation X." But the real derivation was historian Paul Fussell's 1983 book *Class: A Guide Through the American Status System*. "It was about class stratification in American society," Coupland explains. "My mom read it and thought it was really funny, so I read it and thought it was bang on. And at the end of the book, there was this coda that postulated an 'X' class. I actually wrote Fussell a fan letter. Never heard back from him. But everything he said about getting off the class roller coaster felt like the way I thought about the concept of Generation X."

That last thought is telling. The 1990s represented the longest economic expansion in U.S. history; as a consequence, the entire Gen X experience is almost exclusively remembered as socioeconomic. It's become common to classify the sardonic languor associated with Gen Xers as a byproduct of financial privilege, with the built-in assumption that detached political world-views only come from people who don't have to worry about money. This is a minor misreading of history. The prosperity of the nineties didn't begin until slightly later in the decade and rarely included younger adults. In fall of 1992, those in the Gen X demographic possessed only 0.8 percent of American household wealth, slightly less than what they'd held two years prior. For people sharing Coupland's perspective, the onset of the nineties provided little reason to be optimistic or excited about anything professional. The new goal was to emotionally and intellectually remove oneself from an uninteresting mainstream society.

"I didn't have any money in the 1980s. I lived that whole decade without a television," Coupland says. "I remember being in a grocery store in the late eighties and not recognizing a single person on any of the magazine covers. What I mostly remember is a sensation that proved untrue: We had, as a culture, seemingly lost the ability to generate activities or cultural moments that could define time. We had entered this era of timelessness. I would go to my local deli every morning and get the L.A. *Times.* I remember seeing a headline about Communism being officially over, and I was just like, 'Oh.' That Francis Fukuyama meme* was floating around, and it didn't seem strange to be entering an era that wasn't an era. Nothing seemed to be happening in the entire culture. I had this Volkswagen 1600 with a tape deck, and I'd just drive around the desert listening to the Stone Roses.† I think I

---

*Fukuyama, a neoconservative political scientist, is the author of the book *The End of History and the Last Man.* The book argues that liberal democracy will be the final form of human government; the meme that Coupland references is mostly just the title of the book, which was appropriated in different contexts and sometimes taken literally. It must be noted, however, that *The End of History* was not published until 1992 (so if Coupland was already aware of this, it truly was in "meme" form).

†The Stone Roses were among the originators of a genre that would later be dubbed Britpop. Their eponymous debut album was released to critical acclaim in 1989. The band, however, is equally remembered for collapsing into a legal battle with their record label and disappearing for most of the next five years.

chose the desert because it's a metaphor, but also because it's a place of nothingness. I wanted to be back inside time again."

So this, in essence, is how the Generation X identity came into existence: A destitute Canadian writer drives around the California desert in hopes of crawling inside the abstraction of time. He fails to write a nonfiction book, instead producing a novel that is both experimental (which matters) and accessible (which matters more). The characters he invents seem like real people who are coming into everyday existence. The title of the book is easy to remember and a shorthand way to categorize any people who happen to be born within a specific fifteen-year window, many of whom disagree with the qualities associated with that categorization. By 1994, the book title has become a marketing term. By 1999, it becomes an expression that is most often used ironically. Which—even more ironically—is now the main quality associated with the term itself. "There was Richard Linklater's *Slacker*, there was *Generation X*, and then there was Nirvana's *Nevermind*. And it only takes three objects to make a constellation," Coupland says. "So that's what happened to me."

○ ○ ○

Though habitually categorized as self-obsessed, Baby Boomers were slow to self-awareness. *Time* magazine idealistically named every person under the age of twenty-five as 1966's "Man of the Year" and followed that up with a 1967 cover story positively labeling this demographic as "the Inheritors." But the introspective realization that growing up within that specific period of time might generate a host of shared, contradictory personality traits did not fully emerge until the 1980s: The 1983 film *The Big Chill* is the most blatant example, along with TV shows like *Family Ties* and *thirtysomething*. It took some time for Boomers to reach their "uncomfortable analysis" phase. This stands in contrast to Generation X, who entered that phase immediately and never left.

The first national attempts at describing who these new people allegedly were came from the same places that had clumsily defined Baby Boomers in the sixties. *Time* took a stab in July of 1990. The magazine's cover was an image of five people staring in random directions, unified by the word "twentysomething." The headline for the story itself was "Proceeding with Caution." It was published before the term "Generation X" was popularized,* with one source dismissively labeling the demographic as the New Petulants:

> The twentysomething generation is balking at work, marriage and baby-boomer values. Why are today's young adults so skeptical?
>
> They have trouble making decisions. They would rather hike in the Himalayas than climb a corporate ladder. They have few heroes, no anthems, no style to call their own. They crave entertainment, but their attention span is as short as one zap of a TV dial. They hate yuppies, hippies and druggies. They postpone marriage because they dread divorce. They sneer at Range Rovers, Rolexes and red suspenders. What they hold dear are family life, local activism, national parks, penny loafers and mountain bikes. They possess only a hazy sense of their own identity but a monumental preoccupation with all the problems the preceding generation will leave for them to fix.

Trying to encapsulate millions of emerging adults (who are being analyzed precisely *because* they're hard to understand) is infeasible, so the *Time* writers can't be criticized for the dry obliviousness of those paragraphs. Why "red suspenders" are specifically noted as something this demographic dislikes is hard to comprehend, but some of the other projections hold up (for whatever reason, an inexplicable desire to hike across exotic mountain ranges did become a common nineties accusation). The description is most noteworthy for its striking similarity to how Millennials would come to be

---

*The only other major moniker for people born between 1966 and 1981, periodically employed through the early nineties, was "the 13th Generation," based off the book *Generations: The History of America's Future, 1584 to 2069*. The book, written by historians Neil Howe and William Strauss, classified "13ers" as the thirteenth generation of American citizens since the founding of the republic. Though the classification made sense, it did not stick.

categorized* around 2010 (the article goes on to emphasize a supposed desire for political activism). Its boldest psychological assertion was that nineties young people were terrified of romantic relationships and commitment, the consequence of being raised by divorced parents who shielded them from adversity:

> While the baby boomers had a placid childhood in the 1950s, which helped inspire them to start their revolution, today's twentysomething generation grew up in a time of drugs, divorce and economic strain. They virtually reared themselves. TV provided the surrogate parenting, and Ronald Reagan starred as the real-life Mister Rogers, dispensing reassurance during their troubled adolescence. Reagan's message: problems can be shelved until later. A prime characteristic of today's young adults is their desire to avoid risk, pain and rapid change. They feel paralyzed by the social problems they see as their inheritance: racial strife, homelessness, AIDS, fractured families and federal deficits. "It is almost our role to be passive," says Peter Smith, 23, a newspaper reporter in Ventura, Calif.

Almost everything written in this pre-X period portrays the demographic as damaged. A 1991 story in the *Atlanta Journal-Constitution* called twentysomethings "a noun without a definition" and compared them to abused children. "There's no intellectual pride or content to this generation," read a disparaging quote from the article, which is only noteworthy due to the source: Matt Groening, the then thirty-seven-year-old creator of *The Simpsons*. There was, quite suddenly, a shift in how the aesthetic desires of

---

*Part of this is due to a problem inherent with all attempts at generational categorization. Whenever a new demographic comes into prominence, there's a temptation to insist its inhabitants care less about money and material wealth. But this is mostly because any new demographic will always be composed of young people, and young people always care less about acquiring money. If you don't own a house or have children, conspicuous wealth seems gratuitous and shallow.

youth culture were perceived. It was not that Xers were merely thought to have bad taste—the hotter take was that Xers had bad taste *on purpose*.

"The Kids are junk-food connoisseurs," argued the right-wing *Washington Times* in 1991, intentionally capitalizing the letter *K*. "They praise trash as art. High Concept is God." The crux of this increasingly frequent critique went something like this: Andy Warhol had been right about everything. Culture was now a pure commodity, so there was no reason to differentiate between elite culture, consumer culture, and the culture of kitsch. It all served the same popular purpose.

Now . . . were these assessments accurate?

(Yes.)

(No.)

(Sometimes.)

What's historically distinctive about the X era is the overwhelming equivocation toward its own marginalization. The things uninformed people said about who Gen Xers supposedly were often felt reductionist and flawed, but still worthy of examination and not entirely wrong. An internal exploration for generational meaning began almost immediately. Coupland's novel had come out in 1991. By 1994, there was already a 306-page anthology titled *The GenX Reader*, a fossilized example of how understanding the present cannot be achieved until the present has become the past.

Compiled by writer Douglas Rushkoff, *The GenX Reader* can be seen as both an attempt to disprove the conventional wisdom about young people and a way to highlight the rising creative underclass. Rushkoff forcibly tries to rename Xers as "Busters" (as in, the opposite of "Boomers"). The book's hyperbolic introduction portends revolution:

> Until now, Generation X has been explained to the public by people who fear and detest us most. Unable to see through the guise of apathy and anger worn by twentysomethings and unable to understand what's beneath it if they could, the many chroniclers of Generation X

have reduced us to, at best, a market segment and, at worst, the down-
fall of the Western World . . . But we, the members of Generation X,
reject this categorization.

What's odd is that almost everything else anthologized in *The GenX
Reader* responds to this declaration by saying, "We do? Are you sure?" Many
of the best pieces, if published now, would be viewed as spoofs. "Face the
muzak," wrote *Mondo 2000* columnist Andrew Hultkrans. "It's impossible
to retain integrity in the information economy." That sentence is lifted from
a column titled "The Slacker Factor." The compendium has essays on the
cartoon *Ren & Stimpy*, the invention of classic rock as a recognizable radio
format, and the insolvency of Social Security. It excerpts a few pages from
The Morning After, a controversial nonfiction book from a twenty-five-year-
old writer named Katie Roiphe who was intent on "demystifying and even
debunking the notion of a rape crisis." Another excerpt comes from the
I Hate Brenda Newsletter, a postmodern 'zine mocking Shannen Doherty,
the actress portraying Brenda Walsh on *Beverly Hills, 90210* (the selected
issue includes an interview with Eddie Vedder, in which the singer discusses
Doherty's unsuccessful attempt to get backstage at a Pearl Jam concert). One
of the most illuminating perspectives comes from Jefferson Morley of the
Washington City Paper, noting how everything that was experienced by children of the seventies had felt like reruns of events that had happened before:
"I remember wondering why people were surprised that prices were going
up. I thought, that's what prices did. Some people were dismayed that America was losing the war in Vietnam, but to me it seemed like America had
always been losing the war. Some people were scared that George Wallace
was running for president, but he ran every time, didn't he?"

The most retroactively compelling aspect of *The GenX Reader* is not
what the writers got right or wrong, but the intensity of their search for
meaning. Again and again, the anthology grapples with the very stereotypes
it intends to eradicate, only to begrudgingly accept and repurpose the same

clichés (when Rushkoff includes his own work, he chooses a political piece titled "Strength through Apathy"). This was perhaps the most charming Gen X quality: a continual willingness to absorb and internalize its carica-ture. When Boomers were accused of bloated self-interest, they'd remind people they had ended a war; when Millennials would later be accused of entitlement, they would insist they were actually working harder for less reward. With the exception of its introduction, *The GenX Reader* did not provide that type of defiance. It did not really push back.

When informed that they were apathetic, the most common Xer response was disinterest in the accusation, inadvertently validating the original asser-tion. Every fear or concern was assumed to be inevitable. Resistance was hopeless. In 1995, two former *Spin* magazine employees, Steven Daly and Nathaniel Wice, published a reference book titled *Alt.Culture*. Essentially a dictionary of youth-oriented terms and phrases, it was likely influenced by *Spin*'s 1993 eighth-anniversary issue, which included an "A–Z of Alternative Culture" list. *Alt.Culture* was smartly written and nakedly calculating (the intended audience appeared to be marketing executives who wanted to sound hip). Decades later, *Alt.Culture* is a treasure trove of provisionally high-profile trivialities that have otherwise disappeared entirely—the TV show *Studs*,* French philosopher Guy Debord,† Black Death Vodka.‡ An unknowing precursor to Wikipedia, *Alt.Culture* provided countercultural definitions for things that weren't important enough to be defined anywhere else. But this book, despite its content, was never countercultural. In 1997,

---

Studs was a short-lived, mega-popular late-night game show where two male contestants would both go on dates with the same three women, and then all five participants would discuss the dates in the most sexual way possible (but without being explicit, since this was still network television). Winning or losing the game itself was completely irrelevant.

†Debord founded the Situationist International, a Marxist organization comprising avant-garde intellectuals and artists. Partially due to the timing of his 1994 suicide, Debord was an especially popular person among bohemian Gen X film students.

‡This was a brand of Belgian vodka. The bottle was packaged inside a casket. It was endorsed by Slash of Guns N' Roses and almost impossible to find in normal liquor stores.

Wice and Daly partnered with Time Warner and turned *Alt.Culture* into one of the first web-centric databases.

"We didn't sell our souls," Wice told *Wired* when the deal was finalized. "We're just licensing them."

○ ○ ○

It seems quaint, perhaps even ridiculous, that two magazine writers selling Time Warner the licensing rights to a glossary of mediaspeak jargon would require a self-deprecating explanation. It now feels like the logical way to do business. This, however, was not always the case. The concept of "selling out"—and the degree to which that notion altered the meaning and perception of almost everything—is the single most nineties aspect of the nineties. The complexity, nuance, and application of the term *sellout* was both ubiquitous and impossible to grasp. Nothing was more inadvertently detrimental to the Gen X psyche.

The semiotic origin of the *sellout* accusation is technically unknown, though musician/critic Franz Nicolay traces the first citation in the *Oxford English Dictionary* to 1862.* Its application as an artistic epithet was universally known by the time the Who released *The Who Sell Out* in 1967, and Bob Dylan's use of an electric guitar at the 1965 Newport Folk Festival might be ground zero. By 2010, it was hard to illustrate to a young person why this act was once seen as problematic; by 2020, it was difficult to explain what the term literally expressed. But its usage and centrality peaked at the onset of the nineties. What made selling out so psychologically vexing was the level of gradation inherent to its principles: It did not simply mean someone was trying to sell something in order to get rich. It meant someone was compromising the values they originally espoused in exchange for something superficial (which was usually money, but not necessarily). This action was

---

*The piece by Nicolay references Nine Inch Nails frontman Trent Reznor, subsequently described as "a representative of, arguably, the last generation that worried about such things."

particularly bad if the compromised person was still doing the same work they'd done before, except now packaging that work in an attempt to make it palatable to a less discriminating audience. Since the intent mattered more than the result, the success of the attempt was almost irrelevant—selling out and failing was no better or worse than selling out and succeeding.

Every exploit was graded on a sliding scale, and those following the rules most dogmatically were sanctioned most strictly. Conversely, if your *only* core value was conventional success, you would never be seen as credible, but you also couldn't be criticized for abandoning the values you never originally possessed. In 1993, *The Washington Post* wrote this about the DC-based punk band Fugazi.

> There are three facts about Fugazi you must know: It only plays shows where age IDs are not required. It charges $5 admission to its shows, always. It will never, ever sign with a major record label.

Had Fugazi reneged on any of these points (at any time), they would have been crucified. It might have ended the group. An almost fascist refusal to sell out was Fugazi's most critical feature. This, however, only mattered to those who cared about Fugazi for both musical and nonmusical reasons. In 1994, the aging country-rock band the Eagles reunited for the hugely profitable Hell Freezes Over Tour. Ticket prices were around $125 apiece, roughly $100 higher than the national average. There were complaints about the cost, but it didn't change the way anyone felt about the Eagles. The Eagles did not possess the potential to sell out. There was an entrenched personality requirement to this credibility code, intertwined with its stance against compromise: An unvarnished desire to be loved (especially by strangers who looked and acted nothing like your peers) was viewed as desperate and pathetic, so any attempt to alter or soften one's persona was inauthentic and weak.

These imponderable laws and limitations colored every extension of cultural currency. Taken at face value, such rules made life complicated enough. But hipsters of the nineties added one more psychosomatic layer to the conundrum: There was, in real time, an awareness that the whole idea of criticizing people for selling out was ridiculous, even as it was actively happening. It was understood to be a teenage mentality that ignored the realities of adulthood. It punished innovation and ambition, and it was so infused with hypocrisy that the thesis barely hung together. It was a loser's game and everybody knew it. But it was a loser's game *you still had to play*. Perceiving the concept as preposterous did not make it any less pervasive.

The result was a period of communal cognitive dissonance. It was insane to take selling out seriously, yet still unforgivable to actually sell out.

There were micro examples of this everywhere, although none as explicit as the film *Reality Bites*. Structured like a standard romantic comedy, it's now an instruction manual for a transitory set of values that only made sense in 1994. Set in Houston, it's a love triangle involving a talented, unemployable documentarian (Winona Ryder) simultaneously pursued by a supportive but uncool TV executive (Ben Stiller, who also directed the film) and the most paint-by-numbers Gen X character in cinema history (brilliantly embodied by Ethan Hawke). The documentarian's best friend is a jaded pragmatist who works at the Gap and worries that she has AIDS; the best friend's ancillary sidekick is a guy who wants to tell his mom he's gay. Everyone is Caucasian. The entire plot—including the motives driving the love affairs—is a struggle over the meaning and consequence of selling out. The production itself is imbued with this residue: Written by aspiring poet Helen Childress and loosely based on her own friends, the script for *Reality Bites* went through seventy revisions and is sometimes criticized as a plastic, mainstream interpretation of the indie culture it tries to encapsulate. Ryder's fictional character has a similar experience to Childress, allowing her gritty self-made documentary about the lives of her pals to be converted into a garish, high-concept, MTV-like docu-farce. Saturated with product placement, *Reality Bites* is the sellout version of the problem with selling out, which is why it portrays the problem so intuitively.

Throughout *Reality Bites*, we are continually reminded that this could only be happening in a specific historical moment. Nostalgia for the unexperienced seventies is central to everything: The characters dance in public to a hit from 1979. They canoodle in cars while listening to a live album from 1976. They spend their free time quizzing each other about a TV sitcom that debuted in 1974. Hawke* is the Byronic slacker apotheosis—he fronts an unmotivated rock band called Hey That's My Bike, he expertly defines the word *irony* while recognizing the irony in doing so, and he says things like "I am not under any orders to make the world a better place." He's the film's spirit animal, thriving in an era when no one would have considered a term like "spirit animal" remotely offensive. The most generationally instructive element to *Reality Bites* is how the love triangle resolves: Ryder chooses Hawke (who mostly treats her poorly) instead of Stiller (who mostly treats her well). The more mature Stiller buoys her financially, admires her abilities, and only wants to make her happy . . . but he's a nineties sellout, which means he sold out on purpose. "I know why the caged bird sings," Stiller claims, and maybe he does. That's the problem. Meanwhile, Hawke criticizes Ryder in private and humiliates her in public. He's a terrible boyfriend. But in the film's final scene, they move in together, because Hawke's version of love is authentic and Stiller's affections are compromised (and not because of what he does, but because of who he chooses to be).

The initial reaction to *Reality Bites*, particularly among those outside its target market, was that Ryder picked the wrong guy. Writing as a fifty-one-year-old, *Chicago Sun-Times* movie critic Roger Ebert noted the film's "deep-seated prejudices" toward maturity and wondered, "What unwritten law

---

*Hawke's character was named "Troy Dyer." The real Troy Dyer, a financial consultant who attended USC film school with Childress, later sued Childress for defamation. The case was settled out of court.

prevented the makers of *Reality Bites* from observing that their heroine can't shoot video worth a damn, that their hero is a jerk, and that their villain is the most interesting person in the movie?" The consensus in '94 was that this kind of reaction delineated the difference between those who were young and those who were old—twentysomethings viewed the Ryder-Hawke romance as idealistic and intense, while more wizened adults only saw the impractical melodrama of a doomed relationship. It was assumed that such dissonance was eternal. It wasn't. As years have passed, each new crop of young people introduced to *Reality Bites* tends to see the relationship the same way Ebert did. On this one esoteric point, Boomers and Millennials are in lockstep. The language has changed (Hawke is now an example of "toxic masculinity," Stiller a more desirable "beta male"), but the choice seems no less obvious. As it turns out, the mid-nineties were the only time when the validity of this romantic conclusion was the prevailing youth perspective. It's an isolated, freestanding period where a person's unwillingness to view his existence as a commodity was prioritized over another person's actual personality. An authentic jerk was preferable to a likeable sellout.

It was a confusing time to care about things.

The twenty-fifth anniversary of *Reality Bites* coincided with (and likely prompted) a glut of retrospective discussion about the legacy of Gen X, most notably a package in the Style section of *The New York Times* that featured hyperventilating headlines like "Actually, Gen X Did Sell Out, Invent All Things Millennial, and Cause Everything Else That's Great and Awful." Some of the content seemed identical to the much-maligned attempts at describing Generation X in 1990 (the centrality of the Sony Walkman, the colorful diversity of Benetton magazine advertisements, et al.). A common reference point was a CBS infographic from January of 2019 listing all the various generations from 1928 to the present—except for Generation X, which was entirely excluded. This erasure was seen as meaningful, as was the increasing likelihood that Generation X would be the only canonical demographic to never produce an American president.*

What has happened, it seems, is that the portrayal of Generation X has experienced a kind of reverse Mandela Effect. It's not that certain provable truths have been collectively misremembered; it's more that certain abstractions have been so profoundly ingrained that alternate realities can't exist at all. The myths and the facts don't contradict each other. It's the definition of a tautological truth: The generational disinterest in contradicting any allegation of apathy proves that the allegations are correct. Accusations of an overreliance on "irony" are met with ironic rebuttals. It's like a court case where the plaintiff and the defendant are both trying to win by making identical arguments. The portrait is accepted as accurate because no one is particularly invested in arguing otherwise, and that will remain true for as long as the generation is remembered.

It will not matter that most Gen X characteristics only applied to a sliver of the Gen X population.

Reality Bites was a modest success for Universal Pictures, grossing just over $21 million in North America. Another movie from that year was the Tom Hanks vehicle *Forrest Gump*, which made $330 million. The most Gen X TV show from 1994 was the ABC teen drama *My So-Called Life*, canceled after one season. Its Thursday night rival on NBC, *Friends*, ran for ten years. This was not accidental.

"*Friends* plays against the concept of Generation X," the sitcom's co-creator Marta Kauffman told *The Orange County Register* during the show's

---

*Though the future remains unwritten, the most noteworthy Gen Xer to run for president is Beto O'Rourke, the handsome skateboarding Texan who chased the 2020 Democratic nomination and consistently polled at less than 2 percent, dropping out of the race a year before the election. O'Rourke was born in 1972, hates guns, and loves punk bands like the aforementioned Fugazi, although, as Alex Pappademas wrote in an essay titled "Gen X Is Having a (Very Gen X) Moment," "If listening to Fugazi inspires you to run for president . . . you have perhaps not been listening to Fugazi correctly." Entrepreneur Andrew Yang, born in 1975, ultimately lasted longer and fared better than O'Rourke in the Democratic campaign but was rarely portrayed as X-associated, mostly because he was obsessed with new technology and wasn't white.

first season. Such a strategy seems counterintuitive, as *Friends* was a show about people in their twenties trying to navigate life in the nineties. But what Kauffman was playing against was not a demographic. She was playing against the media stereotype of the period, which didn't mesh with the soft reality of most consumers. "[Our characters are] mostly motivated. Their clothes are clean, unlike Ethan Hawke, who wore the dirtiest things in *Reality Bites.*"

In June of 1997, *Time* magazine took a second stab at generational definition, now reconsidering the same clichés they themselves had established in 1990. Another all-or-nothing cover story, this time headlined "Great Xpectations of So-Called Slackers," made the case that Gen Xers were quietly driving entrepreneurship and building a foundation for the coming tech boom. The updated *Time* thesis was that early Gen X categorizations had unfairly misjudged the forces shaping the twentysomething mind-set. What it failed to reconcile was the degree to which most of those categorizations had gone completely unnoticed by most of the people it allegedly categorized. Hardcore Gen X-tacy was a fringe concern. Things regularly cited as generationally totemistic were almost always less popular than things devoid of cultural timeliness. *Bridget Jones's Diary* was more widely read than *Jesus' Son.* For every album sold by Courtney Love, Shania Twain sold fourteen. Over and over, the gap between what's most associated with Generation X dogma and the behavior of Generation X consumers is illogically vast.

This is true even in situations where the product and the audience should have been identical.

In November of 1997, the New Jersey–based independent radio station WFMU broadcast a live forty-seven-minute interview with Ronald Thomas Clontle, the author of an upcoming book titled *Rock, Rot & Rule.* The book, billed as "the ultimate argument settler," was (theoretically) a listing of almost every musical artist of the past fifty years, with each act designated as "rocking," "rotting," or "ruling" (with most of the research conducted in a coffeehouse in Lawrence, Kansas). The interview was, of course, a now semi-famous hoax. The book is not real and "Ronald Thomas Clontle" was actually Jon Wurster, the drummer for indie bands like Superchunk and (later) the Mountain Goats. *Rock, Rot & Rule* is a signature example of what's now awkwardly classified as "late-nineties alt comedy," performed at the highest possible level—the tone is understated, the sensibility is committed and absurd, and the unrehearsed chemistry between Wurster and the program's host (comedian Tom Scharpling) is otherworldly. The sketch would seem like the ideal comedic offering for the insular audience of WFMU, a self-selecting group of sophisticated music obsessives from the New York metropolitan area. Yet when one relistens to the original *Rock, Rot & Rule* broadcast, the most salient element is not the comedy. It's the apoplectic phone calls from random WFMU listeners. The callers do not recognize this interview as a hoax, and they're definitely not "ironic" or "apathetic." They display none of the savvy characteristics now associated with nineties culture. Their anger is almost innocent.

"We had no idea what the reaction there would be," Wurster says now. "With one exception,* the callers were all real, unprompted, and very annoyed. I always felt there was real animosity on the other end of the line . . . back then, things were taken more at face value. People thought, 'It's on the radio, it must be real.' If that show happened today, I think it would only be a matter of seconds before people would start calling in and saying it was a prank."

The audience response to *Rock, Rot & Rule* is a remote event, but it illustrates something critical. The fake WMFU interview is everything we like to remember about what the creative sensibilities of the nineties supposedly were, but the fans listening to that fake interview could not even tell it was fake. One misguided caller makes a series of condescending jokes about "Gen Xers," unaware that the larger joke is directed at condescending Gen Xers exactly like him. What's remembered as universal was, in fact, marginal and specific.

---

*The one fake caller was Scharpling's wife.

Within any generation, there are always two distinct classes: a handful who accept and embody the assigned caricature, and many more others who are caricatured against their will, simply because they happened to be born in a particular year. It was no different for Generation X. The only dissimilarity is that it bothered them less.

[projections of the distortion]

AT THE MOMENT (AND PERHAPS *ONLY* THE MOMENT), THE MOST COMMON candidate for the greatest novel of the nineties is David Foster Wallace's *Infinite Jest*, although that designation comes with a predictably moronic caveat: Its importance is best illustrated by people trying to claim it's actually not that important. Since the criteria for what makes a novel historically "great" are dictated by whatever a minority of unreliable tastemakers happens to care about at a given point in time, the only durable artifacts are the books habitually cited as examples of what needs to be overturned. The 1,079-page *Infinite Jest* has occupied that position since Wallace committed suicide in 2008.

It's impossible to know which nineties writers (if any) will seem significant in one hundred or three hundred years, simply because it's impossible to know what will eventually be considered significant about the time period as a whole. But it *is* possible to identify the writers who seemed most stridently "of the nineties" while those years were happening, and the two strongest nominees were both Wallace adjacent: Elizabeth Wurtzel (whom Wallace knew casually) and Mark Leyner (whom Wallace once called "a kind of antichrist").

Wurtzel was the fully realized incarnation of a personality type that had always existed, but never so completely: an ultra-precocious, highly photogenic woman who was consumed—both personally and artistically—by her own unhappiness. She was the kind of unrelenting talent who could get fired from a newspaper internship for plagiarism and still end up writing for *The New Yorker*. Her 1994 book, *Prozac Nation*, detonated a dazzling style that would become omnipresent in the online world of the early 2000s—a self-aggrandizing candor about intimate events that would normally be viewed as humiliating (in the future, this would be called "oversharing" or "performing vulnerability").

Prozac Nation was published when Wurtzel was twenty-seven, and it defined the philosophical difference between memoir and autobiography. It was the story of Wurtzel's clinical depression, but the veracity of the narrative mattered less than the way the author's illness shaped her own discernment of what was actually happening. It was indulgent and self-absorbed, although according to an epilogue Wurtzel added to the paperback, that was intentional.

"As I found myself saying to not a few people who would tell me they found the book angering and annoying to read: Good. Very good: That means I did what I had set out to do," she wrote. "That means you've felt a frustration and fury reading the book that might even be akin to the sense of futility experienced by most people trying to deal in real life with an actual depressive." The goal, it seemed, was to *force* people to understand her, even if that understanding made people less sympathetic to who she was and what she was dealing with.

In that sense, Leyner was the reverse. There was no way to understand who he was, or at least not through the content of his writing. It was possible to project abstract themes upon his prose, but there were no *obvious* themes. It was kinetic writing, a little like the movie *Airplane!* and a little like Eddie Van Halen playing "Eruption." There was an athletic incomprehensibility to his sentences—a hyperintellectual unorthodoxy that was both undeniable and distancing. In 1992's *Et Tu, Babe*, a fictionalized account of Leyner's grappling with his own celebrity, he abruptly references "Uncle Jack," a character he'd never mentioned before and would never mention again.

"He was my mentor," wrote Leyner. "He taught me to be a writer and to be a man. He said that when you write you march through the reader's mind like Sherman marching to the sea and you burn every neuron and synapse as you go. He taught me a secret style of Kung Fu that's based on ballroom dancing steps—the Foxtrot, Lindy, Waltz, etc.—but that's lethal and terrifying. He had a girlfriend at a nightclub, a cocktail waitress. Her name was Adele."

While Wurtzel wrote about taking drugs, the pages of Leyner's books were made of drugs. But *only* the pages—he didn't seem that interested in debauchery, somehow. It was like he was mocking writers who took amphetamines by writing in the same style, but sober and without pathos.

The reason these authors remain so evocative of the nineties is not that they were popular (though both of them were), not that they were polarizing (which they still are), and not that they were shackled with the "voice of a generation" designation (which is something that happens to young writers so regularly that the title is worthless). It had more to do with how their literary personas—perhaps inadvertently, but perhaps on purpose—caricatured the kind of audacious charisma most vehemently criticized by those who longed to possess it. They were supernatural exaggerations of so many nineties personalities who were just walking around, talking about themselves and driving everyone else crazy. They were the best versions of generational extremes: Wurtzel was the person at the party you couldn't get away from. Leyner was the party guest who wouldn't leave. She was captivating in her brokenness, too smart for her own good. He knew *exactly* how smart he was—but if he was so smart, why was he still here, just making weird jokes about steroids and Mussolini? Wurtzel needed you to know she was self-destructive. Leyner wanted you to believe he was indestructible. There was no one else like them, except for everybody.

As is so often the case with artists who capture the zeitgeist by accidentally inventing it, the lives of Wurtzel and Leyner adopted strange trajectories when the culture moved on. Wurtzel's writing career incrementally dissolved, prompting her to go to Yale Law School and eventually find employment with David Boies. She died from breast cancer in 2020. Leyner disappeared after publishing *The Tetherballs of Bougainville* in 1998, only to reemerge in 2005 as the cowriter of several successful pop-science medical books punctuated by his signature sense of humor (although nothing like the unhinged postmodernism of his earlier period).

The memory of their work is mixed, as is the memory of why it mattered.

2 The Structure of Feeling (Swingin' on the Flippity-Flop)

THE FALL OF THE BERLIN WALL AND THE FALL OF THE TWIN TOWERS. These are supposed be the bookends for when the nineties (really) started and when the nineties (really) stopped. It's symmetrical and it feels intuitively correct, and the fact that both events mattered globally gives the assertion weight. It's the simple, rational description. But there's a problem with this simplicity. The problem is that the Berlin Wall fell in the autumn of '89, and the following eighteen American months remained interlocked with the previous decade. Things changed, but not really.

In spring of 1990, New Kids on the Block started the Magic Summer Tour, a summer that lasted 303 days and earned $57 million. The year's highest-grossing film was *Ghost*, and the ghost of Patrick Swayze was not CGI. David Lynch's *Twin Peaks* debuted on ABC, but its hallucinatory melodrama was disconnected from both linear time and the rest of the TV universe, where *Cheers* remained the most popular show. Joe Montana was still the best player in professional football. The 1990 Sears Holiday Wish Book still pushed Garfield the Cat telephones for $49.99. These high-profile mini-examples should not be surprising: It's not like people rip off the page of a calendar, see a new four-digit number, and decide they want a different life.

There's always an inexact cultural hangover. But what was specifically unsettling about 1990 was the degree to which the future seemed pre-programmed. There was a sensation, mostly unspoken, that the vibe of the eighties would robotically continue.

Ronald Reagan's two-term presidency can be viewed as both upbeat and devastating, but there's no dispute over its dominance. His first win was decisive and his second was a landslide, coming during an economic downturn with high unemployment. Reagan had altered the definition of conservatism, reinventing the Republicans as the party of optimists. His mostly forgotten 1968 book, *The Creative Society*, set the edge for his political philosophy: It promoted the daydream of a decentralized civilization, where the inherent potential of the individual would be allowed to thrive and experience "the privilege of self-government." Time and again, Reagan insisted that American life was improving by becoming more prototypically American, and the collapse of the Soviet Union seemed to validate those values. The visual signifiers of the period—vivid clothing, gravity-defying hair, conspicuous name-brand accessories—became more and more pronounced. This felt less like the temporary taste of the time and more like the orbit fashion would follow in perpetuity. Through most of the seventies, the film industry had been a director's medium; in the eighties, it became a producer's medium, spawning a bland recipe for the manufacture of movies with predictably bankable properties. The public grew to expect formulaic summer blockbusters. Local radio was cautious and conformist, shaped by the national presence of MTV (a network still airing music content nonstop). The line between what was mainstream and what was underground was extraordinarily clear, as was the line between high and low culture. The election of George H. W. Bush extended the Reagan administration and entrenched a sense of permanent normalcy. It was as if certain things about the production of culture had finally been figured out, and 1990 was launched from this static plateau. It was the eighties on autopilot, and the plane wouldn't hit the mountain until September of '91.

○ ○ ○

The songs on Nirvana's *Nevermind* did not tangibly change the world. There are limits to what art can do, to what a record can do, to what sound can do. The video for "Smells Like Teen Spirit" was not more consequential than the reunification of Germany. But *Nevermind* is the inflection point where one style of Western culture ends and another begins, mostly for reasons only vaguely related to music. In the post-*Nevermind* universe, everything had to be filtered through the notion that this specific representation of modernity was the template for what everyone now wanted from everything, and that any attempt to understand young people had to begin with an understanding of why Nirvana frontman Kurt Cobain looked and acted the way that he did. In the same way the breakup of the Beatles was only half-jokingly seen as the end of the British Empire, the public ascension of *Nevermind* is where the nineties became a recognizable time period with immutable values.

Nevermind was released on September 24, 1991, the same day as the Red Hot Chili Peppers' *Blood Sugar Sex Magik* and *The Low End Theory* by A Tribe Called Quest. Only 46,251 copies of *Nevermind* were shipped to stores, generating a brief scarcity of resources (it opened at a quiet 144th on the *Billboard* charts). It didn't explode nationally until Thanksgiving and wasn't certified as the number 1 album in America until the following January. But its ancillary, rippling reconfiguration of the zeitgeist was vast and rapid, even in zones typically immune to the proclivities of youth culture—like car commercials.

In October of 1992, Subaru introduced the Impreza, a compact five-door hatchback. It was considered a marketing dilemma.* "Despite exceeding

---

*The following anecdotes come from the 1995 book *Where the Suckers Moon: The Life and Death of an Advertising Campaign*.

competitors in many, if not most, feature variables, the Impreza is still a Civic-class formula car that lacks a buyer-swaying hook," argued Jim Piedmont of the Wieden+Kennedy advertising firm. Piedmont was outlining the problem for executives from Subaru. "Its upscale refinement qualities are mostly intangibles . . . our challenge is to cut through the advertising clutter and position the car so we can get on the shopping list of Civic-class intenders."

What Piedmont meant by "Civic-class intenders" was "people who actually want a Honda." Such consumers would likely be twentysomethings with entry-level jobs. This prompted a 1993 commercial starring twenty-four-year-old Jeremy Davies (who'd go on to have a nice career as a character actor in films like *Saving Private Ryan* and TV shows like *Lost*). The thirty-second spot features Davies wildly gesticulating around the Impreza in a series of jarring edits, acting like a teenager who's just tried recreational Adderall for the first time. "This car is like punk rock," he insists, and goes on to (sort of) explain that the Impreza will remind people "what's great about a car," in the same way the Ramones reminded people that Jethro Tull used too many time signatures. It's framed like Davies is talking about events from the seventies, but he's actually talking about the present. He is talking about Nirvana without talking about Nirvana, which was the only way to do it. Davies could never have talked about Nirvana directly, because (a) Nirvana would have never participated in a car advertisement, and (b) doing so would have caused the commercial to fail even harder than it did, if that's somehow possible.

It's tempting to dismiss this Subaru commercial as a corporation's clueless attempt at appealing to a demographic they don't comprehend, and that wouldn't be a wholly inaccurate conclusion. But what's really happening here is more complicated. When punk rock was new, almost every TV depiction of punk was negative.* It had no symbolic value to anyone trying to sell any-

---

*The 1978 *WKRP in Cincinnati* episode "Hoodlum Rock," a now-famous 1982 episode of *Quincy, ME* ("Next Stop, Nowhere"), a 1984 telecast of *The Phil Donahue Show*, etc.

thing expensive. By 1991, kids who'd experienced punk firsthand (often through its negative network TV depictions) were now young adults. Nirvana delivers this audience *Nevermind,* an album that is not very punk in practice—it's financed by billionaire David Geffen and sounds, according to Cobain himself, "closer to a Mötley Crüe record than a punk record." And those details embarrass him, because *Nevermind* is completely punk in theory. Everything about its atomic structure is informed by punk values, which have become the default values for all the young adults who recall those early TV depictions of punk as preposterous and wrong. *Nevermind* becomes the most commercially successful punk album ever made, in large part because it doesn't sound like punk music (yet still is). It's the ideal mainstream version of counterculture ideology. Society at large, still trapped in the 1980s, now has a viable art product that can be used as a fulcrum to overturn everything else. The nineties begin in earnest. Companies who sell things like Imprezas see this transformation and conclude, "Nirvana is what people want." But Nirvana isn't interested in being nakedly commoditized. The contradictory values of the band (and its individual members) reject that process. Instead, companies must adopt (or pretend to adopt) the contradictory values themselves. You can't capitalize on the fact that Nirvana is popular. Doing so would have the opposite result. You must focus on the fact that Nirvana is popular against their will, despite all the conscious choices they made in order to become the most popular band in the world.

It was not, as Davies says in the commercial, "like punk rock, but for cars." It was more like cars, but for punk rock.

The first Nirvana album, *Bleach,* came out in 1989. It sold 40,000 copies but cost just $600 to record, so it was successful in a way that went unnoticed. Its claustrophobic, narcoleptic music was widely ignored by the same rock magazines that would later cover Cobain like a sitting president. After *Nevermind* was released in '91, *Bleach* would sell an additional 2 million copies and be

reevaluated as primal and uncompromising (such retrospective reevalua-
tions of Nirvana's material happened constantly). The details behind the
creation of *Bleach* prove how low the stakes were: A second Nirvana guitarist,
Jason Everman, received an album credit and appears on the front cover,
even though he does not play on any of the tracks—he just cut the $606.17
check required for the recording fee. Everman was fired from the band
before the end of '89, briefly playing with Soundgarden before joining the
U.S. military and serving in two wars. The *Bleach*-era drummer, Chad
Channing, was sacked in 1990 over creative differences, setting the stage
for the three-man lineup that would become the definitive incarnation of
Nirvana—Cobain, hulking politicized bassist Krist Novoselic, and cuddly
hardcore drummer Dave Grohl.

The prehistory of *Nevermind* is a series of small events that illuminate
the transition of an underground mentality forced to the surface. Nirvana
left their Seattle-based independent label Sub Pop for Geffen Records, home
to artists like Whitesnake and Elton John. The recording budget was almost
one hundred times greater than the budget for *Bleach*. Cobain requested
Butch Vig to serve as producer, in large part because Vig had produced five
records by the corrosive, comically uncommercial group Killdozer. Cobain
thought a good name for the new album might be *Sheep*, an inside shot
directed at his own fan base. Nirvana initially worked with Vig in Vig's home
state of Wisconsin, but those early tracks were abandoned, rearranged, and
re-recorded in California. The album was mixed by Andy Wallace, selected
because he'd worked with the thrash metal band Slayer. The hope was that
Wallace would make the record super-heavy. That didn't happen, but it still
sounded huge.

There are two ways to consider *Nevermind*. The first is as a collection of
twelve* songs that expertly merge classic rock, subversive music of the 1980s,

---

*A thirteenth song, the hidden track "Endless, Nameless," did not appear on the album's original
pressing and is only classified as a "song" because it involves musicians using musical instru-
ments. It's really just six minutes of noise.

and traditional pop sensibilities. The tempos range from upbeat to funeral dirge, and the dynamics often adopt a quiet-loud-quiet song structure. Many of the lyrics are presumed to be about Tobi Vail, Cobain's ex-girlfriend and the eventual drummer in the riot grrrl act Bikini Kill. The earliest *Nevermind* reviews were detached from what would become its historical reputation (*Rolling Stone* gave it only three out of five stars), but the overall response was positive. It's an excellent reflection of the period, the most far-reaching work of the grunge genre, and the last truly canonical album of the rock era. This constitutes its critical assessment. The second way to consider *Nevermind* is as the specific artifact that happens to include the song "Smells Like Teen Spirit," which is how it will be remembered in fifty or a hundred years.

Explaining the qualities of "Smells Like Teen Spirit" is a little like trying to explain the taste of Coca-Cola: A description of the components cannot reflect the experience. There are details about the song that have been noted so obsessively they've become almost immaterial: the fact that the title is never used in the lyrics, its riff-based similarity to Boston's 1976 hit "More Than a Feeling," the intentional, unstudied raggedness of the guitar solo. The sonic recipe is both stock and singular. It is not, however, an example of something that merely happened to emerge in the right place at the right time. The cultural implications for the nineties aren't the same if the centerpiece is "Jeremy" or "Black Hole Sun" or "Touch Me I'm Sick." The legacy of "Smells Like Teen Spirit" is not transposable. It had to be *this* song, delivered by *this* person.

The song's title derived from Vail's friend (and eventual Bikini Kill bandmate) Kathleen Hanna, who drunkenly wrote the phrase "Kurt Smells Like Teen Spirit" on Cobain's bedroom wall in Olympia, Washington. The joke was that Vail wore Teen Spirit deodorant, thus implying that Cobain and Vail were sleeping together. The significance of this story has, over time, taken on multiple meanings. One reading is that this means "Smells Like Teen Spirit" is technically a feminist artifact with a feminist origin; another reading is that Cobain's misunderstanding of the message (he had no idea

Teen Spirit was a brand of deodorant) proves that any profundity excavated from the language is an inane projection. But of course, when the song was new, there was no knowledge of where it came from, what it meant, or what it was intended to convey. That mystification proved essential. Cobain, disturbed by the magnitude of the song's success, habitually diminished the music as pop and the lyrics as meaningless. That analysis is true, from his perspective. But the music did not sound "pop" to most people listening to pop music in 1991, and the lyrics, despite an aggressive lack of cogency, *almost* made a point. They *almost* seemed like a coded message demanding to be unpacked, even if that was impossible.* In the middle of the song, Cobain casually intones, "Oh well, whatever, never mind," a Gen X aphorism so on-the-nose it would have been ridiculed if the Gen X proboscis were not still in utero. There was a sense he was almost inventing intellectual apathy. The track concludes with the desperate repetition of the phrase "A denial" nine times in a row. What is being denied? It's never explained, which pushes the desperation deeper. It was a version of nothing so close to something it accidentally became everything.

Like all albums of the era, *Nevermind* was released on a Tuesday. The five-minute video for "Smells Like Teen Spirit" debuted five days later on *120 Minutes*, MTV's Sunday night showcase for alternative music. The scene is Nirvana performing at a high school pep rally. The kids watching from the bleachers are the kind of kids who really hate pep rallies. There's a communal memory of Cobain's wearing flannel in this video, and that this image

---

*With the lights out, it's less dangerous
[Seems counterintuitive . . . but is that intentional?]
Here we are now, entertain us
[This was something Cobain liked to say when he arrived at parties . . . but could it also apply to all of society?]
I feel stupid and contagious
[Self-loathing? The realization that life is a bad joke? AIDS?]
Here we are now, entertain us
[Again with this. It must be important. But is the "we" the band or the audience?]
A mulatto, an albino, a mosquito, my libido
[These are definitely disconcerting words that almost rhyme.]

was the dawn of grunge fashion. This, however, is another case of the Mandela Effect—he's just wearing a brown shirt with green stripes. It looks like a shirt a little boy would wear on the first day of third grade. On the kick drum, Grohl has scrawled "Chaka," a reference to a West Coast graffiti artist who'd named himself after a nonhuman character from the seventies children's show *Land of the Lost*. The lighting is bad. It's hard to see people's faces. The burnout teens mosh in slow motion before overrunning the set in a controlled riot. The only authority figure is a pathetic high school janitor. Every visual reflects the same statement: The hedonistic, euphoric, high-gloss 1980s are over. It took five minutes to killdoze an entire decade.

Nevermind would go on to sell 10 million copies. Pearl Jam's *Ten*, released a month prior, eventually sold 13 million. Metallica's self-titled 1991 "Black Album," a more straight-ahead translation of their prototypic thrash-prog fusion, moved 17 million units. Green Day's petulant pop-punk album *Dookie* came out three years after that and moved another 10 million, as did a sweeping 1995 double album by Smashing Pumpkins. Hootie & the Blowfish, an unassuming bar band from South Carolina, got signed to Atlantic Records in '93 and sold 21 million copies of their melodic, much-maligned debut. The nineties were (and shall always remain) the absolute zenith for bands whose goal was selling records.* That success, however, is historical misdirection. Something more significant was happening, openly and without camouflage, though still invisible to everyone involved. Rock music had reached its logical conclusion—not as a genre, but as the pivotal force propelling youth culture. There would be hundreds of consequential rock

---

*In May of 1991, Billboard started using a barcode tracking system called SoundScan to measure album sales, ushering in a new age of knowing exactly which releases were truly selling. Two of the first artists to have number 1 albums in the SoundScan era were N.W.A and Skid Row, unthinkable possibilities in the past. Prior to SoundScan, album sales had been anecdotally "reported" by specific music stores, sometimes based on the personal perception and arbitrary taste of whoever managed the store.

albums recorded in the wake of *Nevermind*, yet none would approach its nonmusical importance. The dominance of Nirvana's paradoxical aesthetic ended the dominance of rock as an ideology. But it would take fifteen years for most people to detect this.

○ ○ ○

"We had grown up admiring punk bands and thinking all those groups on the pop charts were embarrassing . . . and suddenly we were one of those bands."

This is Kurt Cobain, talking to Robert Hilburn of the *Los Angeles Times*. It's 1993. The significance of this quote is not that Cobain is saying something singularly remarkable. It's significant because Cobain will express various versions of this quote incessantly, throughout his three-year career as a public figure. "Famous is the last thing I wanted to be," Cobain says in Michael Azerrad's (essentially authorized) Nirvana biography *Come As You Are*. Such a statement is not a surprising thing to hear from a very famous person. But what was innovative about Nirvana was how central this perspective was to their iconography. It was, ultimately, more important than the music they made.

The trajectory of twentieth-century rock was a continual progression away from simplicity. It was pioneered in the 1950s as unruly, unserious entertainment for teenagers. It matured and peaked in the 1960s, mirroring both the rise of the counterculture and the social maturation of its audience. During the seventies, rock became a big-money business and spawned the identifiable caricature of the Rock Star; in the eighties, that business model was incorporated and the caricature became perfunctory. Throughout the form's existence, there were always truculent artists who positioned themselves against whatever was considered most obviously popular (Lou Reed thought the Beatles were "garbage," the Clash said Led Zeppelin made them want to puke, etc.). Nirvana adopted and internalized that perspective. They believed (or at least expressed the belief) that the hunger for mass fame—

and particularly what an artist was required to do in order to satiate that hunger—was moronic and humiliating. Yet circumstance forced them to bemoan this experience at the same time they experienced it. The second track on *Nevermind*, "In Bloom," directly anticipates how much Cobain will dislike all the thoughtless, antipunk audiences who will inevitably love his album. The song was written and recorded long before those thoughtless antipunk audiences even had a chance to hear it.

"There have been several brief periods where different idiomatic elements of the underground, the *legitimate* music scene, have been brought to the surface and skimmed by the mainstream industry," producer Steve Albini said twenty-five years after Cobain's death. "That sort of culminated with Nirvana becoming the biggest band in the world."

The week before *Nevermind* arrived in stores, Guns N' Roses simultaneously released two albums on the same day. These were the most anticipated albums in years, and fans lined up outside of stores to buy both CDs at midnight. The albums were called *Use Your Illusion I* and *Use Your Illusion II*. It was estimated that almost half a million copies were sold within the first two hours. But as 1991 drifted into '92, the titles of the twin GNR albums started to feel pessimistically symbolic. Guns N' Roses and Nirvana were both offering a manufactured illusion of what rock culture was supposed to be. Axl Rose asked people to *use* that illusion. Cobain was obsessed with telling people that the illusion was stupid, and that he was stupid for letting it happen. Whether he fully believed this is irrelevant. It became the only way to think.

"I don't blame the average seventeen-year-old punk-rock kid for calling me a sellout," Cobain told *Rolling Stone*. This is an understatement. It wasn't just that Cobain forgave the average seventeen-year-old. He still wanted to live inside the average seventeen-year-old's mind. "I have strong feelings towards Pearl Jam and Alice in Chains and bands like that," Cobain said in a 1992 interview with the fanzine *Flipside*. "They're obviously just corporate puppets that are just trying to jump on the alternative bandwagon—and we are being lumped into that category. Those bands have been in the hairspray, cockrock scene for years and all of a sudden they stop washing their hair and start wearing flannel shirts. It doesn't make any sense to me. There are bands moving from L.A. and all over to Seattle and then claiming they've lived there all their life so they can get record deals. It really offends me."

Here again, what's fascinating about these remarks is not that they were made, since there's a long history of musicians attacking other musicians within the same scene. What's fascinating is that the bands Cobain attacked seemed to agree that he had a point. Pearl Jam, the only group rivaling Nirvana's importance to the era, spent most of the decade doing everything they could to mitigate the enormity of their fame. They stopped making music videos for six years and deliberately recorded nonaccessible album tracks. They sued Ticketmaster over monopolization, essentially sabotaging their own ability to tour. They rarely gave interviews. When *Spin* readers named Pearl Jam "Artist of the Year" in 1995, vocalist Eddie Vedder begrudgingly agreed to talk with the magazine's editor, Craig Marks. Vedder expresses nonstop emotional pain throughout the conversation, stressing that he was not the kind of person who wanted "to be validated by the press, and through public opinion."

Why, then, did you decide to go through with this interview?

You know what? I felt it was a real honor that people said we were their favorite band. People should know that it meant a lot to me.

You were also voted the most overrated band.

Well, I totally agree with that.

Near the end of his life, Cobain's view of Vedder softened. He told MTV, "We never had a fight, ever. I've just always hated his band. I consider him a person I really like." Still, this quasi-compliment is a confirmation of his core beliefs. The problem was not the players. The problem was the game. "I don't feel the least bit guilty for commercially exploiting a completely exhausted

Rock youth Culture," he wrote in the liner notes of a Nirvana B-sides collection. For the previous twenty-five years, rock music had flourished as a larger-than-life fantasy, questioned only by its alienated underclass. Now the fantasy and the underclass were the same. Radiohead's Thom Yorke labeled himself "a creep." Beck's breakthrough single insisted he was "a loser." Billy Corgan of Smashing Pumpkins sang that he was "a zero." By 1994, self-flagellation had become a kind of philosophical fashion. It was often a pose, and there was a certain goofiness to megastars lecturing fans about how much they hated themselves. But most of these fans were still undefined young people, and all had been born into a world where rock music was already everywhere. The possibility that the idiom of rock could have some transformative power—that it was rebellious, or revelatory, or even innovative—was off the table. Those qualities could still be experienced through a specific artist (perhaps Nirvana, perhaps someone else), but they weren't intrinsically tied to the art form itself. There was no longer anything exceptional about rock music, even when it was great. Being a so-called Rock Star was embarrassing, and acting like one was even worse. It could only be done as a joke.

Grunge was the de facto soundtrack of the early nineties. It's also sometimes criticized for its sonic limitations—most groups played the same way, at the same speed and with the same worldview, usually mining the same handful of influences. It was, by design, a derivative musical form. But it did introduce at least one new idea to mainstream rock: a collective sense of self-aware skepticism. That was very much a positive, until it became a negative.

Grunge came, more or less, from Seattle.* Its earliest progenitors formed

---

*Obviously, there are exceptions to this statement: Cobain was raised in Aberdeen, Washington. Eddie Vedder had been a surfer in San Diego, and many of the era's other signature musicians originated from different parts of the country. But Seattle was where they all ended up. Many recorded their earliest releases for the Seattle-based label Sub Pop, and all would come to be viewed as extensions of the so-called Seattle sound.

their groups in the late eighties, a time period when the Pacific Northwest was not a prime location for artists with careerist ambition. When Nirvana went nuclear, everything about that changed; record labels would sign a band solely because they happened to reside in the Seattle metro area. It was like the whole town had hit the lottery, and the lives of countless musicians were revamped overnight. Yet even the groups who took advantage of the gold rush were dubious about what was happening. Grunge had the media-age advantage of easy information; for the first time, a rock scene being exploited could fully understand what was happening. The Seattle bands had seen documentaries like Penelope Spheeris's *The Decline of Western Civiliza-tion Part II*. They were aware of what had happened with the pop metal bands on the Sunset Strip during the eighties, when any group with the correct hairstyle was awarded a record deal.* They recognized that the widely expressed desire to find "the next Nirvana" had almost nothing to do with songwriting. The money was fantastic, but the experience seemed stupid. Nothing was more mortifying than success.

How much this directly played into Cobain's 1994 suicide is unknow-able. After "escaping" from the Exodus Recovery Center in Los Angeles on April 1, Cobain flew home to Seattle (coincidentally sitting alongside Guns N' Roses bassist Duff McKagan on the flight). Cobain entered the green-house above his garage, injected a massive dose of heroin, and shot himself in the head with a shotgun. He was twenty-seven. It was shocking, but not surprising (he'd attempted suicide earlier that year in Rome and had famously released a song titled "I Hate Myself and Want to Die"). His suicide note references his unhappiness as an artist, but he was also a chronically depressed opioid addict with debilitating stomach issues, a complicated marriage, and an obsession with guns. His death, mourned by teenage fans

---

*The most egregious example being the (possibly apocryphal) story of the forgotten glam band Pretty Boy Floyd, allegedly signed to MCA Records for almost $1 million after playing only nine shows.

and questioned by curmudgeonly *60 Minutes* commentator Andy Rooney,* became the emblem of grunge as a movement: dark, druggy, and distorted. It was an ironic mode of expression, performed by unironic people.

Had Cobain been the only casualty, such a perception could be viewed as reductionist. But he wasn't the only one. The number of accidental and premeditated deaths by grunge (and grunge-adjacent) artists is staggering. It began with the 1990 heroin overdose of Andrew Wood, the frontman of Mother Love Bone, whose surviving members would later form Pearl Jam.† Cobain's death had been preceded by the rape and murder of Mia Zapata, lead singer of the Gits. Kristen Pfaff, the bass player for Hole, overdosed in her bathtub in the summer of 1994. Two members of Alice in Chains, vocalist Layne Staley and bassist Mike Starr, suffered drug-related deaths early in the twenty-first century.‡ Scott Weiland, the eternally troubled singer of Stone Temple Pilots, died on his tour bus in 2015. The most unexplainable passing was the 2017 suicide of Soundgarden vocalist Chris Cornell, a seemingly well-adjusted artist who'd performed a sold-out concert earlier that day. Grunge, by a wide margin, was the most morbid genre in pop history.

There's no doubt that the timing and circumstances of Cobain's death amplified his legacy. It's possible that his creative output has been posthumously overrated, and that a casual consumer might be more familiar with the work of Foo Fighters, the multi-Grammy-winning group founded by drummer Grohl in the wake of Nirvana's abrupt dissolution. Had Cobain

---

*"Everything about Kurt Cobain makes me suspicious," Rooney said on *60 Minutes* a few days after the suicide. "This picture shows him in a pair of jeans with a hole in the knee. I doubt Kurt Cobain ever did enough work to wear a hole in his pants."

†It's important to note that, in the end, Pearl Jam was the only major group from the grunge scene to succeed over time. They've never broken up, no member of the group has died, their popularity has remained strong, and they've played to massive audiences for thirty years.

‡Roughly half the songs on the 1992 Alice in Chains album *Dirt* are explicitly about heroin. The track "Junkhead" was a virtual mission statement, punctuated by the lyrical passage "What's my drug of choice? / Well, what have you got?" In 1995, Staley sang vocals for the side project Mad Season, a supergroup composed of Seattle musicians connected by their attempts at recovering from heroin addiction.

lived, the intensity of his youthful persona would have muted over time, and it's always easier to lionize a person who isn't around. Five canonical artists who predated him—Neil Young, Van Halen, Cher, Patti Smith, and R.E.M.— wrote songs about his passing.* But even the most cynical observer of Nirvana must accept two things: *Nevermind* transformed the totality of American pop culture, and that transformation initiated rock's recession from the center of society. These results were not Cobain's goal. But, like so many other things in his life, what he wanted and what he got were not the same.

---

*There were also a few less straightforward songs *believed* to be about Cobain's death, most notably the 1995 track "Hey Man Nice Shot" from the industrial group Filter. The song's writer, Richard Patrick, insisted the song was actually about the televised suicide of Pennsylvania state treasurer R. Budd Dwyer. Though unverified, it is generally assumed the caustic 1996 Tori Amos song "Professional Widow" is about Courtney Love.

[i see death around the corner]

IT'S BECOME POSSIBLE—IN FACT, POPULAR—TO ARGUE THAT COBAIN'S
suicide was actually the second most significant musician death of the nineties, and that the 1996 killing of rapper Tupac Shakur mattered more. What's slightly confusing is that this sentiment was already argued at the time of his murder, but always presented as an idea that would inevitably be denied later. A 1996 story in *The Guardian* posited that many Americans viewed Shakur's death as equal to Cobain's, but that "those who railed against his gangsta rap won't mourn him."

It's true that Cobain's death received more attention, and that most of the U.S. music media were more invested in the passing of a white icon from the fading world of rock than the passing of a Black icon within the ascending world of hip-hop.* On the surface, the two deaths seemed unrelated and bluntly metaphoric—one guy hated what his life had become while the other

---

*That criticism could also be made about this book. The previous chapter on grunge is longer and more detailed than this mini-essay, where Shakur's story is almost presented as a coda to that of Cobain (despite the fact that Tupac ultimately sold more records than Nirvana). But this is always a historically tricky problem: If one mediated subculture is imposed upon the culture at large while another subculture is mostly allowed to flourish in its own silo, the former subculture becomes the working language within both spheres, even if the latter ends up having a greater impact twenty-five years later. The way the past is considered in retrospect has almost no relationship to what was assumed to be obvious at the time of the event.

was a victim of the life he pursued. But there's a unifying aspect to both events, fixated on that very nineties obsession over the perception of authenticity.

Cobain had become a tabloid star, a quality he wanted to hide. He could not live with how his fame looked to other people (when his wife, Courtney Love, bought a Lexus, he demanded she return it to the dealer so that they could continue driving an old Volvo). To be the artist he wanted to be, Cobain needed to exist (on some level) as the same person he'd been as a vulnerable adolescent. He could not handle how he had changed. Tupac Shakur had the opposite experience. Shakur changed who he was to fit the artistic character he'd created, because his version of art didn't work if the image wasn't real. And that image was connected to a person living an exceedingly violent life.

Tupac's upbringing was atypical, and not just for a rapper. Both his biological parents were involved with the Black Panther movement during the 1970s. As a teenager, Shakur attended the prestigious Baltimore School for the Arts. He acted in Shakespearean plays, studied ballet, and wrote poetry. There's video footage of a school interview he gave as a seventeen-year-old where he analyzes the concept of poverty with real insight, insists he "deplores" men who speak disrespectfully to women, and directly says, "I try to be as mature as I can be." The soft-spoken seventeen-year-old in that video does not seem like a kid who would not live past the age of twenty-five. There are no signs of the man who would spend eight months in prison for sexual assault. There are no signs of the person who would serve another ten days for attacking someone with a baseball bat, who would punch a film director on the set of a video shoot, who'd survive five gunshot wounds during a robbery attempt, and who would eventually get murdered by an unknown assassin* after attending a Mike Tyson fight in Las Vegas.

The dichotomy of Shakur's life is now understood by almost anyone who cares about his music. But during the zenith of his fame, it was easy to be

---

*An individual once named as a key suspect in Shakur's killing—Compton rapper Orlando Anderson—was shot and killed in 1998.

aware of Tupac Shakur without any knowledge of how he'd grown up or who he used to be.

"[His rap persona] was nothing like the person that I knew," Becky Mossing told the *Baltimore Sun* years after his death. Mossing had been a classmate of Shakur's in high school. "I honestly believe he was playing a part that he probably was made to play."

This categorization, in a broad sense, is plausible. But who was compelling him to play that part, and at what point did this high-stakes Method acting evolve into the actual person he was? Was he, in fact, a casualty of his own ability to appear dangerous? "The whole world's gonna owe me an apology," he said after his '94 sex abuse conviction. "I went through this and ain't blow my brains out like Kurt Cobain. And I should."

As a performer, there's little debate over Shakur's skill. He remains among the bestselling rappers of the nineties, with two albums (1995's *Me Against the World* and 1996's *All Eyez on Me*) regularly classified as classics. His greatness flowed from an emotional intensity bordering on discomfort: Critic Greg Tate called him "the most tortured soul hip-hop has ever known." He was also a naturalistic actor, particularly in his first film, 1992's *Juice*. But this legacy is inseparable from his deliberate transformation into the revolutionary "gangsta" he aspired to be and the central role he played in the nonsensical rivalry between rappers hailing from the West Coast and rappers hailing from the East Coast.

Watching the hip-hop war of the mid-nineties was like watching a cartoon evolve into live action, and then into real life. It initially seemed like a publicity maneuver: Artists from New York would take veiled (or not-so-veiled) shots at artists in Los Angeles, and then the L.A. rappers would respond with dis tracks directed back at artists in NYC. The cities were viewed as having different musical values. Though Tupac was born in Harlem and primarily raised in Baltimore, he joined the Los Angeles–based Death Row Records in 1995 while still serving time in a correctional facility. The coastal conflicts became more personal, especially between Shakur and a four-hundred-pound Brooklyn rapper named Christopher Wallace, professionally known as the Notorious B.I.G. (and perhaps the only hip-hop artist of the era respected as much as Tupac). By spring of 1997, both Shakur and Wallace had been shot and killed, with each artist vaguely implicated in the death of the other (it was speculated, though never proven, that Wallace was killed in retribution for buying the gun used to kill Tupac). It's still hard to accept that an abstract geographic rivalry resulted in the murders of the genre's two biggest stars, but that was what happened. They'd talked themselves into it.

3 Nineteen Percent

GEORGE H. W. BUSH WAS AN EXCEEDINGLY POPULAR PRESIDENT, UNTIL HE tried to continue being president. He then became exceedingly unpopular. This will always be the defining strangeness of Bush's limited tenure in the Oval Office and the single most critical factor in how the nineties ultimately unspooled: How did an elected official with a national approval rating of 89 percent in 1991 decisively lose his job in 1992? There was no major scandal, unless you count the infidelities of the man who beat him. Yes, there was an economic recession. But the heart of that recession ended in March of '91, when his popularity was still peaking. He'd made an optical mistake at the '88 Republican convention, pointing into the camera and saying, "Read my lips: no new taxes." Two years later, taxes went up and the promise became an albatross. But here again—that tax increase happened when his popularity was still formidable, and over half the country hadn't believed that pledge on the day he made it. Bush should have been Kevlar. Part of the reason the Democrats nominated an unproven, unfamiliar Arkansas governor to run against him was the widely accepted notion that Bush was unbeatable. They didn't want to waste a better prospect.

He looked invincible, but he lacked charisma. That was the one intangible everyone seemed to concede, and a deficit that informed everything else

about him. Throughout his successful 1988 campaign against Massachusetts governor Michael Dukakis, Bush was endlessly framed as a "wimp,"
even on the cover of *Newsweek* magazine. It was an odd epithet, considering
how Bush had been shot out of the sky as a pilot in World War II, played
college baseball at Yale, and served as director of the CIA. Yet those biographical details could not compensate for the way he spoke, a nasally delivery that
was rarely confident and never intimidating. He never stopped seeming like
Ronald Reagan's vice president. During a press conference in 1990, he pro-
claimed that he hated broccoli and would never eat it again, banning its
presence on Air Force One. Had Reagan made the same statement, it would
have seemed comedic and candid—prefab proof that he was still a normal
guy who didn't worry about what was (or wasn't) good for him. It would have
scanned as masculine. But for Bush, the same joke made him seem weak,
particularly when he noted how his mother used to make him eat broccoli
against his will. It turned him into a teenager who had to become president
in order to avoid steamed vegetables. That, however, is still not enough to
explain what happened in '92. Bush would have won easily if the election had
happened the year before, and he was classified as presidentially underrated
within a year of his loss. It's hard to fathom how any public figure could
disintegrate so dramatically within the only fleeting period when popularity
objectively mattered.

The Berlin Wall crumbled in November of 1989. The Soviet Union
dissolved two years later. Conservative readings of these events credit Reagan almost entirely: The contention is that Reagan's war-hawk mentality
forced his adversaries into an escalating spending spree that was better
suited for capitalism than communism, eroding the economic structure of
the USSR from within. The liberal reading contradicts this: They assert the
erosion was going to happen no matter who was president, that the real
turning point was Mikhail Gorbachev's 1986 desire for *glasnost* ("political
openness"), and Reagan's aggression only made things worse for everybody
involved. But either way, the timing for George Bush was strategically

perfect—the Soviet collapse and Germany's reunification both occurred while he was in office, and both were initiated by events that had transpired during an administration in which he'd served as vice president. These transformative moments altered everything previously understood about world dominance. They should have remained at the front of public memory for years.

Yet, somehow, they did not.

Something indefinable was changing about the way people processed history, including the history they were actively experiencing. Throughout the eighties, there had been ample criticism about how the popular culture was evolving. The 1980 George W. S. Trow essay "Within the Context of No Context" argued that "the work of television is to establish false contexts and to chronicle the unraveling of existing contexts." It was an unwieldy sentence to grasp, but Trow was explaining something the public could intuitively sense: The way the world was presented through media was increasingly detached from the way the world actually was. Technology was advancing faster than the human condition. When the music network MTV debuted in 1981, the justifiable fear was that an endless stream of four-minute rock videos would destroy the teenage attention span. But could that really be true? Hadn't people expressed the exact same fear when television was first introduced in the fifties? In 1987, the philosopher Allan Bloom published an unexpected bestseller titled *The Closing of the American Mind*, claiming that the modern university system had prioritized relativism over critical thinking, inadvertently leading to nihilism—but Bloom was attacked for being elitist, out of touch, clandestinely conservative,* and not really a philosopher. As is so often the case, any criticism of modernity was marginalized as reac-

---

*It should be noted that some of the high-profile political scientists who would later be viewed as key players in the neoconservative movement—such as writer William Kristol and Iraq War secretary of defense Paul Wolfowitz—were considered acolytes of Bloom when Bloom was teaching at the University of Chicago.

tionary. There was no hard evidence for any of the doomsday claims about how an accelerated culture would change the human relationship to reality.

But then the Gulf War happened, and—suddenly—there was.

○ ○ ○

The explanation behind any war is twofold. On one hand, the twisted guts of a major international conflict are too complicated to fully explain, even within the span of a textbook. That's the historian's view. But there's also the student's view, which unavoidably reduces the entire experience into a single paragraph. Here's one version of the latter perspective: The Gulf War was a successful war, assuming you're willing to classify anything that kills tens of thousands of people as a success. In the summer of 1990, Iraq invaded the tiny, oil-rich nation of Kuwait, ostensibly because (a) Iraq's recent war with Iran had forced them to borrow billions of dollars from Kuwait, which they didn't want to pay back, (b) Iraq believed Kuwait was exporting more petroleum than OPEC regulations permitted and was illegally siphoning Iraqi oil, and (c) Iraqi leader Saddam Hussein assumed he could probably get away with it, because who cared about Kuwait? The invasion was international news, but not the kind of news people in the United States particularly worried about. Had the U.S. done nothing, it would have likely become another interchangeable episode in the long series of Middle Eastern events that Americans accept as problematic without understanding what they are or where they're happening. But Bush, for reasons both understandable and surprising, took an uncharacteristically hard-line stance against the invasion. "This will not stand, this aggression* against Kuwait," he said on August 6. Bush and Secretary of State James Baker spent the rest of the year putting together an international coalition to combat Iraq. The level of co-

---

*This phrase is now more famous for its subtle appropriation by Jeff Bridges in the 1998 Coen brothers film *The Big Lebowski*. It also seems a bit contradictory, in terms of what the U.S. policy actually was: In 1990, the American ambassador to Iraq, April Glaspie, told Hussein directly, "We have no opinion on the Arab-Arab conflicts, like your border disagreement with Kuwait."

operation was higher than anyone expected. Almost forty countries provided military personnel, including previously unthinkable anti-American nations like Syria. A few governments that did not provide manpower (most notably Germany and Japan) offered financial assistance. The political authorization for going to war had predictable critics on the left (among them, Massachusetts Democrat Ted Kennedy and Bernie Sanders of Vermont), but the war resolution was passed* on January 12. Five days later, the U.S.-led alliance initiated its assault, mostly through devastating air strikes illuminating the night sky. Iraq attempted to disrupt the onslaught by firing eighty-eight Scud missiles at Israel, in hopes that Israel would counter with their own military response; this, in theory, would prompt other Arab nations to withdraw from the coalition (based on the premise that Arabs would view fighting *with* Zionists as more distasteful than fighting *against* anyone else). But Israel stood down and absorbed the punishment. The coalition did not crumble. By the end of February 1991, the war was over. The combat period had lasted less than fifty days. Total U.S. casualties were around one hundred fifty, and almost half of those were from random accidents and friendly fire. Oil fields in Kuwait were still in flames and Hussein remained in power, but the victory was unambiguous and—unlike recent American wars in Korea and Vietnam—the outcome was immune to debate. For better or worse, this war worked.

And then it just evaporated, almost as if it had never happened at all.

The Gulf War was a successful war, assuming you're willing to accept its principal illusion: It was seen and unseen at the same time. The war in Vietnam is often referred to as the Television War, but that was a highly curated version of televised combat. Network coverage of Vietnam was akin to a visual newspaper, aggregated for controlled impact—audiences saw specific events that had happened within the past twenty-four to forty-eight

---

*The vote was closer than most people now remember: 250–183 in the House of Representatives and 52–47 in the Senate.

hours. The Gulf War was dynamic. Audiences saw arbitrary events as they were occurring. "The significance in journalism terms," CBS newsman Dan Rather would say years after the fact, "was that it was the first time in which you had extensive *live* coverage of a war."

Watching missiles detonate in real time (for the first time) was a disconcerting experience. It was difficult to reconcile that what was being seen on TV was happening in the present moment, no matter how incessantly embedded broadcasters in Baghdad breathlessly noted that we were seeing and hearing the same explosions they were hiding from. There was an astounding video-game aesthetic to the warfare coverage—cameras were mounted on the noses of missiles, providing the viewer with the sensation of riding weapons directly into their targets. The first air attack was launched at two thirty a.m. local time, so the video images had to be enhanced with futuristic night vision technology; it was seven thirty p.m. in New York, so the action was broadcast in prime time. The destruction of Iraq was unusually watchable, particularly since that destruction seemed to involve no humans whatsoever.

"I'm now going to show you a picture of the luckiest man in Iraq," General Norman Schwarzkopf told a roomful of reporters, pointing at a TV monitor during a press conference in Riyadh, Saudi Arabia. The war was two weeks old and already felt over. Schwarzkopf, a magnetic and heavyset military careerist who seemed like a character from the kind of uncomplicated war movie no longer produced by Hollywood, had emerged as the unexpected star of the invasion. His video showed an Iraqi truck driving across a bridge, directly through the crosshairs of a bomber. Seconds after the truck passed, the bridge was annihilated. The clip was intended to demonstrate the level of precision the modern military now operated with, which is exactly what it did. But this brand of footage distanced the perception of what the war actually entailed. It was as if the war were only fought by machines, devoid of human suffering or existential meaning. The intellectual distancing was intentional. The social and political failure of Vietnam had taught the U.S. military that the public conception of warfare was almost as important as the warfare itself. The Gulf War was shaped to suggest the entire event was a clinical operation with a minimum of bloodshed. In the short term, the framing worked. While only half the country had supported military intervention before the opening attack, the war's approval rating soared to almost 80 percent a week after it began. The Gulf War was a triumph of public relations. But it was forgotten almost instantly.

We tend to assume that seeing an event "live" deepens its imprint on the mind. It should, in theory, make the experience more intense, and the associated emotions should be more ingrained. But the prolonged liveness of the Gulf War produced the opposite effect. Like a CGI action movie with no character development, the plot vaporized as it combusted. In France, cultural critic Jean Baudrillard wrote a series of essays titled *The Gulf War Did Not Take Place*, published while the war was actively happening. Due to the provocative title (and because the essays were not fully translated into English until 1995), the work was mocked. In retrospect, his contention was prescient. Baudrillard was not actually arguing that the war did not take place. He was arguing that the presentation of the war made it feel like a simulation, and that what was really happening in Iraq was instantaneously combined with the interpretation of what was to be expected. The network footage was live and raw, but dependent on the military's willingness to grant those networks access, which meant the rawness was clandestinely cooked. The public saw almost no casualties from either side. The strategic success was robotic. Despite the buildings that were annihilated and the civilian lives that were lost, there was no obvious emotional component to the war, which meant there was no narrative. And since American audiences had been trained to understand the world through the process of storytelling, a war with no story was a war they did not care to remember.

It is, I realize, a bit cavalier to talk about a military conflict as if it were a

TV show that received great reviews before a midseason cancellation. The observation of an event should not be given the same weight as the event itself. Yet that's the only way to understand how little this victory informed George Bush's political future. He had done, seemingly, everything right. He isolated the enemy and built the coalition. He convinced Congress to support the attack and convinced Israel not to jeopardize the plan by retaliating against Saddam's barrage. He won a desert war with almost no U.S. casualties and calibrated how that war was presented to the public. By the end of February, his approval rating crested, six points higher than that of Franklin D. Roosevelt in the days after Pearl Harbor. All he had to do was hang on and remind people that this war had happened. But almost immediately, he started to wither, even among his base. Schwarzkopf's brusque charm and histrionic battle fatigues made him seem like the opposite of Bush (Schwarzkopf was the uncompromising Ditka-esque leader hard-line Republicans had always craved). Neoconservatives were more enamored with the war performance of Colin Powell,* the chair of the Joint Chiefs of Staff, who seemed to embody the polished, composed future of the intellectual right. In the wake of his greatest triumph, Bush devolved into a milquetoast figure no one wanted.

It wasn't his intention, but Baudrillard had been correct: For George Bush, the Gulf War did not happen. And then it got worse.

Though his palpable achievements were minor, H. Ross Perot is an underrated figure in the shaping of modern America. His impingement on the

---

*Though it seems a bit absurd in retrospect, the conventional wisdom of the nineties insisted that the first Black U.S. president would have to come from the Republican Party. The thinking was that a staunchly conservative African-American would still appeal to Black Democrats, but a Black Democrat would alienate white voters on both sides. Powell was inevitably seen as the ideal candidate within this scenario.

1992 presidential election epitomizes the hallucinogenic machinations of partisan politics. It's not simply that opposing sides disagree on the conclusion. It is that each side views their own espoused conclusion as comically obvious. Statistically, it can't be argued that Perot's third-party candidacy cost Bush the election. Perot, an eccentric Texas billionaire obsessed with "common sense," received 19 percent of the vote, and virtually every exit poll painted the same demographic portrait: Had he not run, 38 percent of his supporters would have voted for Bill Clinton, 38 percent would have voted for Bush, and 24 percent would have not voted at all. It's mathematically arguable that Perot stopped Bush from winning Ohio, a state where Perot performed well and Clinton's margin of victory was less than 100,000 people. But Ohio only had 21 electoral votes, and a 1999 analysis by the *American Journal of Political Science* concluded that Perot's only true upshot was slightly reducing Clinton's margin of victory in the overall popular vote. That theory is supported by Bush's late-October approval rating, a number that had eroded to 34 percent. There is no hard data that suggests Perot altered the outcome of the '92 election.

The only problem is that it's impossible to imagine the arc of that election without Perot's presence.

Here's an imperfect metaphor: Hakeem Olajuwon and the Houston Rockets won the NBA title in 1994 and 1995, the two seasons when Michael Jordan was mostly absent from the league in his short-lived attempt at professional baseball. Would Houston have experienced the same success if Jordan had remained with the Chicago Bulls? It's possible. There's statistical evidence suggesting Houston might have won two titles regardless (the Rockets were 5-1 against the Bulls during Jordan's first three title seasons). Yet no one accepts this, regardless of the statistical possibility. If Jordan stays with the Bulls, everything currently understood about those two seasons shifts. In the same way, it's difficult to imagine a Perot-free election that doesn't play to Bush's advantage. While it's possible to argue Perot's campaign damaged both Bush and Clinton, he hurt Bush way more, which means he helped Clinton unintentionally.*

Born in Texarkana, Texas, in 1930, Perot was the kind of man an optimist would cite as an example if forced to explain why being an ambitious workaholic was a good idea. He got his first job when he was eight years old and excelled as a Boy Scout (in an era when being a Boy Scout mattered more). He attended the Naval Academy and became president of his class, serving as an architect of the school's honor code. His decision to attend college at Annapolis illustrates the capricious oddness of his drive and desire. "I had never seen the ocean, and I had never seen a ship," he supposedly said of his appointment, "but I knew I wanted to go to the Naval Academy."

After finishing his naval tenure, Perot took a job with IBM. He could sell anything. His success at IBM led to a life of entrepreneurship in the fledgling field of data processing. By 1968, he was being profiled by *Fortune* magazine, eventually selling his Dallas-based company, Electronic Data Systems, to General Motors for $2.5 billion. But Perot's interests were not limited to the mere accumulation of wealth. He disagreed with U.S. military policy and was particularly obsessed, from the seventies onward, with the possibility that U.S. soldiers were still trapped in Vietnam prison camps (and he believed the Bush administration knew this to be true). He was adamantly against U.S. involvement in the Gulf War. He felt the United States had gone to war against an infantile tyrant they'd purposefully placed in power.

"Our president was sending delegations over to burp and diaper and

---

*Further complicating the prospect of Clinton's inevitability is the presidential predictive system created by American University political scientist Allan Lichtman. By using a series of thirteen true-or-false "keys" regarding the conditions of the country and the composition of the candidates, Lichtman has correctly predicted the outcome of every presidential election since 1980 (although there was one year when he was correct about the popular vote while missing on the electoral map). In April of '92, Lichtman had Bush winning easily, placing eight of the thirteen keys in Bush's favor. But by October of that year, Lichtman had turned three of the keys toward Clinton and predicted that the Democrat would win. At first glance, this seems to suggest Clinton's victory would have happened with or without Perot. But it must also be noted that one of Lichtman's thirteen keys is "There is no significant third-party candidate" (with an answer of "false" favoring the challenger).

pamper Saddam Hussein and tell him how nice he was," Perot said. "[But then] our manhood was questioned and off we go into the wild blue yonder with the lives of our servicemen at risk because of ten years of stupid mistakes and billions of dollars of taxpayer money."

That sentiment is Perot in a nutshell: His language is primitive, colorful, and clear. His larger point is about the war, but it's reframed as practical economics. Most important, he's criticizing Bush with a straightforwardness Bill Clinton would never attempt. Clinton, like any conventional politician, operated from the theory that any mention of America's victory in Kuwait would only make Bush look good. Clinton felt obligated to give Bush credit for his military performance. There appeared to be no strategic alternative. How could winning a war make the president look bad? But Perot saw things differently. He was a "process" guy. The positive outcome of the war did not mean it hadn't been a bad idea to begin with.

Perot launched his third-party campaign in February of '92 on *Larry King Live*, a prime-time CNN talk show that skirted the line between news and entertainment. The program's host was Larry King, an interviewer whose peculiar superpower was knowing next to nothing about the person he happened to be interviewing. It was the ideal venue for someone like Perot. He could just talk. He claimed he wasn't naturally suited for the office of president and would only run if "ordinary people" petitioned to get his name on the ballot in all fifty states. That detail was a foregone conclusion; by April, he was fully invested in the race. With the war evaporating from public consciousness, his platform adopted the usual signifiers of economic populism: Balance the budget, fight globalization, and oversee the government the same way a CEO would oversee a factory. His talent was appearing to understand obvious realities that other people could not see, expressed with the kind of self-assurance that can only come from extreme wealth.

Throughout the nineties, it was not uncommon for armchair historians to note how the winner of previous presidential elections had almost always been whichever candidate was physically taller. Nobody notes this anymore, mostly because it proved untrue in 2000, 2004, and 2020. But it came up all the time in '92, simply because Perot was *so* short. He was usually described as five foot six, although five foot five was more realistic. He had large ears, bad eyesight, and weighed maybe 140 pounds if holding an armadillo. When debating Bush (who was six-two) and Clinton (six–two and a half) onstage, the contrast looked hilarious. Yet his size worked to his advantage. It cast Perot as pugnacious and made his quips more cutting. When explaining why he hated the North American Free Trade Agreement, he said the inevitable migration of American jobs to Mexico would create "a giant sucking sound going south." This wasn't really a joke, but it made people laugh without detracting from the argument. In the weeks before the election, Perot self-financed a series of thirty-minute infomercials where he would sit at a desk and point at line graphs and pie graphs while lecturing about economics. The content was dense and static and seemed like a terrible idea, but 16.5 million people watched the first one (and polling suggested audiences found his infomercials twice as truthful as the predictable thirty-second campaign commercials from Bush and Clinton).

Perot's apex was June. A Gallup poll placed him as the lead dog in a three-dog race with 39 percent of the vote (Bush had 31 and Clinton 25). It is therefore tempting to claim, "For a short time, it really seemed like Perot might win." But this would not be accurate. For one thing, this often cited phone poll only contacted 815 registered voters. For another, Perot's still-unofficial campaign was already in chaos. He was not a normal candidate, and he didn't act like one. He thought the best choice for his campaign theme song was the Willie Nelson ballad "Crazy." He was marginalized as a paranoid control freak (and in this case, stereotypes about his diminutive size fueled that view). A key campaign manager resigned in July and Perot dropped out of the race the very next day, returning to *Larry King Live* to claim that Bush was going to disrupt his daughter's impending wedding if he did not withdraw.* This did not exactly decrease the perception that he was paranoid. Because his entry into the race had been so grassroots and irregular, his departure was taken as a betrayal. *Newsweek* magazine threw him on their July 27 cover with the tagline "The Quitter," as if a struggling candidate withdrawing from a race was somehow unusual. Almost overnight, the perception of his persona shifted from quirky to loony. But then, on the first day of October, he suddenly reentered the race, buying network TV time for his infomercials and generally behaving like he'd never left.

Election Day was November 3. Nobody knew how many votes Perot would get, though only his most fanatical disciples believed he could win. The night was absent of surprise. Clinton did not dominate but still won easily. Though he received only 43 percent of the popular vote, the Arkansas governor murdered the electoral map, taking twenty-two of the states Bush had secured in 1988. Perot did not win any state (his best showing was in Maine). There was a sense he had failed, and that his disorganized exit and return proved he was never a serious prospect. Yet this odd little man from Texas had convinced almost 20 million Americans that he should be president. It was the best showing for a third-party candidate in eighty years.

The U.S. political system operates from the position that a large chunk of the populace will vote along party lines, regardless of who their party nominates (even in landslide elections, like Johnson in 1964 and Nixon in '72, the losing candidate still grabbed around 38 percent of the popular vote). The fact that an independent like Perot successfully appealed to 19

---

*Though Perot never fully explained what he feared Bush was planning, another of his four daughters was quoted in *The New York Times,* saying that her father believed Republicans were going to fabricate a rumor that his soon-to-be-married daughter was a lesbian. Years later, Perot said the Republicans were going to circulate altered photos of his daughter. There is no evidence for any of this, outside of the fact that Bush was the former head of the CIA and it seemed like something the CIA might consider a good tactic.

percent of voters during a period of domestic prosperity simply does not compute.

So who were those 19 percent, and what did they want?

As of the publication of this book, there are still many humans alive who voted for H. Ross Perot in 1992. But asking someone to explain the motives for a decision made three decades ago is asking for a misinterpretation on purpose. People change, and they tend to view past actions through the prism of their current self. Memories are replaced by projections. It's more relevant to examine what people were saying at the time. The only problem is that the amorphous nature of Perot's platform made the desires of his supporters equally imprecise. They wanted an institutional change. That was clear. What's less clear is whether this was a change away from something that was already there or toward something that did not exist.

The earliest and most complete attempt at understanding the phenomenon is an out-of-print book by Albert J. Menendez, *The Perot Voters & the Future of American Politics.* A former statistician with the Bureau of Labor Statistics, Menendez's 1996 abstract is mostly a breakdown of the election's math. The information can seem contradictory or cohesive, depending on your level of apophenia. Menendez saw a lot of meaning in the increase of voter turnout, which went up for the first time in three decades. That could mean Perot convinced people to vote who would not have voted otherwise, but it could also mean that Clinton's outreach to younger people, particularly through MTV's "Choose or Lose" campaign, juiced overall participation (Clinton was, for anyone under twenty-five, the first presidential nominee in memory to resemble a father more than a grandfather). Perot performed better in states where the population was increasing. He exceeded his national average of 19 percent in the ten states with the lowest percentage of citizens who were born native to that state. He also tended to underperform in the most urban areas within every state, regardless of its size or geographic location (he did worse in Manhattan than in upstate New York, and he did worse in Fargo than in western North Dakota). Most of his support came from white people in their twenties and thirties (he was abysmal with Black people and the elderly). He was most effective with manufacturers (understandable), farmers (somewhat understandable), and people with German heritage (weird, unfathomable, and possibly coincidental). The author's conclusion is that Perot irrefutably harmed Bush more than Clinton, despite what the exit polls indicated. Every county Perot managed to carry in '92 had been won by Bush in '88.

What these numbers cannot illustrate, of course, are the underserved ideas these people shared. Typically, people who support third-party candidates are unified by their prioritization of idealistic issues that fall outside mainstream politics (Ralph Nader in 2000, Jill Stein in 2016, et al.). Perot's people did not fit this profile. He was a radical centrist—the overlapping intersection of a Venn diagram involving two interloping rivals who had nothing else in common (ultra-liberal Jerry Brown and paleo-conservative Pat Buchanan). Perot's espoused motive for entering the race was his distaste for the Gulf War, but he wasn't embraced as an antiwar champion; his view of Kuwait, much like the war itself, was rapidly swallowed by the memory hole.* Instead, he was seen as the guy who wanted to reduce the national debt and brutally balance the budget (tax the rich, tax gasoline, and cut into every program, including the military and Medicare). It was the kind of populist thinking that always appeals to those who prefer to think of the country

---

*In the process of writing this chapter, I had many casual conversations about the legacy of Perot. No nonhistorian I spoke with remembered that Perot had entered the race due to his displeasure with the Gulf War (or even that he had a strong position on it). There was, however, a high degree of recall for Perot's selection of Vice Admiral James Stockdale as his running mate, and particularly Stockdale's terrible performance in the October 11 vice presidential debate. At one point in the televised debate, Stockdale rhetorically asked, "Who am I? Why am I here?" The line backfired and became the principal sound bite for news organizations. The '92 election is the rare example of a presidential race where a candidate's running mate choice may have actually made a difference in how people voted. Perot wanted to be an outsider, but a more traditional veep selection would have increased voter confidence in his ability to work within the constraints of traditional government.

as a nuclear household. Around the same time, militant economists like Warren Mosler were constructing the academic foundation for Modern Monetary Theory,* a philosophy that destroys the value of Perot's premise. But in 1992, most people agreed with his general logic, even if they didn't like Perot as a person or see him as qualified to lead. It seemed like a bad idea to spend more money than you made. How could this little fellow from Texas be the only person who realized that?

There was, however, something else at play here—something reflective of the era, and something antithetical to how presidential elections have come to be covered. Part of the reason 20 million people voted for Ross Perot was because it didn't seem like a particularly big deal to do so. Communism, and whatever threat it allegedly posed, was over. There was only one super-power remaining, and that was the U.S. (China was still in its "sleeping giant" phase). The Republicans had been in power for a long twelve years, and Bush's approval rating was in the tank, in large part due to fatigue. The '92 election was a "change election," where voters mainly wanted something unlike what they already had. Did the direction of that change even matter? What's the worst that could happen? There had been good presidents and there had been bad presidents, but the net deviation was akin to Richard Linklater's description of fingerprints in the 1991 film *Slacker*: The differences were minor compared to the similarities.

○ ○ ○

If, as the exit polling statistics suggest, Perot did not actually alter the outcome of the 1992 election, his current status in history is probably where it belongs—somewhere between a curiosity and a trivia question. He ran again

---

*In the simplest terms possible, Modern Monetary Theory (MMT) promotes the following idea: A nation is not like a household, and comparing its budget to a family budget is stupid. For a nation, debt is meaningless. A government can print its own money and should do so whenever the need arises, as long as prices don't escalate. Government spending does not matter. The only concern is keeping down inflation.

in 1996 and was not even half as successful (he took roughly 8 million votes, 8.4 percent of the total). He founded the Reform Party in 1995, constructed as a collection of his values. The party was still active in the wake of Perot's vacancy, but just barely (in 2008 and 2012, the Reform Party's nominee received less than 1,000 votes nationally). Within this framework, his legacy is not that different from that of Congressman John B. Anderson (a third-party candidate from Illinois who got 6.6 percent of the vote in 1980). But if the 1992 exit polling only illustrates the final outcome without reflecting how much Perot warped the election cycle, his rippling influence on the nineties is almost too large to calculate.

Bush, unbeatable in the summer of 1991, had blown it all by the summer of '92. But if there's no Perot incessantly nipping at his heels, perhaps Bush wins a campaign of attrition. Without the adversarial presence of Perot, Clinton can't unceasingly exhibit the charming idealism that came to define his early persona (and was so appealing to voters under the age of thirty). Instead, Clinton has to attack. The race becomes darker and more traditional. Bush wins Ohio and does better in the industrial Northeast. Even if the margin of victory is narrow, a fourth straight Republican win forces a deep-seated reinvention of the Democratic Party. The Democratic Leadership Council (essentially a liberal think tank launched in 1985) was already pushing the party in a centrist direction. The DLC's agenda was succinctly outlined in a 1989 paper titled "The Politics of Evasion," published by the Progressive Policy Institute: "Democrats must now come face to face with reality: too many Americans have come to see the party as inattentive to their economic interests, indifferent if not hostile to their moral sentiments and ineffective in defense of their national security." Clinton adopted the DLC perspective and positioned himself as a New Democrat who would distance the party from its tax-and-spend, morally ambivalent identity. It proved to be a winning strategy in a three-man race, although not overwhelmingly, and it's hard to predict in which direction the party would have moved if Clinton had lost (or whom the Democrats would have run in 1996). Equally opaque is the path of the Republican Party without a Clinton presidency to push against. In the off-year election of 1994, the GOP gained 54 seats in the House of Representatives and 8 seats in the Senate. The tectonic shift vaulted combative Georgia representative Newt Gingrich to Speaker of the House, laying the groundwork for the intense partisan polarization that would flourish throughout the twenty-first century. If Bush remains in the Oval Office, this so-called Republican Revolution isn't necessary and never happens. It seems counterintuitive, but the modern Republican Party would likely be much less extreme if George H. W. Bush had been reelected in a landslide. This can't be blamed on Perot, assuming you believe the 20 million people who voted for him ultimately did not matter. But if you believe otherwise, the prospect becomes more complex.

Perot died on July 9, 2019. He was eighty-nine. Because he passed in the midst of Donald Trump's presidency (and because all news events that happened during that period could only be viewed through the prism of Trump's existence), it was common for obituary writers to draw parallels between the man who became the forty-fifth president and the man who failed at becoming the forty-second. Certain symmetries made this easy: Both were billionaires. Both were against free trade and immigration. Both were willing to propagate conspiracies. Both used unorthodox media platforms to launch their campaigns, and both attacked the press when faced with adversity. Both appealed to people who otherwise may not have voted, and both utilized a colorful lexicon that made them seem unlike normal politicians (Perot once compared the national debt to a "crazy aunt" living in a basement). Perot did better with the young than the old; Trump did better with the old than the young. Was it possible that the thirty-year-old white males who voted for Perot in 1992 had become the disenfranchised fifty-four-year-olds who elected Trump in 2016? It is, I suppose, possible. There were undoubtedly a few voters who fit that description. But if they did, it was an irrational coincidence. In the years immediately following the '92 campaign, a true believer in Perot's vision would have almost certainly moved away from Republican politics and toward the New Democrats. Clinton and Perot were much more aligned on cultural issues (Perot was pro-choice and claimed to support gay rights), and Clinton ultimately achieved many of Perot's espoused goals (he balanced the budget and decreased the debt). Perot people and Trump people were not the same people.

But were they the same *kind* of people?

There is, for a variety of self-serving reasons, a desire for this to be true, particularly among those who work within the insulated institutions outsiders always attack. "If Donald Trump is the Jesus of the disenchanted, displaced non-college white voter," former Clinton campaign strategist James Carville said in a short documentary just before the 2016 election, "then Perot was the John the Baptist of that sort of movement." The first counter to any unconventional candidate is to marginalize that candidate as unreasonable and crazy; if that approach fails, the next response is to do the same to the candidate's base. No one believed someone like Trump could win in 2016, so the unexpected victory forced his opponents to hastily construct a cultic caricature of the 63 million people who voted him into office: anti-intellectual, a bit deranged, desperate, and—above all—willing to blow up the entire political system (sometimes, depending on the level of sympathy from the accuser, modifiers ranging from "working-class" to "racist" might also be applied). It's certainly possible to argue these qualities don't always apply to Trump voters. But it's straight-up wrong to apply them to Perot voters. He did not emerge in a deranged, desperate era. He was folksy, but his appeal was not anti-intellectual (relative to his opponents, Perot's charts and graphs positioned him more as a wonk). He did not want to become president to blow up the system—in fact, he feared the system would explode if he *didn't* get involved.

Perot overestimated the risk of the national debt and his own potential ability to solve the problem. It could be argued that his main similarity to Trump was an overdriven ego, but that's hardly worth mentioning: An egoless presidential candidate cannot exist. It would have been far more remarkable if Perot had seemed humble while insisting he alone could fix America.

That ambition, when considered retroactively, is central to what's so compelling about Perot, and perhaps why he has been mostly cast aside: Despite his deep influence on the landscape of the nineties, he was not really a "nineties person." This was not the right person emerging at the right time. He was more like the wrong person, emerging at random. He was sixty-two when he ran for president but already seemed older. The nineties were not a time for the aspirant, yet here was a billionaire who always wanted more. His identity was built around modernized interpretations of Depression-era values—increasing austerity, staying out of foreign wars, cracking down on marijuana, cutting your hair and wearing a tie to the office. It was the ideological opposite of where the country was going. It was also what 1 out of 5 voters preferred.

There's a belief in America that a third-party candidate can't become president, and Perot is both the refutation and the proof. On one hand, he was an independent iconoclast who used his own money to pull 20 million votes from both liberals and conservatives. He proved it was possible. On the other hand, he had unlimited financial resources and massive media support, yet still couldn't win a single electoral vote. He proved it was impossible. Either way, Perot's performance embodies the low-level dissonance built into any culture of change: In 1992, the U.S. was evolving in a manner that was both conformist and unpredictable, and 19 percent of its citizens weren't happy about that. They wanted an alternative, which was the only thing you were supposed to want, even if it was packaged as a strange little man from Texas.

[casual determinism]

"THERE ARE DECADES WHEN NOTHING HAPPENS," VLADIMIR LENIN ALLEGEDLY claimed, "and there are weeks when decades happen." But there are also weeks when decades of meaning disappear into mist. The onset of 1993 was punctuated by a collection of seemingly unforgettable events that have been forgotten almost completely, mostly due to future events that would make the affairs of '93 feel minor and insignificant.

The February 26 attempt to blow up the World Trade Center is the epitome of this shift. A van carrying more than 1,300 pounds of urea nitrate was driven into the parking garage of the North Tower in lower Manhattan and detonated with a twenty-foot fuse. The intention was to collapse the North Tower into the South Tower and destroy both buildings. It failed, although the damage was considerable (the entire 110-story structure shook and the electricity went out, trapping some occupants in the dark for twelve hours). Six people died (seven if you count an unborn child). It was a brazen attack with unclear motives. One of the main terrorists on the ground, Ramzi Yousef, was able to escape to Pakistan (though later captured, extradited to the U.S., and sentenced to 240 years in prison). The financial architect was Khalid Sheikh Mohammed, Yousef's uncle. Mohammed would later confess to directing this bombing attempt and the successful 2001 attack on the WTC (although he made this confession while being tortured in a secret CIA prison in Poland, subsequently confessing to many, many things).

The assault on the Twin Towers was, understandably, huge news. But because the death toll was "only" seven people, many stories in the immediate aftermath focused on the least emotional aspects: how the explosion affected the stock market, WTC businesses that needed to find temporary office space, and the realization that the Trade Center buildings had numerous code violations. And there was, or so it seemed, one upside to the event: The skyscrapers were clearly too stable to destroy. Did these terrorists really believe they could knock down two of the tallest buildings in the Western Hemisphere? It was an inconceivable fantasy. They were amateurs.

Two weeks after the bombing, the East Coast experienced another cataclysm: the most intense weather event of the twentieth century. The 1993 Superstorm, experienced over four days in March, was the rare meteorological trifecta—a low-pressure system simultaneously generating a multistate blizzard, a collection of tornadoes, and a tropical storm on par with a hurricane. The conditions were mercurial. A town in east Tennessee received 60 inches of snow, while Nashville received less than 3. In Texas, heavy snowfall was accompanied by thunder. Winds in North Carolina exceeded 90 miles per hour. There were 11 tornadoes spotted across Florida. A cargo ship off the coast of Nova Scotia capsized and the entire crew was lost at sea. Two thousand miles away, another freighter sank off the coast of Florida. Because the weather system encompassed so many dense population centers, 40 percent of the American public was affected. The death toll was considerable: More than 250 people perished (49 in Pennsylvania alone). Many deaths were attributed to people having heart attacks while shoveling snow. Still, the legacy of this tempest is improbably positive: It's considered the first time the National Weather Service was able to predict a storm of this magnitude a full five days before it hit. Local governments in the Northeast were able to declare a state of emergency before the snow even started to fall.

The reason these events have been so collectively erased has to do with other events that came later. The failed 1993 bombing of the WTC became a footnote to the 2001 attack that worked. The superstorm now seems minor when compared to the damage from 2005's Hurricane Katrina, when 1,800 people died and New Orleans was evacuated. But some of this erasure had to do with perspective. There was, in 1993, a greater willingness to view reality as something that was only happening to oneself. History was an individual experience. One of the most striking examples of this worldview was a film released just after the WTC explosion and just before the Texas thunder snow.

Falling Down was not a great movie, nor was it an unwatchable movie. What it was, mostly, was a movie that seemed important enough to be featured on the cover of *Newsweek*, even though it could never possibly be made today without a rewrite of almost every scene. The plot of *Falling Down* followed a character played by Michael Douglas, a middle-aged white male who gets stuck in traffic, experiences a mental breakdown, and attacks Los Angeles by himself. The most memorable moment involves Douglas entering a fast-food restaurant and trying to order breakfast, only to be told the restaurant stopped serving breakfast at eleven thirty a.m. and was now offering lunch. He responds by pulling out a TEC-9 machine gun. There is a ludicrous *Metal Gear* quality to the narrative—the main character acquires increasingly powerful weapons as he moves from location to location (he starts with a bat, uses the bat to get a knife, miraculously acquires a bag of guns, and eventually ends up with a rocket launcher). In the end, Douglas is killed in a suicide-by-cop scenario.

Falling Down has aged poorly. It's saturated with details that now seem unthinkable: the fact that Douglas's character claims to be against racism while killing minorities, the fact that the film was sometimes publicized as a comedy, the fact that it received mostly positive reviews and was briefly the number 1 film in the country. Contemporary critics tend to be appalled by the film's themes and won't even engage with the premise, often unaware of its unusual scope of influence (it inspired a song by Iron Maiden, a video by

Foo Fighters, and a character in *The Simpsons*). What makes *Falling Down* generationally noteworthy, however, has less to do with its reactionary politics and more to do with the way it allows the viewer to sympathize with a violent person who overreacts to mundane inconveniences. The abstract rage Douglas feels is not depicted as reasonable or justifiable but is still supposed to be relatable. The main cover line on the issue of *Newsweek* featuring Douglas's face screams "WHITE MALE PARANOIA" in capital letters, but the subhead is more generous: "Are They the Newest Victims—or Just Bad Sports?"

The protagonist in *Falling Down* was not presented as a sociopath damaging the world. He was presented as a man pushed to lunacy by a world that isn't perfect, but is by no means unlivable. Douglas is infuriated by exterior problems that barely qualify as problems, the manifestation of flaws in his own interior life. Within the framework of his belief system, what is happening in society is *only* happening to him. He is a terrorist and he is a superstorm, and if we forget the explanation as to why that was supposed to translate to other people, it's because the explanation was never there to begin with. It was just something to harmlessly consider, for 113 minutes, until there was something better to complain about.

4 The Edge, as Viewed from the Middle

IN 1993, THE *LOS ANGELES TIMES* MADE A DECISION ABOUT ITSELF. THE newspaper internally distributed a document titled "Guidelines on Ethnic, Racial, Sexual and Other Identification," instructing its writers and editors on roughly 150 words or phrases that would either be banned or restricted from publication in the newspaper. The nineteen-page booklet was drafted by a twenty-two-member committee and issued by editor Shelby Coffey III. Some of what was eliminated now seems obvious and arcane (the idiom "Chinese fire drill," the description of someone as an "admitted homosexual"). Other citations remain debatable (the elimination of the modifier "normal" and the use of the euphemism "inner city" to describe residential districts at the geographic center of a large community).

The implementation of these rules was not remarkable. All publications sporadically update their style guides and language parameters, a practice typically noticed by no one outside the office. But these changes were made in one swoop, delivered as a package, and labeled with a title that appeared to openly embrace the burgeoning notion of "political correctness," an academic term that had been adopted into the mainstream lexicon during the last half of the 1980s. It prompted an unusually high-volume response to an otherwise small decision, mostly from other journalists and almost entirely negative. A *Los Angeles Times* columnist working in the San Fernando bureau wrote a column criticizing the intent of the style manual, only to have the column killed before publication. The decision to stop its own staff from criticizing the new policy inflamed the opinion that the newspaper was now trying to control language in an awkwardly Orwellian manner.

The most measured reaction to the manual, however, came from a Canadian cognitive psychologist with a rising profile as a public intellectual. MIT linguist Steven Pinker had just released his sixth book, *The Language Instinct*. He was commissioned to write an op-ed for *The New York Times* about how the newly imposed guidelines should be received by a reasonable reader. Though it's difficult to deduce Pinker's personal feelings about the conflict, his essay made three points that applied to almost all extensions of the debate. The first was, "words are not thoughts," and that there's no scientific evidence that language determines thought. The second was that words are arbitrary, an actuality that connected to his third point: "Concepts, not words, are in charge," wrote Pinker. "Give a concept a new name, and the name becomes colored by the concept; the concept does not become freshened by the name."

There's a level of obviousness to what Pinker was asserting here: If you call a cow a horse, it won't make people think a cow *is* a horse, and if you somehow coerce people to say "horse" every time they see a cow, all it will change is the definition of the word *horse*. It seems to support the argument that limits on language have no impact on how people actually think or how the world works, and that these changes are superficial capitulations. But it can also be read in the opposite way: If words are arbitrary and only serve as signifiers for their underlying concepts, there's no reason to get upset over changes to the language, since the real issue is the problematic concept that specific language is being used to uphold and enforce.

This is why Pinker's assertion was not really obvious at all. There was, throughout the nineties, ongoing discomfort over the alleged dangers and espoused necessity of unsanctioned expression. It was increasingly unclear whether that discomfort came from the words being used or the concepts being interrogated, and increasingly transparent that those most invested in the debate preferred to view the terms interchangeably. There was language and there were concepts. But there was also circumstance, and that was the wild card.

○ ○ ○

As Nasty As They Wanna Be showed up in record stores in February of 1989. The third album from the Miami-based rap group 2 Live Crew, it was a hugely successful record at a time when rap still had a hard commercial ceiling, selling over 2 million copies (twice as many as Public Enemy's *It Takes a Nation of Millions to Hold Us Back*, a release from 1988 that remains the greatest hip-hop album ever made). *As Nasty As They Wanna Be* was also the first pop album to be classified as legally obscene, a categorization even its ideological supporters could not dispute ("This record is pornographic," wrote Robert Christgau of *The Village Voice*. "That's one of the few good things about it"). The popularity of 2 Live Crew, much like the contemporaneous success of comedian Andrew Dice Clay, was almost entirely due to the unrelenting onslaught of graphic obscenity expressed in the lyrics, along with the tacit understanding that this obscenity was (more or less) the whole artistic idea.

In 1990, Florida district judge Jose Gonzalez declared that the album qualified as obscenity and was not protected by the First Amendment, claiming the record was an "appeal to dirty thoughts and the loins, not to the intellect and the mind." It was a nonsensical legal argument that was difficult to enforce, but it terrified retailers (especially those in South Florida), prompting the removal of *As Nasty As They Wanna Be* from many stores. A shop owner in Fort Lauderdale was actually arrested two days after the ruling when he sold a copy of *As Nasty As They Wanna Be* to an undercover policeman.

2 Live Crew's criminality was a temporary condition. Within three years,

the Eleventh Circuit Court of Appeals overturned the decision. This case was never a battle over a concept. It was solely a battle over language. There isn't any *concept* within a song like "The Fuck Shop." There was no fear that "The Fuck Shop" would motivate the public to visit brothels or launch family-owned businesses where "the price is right just to fuck a ho." It did not, in any way, represent a clear and present danger to the government. This was *only* an obscenity case, which meant there were only three points of contention:

1. Did *As Nasty As They Wanna Be* appeal to prurient interests (probably)

2. Did it depict or describe sex in a patently offensive way (absolutely)

3. Did it lack serious literary, artistic value (maybe, but not necessarily)

The original Gonzalez verdict hinged on the third point; the appeal succeeded on the basis that the third point was never satisfactorily proven. To First Amendment scholars, this was wonderful news. But it meant less to everyone else. The content of the album was (literally) the presentation of profane nursery rhymes. It seemed wrong to stop its distribution, and it seemed constitutionally correct to support its existence. But what was the specific loss or gain? There was an overwhelming sense that all this legal trouble* was good for 2 Live Crew, providing them with a nonmusical significance they would have never achieved on their own. A few days after the Gonzalez verdict, two of the group members were arrested for violating a prohibition against lewd behavior during a late-night club show in Holly-

---

*A different case involving 2 Live Crew, this one over the Roy Orbison song "Oh, Pretty Woman," went all the way to the U.S. Supreme Court. That case, however, had nothing to do with obscenity. It was a dispute over whether making a commercial parody version of a copyrighted song should be classified as fair use. The court sided with the Crew.

wood, Florida. They spent two hours in a Broward County jail, were not required to post bail, and were released in time to catch a flight to Phoenix for another concert. None of this seemed important.

But another song, released between the 1990 Gonzalez verdict and the successful '92 appeal, tested similar principles in a more combustible way.

Ice-T (born Tracy Marrow in 1958) was a hip-hop artist who'd spent his teen years in Los Angeles and pioneered the genre of gangsta rap throughout the 1980s. Ice-T's musical taste, however, was considered expansive and eclectic. He would often note the narrative similarities between rap and country, and between rap and hard rock. In 1991, he formed a heavy metal group called Body Count, influenced by bands like Black Sabbath and Slayer. In March of 1992, Body Count released a self-titled album that concluded with a track called "Cop Killer." It was divisive, for reasons that went beyond language. This conflict was *all* concept.

The expository, nonmetaphorical lyrics to "Cop Killer" were dedicated to the Los Angeles Police Department: The narrator puts on black gloves and a ski mask, turns off the headlights of his car, and prepares to shoot himself some cops. The song's central refrains are "Fuck the police" and "Tonight we get even," punctuated by a sample of gunshots from an automatic weapon. The song would have been marginally controversial in 1982 or 2002. It would be marginally controversial if released tomorrow. But in 1992, it was the most contentious work of art about the most contentious quandary in America. Timing, as always, was everything.

In 1991, Black motorist Rodney King was beaten by several white LAPD officers following a high-speed chase through the San Fernando Valley. Four police officers were charged with assault and use of excessive force. The trial concluded on April 29 of the following year. All four officers were acquitted of assault, despite a widely seen twelve-minute videotape of King being pummeled. That verdict immediately led to the Los Angeles riots, a six-day affair that killed sixty-three people and incinerated huge sections of South Central Los Angeles, particularly ravaging businesses in the neighborhood of Koreatown. The most graphic footage was captured by news helicopters hovering above the riot, notably a truck driver named Reginald Denny who was violently dragged out of his vehicle and struck in the head with a cinder block. President Bush dispatched over four thousand military personnel to restore order.

The beating of King, the trial of the officers, and the devastation of the protests were all used as validation for every possible view about law enforcement and racism. The assault on King showed that Black people were targeted and abused by the police; the trial indicated that white juries were biased toward white defendants, regardless of the evidence; the riot suggested that the city of Los Angeles was self-destructive and out of control, requiring authorities to employ permissible force. The perception was that everyone involved was partially at fault: A poll by the *Los Angeles Times* found that 71 percent of local residents "strongly disagreed" with the King verdict, but 75 percent classified the subsequent protests as "totally unjustified."

This was the maelstrom "Cop Killer" parachuted into, forcing a theoretical puzzle that suddenly felt plausible: Considering the condition of the country, could a song about killing cops directly convince someone to kill a cop?

Questions over the real-world culpability of entertainers had come up before, throughout the eighties. Metal artists Ozzy Osbourne and Judas Priest were both accused of recording music that led to teenagers committing suicide. The question would surface again in 1993, twice: An episode of MTV's *Beavis and Butt-Head* was accused of prompting a five-year-old boy to set a fire that killed his sister, and a scene (later deleted) from the college football movie *The Program* led to a teenager lying down on the highway and being killed by a car. The scenario posed by "Cop Killer," however, was more unnerving. All those other cases required a misinterpretation of the content. The message of "Cop Killer" was considerably less interpretative. It bordered on instructional, even mentioning Los Angeles chief of police Daryl Gates by name. Yet the song was also indisputably commenting on police brutality and the present-tense political climate, making it more than mere entertainment. In terms of the First Amendment, "Cop Killer" was bulletproof (Vice President Dan Quayle called the song "obscene," willfully ignoring the legal meaning of that term). That airtight constitutionality deepened the problem. The only way for opponents to stop the song was to go after Time Warner, the parent company that released the Body Count album on its imprint Sire. The pressure was applied by police organizations, initially coming from Texas (the Dallas Police Association was among the first to demand a boycott). Here's where the complexity escalated—pressure from police organizations equated to pressure from the executive branch of government, and that seemed like a straightforward First Amendment violation. But this possibility was convoluted by Ice-T's disinterest in protection from First Amendment advocates. He argued that the issue was not the legality of the record but the subject it addressed.

"I think that people who are backers of the First Amendment and anti-censorship have to realize that when you jump on the First Amendment, what you're doing is trying to use the system's tool, the Constitution, to defend you. We need to just get away from that," Ice-T would later say during a speech at Ohio University. "I have human rights, so fuck the First Amendment."

The precariousness of "Cop Killer" proved too dangerous, however. Fearing the government might actually charge him with sedition or incitement, Ice-T pulled the track from future pressings of the album late in July, replacing it with a metalized version of an old rap song called "Freedom of Speech." A year later, Ice-T ended his relationship with Time Warner altogether and became more involved with film and television (though he still released records on an independent label). Since all these decisions were (technically) his own choice, the drama around "Cop Killer" disappeared.

The album was certified gold a few days later, but—with the highest-profile song deleted from a disc that had limited commercial appeal to begin with—Body Count receded from the public consciousness.

Still, the latent potency of "Cop Killer" was profound. The song instantaneously normalized ideas that had previously been unconsidered by much of the country.

"Cop Killer" was not, certainly, the first time somebody had written a song expressing distaste for the police. From 1950 onward, the majority of rock and pop songs referencing police were stridently anti-cop.* This was even more true in hip-hop, where artists increasingly described negative interactions with law enforcement: Public Enemy's "911 Is a Joke" and LL Cool J's "Illegal Search" had both come out in 1990. Two years before that, the group N.W.A had released "Fuck tha Police," a song that discussed shooting LAPD officers even more casually than "Cop Killer."† So what made the Body Count track different? Part of it was the coincidental fact that the record arrived a month after the riots. Another part was that Body Count had infused hard rock (i.e., "white music") with ideas previously associated with hip-hop (i.e., "Black music"), making it more of a suburban concern.‡ But the real catalyst may have been the repetition and implication of one specific lyric: "Tonight we get even."

---

*The only time this was (temporarily) reversed was in the confusing period immediately following the September 11, 2001, terrorist attacks, when support for law enforcement was so high that the Strokes' debut album, released on October 9, had to remove the song "New York City Cops" from the track listing, because of its suggestion that members of the NYPD "ain't too smart."

†"When I'm finished, it's gonna be a bloodbath of cops dying in L.A.," rapped N.W.A member Ice Cube, whose 1991 solo album *Death Certificate* managed to push the antagonism even further.

‡It's possible that Ice-T's Blackness and entrenched relationship to rap was the only real reason this song received as much attention as it did. Had "Cop Killer" been written by (say) Metallica, it would have been considered troubling and antiauthoritarian, but any racial implications would have been nonexistent. It's worth noting that "Cop Killer" was sometimes covered live by the white grunge band Soundgarden and no one cared at all. Ice-T explained it like this: "The fact that 'Cop Killer' was a rock record, but they called it a rap record, was a way to rally people behind it. Because if you say a rock record came out with a song called 'Cop Killer,' a lot of the white people with power would say, 'I like Aerosmith. I like Fleetwood Mac. Maybe I'd like this song,' But if you say *rap*, that means niggas and I don't like it."

In almost every other example of an artist celebrating violence toward law enforcement, the narrative begins with a description of mistreatment initiated by the police. It's typically a direct response to something that just happened—a song would begin with the protagonist innocently minding his own business before being *forced* to respond to groundless harassment. "Cop Killer" isn't like that. "Cop Killer" is proactive. "Cop Killer" operates from the literary premise that all cops are the same, that police brutality is inherent to police activity, and that the only justification required for killing a cop was that the cop was, in fact, a cop.

"It was the epitome of a protest record," Ice-T would later explain. "*Better you than me*. If I'm gonna die, then I think you're gonna die. I'm not just going to let you kill me."

The song's cartoonish directness was almost confusing. "Cop Killer" was received by the public a little like the Bret Easton Ellis novel *American Psycho*, a book released in the previous year: The straightforward language defied allegorical analysis, prompting both detractors and supporters to view a fictional work of satire with rigid literalism. Consumed in concert with the nonfictional events of King's beating and the protest that followed, "Cop Killer" popularized a philosophy that had once lived only on the politicized fringe: In the city of Los Angeles, young Black males were actively at war with the police force, and an explanation as to why was no longer required. The war was perpetual, the cops were on the wrong side, and whatever happened to those cops was warranted.

Not everyone accepted this, of course. Racial views during the "Cop Killer" era were not that different from racial views during the early seventies (in 1992, polling indicated that almost half of all Americans still disapproved of interracial marriage). National crime figures decreased during the nineties while the prison population increased by almost 70 percent. To a person with no firsthand exposure to police, those seemed like positive trends. The Fox television show *Cops*, a real-life depiction of working police officers exclusively delivered from the perspective of law enforcement, was the most ubiquitous reality show of the era.* An anti-cop viewpoint was not universal. But what mattered was this was now a possible viewpoint to hold, even if you weren't young or Black or living in Los Angeles.

○ ○ ○

This phenomenon of white-bread audiences suddenly confronting ideologies that minority groups had long considered inescapable parts of life accelerated during the first half of the nineties. It tended to happen in bunches: The Body Count album was preceded by *Boyz n the Hood* and followed by *Menace II Society*, two films illuminating the violent existence of Black adolescents in gang-ravaged Los Angeles. Realities once ignored were rapidly transformed into narrative tropes, and this mass recognition of inequality would generate a parallel period of frustration and confusion. The frustration came from the marginalized, aghast that problems intrinsic to their lived experience were being turned into entertainment within the same moment they were acknowledged to exist. The confusion came from white consumers, many of whom did not understand the insular rules governing the cultural worldscapes they were absorbing for the first time.

Arrested Development's *3 Years, 5 Months and 2 Days in the Life of . . .* reflected that dissonance. Steeped in Southern spiritual Blackness, it was the epitome of a success story that could only have occurred in 1992: An Afrocentric, politically conscious record that sold millions of copies to boring suburbanites while also being named album of the year by *The Village Voice*

Cops aired for thirty-two seasons and was canceled by Fox in the wake of the 2020 murder of George Floyd by a Minneapolis police officer. For years prior, *Cops* had been criticized as evidence of an unholy alliance between law enforcement and media—the show was dependent on the police allowing TV crews to shadow their street work, which would only be allowed if the police were featured in a positive light. When public sentiment toward law enforcement collapsed, the very premise of a program delivered from that viewpoint was seen as irredeemable. There was, however, an ancillary aspect to *Cops* that played an underrated role in its watchability: the uniqueness of its geography. *Cops* was filmed in multiple cities across multiple states, and since the sole focus was on criminal activity, it ended up featuring neighborhoods and communities that would never appear on TV for any other reason. It's possible to argue that *Cops* was a soft form of fascism, but that it was also an unorthodox form of tourism.

and *The Wire*. It was a positive, melodic hip-hop album that appealed to white audiences, some of whom had never before listened to rap music. But that didn't mean white audiences understood how to read it. At the end of the single "People Everyday," the group's pacifist frontman (Todd Thomas, who referred to himself as Speech) describes his victory in an unwanted brawl versus a hypermasculine peer as the story of "a Black man acting like a nigga and getting stomped by an African." The internal nuance of those designations was not necessarily clear to white people, particularly those who had never considered what nomenclature was (or wasn't) acceptable. When MTV aired the video for "People Everyday," the network edited out the N-word from the lyrical phrase, creating the odd impression that Arrested Development was using verbiage that would be offensive to Black people.

Here again, the friction was contextual. When white people engaged with new language through a hip-hop album, it was seen as enlightening and mind-expanding. But the moment that engagement encroached upon regular day-to-day life, the response turned negative. The fleeting 1997 panic over Ebonics was proof.

The term was invented in the mid-1970s, a blending of the words *ebony* and *phonics*. The premise was that differences between traditional English and the way the English language was used in segments of the Black community were not errors or flaws, but part of an organized vernacular built over time and governed by its own grammatical rules (pronouncing the word "ask" as "ax," for example, or the purposeful employment of double negatives). The academic version of the term was African American Vernacular English, and nobody outside of academia paid much attention to the theory for twenty years. But then, in December of 1996, seemingly out of nowhere, the Oakland, California, school board publicly recognized Ebonics as the primary language for the majority of its Black students and that this linguistic difference needed to be considered within the education process.

The news was not exactly greeted with bemused curiosity. It prompted a national freak-out over the sanctity of language, driven by a detail that wasn't even accurate: The popular assumption was that Oakland public schools were not simply recognizing Ebonics but *replacing* traditional English education *with* Ebonics. It was somehow believed that kids in the Oakland school system would now be taught in Ebonics, and that the grammatical rules of Ebonics would supersede all other preexisting grammatical rules. The whole notion of Ebonics was ridiculed so relentlessly that the term ended up having the opposite effect of its intention: Instead of legitimizing the dialect, it became a facile way of mocking the vernacular as a demented academic construction. By the end of the decade, the term had fallen out of favor with almost everyone, and even positive references to Ebonics would often be placed in quotes ("Ebonics") to signify its cultural illegitimacy.

Language and concepts were advancing at different speeds.

An even easier example of this asynchronous evolution is the word *queer*. For roughly a hundred years, it was pejorative slang for *homosexual*. Among the heterosexual populace, that colloquial connotation was unambiguous and inflexible. But in the gay community, the meaning of *queer* had been incrementally changing throughout the seventies and eighties. The critical turn was the 1987 formation of the AIDS Coalition to Unleash Power, better known by the acronym ACT UP. It culminated with two key events in 1990: the formation of the splinter activist group Queer Nation* and the distribution of the combative leaflet *Queers Read This!* during the New York City Pride March. Published anonymously, *Queers Read This!* is eternally provocative— it calls for "a moratorium on straight marriage, on babies, on public displays of affection among the opposite sex and media images that promote heterosexuality." It outlines "Rules of Conduct for Straight People" and explicitly explains the adoption of *queer* as a means of self-identification:

---

*Queer Nation members are usually cited as the originators of the chant "We're here! We're queer! Get used to it!" The inclusion of that final demand ("*Get used to it!*") illustrates just how new and outside the norm this phrasing was at the time.

Ah, do we really have to use that word? It's trouble. Every gay person has his or her own take on it. For some it means strange and eccentric and kind of mysterious. That's okay, we like that. But some gay girls and boys don't. They think they're more normal than strange. And for others "queer" conjures up those awful memories of adolescent suffering. *Queer.* It's forcibly bittersweet and quaint at best— weakening and painful at worst. Couldn't we just use "gay" instead? It's a much brighter word and isn't it synonymous with "happy"? When will you militants grow up and get over the novelty of being different? Well, yes, "gay" is great. It has its place. But when a lot of lesbians and gay men wake up in the morning we feel angry and disgusted, not gay. So we've chosen to call ourselves queer. Using "queer" is a way of reminding us how we are perceived by the rest of the world. It's a way of telling ourselves we don't have to be witty and charming people who keep our lives discreet and marginalized in the straight world . . . it is also a sly and ironic weapon we can steal from the homophobe's hands and use against him.

The intensity of *Queers Read This!* reflects the conditions of 1990, which were still the conditions of the previous decade. To say homophobia was "more common" in the eighties wildly underrates the degree to which it was ingrained. Unconcealed homophobia was still an acceptable topic for commercial entertainment. The 1988 family-oriented action film *Crocodile Dundee II* jokes that being gay is a valid reason for committing suicide. The Beastie Boys, a musical group who'd eventually become progressive icons of inclusion, wanted to title their 1986 debut album *Don't Be a Faggot.* Eddie Murphy, whose stand-up routines mocked gays with obsessive regularity, was (by far) the most popular comedian of the eighties. All those retrograde sensibilities were about to transform at an astonishing pace: Within ten years, the notion of nonchalantly using homophobia as a vehicle for unironic humor would disappear almost entirely (at least in the entertainment

89

industry).* But when the nineties were new, the heterosexual relationship to gay culture was still nonsensical. There was a disconnect between what it meant to know an actual gay person and what it meant to refer to something as "gay" in the abstract. The adoption of *queer* by queers added still another layer to the tiramisu of heteronormative befuddlement.

Within the queer community, "queer" seemed better suited for the intricacy of the designation: It was less overtly male and encompassed a wider spectrum of identities and orientations. To the straight community, and particularly to straight liberals, the linguistic transition felt unnatural. How could a word that had always been used as an insult against gay people suddenly become the preferred terminology? Was a straight person now supposed to call all gay people *queer,* or was that a word only acceptable for queer people to use among themselves? If *queer* was more encompassing than *gay,* did that mean a straight person could potentially claim to be queer? Would doing so indicate solidarity, or would that be the most offensive move possible? In 1995, the band Garbage released a single titled "Queer," but singer Shirley Manson claimed the song was not about being gay. Guitarist Duke Erikson said the track was about a loss of innocence. Were these elastic interpretations still on the table?

Here again, nothing about the concept had changed. The material difference between being gay in the summer of 1989 and being queer in the summer of 1990 was negligible. But the language was different, so static concepts became dynamic concepts. What seemed to happen was what so often happens with radical activism: Outrage from the periphery moved the needle beyond the comfort zone of Middle America, prompting pushback.

---

*What you would see instead were things like 1996's *The Ambiguously Gay Duo,* a cartoon sketch that started in prime time on *The Dana Carvey Show* and would later became more familiar on *Saturday Night Live.* The focus of the cartoon was a pair of superhero partners (voiced by the then barely known Steve Carell and Stephen Colbert) who kept saying and doing things that made them appear outrageously gay, but always as if this were accidental and unconscious. In the distant past (and in the not-so-distant future), such a sketch might have seemed cheap and homophobic, but the creative intent in 1996 was viewed as supportive and knowing. The target of the humor was assumed to be homophobes, even if that wasn't always the outcome in practice.

But when the needle drifted back, its home position had shifted. The uncompromising platforms of *Queers Read This!* and Queer Nation were too much for most middle-of-the-road straight people to process, but they cracked open the door for less antagonistic depictions of lifestyles previously verboten in any mass milieu.

Broadway plays had always been driven by gay culture, but usually subtextually and behind the scenes. That limitation disappeared. In 1994, the AIDS-centric musical *Rent* debuted in New York's East Village before moving to Broadway and running for over 5,000 performances, winning the Pulitzer Prize, and earning around $280 million. In 1997, Ellen DeGeneres came out as a lesbian on her ABC sitcom, *Ellen*, both as a character and in real life. It was the first time the marquee star of a major network show had ever done so. A year later, NBC debuted the situation comedy *Will & Grace*, the story of a gay man living with a straight woman in New York. Over its eleven-season run, *Will & Grace* would sometimes face criticism from progressives for its willingness to traffic in caricature, and for the fact that its central gay character was played by a straight actor (Eric McCormack). It would, however, often rank among the ten most popular shows in the country. By the year 2000, the linguistic battleground of 1990 had been fully integrated into unremarkable televised entertainment: The premium cable network Showtime created the U.S. version of a show that had already aired in Britain. This one-hour drama exclusively examined the lives of gay men and women living in Pittsburgh. The show was *Queer as Folk*, and everyone who knew what it was knew exactly what it meant.

○ ○ ○

There was uncertainty, always. There was uncertainty about what was real and what was unreal, though not in the way that ambiguity has come to infiltrate modern political discourse. The old uncertainty had been based on the *reliability* of language, particularly in fiction: Were the ideas being expressed by transgressive characters the way things actually were, or

were those ideas merely the most extreme version of what might potentially be true?

The 1995 movie *Kids* was designed to shock people. It was, according to
disgraced Miramax executive Harvey Weinstein, the most controversial film
he ever distributed (so controversial that he set up a separate stand-alone
studio, Shining Excalibur, just for this release). Part of its confrontational
force was that it was possible to make two diametrically opposing arguments
as to why *Kids* was so disturbing. To people like *Kids* director Larry Clark, the
film was a forbidden glimpse into how modern young people secretly lived.
Critics saw the film as important and intuitive. To just about everyone else,
it seemed like an exploitative, quasi-pornographic depiction of hypothetical
teenagers who could only exist in a false dystopia. *Kids* could be hated for
being too real as easily as it could be hated for being too fake.

Kids was shot documentary-style over a twenty-four-hour span in the
most unglamorous environs of New York. The ensemble of (often shirtless)
young people spend most of the film drinking malt liquor, taking drugs,
robbing bodegas, assaulting skateboarders, and (especially) having and discussing sex. None of the adolescents were professional actors. The central
male character is obsessed with deflowering virgins; in the film's final
scene, his best friend rapes an unconscious girl and presumably contracts
HIV. Written by a then nineteen-year-old Harmony Korine, the meaning of
Kids was that there was no meaning *to anything*, ever. Its all-encompassing
title suggested a universal unspecificity to the on-screen images—this was,
allegedly, a straightforward depiction of what it was like to be any kid in
1995. The implication is that the way these teenagers talk is the way all
teenagers think.

Another movie from this period, Neil LaBute's *In the Company of Men*,
was more nuanced and (perhaps) even more traumatizing. Two nondescript
businessmen are temporarily assigned to a branch office in a nameless city
(here again, the unspoken message is that these men could be *any* men, and
that this story could happen in any place). One man, Chad, is good-looking,

misanthropic, and dominant. He represents the worst possible version of masculinity. The second man, Howard, is submissive and weak. Both are angry at women. Chad convinces Howard that they should play a game on this business trip: They will select a vulnerable woman at random, pretend to romantically pursue her, and then obliterate her heart for sport. This is exactly what they proceed to do (and the woman they select is deaf, amplifying the psychological brutality). The final twist is that the trick is not just on the woman, but also on Howard. The insinuation is that the way men talk when women aren't around is the only time men are actually honest.

Though the cinematic realities of *Kids* and *In the Company of Men* are different, the mediated similarities run parallel. Both were small, independent productions that were talked about more than they were seen (their combined box office take was only around $10 million). Both cinematic debuts delineated the subsequent trajectories of their creators: Clark would make multiple films about deranged adolescents, Korine became a specialist in the comedic exploration of the depraved, and LaBute's scriptwriting would repeatedly dissect the nature of interpersonal cruelty. Both launched the screen careers of unknowns who'd eventually become famous (Chloë Sevigny, Rosario Dawson, Aaron Eckhart). But the deepest connection was the discrepancy between the future value of their expressed ideas and the impossibility of those ideas being expressed in the future. When first consumed in theaters, *Kids* and *In the Company of Men* felt like provoking exaggerations. The kids in *Kids* seemed too wild and nihilistic to be normal; the men from *In the Company of Men* seemed too hateful and misogynist to be typical guys.

Decades later, the themes and personalities in both movies have been systematically accepted as endemic and incontrovertible.

Few teenagers born after the year 1995 would be shocked by the dialogue in *Kids* (although some might claim to be offended and disappointed). Much of *In the Company of Men* was so intellectually advanced that some of its issues were not yet recognized as social problems (the notion of microaggressions, the toxicity of male secrecy, the assertion that patriarchal societies can also be destructive to men, etc.). The ideological perspectives within these films are more relevant now than they were in the nineties. Yet it's almost impossible to imagine either movie being made today. The content would be too problematic. Multiple scenes in *Kids* would now qualify as triggering, and the use of such young actors in scenes so graphic would be considered damaging to the performers. The elements of satire lodged within *In the Company of Men* would be willfully misinterpreted. Its dialogue would be classified as abuse, and the fact that its antagonist is never punished would be seen (by some) as a validation of his persona.*

Conceptually, *Kids* and *In the Company of Men* were too prescient for most audiences in the mid-nineties to fully appreciate. But the incendiary language used to express those concepts? That was totally fine. People *wanted* to hear those words. They wanted people to talk like that, especially if they weren't expected to agree with what those people were saying. It was fun to be shocked, or to pretend to be shocked, or to feign a lack of shock to prove you were unshockable. The words themselves were not the problem, as long as you didn't believe them.

○ ○ ○

The alarm over political correctness was grounded in the fear that people were losing control over what they could casually say in public, and there was some truth in that. That did happen. But the freedom to use coarse, non-political language in middle-of-the-road entertainment was actually expanding, and that freedom felt novel. In the 1993 pilot episode of the cop show *NYPD Blue*, a character refers to another as "a pissy little bitch." Nothing like

---

*The 1998 film *American History X* is another example of a nineties movie that expressed an overt progressive message about tolerance, yet would still be too discomforting to produce or promote in the modern era. *American History X* is about a white supremacist, portrayed by Edward Norton, who goes to prison for murdering two Black men and slowly comes to realize the error of his ideology. Nothing about the movie's thesis is unclear. However, Norton's performance and rhetoric during the first half of the film—before his rehabilitation—would almost certainly be seen as fetishistic, dangerously persuasive, and far too respectful. *American History X* is an antiracist film that could potentially be enjoyed by a racist.

that had ever been said on prime-time network television. But, like all fabricated freedoms, the new parameters were immediately reconfigured into a prison.

A comedian like Roseanne Barr could ascend to the top of her industry, fueled by a willingness to say things that felt both honest and bombastic, particularly considering the source (Barr presented herself as a typical housewife from Colorado). Yet as soon as that apex was reached, bombast became the entirety of her being. The merit of her comedy was usurped by a categorization that she was a woman "without boundaries" who would say anything, just to hear herself say it. Over time, the public grew disinterested in anything Barr said that *wasn't* overtly provocative or potentially treasonous. The more intellectual version of this entrapment was experienced by Camille Paglia, a brilliant polemicist who became an academic celebrity upon the publication of her 1990 book *Sexual Personae,* only to spend the next twenty-five years facing constant criticism for championing an incendiary version of feminism that often appealed to men more than women.

This backdoor imprisonment was even more pronounced in music. There was a newfound hunger for female artists who would talk about sex with frankness and unvarnished clarity. The hip-hop trio Salt-N-Pepa had a 1991 single that was literally titled "Let's Talk About Sex," but the song's responsible message was too abstract and impersonal to resonate beyond Top 40 radio. What people really wanted were young women who seemed to be talking about sex from the most personal perspective possible. In the short term, autobiographical rawness was a bridge to instant credibility. But the long-term consequence was almost always converted into an artistic impediment. It would inevitably become the only aspect of their work anyone wanted to consider and the prism through which the totality of their personality would be pushed.

Throughout most of the nineties, there was an unambiguous bifurcation within pop music: There was mainstream radio fare, and there was indie college rock. The towering female figure in the first category was twenty-one-year-old Canadian Alanis Morissette, whose 1995 album *Jagged Little Pill* would eventually sell a whopping 33 million copies worldwide. The most significant female artist in the second category was Liz Phair, whose debut, *Exile in Guyville*, defined (and, to an extent, invented) the archetype of what an ultra-cool, uncannily clever woman was supposed to be like in 1993. What Morissette and Phair were doing musically was not that similar*— both of their albums were excellent, but for different reasons. What they shared was the experience of being trapped by their own willingness to use language that was too visceral for audiences (and particularly male audiences) to move beyond.

Morissette entered the public consciousness through the song "You Oughta Know." She instantly seemed super-famous, though she'd technically been semi-famous for years (she'd made a dance record that got attention in Canada, toured with multiplatinum poseur Vanilla Ice, and—as an adolescent—appeared on the kids show *You Can't Do That on Television*).†
"You Oughta Know" was sung from the perspective of a woman who'd been dumped by her partner and needed her ex to realize just how much pain the breakup had inflicted. The plot wasn't original, but the details were rich and disarmingly explicit. One of Morissette's rhetorical questions was whether the man's new girlfriend was willing to perform oral sex inside a movie theater. The implication was not unclear—this question was being

---

*In 2020, the *Los Angeles Times* published a conversation between Phair and Morissette, connecting their experiences and noting how they'd briefly toured together in the mid-nineties. The media relationship seems natural. But this relationship only exists because of gender. It's hard to imagine a male version of Morissette (such as the band Candlebox, who were on the same record label as Alanis) viewed as even vaguely analogous to a male version of Phair (a group like Guided by Voices, Phair's prolific peers who also recorded for Matador Records).

†Morissette's past as a teen television performer is illustrative of how differently the aforementioned idea of credibility and "selling out" was during this period. In the music community, Morissette's involvement with *You Can't Do That on Television* was seen as an embarrassing detail her critics could wield as evidence that she wasn't a real artist, and that she was a manufactured celebrity who'd been meticulously groomed for pop stardom. It stands in stark contrast to the more modern biography of someone like Drake, a twenty-first-century rap star who started his career as an actor on a Canadian kids show (the soap opera *Degrassi*) and is not only never mocked for doing so but generally appreciated more.

posed as a reminder of something Morissette herself had done when they were still a couple. It was too specific to be a metaphor. "Are you thinking of me when you fuck her?" she asked in the next verse, and (of course) the word *fuck* was removed for the radio edit. But that edited *fuck* was not replaced by some other word—it was just a blank space near the end of the phrase, meaning anyone who heard the line didn't need to hear the *fuck* to realize it was there. There was no other word that fit. Alanis was subliminally saying *fuck* on Top 40 radio every other hour for an entire summer.

There are many reasons why "You Oughta Know" warrants reflection. One is the notion of a breakup being a legitimate form of psychological trauma, a view not taken seriously by most people of the era (such a reaction was discounted as hysterical). Another was the sense that the relationship she described involved an inherent power imbalance, assumedly based on the man's age (the new girlfriend is described by Alanis as "an older version of me"). Still another was the use of outrage as a viable form of feminine pop expression (when *Rolling Stone* magazine put Morissette on the cover, the tagline was "Angry White Female"). Within the environment of a song this commercially massive, all of these things were new. Still, the central media obsession with "You Oughta Know" was antiquated: *Who was the man she was talking about?* The unnamed womanizer at the song's center became the most compelling blind item since Carly Simon's "You're So Vain." It epitomized the long-standing complaint that a male artist's experience is seen as universal while any female experience is inexorably viewed as personal—instead of becoming a song about breakups, it became a song about this specific breakup. Morissette was asked about this anonymous man constantly and always declined to say whom the story was about. When a gossipy consensus about the man's identity was finally reached, the answer—Dave Coulier, an edgeless comedian from the family sitcom *Full House*—was unexpected and deflating. It was not the answer people wanted, though there was probably no answer that would have sufficed.

For Phair, the interplay of who she was and the words she chose was even more convoluted, magnified by the dichotomy of her elevated cultural position. Her commercial success paled in comparison to her public profile. It was the worst of both worlds—*Exile in Guyville* sold only a fraction as much as *Jagged Little Pill*, but it was dissected more obsessively and analyzed with a critical seriousness that warped the framework of pop's true potentiality.

Exile in Guyville was presented as a track-for-track response to the Rolling Stones' 1972 album *Exile on Main St.* That sonic relationship did not always cohere, but the intent was enough to confirm her integrity. Morissette was sometimes accused of not having a deep knowledge of music history.* Phair, conversely, had made a record for dudes who collect records about dudes. Even the homemade demo versions of the unfinished songs, recorded on cassette under the moniker Girly-Sound, were prized bootlegs. It was as if she'd been genetically engineered in some kind of indie rock laboratory: a Midwestern feminist who eviscerated male hipster oppression while embodying the unrealistic fantasies of every male hipster. She appeared topless on the album's cover, but not in a way that could be construed as gratuitous. Her songwriting was deft and the delivery was deadpan. The self-aware lyrics displayed an innate ability to reflect not only how she felt, but how those feelings would be interpreted by others. Yet it was the intermittent crassness of her language that was always pushed to the front of the conversation. When the album was first reviewed (positively) by *Spin* magazine, the success of the music was credited to the production acumen of her male drummer. Meanwhile, Phair's contribution was described like this:

> With [the song] "Flower" declaring "I want to be your blow job queen"
> and [the song] "Fuck and Run" wondering "Whatever happened to a
> boyfriend," the glaringly inconsistent lyrics make Phair sound like
> a Freudian wet dream.

---

*When asked what she would say to critics who argued that an artist needed to understand the history of rock music in order to create new rock music, Morissette responded, "I would say, 'Apparently not.'"

That review was from 1993. Five years later, Phair was releasing her third album. *Spin* wrote about her again,* this time in a short profile before the record showed up in stores. Now the emphasis was on how Phair wasn't talking about sex *enough*. "The rock 'n' roll mama is keeping it PG-13 this time around," noted the caption to her photograph. A (not-so-positive) album review in the same issue argued that "her brainy-slut persona was much more compelling than her new role as a sincere adult." There was no possibility that Phair might be singing from the perspective of a fictional character or as the avatar for a collective experience. Her work could only be about her, to a point where the artist and the art were transposable. There was no gap between the language and the concept. The language *was* the concept.

Over time, Phair's adoration from the same male audiences she criticized became a weapon used against her. How could she be dismantling the patriarchy if the patriarchy had a crush on her? As with Paglia, there was a sense that her sexualized, self-contained form of feminism was designed for men more than women. Feminist criticisms of Morissette evoked a similar contradiction, though more tied to her commercial triumph. Her radio-friendly anger was sometimes belittled as a sanitized commodity, a non-political reproduction of confrontational female artists like Bratmobile and Babes in Toyland:

> Morissette and [Fiona] Apple† focused their anger on many of the same issues as Riot Grrrl; however, they were carefully constructed as non-threatening and their form of female empowerment was something

---

*Her second album, 1994's *Whip-Smart*, had been effectively ignored by *Spin* entirely. The magazine killed a review of the record when Phair reneged on an agreement to appear on the cover of *Spin*, opting instead for the cover of *Rolling Stone*. At the time, the two publications were extremely competitive.

†Fiona Apple fell somewhere between Morissette and Phair—very young and hugely successful (like Alanis), but often erotic and always credible (like Phair). She was another casualty of language: In 1997, Apple was mocked as immature and kooky for accepting an award on MTV and telling the live audience, "This world is bullshit." Twenty years later, she would be reconsidered as a generational genius.

to buy in CD format rather than something to actively produce. . . . Morissette is unusual only in that she is a woman expressing the same ideas. But how strong does that make her? Her discussion of sexuality in "You Oughta Know" suggests that a good girlfriend is one who will perform sexual acts for a man at any time, even in a movie theater. She offers no examples of a woman receiving sexual pleasure, which casts women back into the traditional sexually passive role. Also, if Morissette is truly a feminist rock heroine as the papers claim, is being unable to let go of a relationship a positive message for young girls?

That analysis comes from sociologist Kristen Schilt's paper "'A Little Too Ironic': The Appropriation and Packaging of Riot Grrrl Politics by Mainstream Female Musicians." Some of its content now seems perilously close to academic satire. It was not written at the time of *Jagged Little Pill*'s release, nor did it appear in any general-interest publication (it was published in the journal *Popular Music and Society* in 2003). But the crux is an accurate summation of what some people didn't like about Morissette. Versions of those expressed sentiments were always around, even if most music fans didn't have the lexicon or desire to explain the problem. There was just something about Alanis's outsized success that felt like an exception that proved the rule. Her outrage scanned as the calculated version of an emotional response—the most acceptable form of an unhinged reaction. Any record that sells 33 million copies is the definition of monoculture . . . so maybe it was never that personal to begin with? How could this be real? The Gen X mind-set demanded that success always necessitated skepticism.

The title of Schilt's paper ("'A Little Too Ironic'") was a reference to Morissette's highest-charting single off *Jagged Little Pill*, the mid-tempo, hook-laden "Ironic." The song is now most remembered for its flaws. It was too on-the-nose (*ironic* was the most overused word of the decade, and the most overused word in this book). More pressingly, the lyrics kept describing ironic scenarios that were not technically ironic. The track became the nineties equivalent of a self-own: Here, it seemed, was a woman singing about irony without knowing what irony was. What we know now is that this analysis was cheap and lazy. Irony was the one quality Alanis Morissette would come to understand more deeply than almost any artist of her generation. She was successful because of her honesty, but anyone that successful had to be lying.

[the slow cancellation of the future and the fast homogenization of the past]

IN THE SEVENTIES, PEOPLE LOVED THE FIFTIES, REMINISCING OVER THE preordained conclusion that it had been a better time to be alive (*Happy Days* and *Laverne & Shirley* on TV, *American Graffiti* and *Grease* in movie houses). In the eighties, people fixated on the sixties, and particularly what it meant to have lived through a failed social revolution that now looked inconsistent and antiquated. The pattern is dependable: Every new generation tends to be intrigued by whatever generation existed twenty years earlier. The nineties were no different, except in the way that interest was performed. A fascination with the 1970s was predictable, but not because that era was seen as more wholesome or more political. The appeal was in the conviction that it had been neither.

Grunge musicians viewed the polished, anything-to-make-it aspirations of eighties arena rock with contempt. Down-tuned bands of the nineties were more interested in recapturing the fuzzy sound of the seventies, and really just the distorted anti-pop center of those particular years (a combination of Black Sabbath in '73 and Neil Young in '78). In 1990, an emaciated Southern rock band called the Black Crowes released an album resembling the undistinguished mid-seventies period of the Rolling Stones. It sold 5 million copies. *Dazed and Confused*, an ensemble 1993 teen movie set in 1976

Texas, was intended as an anti-nostalgia project that would eviscerate the seventies as a boring, homogeneous purgatory. The director's goal backfired. Those specific qualities were consumed as delightful. The fact that the characters in *Dazed* smoked pot constantly (and casually) was especially appealing at the time of the film's release: Recreational marijuana was still illegal in all fifty states and would not be legalized for medical purposes until 1996 (and initially, only in California).

The nineties, or at least the first half of the nineties, adopted the look and feel of the seventies with uncalculated orthodoxy. It was trendy to wear bell-bottom pants and crop tops. It was standard to buy the 1990 Led Zeppelin box set, a four-disc best-of collection that cost (a then astronomical) $65 and still moved 10 million units. The retro escalation was earnest, for a while. But there was no way full-on sincerity could withstand the onslaught of the larger zeitgeist. By the decade's midpoint, even pleasant childhood memories required heavy injections of emotional distance. *The Brady Bunch Movie*, released in February of 1995, was built on this ambivalence: It was both an affectionate appreciation of the 1970s family sitcom and a parody of everything that made it cornball and outdated. The film's plot points were adapted from old episodes, the visual details were painstakingly re-created, and original cast members had cameos—but the content was recast as sexual, subversive, and obsessed with reminding the audience that most of what qualified as mainstream entertainment in 1972 was terrible. Some of the jokes were funny, but the main joke was directed at the audience: *"You know, you actually used to like this."*

Smashing Pumpkins released a single titled "1979" in January of 1996. It was a gorgeous song with a wistful ambiance, but it wasn't particularly reminiscent of music from the late seventies, nor did it lyrically evoke anything identifiable from that particular year. It was just called "1979." That was enough. Nothing, however, capitalized on the sarcastic/sincere interest in the seventies as explicitly as *That '70s Show*. The title of the program *was* the program, defying all possibilities for deconstruction. Debuting in the

Fox fall TV season of 1998, it originally looked like a small-screen rip-off of *Dazed and Confused,* and it would similarly serve as a launching pad for its collection of unknown actors (half of whom became Hollywood commodities, most visibly Ashton Kutcher). But unlike *Dazed,* the TV version of the seventies did not invest much thought into what the seventies meant: The main point of *That '70s Show* was that the seventies had, in fact, happened. Every character dressed like someone attending a seventies-themed Halloween party. Every scene was supersaturated with unsubtle references to anything that had come into existence over the last half of the decade—there was an episode about the release of *Star Wars,* an episode about rebuilding a Pong gaming console, an episode about disrupting a rally for Gerald Ford by streaking. The two most durable joke constructions were (a) casually dismissing something new that would later become extremely common, and (b) referring to some forgotten triviality as if it were destined to be timeless.

This is not necessarily a criticism of *That '70s Show.* It was better than most network sitcoms of the time, and it was exceptionally well cast. *That '70s Show* merely exemplifies the psychological duality of how the seventies had come to be considered by the end of the nineties. The seventies were beloved, but not as a historical period; the seventies were beloved as a collection of *stuff,* some of which was cherished precisely because it now seemed dumb. The kids on *That '70s Show* hung out in basements and killed time by driving the family car around in circles, but those pastimes were not bygone pursuits—teenagers in the nineties were still hanging out in basements and still aimlessly cruising around. This was not some portal into an alien unknown. *That '70s Show* could have instantly been remade as *That '80s Show** or *That '90s Show* if the references were changed and the fashions were updated. The characters and the conflicts were not entrenched in the seventies but ubiquitous to the entire last quarter of the twentieth century.

---

*This was, in fact, attempted: *That '80s Show* debuted on Fox in 2002, using the same format and much of the same writing staff as *That '70s Show.* It was canceled after thirteen episodes.

The only distinction was the ephemera. Which, to both discerning and undiscerning audiences, seemed vastly superior to the ephemera of the present—and that was because of what had happened in the eighties.

What the 1980s destroyed was the fantasy that culture could happen by accident. A band like Led Zeppelin had (seemingly) come into existence organically, but the bands that followed looked and acted like photocopies modeled off the original.* Blockbuster movies in the seventies occurred when people loved a movie so much that they had to see it again, but now it felt like manufacturing viewer repetition was the whole idea. What seemed enticing about the seventies was that life experiences were still unscripted, and that no one had figured out how to give the people what they wanted before the people even knew what that was.

Now, was this true? Not really. Led Zeppelin was no accident. *Jaws* was no accident. But throughout the 1980s, the concept of commodifying pop culture had become so widespread—and so undisguised—that it was difficult to see anything emerging in the nineties as a naturally occurring phenomenon. Part of the Gen X irony fixation was the result of so much accepted obviousness: When you made a TV show about the seventies, you could just call it *That '70s Show*. Was that title clever, or was that title lazy? It was impossible to know. But it was clear that the show would refer to things from the seventies, sometimes as a joke and sometimes as a heartfelt expression of joy. So did that make it satire? Was it a tribute? Maybe both. Maybe neither. Maybe it didn't matter. Whatever. Who cares? Just get on with it. Just look at the pants.

---

*In 1988, the band Kingdom Come released their first single, "Get It On." It sounded so much like Led Zeppelin that some fans erroneously suspected the surviving members of Led Zeppelin had secretly re-formed. Kingdom Come was widely mocked for this, but the idea did not disappear. Producing new bands to sound indistinguishable from preexisting popular acts became a standard practice.

5 The Movie Was about a Movie

THE STORY OF THE VCR IS AN EIGHTIES STORY. PIONEERED BY THE JAPA-
nese in the 1950s, streamlined by the British in the sixties, and engineered
for worldwide consumers in the seventies, videocassette recorders were still
cutting-edge technology at the dawn of 1980, when less than 1 percent of
American households owned their own VCR. The reason was cost: In 1975,
the earliest retail VCRs were priced between $1,000 and $1,400. By 1985, that
price had incrementally dropped to under $400, with some models as cheap
as $169. By 1990, 65 percent of U.S. homes had multiple televisions and the
majority had at least one VCR. The defining technological conflict of the
videotape era—the format war between VHS and Betamax—was already
over by 1988. As a machine, the VCR historically denotes the 1980s.

But the visual civilization it engineered emerged later.

No movie or director influenced nineties film culture as much as the
advent and everywhereness of the video store. It altered everything about
how movies were consumed and considered, spawning a new type of working-
class cinephile who would come to dominate critical thought about the entire
medium. Here again, the origins predate the nineties: The first American
video store opened in Los Angeles in the late seventies. The first Blockbuster Video appeared in Dallas in 1985. The immediate popularity of movie

rentals was not surprising to anyone. It was something people had awaited from the first moment VCR technology was described. What was not antici- pated, however, was how that experience would shift the way people thought about the art form, particularly for those who turned the VCR into an auto- didactic means for the reconstitution of history.

Prior to the VCR, it was difficult for average people to develop a personal, intimate relationship with non-obvious filmmaking. Outside of New York, Los Angeles, and a handful of university towns, there was just no way to see any movie that wasn't being simultaneously experienced by large numbers of people. For one thing, there were fewer movies to see—in 1980, only 161 total films were released in North American movie houses. Movies also stayed in theaters much longer: 1985's *Back to the Future* played in public for thirty-seven straight weeks. It was possible to see older movies on network television, but that was like trying to learn a language by flipping through a dictionary. Certain classics were on every year: *The Wizard of Oz, Gone with the Wind,* and *The Ten Commandments* on Easter. Other entries seemed to be selected haphazardly, often airing late at night and heavily edited for content (key scenes from teen films like *Halloween* and *Fast Times at Ridgemont High* became incomprehensible in their sanitized network form). Cable subscrib- ers could get HBO, but the audience was small (12 million total subscribers in 1983), the schedule was limited (until 1981, HBO was only available for nine hours a day), and some movies were repeated constantly (*The Beast- master, Clash of the Titans*). The majority of film history was extremely diffi- cult to access. It was monoculture by default. For a movie fanatic living in a small town, the experience of reading *Leonard Maltin's Movie Guide* was more mind-expanding than spending twelve months trying to see every movie within driving distance.

But then, within a span of five years, the entire ecosystem was reversed. When that first Blockbuster opened its doors in Texas, it carried ten thou- sand videotapes. Granted, many of those tapes were duplicates—and over time, it became increasingly common for chain stores to fill entire walls with copies of the same new release. Inventory was always weighted toward pre-existing popularity. But the ideological transformation was nonetheless total. It was now possible to peruse a shelf with dozens of subtitled foreign films in communities where a foreign-language film had never previously screened, ever. There was a preponderance of VHS movies specifically available due to their commercial limitations as theatrical releases: blaxploitation cinema, retrograde slasher flicks, comedic soft-core pornography. More important, there were many films (particularly from the 1970s) that had been released in a limited capacity and were not successful enough (or appropriate) for television and would have been lost to history had it not been for these emerging rental repositories.

The fact that the videotape industry was based around renting (as opposed to selling) was critical. Throughout the eighties and early nineties, the retail cost of a VHS movie was inordinately high—usually around $79 to $90. *Top Gun*, released on video in 1987, made national news for being "only" $26.95, the lowest introductory price ever for a major release (McDonald's received similar attention in 1992 when the fast-food chain distributed copies of *Dances with Wolves* on VHS for $7.99, if the buyer also purchased food). Conversely, the cost of individual three-day rentals hovered around $1.99 to $2.99. It was hard to justify buying any film for $80 if the same money could to be directed toward the temporary possession of twenty-five different titles. Renting fostered a culture of aesthetic diversity, to the point of pure randomness. Most available titles were older, so the only source of promotion was the cardboard box the videotape was packaged in. The rental experience was locked within the physical world, and there was no algorithm coercing consumers toward things they were predisposed to enjoy. The most common way to select a movie was to aimlessly meander around the video store, glance at the covers of various boxes, read the cursory plot descriptions on the back of those boxes, and select the most appealing option that happened to be available. There was no system or logic. But the effect on filmmaking was profound. Video stores invented a new kind of independent director that became so pervasive it instantly became a caricature: the fiscally insolvent, vociferously unglamorous dude (and it was always a dude) who used his video store experience to build an encyclopedic, unorthodox, pretentious cinematic worldview. The 1995 coming-of-age comedy *Kicking and Screaming* includes a minor character who manages a video store while preparing to direct his own feature film, yet plans to continue working in the video store after his movie is released so that he can properly stock it on the shelves.

"The video store was the beginning of everything. It was the cradle of civilization," director Kevin Smith says in the 2015 oral history *I Lost It at the Video Store.* "It was like having a film library. You could watch anything and you could watch it over and over again."

Smith was the insolvent, unglamorous indie director sent from central casting. He made his black-and-white 1994 debut, *Clerks,* in New Jersey, for $27,575 financed on credit cards.* He was twenty-four years old. One of its two principal characters works in a video store, and the film's most memorable scene involves an extended conversation about un-unionized labor complications within *Return of the Jedi.* Much of the film involves static shots of people debating trivialities, a quality Smith credits to his experience working at a store called RST Video—movies were constantly playing inside the shop while he worked, but because he was working the counter (and could not look at the TV while dealing with customers), he "re-watched" and memorized many films as a solely audio experience. *Clerks* did not look or sound like other films, or at least not like films made by professionals. It was crude, visually and emotionally. Its dialogue aged quickly (and sometimes awk-

---

*The relationship between indie filmmaking and credit cards exploded during this period. Throughout the 1970s and early '80s, it was difficult for people under the age of twenty-one to get a credit card unless their parents were willing to cosign the application. Banking outlets eventually dropped those policies and started targeting young adults, especially on college campuses. This (somewhat predatory) practice had the unexpected upside of giving independent filmmakers instant access to capital they could have never raised on their own. In the trailer for Robert Townsend's 1987 film *Hollywood Shuffle,* Townsend looks directly into the camera and admits that his film was financed on credit cards. Within five years, this practice had become the cheat code for making movies without a Hollywood studio.

wardly). But *Clerks* exhibits an almost supernatural commitment to Smith's own sense of aesthetics and taste. It's immersed in his heavily stoned, highly specific actuality, built on the lived experience of endless hours spent in a room filled with thousands of disposable movies. It was now possible for *anything* to be culturally important, based on the personal proclivities of the viewer. Which, depending on your perspective, was either exhilarating or idiotic.

"I am from a generation that very much wants to consume and reconsume its own shit," said director Joe Swanberg. Swanberg was thirteen when *Clerks* came out in 1994. He released his first feature in 2005, helping forge the so-called Mumblecore movement, a word-heavy style influenced by indie filmmakers of the nineties. Swanberg now dismisses his own period of rental-based self-education as inherently uncreative. "The video store, for me growing up, was access to watch and rewatch shit. What happens to my generation is, we don't just watch *The Breakfast Club** two times while it's in movie theaters. We watch *The Breakfast Club* sixty-nine times between the ages of twelve and twenty-five and convince ourselves that *The Breakfast Club* is a genius movie. You have this wrapped-up nostalgia and regurgitation and overcompensation of mediocre shit . . . and I directly tie that to the video store."

Swanberg's accusation is not invalid. The backbone of his argument, however, is not far removed from the same argument one would make in favor of this experience. Rewatching *The Breakfast Club* (or any film) sixty-nine times *does* change the meaning of what it is and how it's understood. It shifts the focus away from the straightforward message received by the audience ("This is a story about why high school is hard") and amplifies the components generating those messages (musical cues, shot framing, and

---

**The Breakfast Club* was a 1985 teen movie directed by John Hughes. It's most notable for its depiction of each character as having one identifiable social trait that defines everything else about their personality, a template that became integral to the construction of reality television throughout the nineties.

the casual integration of minor pop culture references carrying their own autonomous meanings). Video stores opened this deconstructive process to anyone who cared enough to try. They also created the opportunity to conduct this level of mental surgery on any random film—*The Breakfast Club*, but also *Citizen Kane* and *Chinatown*, but also *Bloodsport* and *Troll 2* and *Rocky III*. There was no syllabus to follow and no tradition to respect. VCR culture obliterated the traditional understanding of what was canonically significant: A film could be important for what it was, but also for what it prompted other people to inexplicably invent. A single redeeming detail could be taken from an immaterial B movie, repurposed within the context of a good movie, and drastically change the meaning of both pictures. Which had always been possible—it's just that most people didn't care or notice until the arrival of Quentin Tarantino.

Tarantino made it impossible not to notice.

It would be wrong to claim Quentin Tarantino learned about film history by working at Video Archives in Manhattan Beach, California ("I was already a movie expert," he explained. "That's how I got hired"). He'd started privately collecting films on videotape in 1978, years before he owned a VCR. As a sixteen-year-old in 1979, he seemingly saw every film screened in greater Los Angeles and can still recall in which theater he saw each picture. But Tarantino's association with the video store ethos (and the imagined iconography of the overbearing video store clerk) defines the archetype. Here was a gangly, ultra-confident person who spoke so fast it seemed as if he was trying to answer questions that had not yet been asked. He knew *everything* about movies, particularly movies that were considered irrelevant, always expressing his arcane knowledge as if it were somehow obvious and unconditional. He made offhand remarks like "Brian De Palma is the greatest director of his generation," a sentiment that could only come from a guy who'd read every sentence Pauline Kael had ever written and somehow concluded she was too understated. What Tarantino could express, more explicitly than any of his peers, was the intensity of his own perspective. He became the most important filmmaker of the nineties by making movies exclusively designed for his own idiosyncratic pleasure.

"What you find out fairly quickly in Hollywood," Tarantino told the BBC in 1994, "is that this is a community where hardly anybody trusts their own opinion. People want people to tell them what is good. What to like, what not to like. But here I come. I'm a film geek. My opinion is *everything*. You can all disagree with me. I don't care."

The best way to understand Tarantino's impact on the movie industry is through the three scripts he wrote while working at Video Archives in the eighties: *True Romance* (eventually directed by Tony Scott in 1993), *Natural Born Killers* (drastically rewritten and directed by Oliver Stone in 1994), and *Reservoir Dogs* (Tarantino's directorial debut, released in 1992). The first two offer incomplete glimpses into the Tarantino toolbox. *True Romance* stars Christian Slater as an avatar for its screenwriter, a comic book store employee obsessed with old movies, Elvis Presley,* and an idealized girlfriend who couldn't exist in real life. *Natural Born Killers* is an avalanche of comedic violence that almost seems real and realistic violence almost presented as comedy. There are hints of his proclivities in both scripts. Neither movie, however, *feels* like a Tarantino movie, or how that designation has come to be understood. *True Romance* has Tarantino-esque language, but the narrative is presented like a fairy tale. It's supposed to remind the viewer of the first time they fell in love and the emotional psychosis that accompanies that experience. *Natural Born Killers* is the story of two lovers on a killing spree, but it's thematically "about" many other things: the collective desensitizing to violence, the illusion of the nuclear family, and a heavy-

---

*Before becoming a writer and director, Tarantino tried to make it as an actor. His acting teacher was James Best, best known for playing sheriff Roscoe P. Coltrane on *The Dukes of Hazzard*. During this period, Tarantino appeared on a two-part episode of *The Golden Girls* as an Elvis impersonator. It was a nonspeaking role.

handed critique of media. In both cases, the films are supposed to serve as bridges to other realizations. Audiences were supposed to leave the theater and think other thoughts about other things. What was different about *Reservoir Dogs* is that the movie was about *the movie*. It was not an attempt to make anyone rethink the notion of crime, or the complexity of masculine relationships, or the psychological consequences of witnessing torture; a viewer might well consider those concepts, but such considerations were ancillary. *Reservoir Dogs* is a wholesale captivation of the universe it constructs. It's not a fictional version of life. It's the nonfictional representation of a life that only exists within the mind of the filmmaker. It has more to do with the experience of watching and internalizing the 1987 Hong Kong thriller *City on Fire* than with any personal experience in the physical, nonnegotiable world.

Reservoir Dogs is about a jewel heist that goes awry. Its six characters are identified only by their color-coded aliases ("Mr. Pink," "Mr. Blonde," etc.). One of the six is an undercover cop. Part of the reason *Reservoir Dogs* was green-lit had to do with the involvement of Harvey Keitel, an actor who'd already been famous for fifteen years. Keitel read the script and attached himself to the production, portraying the character "Mr. White." Keitel's recollection of reading the script is telling; he assumed (having never met him) that Tarantino must have had some kind of family connection to the world of organized crime. The narrative details were so rich and specific that it seemed like a story that had to have come from familial memory, particularly since the author had an Italian last name. He was shocked to learn that Tarantino was born in Tennessee, moved to L.A. with his mom as a child, and had never met a real criminal in his life. Tarantino's understanding and interpretation of the underworld was exclusively generated by other movies. And this, as it turns out, was the catalyst for almost everything he'd ever make.

The opening scene of *Reservoir Dogs* takes place in a diner. There are two topics of conversation at the table: the subtext of the Madonna song "Like a Virgin" and the morality of tipping waitresses. The dialogue is delivered convincingly. It has all the semiotic qualities of a real conversation among uneducated felons. Yet the *quality* of the content—the insights the characters present and what those sentiments reflect about the people articulating the opinions—is implausible. It's too perfect. These are people who casually talk with a studied eloquence that can only happen in movies. They are symbolic extensions of the video clerk experience, where the author's primary guide to human interaction comes from the consumption of meticulously crafted conversations, expressed through performances designed to make the craftsmanship invisible. What Tarantino captured was something that was accelerating across all popular culture: not reality, but a kind of hyperreality, where the secondary meaning always mattered more than the first. Kurt Cobain was a rock star whose essential purpose was critiquing the concept of rock stardom. *Seinfeld* was a TV show where the characters aspired to make a TV show exactly like the TV show that framed their fictional existence. *Reservoir Dogs* was a fake crime story with another fake crime story built inside of it, and that layered pathos is the essence of the Tarantino attack.

The undercover cop in *Reservoir Dogs* is played by British actor Tim Roth. In order to infiltrate the crime ring, Roth needs to convince the other criminals he's an authentic thief. To do this, his superior officer (Randy Brooks) gives Roth a four-page script describing a phony anecdote about a past drug deal that almost got him arrested. He's told to memorize the anecdote, because "an undercover cop has gotta be Marlon Brando—to do this job, you gotta be a great actor." What's essential, Roth is instructed, is the naturalistic nuance; he's supposed to internalize the main story while making the specific details his own. It's an extraordinary seven-minute sequence: Roth is an actor pretending to be a policeman who's learning how to pretend to act like a drug dealer, employing the same techniques Tarantino used in order to make Harvey Keitel believe he must have a familial relationship with actual crime.

In 1992, people referred to this kind of thing as "postmodern," partially because 1992 was the golden age of classifying anything as possibly postmodern. And in some academic sense, *Reservoir Dogs* absolutely was postmodern; it rejected the limitations of modernism and prioritized the subjective viewpoint of the artist. But what was really happening here was more basic. For all of the twentieth century—and particularly in the decades following World War II—the volume of manufactured consumer art had exponentially increased. The volume was now vast enough to replace the natural world in totality. A fixed reality was no longer needed; there was enough unfixed reality inside a single Blockbuster to sustain the entire cinematic multiverse. Content could be made from content.

○ ○ ○

Reservoir Dogs was well reviewed in America but earned more in the UK (its box office gross in the city of London alone was greater than the $3 million it made in all of the United States). But, perhaps predictably, it did extremely well on home video. It had strong word-of-mouth support. The only hitch was that the word of mouth, though effective, usually seemed to focus on the same detail: "Have you seen that movie where a guy gets his ear chopped off?"

As years have passed and his catalog has deepened, the relationship between Tarantino and violence has become less pervasive, even if the violence in his films has not. When people argue about him today, they argue about many things. But in 1992, violence was pretty much the only aspect of his work that people always wanted to discuss. The scene from *Reservoir Dogs* that resonated most arrestingly with casual audiences involved Michael Madsen ("Mr. Blonde"), the film's unabashed sociopath. After dancing to the lighthearted pop song "Stuck in the Middle with You," Madsen covers a kidnapped policeman's mouth with duct tape, slices off the man's ear with a straight razor, douses him with gasoline, and is killed (by Roth) moments before he burns the cop alive. Technically, the viewer does not witness the carving of the ear; the shot is blocked in a way that hides the assault. But you can *hear* the torture, so it feels like you saw it. And this raised a lot of questions about how people were supposed to think about transgressive art (although not in the way such questions are asked today).

In the eighties, violent cinema was mostly a matter of body count. A mind-numbing number of humans could be killed in a commercially viable film, simply because (a) the anonymous victims often did not speak English, and (b) the methods of termination were explosive and cartoonish. In 1984's *Red Dawn*, 118 people are killed, almost none of whom have speaking roles. Around 146 people die in the Chuck Norris vehicle *Invasion U.S.A.* In 1985's *Rambo: First Blood Part II*, 67 people are slaughtered, 51 of them by the titular protagonist. This style of wide-angle ultraviolent action flick was not viewed as legitimately controversial, in the same way teen sex romps of the time were considered gratuitous and stupid but not especially harmful. The Motion Picture Association of America had added the PG-13 rating classification in July of 1984, ostensibly limiting very young children from seeing nudity or excessive horror without a guardian (at least in public). And though there were significant exceptions, the eighties were—in general—an astonishingly unimaginative period for mainstream film, certainly when compared to the decade that came before and the decade that came after. Complaining about the social ramifications of the sex and violence from this era of moviemaking almost seemed to give the movies too much credit.

That changed in the nineties. The explosion of independent film during the first half of the decade reenergized the 1970s impulse of taking movies seriously. It climaxed in 1994, with the release of two films in the same three-month window: Tarantino's second directorial effort, *Pulp Fiction*, and Oliver Stone's *Natural Born Killers* (written by Tarantino in the eighties, rewritten several times in the interim, and now crediting Tarantino only as the story's original source). Pre-release interest in the two films was bifurcated: Critics were waiting for *Pulp Fiction*, but the general populace assumed *Natural Born Killers* would be a bigger deal. Stone was seen as the most socially engaged American director of the previous ten years. His war film *Platoon* (based on his own experience in Vietnam) won the Academy Award for both picture and director, and 1987's *Wall Street* had become a shorthand encapsulation of how the eighties would be remembered. He'd put out two polarizing movies in 1991, both based on real events from the sixties (a biopic about the Doors and a conspiratorial retelling of the John F. Kennedy assassination). There was widespread anticipation that *Natural Born Killers* might be Stone's masterwork. Everything about it seemed politically charged and emotionally paradoxical. The star would be Woody Harrelson, playing a nihilistic mass murderer. The casting decision was bold: Harrelson was internationally famous for his role as Woody Boyd on *Cheers*, one of the sweetest, least threatening characters in the history of television. His equally malevolent female companion would be played by twenty-one-year-old Juliette Lewis, a former child actor still described as childlike. Robert Downey Jr., coming off his acclaimed portrayal of Charlie Chaplin in *Chaplin*, would provide a critical supporting role in *NBK*. The soundtrack was produced by Trent Reznor, operating at the apex of his rock power. All the dominos were aligned. *Natural Born Killers* was going to matter. It was going to be important.

But then it came out, and it didn't, and it wasn't.

There were three problems with *Natural Born Killers*. The first was that it wasn't very good. There was a sense of visual overkill and the tone was inconsistent. It made points about society that were clumsy and obvious, along with a few radical assertions that didn't seem accurate and a couple that contradicted the film's core intention. The second problem was that *NBK* and *Pulp Fiction* came out at roughly the same time. The movies were constantly compared, almost never in Stone's favor (and the fact that Tarantino said he "fucking hated" *NBK* compounded that dissonance). Third, all those various comparisons inevitably (and sometimes obsessively) dwelled on the one quality both pictures had in abundance—excessive, graphic violence. Critics could not get over this. But audiences could, and the difference between the two filmmakers' humor made it much easier to justify the auxiliary violence in *Pulp Fiction* than the necessary violence in *Natural Born Killers*. Something had changed in the way this kind of material was consumed. It was an evolution that would become more and more pronounced as time crawled forward.

○ ○ ○

There's a central incongruity to the way movie violence is perceived by those who cover it: The criticism is always greater if the depiction is especially realistic. Verisimilitude is actually a detriment. Early reviews of *Pulp Fiction* are a clear example. Though its retrospective reputation is exceedingly positive (the American Film Institute places it among the one hundred finest films ever made), early reviews were mixed. "What's most bothersome about *Pulp Fiction*," snarked Stanley Kauffmann in *The New Republic*, "is its success."

"This is a movie about a collection of morons who move through life dispassionately executing the guilty and the innocent," claimed one writer for *USA Today*.* Versions of this moralistic take were surprisingly common. "The experience overall is like laughing down a gun barrel, a little bit tiring, a lot sick and maybe far too perverse for less jaded moviegoers," wrote Rita Kempley in *The Washington Post*. Roger Ebert, traditionally open to this brand of on-screen carnage, expressed confusion over its "unrelenting violence and bloodshed, interrupted on occasion by mordant humor, broad adolescent satire, and grim warnings from the Old Testament. . . . I have no idea at all whether I liked *Pulp Fiction* or not." Discomfort with the imagery and

---

*USA Today really, really hated *Pulp Fiction*. The above quote was from a critic named Joe Urschel, reviewing the film upon its release. But just in case anyone missed that article, they had another writer, future Fox News pundit Linda Chavez, eviscerate the film again in January of 1995: "What is most objectionable about *Pulp Fiction* is its reprehensibly amoral vision. . . . [Tarantino] displays the ethical judgment and moral sensibility of a hyena. There is not a single redeeming character in the cast of *Pulp Fiction*, only killers, thieves, dope addicts, sadists, hustlers and quislings. There are no heroes and villains, only bad guys and worse." One almost wonders if, this being *USA Today*, there was a state-by-state breakdown of everyone in the country who was offended by this movie.

the language sometimes morphed into harder questions about the director's intent. Kenneth Turan of the *Los Angeles Times*, while conceding that *Pulp Fiction* was "sporadically effective," ultimately concluded, "This is a noticeably uneven film, both too inward-looking and self-centered in its concerns and too outward-bound in the way it strains to outrage an audience."

Two critical notes on all those newspaper accusations: The first is that most of them are partially true. The second is that they inadvertently explain why *Pulp Fiction* worked. In an attempt to point out traditional flaws, the critics (Turan especially) were unknowingly describing the incendiary power of the Video Store Aesthetic. The elements they deride would have been problems for any movie that aspired to be other things. They were strengths for a movie that aspired to be a movie.

Pulp Fiction was an ensemble piece with no obvious star. The best performance came from Samuel L. Jackson, a journeyman who'd been in more than thirty previous movies before emerging as the ideal mouthpiece for Tarantino's stylized dialogue. But the casting decision that seemed most irregular was the high-profile inclusion of John Travolta. In 1994, it would have been hard to come up with a less cool person to include in a movie where coolness was everything. Travolta had not been a serious performer for almost a decade, scarcely subsisting on a trio of movies about a baby with the voice of Bruce Willis (*Look Who's Talking, Look Who's Talking Too,* and *Look Who's Talking Now*). Cynical pre-release suspicion hinted that Travolta had been cast in *Pulp Fiction* for unkind comedic value.* But this was not the case at all. Tarantino had loved Travolta's early work, particularly his performance in the 1981 De Palma thriller *Blow Out*. The thirteen barren years in between were beside the point. He didn't view Travolta as a commodity whose value had plummeted, nor was it like the casting of Harrelson in *Natural Born Killers*, where the existing awareness of his TV career was sup-

---

*Disgraced sexual predator Harvey Weinstein, cofounder of Miramax and producer of *Pulp Fiction*, approved every casting decision Tarantino wanted *except* Travolta and unsuccessfully tried to cut him from the film, pushing instead for Daniel Day-Lewis.

posed to complicate our understanding of his character. Tarantino wanted Travolta in *Pulp Fiction* for the same reasons he'd liked Travolta in *Urban Cowboy* and *Saturday Night Fever* and *Welcome Back, Kotter*. The culture may have shifted, but—within the aisles of the video store—all those performances remained unchanged. It's like the philosophical difference between viewing time as linear and believing all time is happening at once: Travolta was still Travolta, and Travolta was what Tarantino wanted. That desire, as Turan noted, was "inward-looking and self-centered." But it's also why Tarantino was the only person who could have made that movie.

For a fleeting moment in time, this attitude was everywhere. The nineties were a fertile period for the self-indulgent genius and an amazing decade for high-gloss unconventional film, saturated with anti-cliché, self-contained projects defined by the interiority of their creators: Danny Boyle's drug exploration *Trainspotting*. P. T. Anderson's fictional porn biopic *Boogie Nights*. The discomfiting atmospheres of Jane Campion's *The Piano* and Vincent Gallo's *Buffalo '66*. Spike Jonze and Charlie Kaufman's brainfuck *Being John Malkovich*. Sofia Coppola's essayistic *The Virgin Suicides*, Darren Aronofsky's mathematically obsessed *Pi*, and Christopher Nolan's memory-inverted *Memento*. Spike Lee's prescient *Bamboozled*, overlooked during its initial 2000 release. Wes Anderson's esoteric character studies. Even directors with more formal aesthetics—the Kubrickian perfectionist David Fincher and the interpersonal realist Noah Baumbach—did not make rote, familiar-feeling movies. Their manufactured realities were lifelike, but not transposable with life itself. They demanded to be seen (and considered) as isolated and nontransferable. Time and again, the movie was about the movie.

But this, as it turns out, was an impermanent condition. What came from the nineties stayed in the nineties: By 2015, the notion of seeing a film (or any art) as separate from real-life morality and present-day politics had become increasingly unpopular. By 2020, it was verboten. A movie like 1992's *The Crying Game*, which would have been unmakeable in the remote past, became unmakeable again. Tarantino, once lionized for his uncompromising singularity, would be regularly attacked for using racially abhorrent language and prioritizing his own internal fantasies above the external message his work seemed to project. The possibility of a movie being only about itself was out of business, along with all the video stores.

[the power of myth]

THE ATTRACTION TO SPORTS IS SO INDIVIDUAL AND MULTIFACETED THAT trying to explain why the attraction exists is like trying to explain why people enjoy falling in love. Sports can be whatever you want them to be—escapist, political, symbolic, inspirational. But the one quality that coincides with all of those projections is the degree to which sports are *clear*, at least when compared to conventional reality: The rules are outlined in a book, the outcomes are nonnegotiable, and success or failure is a direct extension of physiological meritocracy. Unlike life, sports make it simple for the ordinary person to deduce who is good and who is bad, who has won and who has lost. Which is why it's so fascinating that—until 1998—Division I college football purposefully stopped that from happening.

Throughout the twentieth century, college basketball was significantly more popular than pro basketball, largely due to its postseason tournament. Interest in the collegiate regular season was (and is) dwarfed by interest in the sixty-eight-team tournament staged over the end of March. For most college basketball programs of the nineties, the primary goal of the entire season was qualifying for the NCAA tournament. Major college football, however, was still using a system that now seems antithetical to the concept of competition: There was no playoff at all. The postseason involved thirty-eight teams all playing a single bowl game, and the national champion was a box of smoke.

Where (and who) the thirty-eight teams played was either inflexibly assigned or capriciously selected. The champion of the Big Ten conference played the champion of the Pac-10 conference in the Rose Bowl, always. That was the easy one. The winner of the Southeastern Conference was sent to the Sugar Bowl, almost without exception, but their opponent could be pretty much anyone. The Orange Bowl traditionally featured whoever won the Big 8 Conference facing whoever won the Atlantic Coast Conference, but only if the ACC champion was legitimately strong and there was no better alternative. The Cotton Bowl was the winner of the Southwest Conference, usually pitted against the second-best team from the SEC or a major independent like Notre Dame. The Fiesta Bowl could involve any two teams the Fiesta Bowl committee desired, assuming those teams agreed to participate and weren't already obligated to go elsewhere.

After all nineteen bowl games were complete, a national champion was selected by voting. But there were two polls, one comprising the media and one comprising the coaches. The two polls did not have to align, so it was possible for one season to have two champions. There was nothing even tenuously similar to this system in any other sport, including every other echelon of football: Playoffs were used in the NFL, at the high school level in all fifty states, and even in all the lower divisions of college football. Only Division I football was opposed to a playoff. The bureaucratic singularity of this system was not some taboo subject nobody questioned. It was questioned constantly, in every season when there was more than one outstanding team (which was almost every season).

"I think Division I football is the only sport in America where they don't have a tournament or a playoff to determine the champion," Florida Gators head coach Steve Spurrier said in 1990. "I don't see how we can say we're right and everyone else is wrong."

The defects of the no-playoff system had always been understood. In

1984, undefeated Brigham Young University was crowned national champ, even though they didn't face any team who finished the year with less than four losses. The possibility for an imperfect champion was always there. But the problem escalated with the onset of the nineties, sometimes in embarrassing ways. In 1990, the national title was shared between Georgia Tech (a second-tier football program, unranked before the season began) and Colorado (another nontraditional power who'd won a critical regular-season game against Missouri when the officiating crew accidentally gave the Buffaloes an extra down on the last play of the game). The trophy was split again in 1991, when Miami and Washington both went undefeated but were required to play in different bowl games.

In 1994, undefeated Nebraska and undefeated Penn State were the two best teams in the country, and most of the major conferences had finally agreed to release teams from fixed bowl obligations if there was an opportunity for a matchup between the two top teams in the nation. This agreement was called "the Bowl Coalition." The Big Ten, however, did not agree to the terms of the coalition and forced Penn State to play twelfth-ranked Oregon in the Rose Bowl. Nebraska beat third-ranked Miami in the Orange Bowl and was named national champ in both polls. The trophy was shared again in 1997, when both Michigan and Nebraska were unbeaten but unable to play each other on January 1: Michigan was from the Big Ten and (here again) required to play in the Rose Bowl. Michigan was still awarded the national title by the media, but Nebraska won the coaches' poll, an outcome even more controversial than usual—some believed the coaches voted for the Cornhuskers only because longtime Husker head coach Tom Osborne was retiring after the season.

Why major college football refused to relent from this restrictive, highly unpopular postseason structure can be viewed as either simple or confounding, depending on how long you want to think about it. The simple answer was money. The confounding part was trying to understand how *not* having a playoff was more lucrative than the opposite. It made no obvious sense. By

1995, annual TV revenue from the NCAA men's basketball tournament had already climbed over $200 million, and college football was worth way more than college hoops. And while it's true that a minor bowl game (such as the Independence Bowl) is good for the local economy of the host city, it's hard to understand why that would matter to the NCAA (or why the economic needs of a community like Shreveport, Louisiana, should have any influence on how college football decides a champion). Bowl games were, and still are, something of a financial boondoggle: Bowl organizers pay participating colleges for playing, and that money is distributed among all the teams from that program's conference (thereby incentivizing the various conferences to keep their bowl relationships intact). The rest of the revenue stays with local bowl executives, and the games themselves are inexplicably classified as tax-exempt nonprofits.

It was not until 1998 that all six major bowl games and the five major conferences (along with Notre Dame, who remained independent) agreed to form the Bowl Championship Series, commonly referred to as the BCS. The upshot of the BCS was that (a) the two top-ranked teams would *always* play for the national title, regardless of conference affiliation, and (b) all the minor bowl games would continue, even if people stopped caring about them.

The first champion decided in this new era was Tennessee, and the BCS system was used for the next fifteen years, until the NCAA adopted a conventional four-team playoff in 2014. Almost every fan and analyst now agrees that deciding the champion on the field, as opposed to begrudgingly accepting the results of two unaffiliated polls, is a more reasonable way to decide who is the best team in the country. But certain eccentricities were lost in the transition, and it's tricky to discern whether making college football more logical actually made it more compelling.

Part of what had always made college football so emotionally explosive was its willful lack of definition. By allowing the national champion to stand as a mythical abstraction, multiple schools could justifiably argue that they were the best program in the country, even if the polls said otherwise. In 1993, the one-loss Florida State Seminoles were awarded the national title, even though a one-loss Notre Dame beat them in the regular season and Auburn (a school on probation) finished the year undefeated. There was sometimes a cachet to *not* finishing number 1, since winning a human poll didn't "prove" anything at all. By creating an officially sanctioned title game, the NCAA removed college football's existential tension. But perhaps even more historically deflating was the erosion of its unique brand of idiosyncrasy.

Until the '98 season, it was still possible to look at college football as wholly separate from every other dominant sport—a national fascination where regional tradition mattered more than logic. For roughly a hundred years, establishing an airtight champion was seen as less essential than perpetuating the semi-irrational construction of how the sport had been originally conceived, even when that frustrated everyone who cared about it. By never *really* verifying the champion, college football was able to sustain an illusion of old-school amateurism that belied its economic superstructure (and its negative academic influence). A playoff was fine for the pros, but maybe college kids didn't need it. Maybe it was okay to end every season with an essay question that could not be answered. It was something to talk about when there was nothing else to talk about. It was an acceptable thing not to know.

But the age of not knowing things was ending.

6 CTRL + ALT + DELETE

THE SOUND OF THE INSURRECTION WAS NOT MUSICAL. THE SOUND OF THE insurrection was annoying, until it was begrudgingly zapped into nonexistence and turned into a thirty-two-second YouTube demonstration of nostalgia induction. The sequencing of the sound is "nostalgic" in the truest definition of the word, as it cannot be argued that the emotional memory it represents was in any way superior to the modern version: First, a dial tone, followed by eleven rapid beeps from an invisible push-button telephone. This was followed by three or four high-pitched electronic whistles, collapsing into a longer whistle resembling the flatlining of a dying patient hooked to an EKG machine (this was the sound of the phone line's echo suppression being disabled). There were a few more beeps absorbed into a wall of white noise, and then the white noise abruptly doubled, meaning the receiving modem was now interacting with the calling modem. There was an instant where it sounded like something inside the computer had broken, spontaneously repaired by the digital interplay of two probing modulators, similar in pitch to a metal detector passing over a pocket watch. This was bookended by another fleeting second of white noise, and then . . . silence. The wall had been breached. The floodgates were open. And then, depending on who you were and the year in which you were living, there was a high likelihood the next sound was a one-word welcome from Elwood Edwards, a voice actor living in Orrville, Ohio. His affable greeting would be followed by a grammatically incorrect phrase: "You've got mail."

In a year like 1998, this sequence happened around 27 million times a day. Elwood Edwards—the faceless, bloodless, unofficial spokesman for America Online—was the most heard voice on the planet. "I think of myself as a postman," Edwards said. "My attitude never changes."

This is true. His attitude did not change. But it was the only thing that didn't.

○ ○ ○

The wheel was invented in 3500 BC, a few hundred years before the Bronze Age. It's the pinnacle example of something very old that still seems uncomfortably recent: While it's impossible to pinpoint exactly when the earliest hominids transitioned into a version of what we now understand as humans, even conservative estimates place the inception at around 70,000 years ago. That's a long time for people not to notice that rocks roll down hills. How was it possible that creatures with enough intellectual capacity to fuse copper and tin did not have the intellectual ability to advance beyond the art of dragging things across the ground? The answer is that the invention of the wheel was not the key to wheeling things around. The key was the invention of the axle. Within the carpentry limitations of the pre-Bronze era, it was extraordinarily difficult to engineer a mechanism where revolving cylinders could be affixed to stationary wagons. The wheel, as a concept, was always just sitting there. It merely took a few millennia to figure out how to make it do all the things wheels are supposed to do.

The internet can be viewed in a similar way, accelerated by a factor of 1,000. When and how the internet technically came into existence is a semantic argument over the definition of the word *internet*. The first "node to node" communication was conducted by the military in 1969. The protocols for how digital information is packaged, translated, and routed were developed in the late seventies by Vinton Cerf, the so-called Father of the Internet, eventually awarded the Presidential Medal of Freedom. When Al Gore ran for president in 2000, he was mocked for casually claiming on CNN that he "took the initiative in creating the Internet," an inaccurate statement that was also willfully misunderstood (what Gore was referencing was a $600 million bill he'd sponsored as a senator* that expanded the internet into schools and libraries). As with the wheel, there is no singular point of origin. But what we do know is this: When the hypothesis of a World Wide Web was first proposed in Switzerland in 1989, almost no one in the United States who wasn't a computer scientist had any idea what that meant or what it could be. Twelve years later, almost every American adult would know what it was, even if they'd never used it and never would. Within our aforementioned analogy, the wheel represents the internet and the axle represents the human relationship to computerized technology.

It's possible to imagine a distant future in which the only achievement most people associate with the nineties is the foundational rise of the internet. Part of this has to do with the speed at which it happened—while the Industrial Revolution unspooled over fifty years, the Internet Revolution took ten (plus or minus two years in either direction, depending on the age and education of the consumer). The speed of this transformation trifurcated the populace. If someone had already reached middle age by 1995 (say, any person born before World War II), it was possible to view the internet as an interesting outgrowth of modernity that could be ignored entirely. It was neither a necessity nor an obligation. We'll classify these individuals as "Group A." Another set comprises those people born after 1985, whom we'll call "Group C." Individuals in Group C have almost no educational memory that isn't vaguely tied to network computing. They have no concept of a purely analog existence that isn't anecdotal. Upon reaching adulthood,

---

*Because of his legislative fixation on technology, Gore was sometimes lumped into the subset of "Atari Democrats." That classification started to disappear around 1992, after Atari lost a copyright suit against Nintendo.

Group C individuals would be classified as "internet natives" (until they became the dominant class and such a designation became superfluous).

It was only the middle cluster, Group B, who were forced to wrestle with an experience that reconstituted reality without changing anything about the physical world. These interlocked generations—Boomers and Xers— will be the only people who experienced this shift as it happened, with total recall of both the previous world and the world that came next. "If we're the last people in history to know life before the Internet," wrote Michael Harris in his book *The End of Absence*, "we are also the only ones who will ever speak, as it were, both languages. We are the only fluent translators of Before and After."

What's odd about this transformation is that the concrete differences don't seem especially dramatic. Instead of mailing a stamped paper enve- lope, you could now send the same letter as an email (and it was three days faster). If you wanted to fly to Hawaii, you no longer had to call a travel agent in order to book a flight (everyone had access to the same airline listings). If you ran a fantasy football league, you didn't need to find the sports section of the Monday newspaper and do the math by hand. Driving directions, cake recipes, and nontraditional pornography could all be found within the same portal, at no cost, instantly and temporarily. It was easier to buy things and it was easier to sell things. The litany of mechanical differences between daily life in 1993 and daily life in 1998 is mostly a list of minor advancements expediting activities that weren't that difficult in the first place. But this is a little like saying the main impact of the automobile was a decline in horse ownership. The full spectrum of social and psychological consequences that accompanied the advent of the internet is too profound to explain or under- stand (then, now, or ever). It exponentially expanded the parameters of exter- nal existence while decreasing the material size of interior existence. It allowed any person to simultaneously possess two competing identities— one actual and one virtual. It altered the value of concepts whose value had once been stable and self-evident (solitude, distance, memory, knowledge).

Most critically, it recontextualized every fragment of data that moved through its sphere, which eventually encompassed all data available.

This process, to varying degrees, had happened before. Similar arguments had been made about television and the radio and the printing press. No one disputes that technology has continually changed the structure of society. But the difference this time was the scale, the depth, and the intensity.

In 1972, the BBC broadcast a four-episode TV series titled *Ways of Seeing*, hosted by art critic John Berger (the series was later adapted into a book with the same name). The first episode was built off the work of German philosopher Walter Benjamin. It argued that the modern capability to easily "reproduce" any canonical painting via photography changes the meanings of the original artifact, detaching it from the artist's original intent. In the episode's final ten minutes, Berger speaks directly into the camera and makes two points. The first is that the meaning of a painting is manipulated not only by how it is seen, but by whatever is seen directly before and directly after. He explains how any sound or text accompanying the image can have the alienating effect of turning something accessible into something inaccessible. But then he says something else, a warning about his own televised argument:

> Remember that I am controlling and using, for my own purposes, the means of reproduction needed for these [television] programs. The images may be like words, but there is no dialogue. *You* cannot reply to *me*. For that to become possible in the modern media of communication, access to television must be extended beyond its present narrow limits.

Berger was analyzing oil paintings that were hundreds of years old, but he inadvertently explained what would eventually make the exploration of culture in the Internet Age so unlike the same experience in the 1972 world where *Ways of Seeing* was produced. The majority of internet content is an incomplete reproduction of something that already exists elsewhere, delivered in a capricious sequence self-directed by the user. Every message or image is preceded and followed by a different message or image with which it has no natural relationship, except to modify the meaning of whatever is currently being experienced. It is literally a context of no context, thus negating the very notion of contextual meaning. Berger's hypothetical future is our inescapable present. Yet it was his second point, about the "narrow limits" of television, that was even more prescient, probably by accident. Those narrow limits have been obliterated. The internet turned every computer into an object that was almost (but not entirely) unimaginable in 1972: a television you could talk to, and a television that would listen. A television that knew everything. A television built out of people.

Things that are astonishing to the members of Group B aren't astonishing to anyone else. It is only those adults who lived both before and after the internet who find themselves fixated on how random activities were conducted differently before the computer and the cell phone. So many prior pursuits now seem needlessly convoluted, or even dangerous. It sometimes doesn't seem possible that the postal service and landline telephones were enough to perpetuate society. But they were, and there was no sense whatsoever that communication was not happening fast enough. In 1990, a ten-minute phone call from Chicago to Los Angeles cost $1.58 during evening hours and slightly more during the afternoon. While it was always possible to disagree over whether this long-distance rate was reasonable or expensive, no one assumed phone calls should be free. The limitations of time and space were ingrained, as was the concept of a telephone's calcifying geography in nonnegotiable terms.

Take, for example, the premise of using one's native area code as an expression of identity. Today, this practice is often employed as a form of sarcasm. But before a phone could be placed inside a pocket and walked onto an airplane, it signified more. One of the earliest illustrations was the hip-hop group 213, the three-man collaboration of Snoop Dogg, Nate Dogg, and Warren G. Although 213 (expressed as the singular digits "2-1-3") did not release an official album until 2004, the trio formed in 1990, inspired by the Oakland-based hip-hop group 415. The reason 415 called itself "4-1-5" is that 415 was the old area code for Oakland. Snoop, Nate, and Warren were all from Long Beach, California, so they adopted the local prefix, 213. Over time, this type of branding became so common that it moved into self-parody. It was banal enough to be included as a plot point in the first *Sex and the City* movie (Carrie Bradshaw refuses to accept a 347 area code, classifying herself as a "9-1-7 gal"). That might seem like just another example of rap slang being co-opted by white culture (and it is). But it's more than that. It is, in a way, a bizarre symbol of victory for the North American telecommunications industry.

Area codes were introduced in 1947. The lowest digits were assigned to regions with the highest population density, based on the principle that people living in highly populated areas would make more phone calls and should have to "work" less (this was the era of rotary phones, when dialing a number could hurt your index finger). Large expanses of land might share a single area code (the code for the entire state of Florida was 305). Over time, area codes became more and more specific (Florida now has seventeen codes, with 305 applying only to Miami-Dade County and the Florida Keys). This enhanced specificity generated multiple meanings. Telling a rap audience you were born in Long Beach is the equivalent of vaguely pointing at a map, but saying you "represent the 2-1-3" requires the audience to (a) have deep familiarity with California, since most area codes aren't familiar to outsiders, and (b) understand that this particular prefix also encompassed South Central Los Angeles and the depressed economic status therein. If you didn't hear about the group 213 until all its members had become indi- vidually famous, you also needed to know that the California code maps were redrawn in 1998, and that "213" now only includes a sliver of down- town L.A., and that the group's allegiance to the discontinued code was historical and honorary.

Something that was once emotionless and practical had become per- sonal and expository. Lines drawn by the phone company were more impor- tant than signposts denoting a community's city limits. And what makes this notable is its correlation to how much phone culture changed in such a short period of time.

For the (so-called) average nineties person living a (so-called) normal nineties life, no part of day-to-day existence changed as radically as their relationship to the telephone. It's not just that only 4.3 million Americans had a cellular phone in 1990 and 97 million had one by 2000, although that's part of it. What changed even more was the psychology of how the telephone was viewed and prioritized. The primacy of a landline connection dictated how life was lived, with such deep-rooted universality that its role in shaping humanity was virtually unconsidered. It was the single most important fea- ture of every home, and nobody cared.

There are no statistics illustrating how rare it was for someone to ignore a ringing telephone in 1990. This is because such a question would never have been asked (or even pondered). To do so was unthinkable. For one thing, the ring of a conventional rotary telephone was set at 80 decibels, engineered to be audibly noticed in every room of a two-story house. For another, a phone without an answering machine would ring incessantly until the caller gave up. You had to answer the phone in order to *stop* the phone. But the main reason everyone always answered the telephone was the impossibility of knowing who was on the line. Every ringing phone was, potentially, a life-altering event. It might be a telemarketer, but it also might be a death in the family. It could be your next-door neighbor, but it could also be the governor, and there was only one way to find out.* It was a remarkably democratic device: Every incoming call was equally important, until proven otherwise. If a homebound person wanted to avoid a specific conversation, the only solution was to take the phone off the hook and receive no calls whatsoever.

Times change, because that's what times do. There's always a preciousness to writing about the recent past, inexorably consumed with how something slightly different was either far better or far worse. It's easy to argue that a world without cell phones was charming, and easier still to argue that it was inferior. But it was mostly just immutable. Modern people worry about smartphone addiction, despite the fact that landlines exercised much more control over the owner. If you needed to take an important call, you just had to sit in the living room and wait for it. There was no other option. If you didn't know where someone was, you had to wait until that person wanted to be found. You had to trust people, and they had to trust you. If you made plans over the phone and left the house, those plans could not be changed—everyone had to be where they said they'd be, and everyone had to arrive when they said they'd arrive. Life was more scripted and less fluid, dictated by a machine that would not (and could not) compromise its location. Yet within these fascistic limitations, the machine itself somehow mattered less. It was an appliance, not that different from the dishwasher. The concept of buying a new phone every other year† would have seemed as crazy as

---

*This would change with the introduction and proliferation of caller ID, first established in New Jersey in 1987 but not widely available everywhere until the middle nineties. There was, however, an especially goofy period in between not knowing and knowing: the fleeting era of "*69." Around 1993, many phone companies introduced a feature by which you could find out who was the last person who called your number, by dialing "*69." It was supposed to be a way to track abusive callers, but its main utility was for romantic obsessives trying to see if the object of their desire had called without leaving a message. In 1994, R.E.M. wrote a song about the feature ("Star 69").

†My childhood home had one phone, on the wall in the kitchen. We had the same phone for all eighteen years I lived there. I suppose it's possible we replaced the phone at some point and I simply didn't notice, but—if we did—my mother selected the exact same model, in the exact same color, with the exact same features.

installing a new toilet every other Thanksgiving. There was nothing exciting or provocative about a telephone. It had no relationship to taste or independence (every member of a household shared the same telephone number). A phone was supposed to serve one concrete function, and it wasn't even assumed to be particularly reliable. In the 1992 film *Singles*, the romantic lead (Campbell Scott) drunkenly calls the woman he loves (Kyra Sedgwick) from a pay phone in a rock club, only to have his rambling confession destroyed when the answering machine's audiotape unravels. In just over a decade, both sides of that equation would be moot. Pay phones would vanish and analog answering machines would be replaced by digital voice mail. But the scene remains as a deft depiction of landline communication at the onset of the nineties: It *seemed* as good as it could possibly be, with flaws that didn't seem unacceptable until they were already eradicated. If a phone call was critical, you simply had to stay home. It was the only way to control the experience and the only way to ensure that the message would be received. And why would anyone have expected otherwise? Cell phones were the size of a brick and cost $4,000. They were gratuitous, even for millionaires. A TV commercial for the Canadian beer Labatt Blue was plotted on the premise that anyone who brought a cell phone into a bar was automatically an asshole,* much in the same way Ben Stiller's character from *Reality Bites* is introduced as self-absorbed by talking on a car phone in his very first scene. Zack Morris carried a cell phone to school on the adolescent sitcom *Saved by the Bell*, and that seemed no less ridiculous than his ability to freeze time. You had to be at home to talk on the phone. Home was where the phone was.

Until (of course) it wasn't. In 1992, bragging about your area code was a collective expression of the community where you were. By 2002, it was an individual connection to the place you had left. The machine that trapped

---

*The alleged asshole in the Labatt advertisement was played by Mark DeCarlo, who'd later host the salacious syndicated game show *Studs*.

people in the living room had been converted into a machine that offered liberation, akin to the rise of car ownership in the 1920s: Suddenly, anyone could go anywhere, whenever they wanted. The shackles were gone, until we replaced them on purpose.

○ ○ ○

It sometimes seems like 1995 was the year the future began. This is particularly true if the last book you happened to read was W. Joseph Campbell's *1995: The Year the Future Began.*

It was, irrefutably, a critical year for the elementary operations of the internet. Netscape Navigator emerged as a viable, practical web browser (the software to install it cost $39). A balding San Francisco entrepreneur named Craig Newmark started a tiny website called Craigslist, an alternative to classified advertising that would go on to inadvertently annihilate the American newspaper industry. Amazon went live that summer, although only as a bookstore. The American Dialect Society declared "World Wide Web" one of the words of the year, having already bestowed that declaration on "cyber" in 1994 and "information superhighway" in 1993 (they'd break the mold in 1996, when the word of the year was "mom" as a pejorative term, as in "soccer mom"). But 1995 was still a period when the internet was mainly something to speculate about, as opposed to something to use. Only 14 percent of American adults had ever been online.

Growth in public understanding of the internet was asymmetrical. The chronology worked in reverse: Early coverage was insular and esoteric to anyone not already familiar with what was being covered. Late in 1993, *The New York Times* ran a small story about Mosaic, the pre-Netscape web browser now credited as a catalyst for what the internet would become. Within technology circles, Mosaic was immediately perceived as a game-changing software application. It added graphic elements to what had been a purely textual experience and increased the reach of where the web could go. But the article also noted its limitations:

There remain, however, significant barriers to using Mosaic. It requires that the user have a computer that is directly connected to the global Internet. Many businesses and almost all universities now have such connections, but the majority of personal computer users currently connect to the Internet only indirectly through on-line information services like Delphi or America Online.

Though it's easy to understand this problem now, imagine how confusing it would seem to a nation where less than a quarter of its households possessed a home computer. It was perplexing even to early adopters of dial-up providers like AOL. If they weren't already reaching the "global" internet, what level of internet were they reaching? What would be the difference? There was a pedantic tedium to the way the internet was described—a continual onslaught of jargon that insisted something important was happening without fully elucidating what the important thing was. It was mechanics for mechanics. *Wired* magazine, launched in 1993, provided in-depth journalism about a technological landscape many of its readers had no ability to access or visualize. But then, for reasons both intellectual and commercial, the approach to coverage reversed. It suddenly became essential to describe the internet as simple, and to assert that the user did not need to understand how it worked in order to enjoy it.

The 1995 television program *The Internet Show* was the apotheosis of this movement. Filmed around Houston, it was hosted by John Levine (the author of *The Internet for Dummies*) and Gina Smith (a tech journalist who would later cowrite the autobiography of Steve Wozniak, who cofounded Apple with Steve Jobs). Its production values were rooted in the 1980s. The posture of *The Internet Show* felt promotional, although it aired on public television and promoted a digital abstraction that wasn't owned by anyone. The internet, the hosts explained, was merely a "network of networks." Their message was that any understanding beyond that was potentially interesting but not really necessary. *The Internet Show* was patterned to resemble the kind of video a teenager would watch in a driver's education class. "In some ways it's a lot like your car," Levine said of the internet. "You don't have to know how every single part works in order to drive to some wonderful places." How many places? Not that many, actually. "There are hundreds, if not thousands, of neat things you can do on the Internet," noted Smith. But in 1995, any number greater than seven sounded like a lot.

Within ten years, footage of *The Internet Show* would scan as deadpan satire. It's a prehistoric objet d'art, and most of its information is so obsolete it can't even be classified as incorrect. Yet it still offers moments of inadvertent insight. At one point, Smith tries to explain the difference between "nerds" and "geeks." While there's arguably a semantic difference between these two classifications,* Smith draws the line of demarcation as a disparity over enthusiasm: "A *nerd*," asserts Smith, "is someone whose life is focused on computers and technology. But a *geek* is someone whose life is focused on computers and technology and likes ît that way."

What's telling about this contrast is that—because it was 1995—Smith worked from the premise that the only people engaged with the internet would undoubtedly fall into one of these two camps. Having a life focused on computers and technology was still an unorthodox way to live. But within half a decade, such an experience would encompass millions and millions of lives, often against their will. That forced a lot of people to reluctantly become what Smith labeled as nerds, controlled and oppressed by a minority of geeks who insisted the nerds should be thrilled about it.

"It almost doesn't matter whether the Internet is likely to deliver on the hopes that many people invested in it, as, for the time being, it focuses on the *aspirations* of millions," British tech entrepreneur Keith Teare wrote in

---

*In theory, nerds are supposedly more introverted and self-involved, while geeks are more socially comfortable and performative about their nerdlike interests.

1996. Two years prior, Teare had opened Cyberia, one of the UK's earliest internet cafés. "The optimism among Internet users contrasts starkly with the general pessimism in society."

Mid-nineties web adopters were optimistic about the internet to the same degree Alexander the Great was enthusiastic about the acquisition of real estate. It is perhaps the hardest aspect to retrospectively reconcile about the time period—within a decade relentlessly categorized as cynical and underwhelming, the cult of the internet was evangelical in its belief that this technology was not just positive but unassailable and limitless. There was nothing it did not have the capability to reinvent. "The Internet will be to women in the '90s what the vibrator was to women in the '70s," self-described cyberporn editor Lisa Palac said in a 1994 *GQ* story. "It's going to have that power."

This hyperbolic hopefulness was forged by intellectual separation. The theoretical magnitude of what a network of networks could achieve was already massive, and the potential of its ever-expanding influence could be expanded further still. However, the number of people who perceived the scope of this power was still small. The internet was a medium that could not be understood through casual observation; you had to be inside in order to see the outside. As a result, the fragment of the populace who knew society was about to change was free to assume the rest of the world would want to use the internet in the same way (and for the same purposes) that they did. An inward-looking adoration of the internet was projected as the predestined status quo for everyone else.

"Like a force of nature, the digital age cannot be denied or stopped," wrote Nicholas Negroponte in his 1995 book *Being Digital.* "It has four very powerful qualities that will result in its ultimate triumph: decentralizing, globalizing, harmonizing, and empowering."

What's compelling about this assertion is not what it suggests, or the fact that Negroponte was (mostly) correct. What's compelling is the vigor of his conviction. Negroponte was not predicting that this was something that *could* happen. He was stating that there was no way it wouldn't, and that this inescapable transformation was inherently good. That same year, tech billionaire Bill Gates published *The Road Ahead*, another book presenting technological change in a maniacally upbeat manner. In his book, Gates employs the same language he used in a memo to his employees at Microsoft, comparing the internet to a tidal wave that would kill anyone who couldn't learn to "swim in its waves." Here again, a seemingly draconian sentiment is expressed as a positive, since one is supposed to concede that the metaphorical "waves" are intrinsically awesome.

The optimism was fueled by a simplistic brand of ad hoc Marxism crossed with social libertarianism, though such political terminology was still verboten and rarely expressed: The internet would eradicate the institutional obstacles that could traditionally be overcome only with money or status. This process would democratize the culture as a whole. It would reset society by flattening the hierarchy. Within the digital sphere, that premise was already self-evident, at least socially: Becoming "internet famous" had no connection to fame in the conventional world (in 1993, *Wired* claimed "the best-known online personality in the country" was a sixty-four-year-old retired army colonel named Dave Hughes). It would now be possible, or so it was believed, to construct a competing version of reality that would be governed by the morally neutral meritocracy of an agenda-free network. Every online citizen would be exactly the same. Handing the reins of society over to the machines was not seen as a risk. The risks came from conventional society. Internet pioneers believed governments would try to invade the virtual sphere and legally impose the same constrictions the web had eliminated. That was the inside view. The outside view was that what internet insiders valued was the central danger.

When *Time* magazine ran its first major article on the subject, a 1994 cover story ominously titled "The Strange New World of the Internet," its inadvertent emphasis was on the potential chaos generated by an enterprise where freedom was the principal goal:

The Net was built without a central command authority. That means that nobody owns it, nobody runs it, nobody has the power to kick anybody off for good. There isn't even a master switch that can shut it down in case of emergency. "It's the closest thing to true anarchy that ever existed," says Clifford Stoll, a Berkeley astronomer famous on the Internet for having trapped a German spy who was trying to use it to break into U.S. military computers.

There were, here and there, political attempts to control the uncontrollable. They didn't work, and the pushback was usually more extreme than the sanction. Congress passed the Communications Decency Act in 1996, an attempt to regulate online pornography. That legislation had almost no bearing on anything sexual or profane, except to make the internet even harder to control.* But it did prompt the writing of *A Declaration of the Independence of Cyberspace*, a straightforward portrait of the internet as utopia. It was authored by John Perry Barlow, a forty-eight-year-old poet who'd written lyrics for the Grateful Dead† before cofounding the San Francisco–based Electronic Frontier Foundation. The declaration was less than a thousand words, composed in Davos, Switzerland, and heavily shared by like-minded technocrats (it is among the earliest examples of online virality). The paragraphs were short and not particularly conversational—it was crafted to feel older than it was. The internet is described as "transactions, relationships, and thought itself." Its enemies are marginalized as "weary giants of flesh and steel." Governments, argued Barlow, derive power from the consent of the

---

*In the years since 1996, the most critical detail of the Communications Decency Act has become twenty-six words known as "Section 230." What Section 230 dictates is that third-party internet platforms cannot be held legally liable for the content posted by their individual users. Since things like Facebook, Twitter, and TikTok were still a decade away, the legislation did not seem as significant as it would later become. But without Section 230, social media could probably not exist (or certainly not in the manner to which we are now accustomed).

†An amusing factoid about the early internet was how much of its philosophy was created by tech-obsessed hippies.

governed, and the citizens of the internet never consented to anything of the sort. Here's a section from the middle of the document:

> We are creating a world that all may enter without privilege or prejudice accorded by race, economic power, military force, or station of birth.

> We are creating a world where anyone, anywhere may express his or her beliefs, no matter how singular, without fear of being coerced into silence or conformity.

> Your legal concepts of property, expression, identity, movement, and context do not apply to us. They are all based on matter, and there is no matter here.

The contemporary appreciation of these goals can be viewed in three different ways, depending on the political proclivities of the viewer: They can be seen as things that mostly happened, things that clearly didn't happen at all, or things that are still being debated in exactly the same way. It does, in retrospect, read like an attempt at starting another country or seceding from the existing one, neither of which happened. Instead, a suspension bridge was built between the Old World and the New World. The bridge was an index.

○ ○ ○

The words and phrases used by the original internet apostles are now the words and phrases used to mock the internet. Their employment in modern conversation is a signal that the person talking doesn't know what they're talking about, or as a way to indicate sarcastic self-deprecation. Some of this happened immediately, even when there was no better option. The first story *The Nation* ever published about the internet (July 12, 1993) includes a

sentence that starts by asserting, "Internet experts deride the term 'information superhighway' as an empty soundbite," but nonetheless ends that same
sentence by conceding that "the concept works as an analogy to understand
how the Internet functions." The prevalence of the imperfect neologism *superhighway* probably did help casual people visualize how a network of networks
would be connected, assuming they actually cared. It became the omnipresent
internet noun. The omnipresent internet verb was *surf* (as in "surfing the
web"). Though rarely noted at the time, there was an undeniable contradiction between these two descriptions. A *superhighway* implies the organiza-
tional qualities of an atlas, as if the internet could be mapped and followed
from destination to destination. *Surfing* suggests a kind of travel that's hard to
predict or control, where riders try to maintain balance while swept along by
forces beyond their understanding. Here again, the comparison is imperfect.
But the latter imperfection was closer than the former.

It would be wrong to claim you couldn't conduct internet searches before
the invention of Google. You could. It's just that it didn't really work, and no one
really cared. The best pre-Google search engine was AltaVista, which felt like
a significant leap forward when it appeared in 1995. It was a searchable text
database with a simple interface. If someone typed the word "bear" into the
search box, they'd get a list of web pages that included the word *bear*. But this
was only valuable to a person who wanted random bear information, potentially encompassing omnivorous animals roaming Alaska, the professional
football team in Chicago, and husky gay men with facial hair. It was impressive without being helpful. Imagine a library of physical books that didn't have
any shelves—instead, it just stored the books in various piles throughout the
facility. AltaVista was like a reference librarian who'd dreamily point at a heap
of books and say, "I know there is some stuff over there about bears."

This is not a denigration of AltaVista. In 1995, being pushed toward a
pile of books that might be about grizzlies was a real breakthrough. But
consider whom this would interest, and how that would shape the kind of
person who cared most about the internet.

An unorganized public library wouldn't be as practical (or as popular) as a library with alphabetized shelves and the Dewey decimal system. But an unorganized library would still attract the type of exploratory patron who didn't mind a haphazard afternoon of paging through dozens of books that might only have a peripheral connection to their area of interest. There was, philosophically, a surfer-like mentality to using the early internet, where the experiential key was surrendering the desire for order and embracing the avalanche of information. Ten minutes on AltaVista could easily turn into three hours. Time disappeared. It was a shapeless process that attracted shapeless thinkers.

But then Google gave the internet a shape.

The Google search engine was invented by two Stanford PhD students, Larry Page and Sergey Brin. Both were born in 1973, dead center of the Generation X demo. Relative to their influence on society, neither man is particularly recognizable. Page was raised in Michigan and is usually described as socially awkward. Brin was born in Russia before immigrating to the U.S. in 1979. He's typically described as more intense. When analyzed in tandem, they're cast as two distinct-but-interlocking personality tropes, as in this early passage from Richard L. Brandt's hagiographic biography *The Google Guys*. It was published in 2009, when Google Inc. was valued at around $140 billion and about to ascend upward.

Larry, as president of Products, is the primary thinker about the company's future direction, and weighs heavily on key hiring decisions. Sergey, a mathematical wizard and president of Technology, is the arbiter of Google's technological approach and shows deep interest in the company's moral stance.

Originally called "BackRub," the search engine was renamed "Google" after the accidental misspelling of the mathematical term "googol" (the number 1 followed by 100 zeros). The reason Google is so much better—and so much more popular—than every other searching tool is unsurprisingly complicated. A complete answer might not be possible. But the incomplete answer is sufficient enough: its ability to algorithmically "rank" search results in a meaningful way, elegantly classified as PageRank. The origin of this development can be found in a paper Page and Brin wrote at Stanford, less elegantly titled "The Anatomy of a Large-Scale Hypertextual Web Search Engine." The critical advance was how the algorithm measured the quantity and quality of content on *other* websites; when searching for a given term, Google users receive the most relevant "primary" sources first, in descending order of importance. This process mathematically perpetuates itself—by showcasing the most relevant results, additional web traffic is driven to those results, making them even more relevant. Google was better because it was less human. There was also no advertising on the Google home page, generating the sense (or maybe the delusion) that this was an impartial system with a singular purpose. Over time,* the Google algorithm created something that had never previously existed: a *consensus* about the shared understanding of *everything*. If somebody asks a question and the questioner is told to "just go ahead and Google it," whatever loads at the top of the first page is the surrogate for an airtight answer.

The value or tragedy of this shift is debatable. An algorithm dictating the construction of reality is an easy thing to worry about, though probably not as easy as Google has made so many other aspects of everyday life. We are still, decades later, assessing the mental and sociological mutation of a technology that gave all people equal access to a communal corpus callosum. It inverted the definition of what it meant to be a smart person: It was now possible to know a little bit about everything without remembering anything. In the coming years, soft scientists would give this phenomenon a name—"the Google Effect," sometimes called "digital amnesia." But the

---

*It's important to note that this sea change did not happen instantly, even if it feels like that in retrospect. Many daily newspaper references to "Google" in 1996 were actually about "Barney Google," a cartoon character from 1919 that had become a hot commodity in the collectible market.

deterioration of memory was only a fraction of the makeover. There was a flattening of society, where all forms of data became identically accessible. Arbitrary online thoughts did not disappear, generating the false impression that those thoughts had never been arbitrary to begin with. The internet was now a universal tool of convenience, in no way exclusive to the so-called geeks and nerds. It was a tool for anyone, capable of achieving highly specific goals in fast, novel ways. In the pre-Google world, the internet had changed the way people thought about computers and communication. In the post-Google world, the internet changed the way people thought about life.

○ ○ ○

The difficult question here is not about the way technology mechanically changed over the expanse of the nineties, because that can be grasped by anyone. What's harder is understanding what those mechanics did to the psychology of people who experienced the shift.

There's an intuitive belief that technology changes people, and the internet feels like an unusually straightforward example of this process. But it's also possible that the relationship between the internet and the evolution of society was more epiphenomenal: It's possible that society is *always* changing, and that the rise of the internet was a coincidental event that merely made that natural process more visible. The nineties were technologically defined by a reinvention of human communication and the expanding power of network computing. It stands to reason that this reinvention must explain any psychological difference between a twenty-five-year-old in 1989 and a twenty-five-year-old in 2001. But then again, the difference between a young adult in 1969 and a young adult in 1981 was equally dramatic, and both versions of that twenty-five-year-old used tools of telecommunication that were essentially identical. So how do we know it was the internet that changed people's brains? How do we know those brains weren't going to change anyway? The short answer is that we don't. The long answer is that certain social dynamics reversed so quickly that the inversion could not have happened without some kind of unnatural cause, and every reasonable explanation eventually connects with online communication.

Take, for example, the conception of privacy, as it applies to the notion of "doxing." The word "dox" comes from early nineties hacker culture, an abbreviation of the word "documents." A person gets "doxed" when someone publicly "documents" their personal information online, potentially exposing the individual to all kinds of real-world threats and attacks. Doxing has come to be classified as a form of violence, in and of itself. What's mildly amusing is that, prior to the internet, most Americans doxed themselves. Home addresses and telephone numbers were listed in the phone book, annually distributed to every local home for free. Phone customers were charged a monthly fee if they *didn't* want their home number included in the directory.* And possession of the physical directory wasn't even necessary. It was possible to dial the telephone operator and request an immediate connection to almost anyone's home phone, without consent. All that was needed was the spelling of the person's last name and an educated guess as to the area code in which they lived.

How did something once considered a normal extension of establishing residence become a disturbing act of aggression, during a decade when crime statistically decreased? The explanation is twofold. The first is that the early internet was built around anonymity. It was populated by people known only by their fabricated screen names, interacting with anonymous strangers they knew nothing about. This established a new expectation of confidentiality, where it was assumed everyone had the inherent right to say or do whatever they wanted online, without those words or actions impinging on life in the real world. The doxing process obliterated the wall between the

---

*Throughout the 1980s, the percentage of Americans with unlisted phone numbers was estimated to be in the low teens, though that number varied by region. The highest number of unlisted numbers was in California, where needing an unlisted number was sometimes viewed as a status symbol.

persona someone created online and the personage they inhabited by default, amplifying the belief that such a wall was necessary. A second factor was the realization that holding two disassociated realities simultaneously made both of those realities less secure, and that the entire globe was now inter-connected in a way that *felt* dangerous and unmanageable. Engaging with an invisible cyberworld required the user to surrender control over what they understood about their own decisions. It took a long time for many people to get comfortable using their credit card to buy a book on Amazon, even if they had no qualms about making an identical transaction over the telephone. In the same way, typing biographical information into a network of networks seemed totally unlike having that same information published in a phone book, even if that book was distributed to millions of people living within driving distance of your front door. The incomprehensible scope of the inter-net produced entirely new genres of invisible anxiety.

But some other reversals were more concrete.

The easiest illustration of how the internet reinvented industries outside of itself was the advent of Napster in 1999. Created by eighteen-year-old col-lege dropout Shawn Fanning, Napster altered popular music irrevocably. This is partially because the song-sharing program Fanning designed was so efficient. People downloading MP3 files on Napster for the first time always had the same reaction: *I can't believe how fast and easy this is.* But the larger reason was that it was free. The original incarnation of Napster lasted only two years. It was replaced by similar pirating services that were even faster (LimeWire, Megaupload, et al.), and the rudiments of its streaming mechanics were eventually replicated by traditional corporations. But its influence on the *meaning* of music was extraordinary and unanticipated. It made single songs more important than albums, which hadn't been the case since the early sixties. It eroded the cultural significance of genres and anni-hilated nonvirtual musical subcultures. It radically expanded the hori-zons of pop consumption, exposing people to music they would have never purchased or investigated. It reestablished the way musical history was considered and remembered. And—most significant—it made the tangible value of recorded music almost zero.

When discussing the twenty-first-century collapse of the music industry, it's always tempting to blame the industry itself. Without question, there were problems with how music was sold throughout the 1990s that justified the desire to create a new system, most conspicuously the retail price of compact discs. When CDs were introduced in the 1980s, they cost a little more than vinyl records or cassettes, ostensibly because CDs were a high-end laser product that offered better sound quality than all preexisting formats.* By the end of 1991, compact discs had become the dominant medium. At first, the manufacturing cost of CDs was around $4 a disc. But by the mid-nineties, the raw materials required to manufacture a CD cost less than 20 cents. Its packaging† cost about 30 cents. Yet the list price for new CDs inexplicably increased, to around $17.‡ The explanation from record labels was that digital CDs offered the potential to hold more data, so new releases could now be longer. This was an upside that often became a downside.

---

*A mostly forgotten side note in the history of compact discs was the brief excitement over the CD-ROM. These were data-rich CDs with "read-only memory," meaning they could not be overwritten or changed. They were developed in the late eighties but took off during the nineties, often as a platform for computer games like *Myst*. "The CD-ROM is like manna from heaven for us," the president of Virgin Interactive Entertainment Inc. said in 1994. The *Encyclopædia Britannica* was introduced on CD-ROM in 1995, debuting a searchable interactive encyclopedia. Mattel launched a CD-ROM in 1997 titled Barbie Fashion Designer that allowed kids to create original Barbie outfits on the computer screen. Barbie Fashion Designer sold 1 million copies in a year. But the closed, one-way experience of the CD-ROM was obliterated by the open, two-way experience of the Internet, particularly when high-speed online connections became common. By the start of the twenty-first century, the relationship between home computing and the CD-ROM was equivalent to the relationship between home cinema and the laser disc—a transitional technology that disappeared almost entirely.

†Initial CD packaging was wasteful and stupid. The size and width of compact discs made them easy to steal, so they were packaged in cardboard "long boxes" that were twelve inches long. It was like buying a pair of shoelaces packaged inside a shoebox. Long boxes were discontinued around 1993, but the replacement was almost as frustrating: Plastic CD jewel cases were sealed with a long, narrow sticker that was maddening to remove, sometimes causing the consumer to break the case during the first attempt to open it.

‡These figures come from a July 1995 *New York Times* article by Neil Strauss. Even at the time, people realized the inflated cost of CDs was illogical. There just wasn't a reasonable alternative.

Many artists could not resist using all of that potential extra space, filling CDs with lesser songs that no one wanted (the third Oasis album, 1997's widely criticized *Be Here Now*, clocked in at over seventy-one minutes). Consumers were led to believe that one of the advantages of CDs was that they'd last forever. That slowly proved untrue (and a scratched compact disc was even more useless than scratched vinyl, since a damaged CD wouldn't play at all). Equally frustrating was the wholesale transition to a CD-only world, forcing collectors to repurchase music on disc they'd previously owned on vinyl or cassette. This large-scale repurchasing, more than anything else, explains why overall revenue from music sales almost doubled within the span of the decade—people buying new releases were also constantly rebuying old ones. The Eagles' *Their Greatest Hits 1971–1975* was certified platinum by the Recording Industry Association of America in February of 1976. In 1990, its career sales pushed past 12 million copies. But by 1999, that number had ballooned to 26 million. It would appear that most people who bought *Their Greatest Hits 1971–1975* once eventually bought it twice. It became increasingly common for legacy artists to remaster and re-release their old catalogs on CD, often resulting in "new" versions of old albums that merely sounded slightly louder than before.

The greed was unyielding. Still, no amount of corporate avarice can fully explain the mental transformation that emerged from the Napster era. Once consumers experienced free music, they came to view music as something that was *supposed* to be free. The newness of the technology allowed people to adopt a seemingly impossible ideological position: Yes, they were getting something for nothing, without the consent of the creator—but this was not theft. It was not "stealing." It was "sharing." The argument had three prongs. The core contention was that this could not be considered theft if nothing was being physically taken. Nobody who possessed a Matchbox 20 album was losing what they already owned. Retail stores weren't hemorrhaging inventory, and warehouses weren't being ransacked. It was just the digital liberation of ones and zeros. The second prong was that all this sharing was consensual, making it no different from the accepted practice of dubbing a vinyl record onto a blank Maxell audiocassette. The third argument wasn't really an argument at all, but more of an economic rationalization—music labels were deliberately gouging consumers and undercompensating musicians, so any revenue the labels lost was money they never deserved to earn.

That third non-argument was actually Napster's cleanest defense. Recording contracts were notoriously unfair to the talent who made the music, generally providing musicians and songwriters with less than 10 percent of CD sales revenue (and even those royalties couldn't be received until the artist had recouped all the up-front money advanced to them in order to record and promote the music, a cost regularly stretching into six figures). To make real money from album sales, a major-label artist generally needed to sell a minimum of one million units, which is why the bands most against downloading were superstar acts like Metallica. Midlevel artists lost much less from illegal downloading, and minor artists were usually helped by it. Conversely, the argument's second prong—the claim that sharing music over the internet was no different from physically duplicating music on cassette—only made sense on an academic level. The speed of technology rendered that analogy irrelevant. By 2000, Napster users regularly shared about 14,000 tracks every minute (in an era when most users were still on dial-up connections).

The first contention, however, remains troubling and complex.

The logic supporting illegal file sharing was not unfathomable. If one accepts the traditional definition of theft, somebody needs to lose something, and that something has to be taken against the victim's will. That's not what was happening with Napster. There's also the theory of owner agency: Once someone buys a product legally, she gets to decide who does or doesn't have access to the product she purchased. If, for example, a woman were to buy a Ford Mustang, it would be her right to let everyone in her neighborhood borrow that car whenever they wanted, and Ford couldn't claim her generosity was hurting potential car sales. Napster advocates made the same claim about CDs. If someone spent $17 on a Tool album, didn't they have the right to decide what they did with it? How could someone be classified as a pirate if they were giving something away for free?

In a physical world, these points would have been unassailable. But this was not a physical world.

This world was closer to the imaginary world of money. Right now, over 90 percent of the world's currency is digital. It exists as a numeric concept: Money has value only because we agree that it's valuable. The value is illusory and dependent on our collective willingness to agree that the illusion is real. And for that illusion to work in perpetuity, money needs to be somewhat finite. If it were possible for a random citizen to flawlessly photocopy a $1 bill ten thousand times, it would not create ten thousand new dollars of equal value. It would imperceptibly devalue all available currency, and if fourteen thousand people did the same thing every minute, the perceived value of a $1 bill would microscope to nothing.

This is what file sharing did to music.

Napster did not make people like songs less. It probably made people like songs more. But it turned the larger concept of music into an abstraction that signified less. Music was never intended to be a pure commodity, but its commoditization created the framework for how it was understood and what it represented to individual people. "You can see the 21st century as a disaster for musicians," anticapitalist theorist Mark Fisher conceded in 2014. "The key technological shifts are with the consumption and distribution of music, rather than in its production. It's not that the 20th century was an ideal situation for musicians . . . but in retrospect, it's looking better and better. Because paradoxically, big record companies did insulate some musicians from market pressure."

The free democratizing of songs eliminated the experience of categorizing music as a reflection of who the listener was. Inside a store like Tower Records, most CDs were priced at around $17. The average Tower Records patron might only have $20 to spend, so a decision had to be made: Did this person want Korn or did they want the Dixie Chicks? Was a new album by the Cardigans a better investment than an old album by Bill Evans? Did this consumer relate to pothead peers who liked Sublime or peevish peers who liked Neutral Milk Hotel? Browsing through someone's album collection was a low-level Rorschach test. Limitations and scarcity made subjective distinctions meaningful. Napster made subjective distinctions unnecessary. A person could now have the complete catalog of all those artists, at almost no cost, without leaving the house. A college kid could possess all of Tower Records inside his dorm room, limited only by the size of his hard drive and his willingness to methodically type song titles into a search field. There were no limitations, and there was no scarcity. It changed how people viewed what music was, in a way that would never change back.

Walter Benjamin at the Dairy Queen, a short work of nonfiction by Western writer Larry McMurtry, was published in 1999. The book's title was the book's premise—sitting on a bench inside a small-town Dairy Queen, McMurtry reads a 1936 essay titled "The Storyteller" by Walter Benjamin (the same critic who'd inspired the first episode of *Ways of Seeing*). This essay prompts McMurtry to have big thoughts about his own life. *Walter Benjamin at the Dairy Queen* was the closest McMurtry ever came to writing a memoir, although his book was mostly about other things: the identity of Texas, the myth of the American cowboy, the pleasure of reading, and the obsessiveness of book collecting. There's particular focus on the meaning of memory. "Walter Benjamin was a farseeing man," writes McMurtry, "but I suspect that even he would be a little surprised by the extent to which what's given us by the media *is* our memory now. The media not only supplies us with memories of all significant events (political, sporting, catastrophic), but edits these memories, too."

McMurtry was sixty-three when *Walter Benjamin at the Dairy Queen* was released. He wasn't that engaged with the internet—McMurtry was a long-confirmed citizen of Group A. He was writing about television news. But what McMurtry argues (and what Benjamin projected) is more applicable to online discourse than it was to TV or radio or print. It was possible, perhaps as late as 1995, to view the internet as only an extension of computer technology. By the end of the decade, the internet operated as its own form of mass media, with computers merely serving as the host. And what was so different about this new form of media was its capacity to *hold* information. Nothing is truly temporary. Moments are fleeting, but the record of that moment remains locked. When McMurtry expressed apprehension over the way media warps memory, his fear was that this exchange transmogrified the interior process of how people recalled their own lives:

> Anyone who has ever taken part in a large public demonstration—a civil rights march, a war protest—and then gone home to see the same demonstration as reconstructed by television will know what I mean. What to the participant may seem merely an inchoate surging of masses of people will look, on television, ordered and effective, though if there was any violence it will always be shown first.

What he's describing is a process familiar to most modern people: the sensation that the mediated version of an event will overwrite one's own personal memory of the same experience, forcing the individual to reinterpret the way that memory sits within their own mind. The internet abbreviated this equation by eliminating the need for a mind. The software does the remembering, relentlessly and inflexibly, for you and for everybody else. The words and images never dissolve (the link might break, but the data is still cached). There is no interpretation and there is no misinterpretation. The mediated version of the event *is* the memory, even if the context is false or invisible.

This is even true of the internet itself.

What's so disorienting about the internet of the 1990s is the paradox of its centrality: It was the most important thing that happened, but its importance is still overrated. The facts don't align with the atmosphere of the memory.

The trajectory of the web can be traced across the decade, guided by a history provided by the web itself. There's almost nothing easier to research than the growth of the internet. Every industrial advance can be verified and every forward-thinking futurist can be identified. All of that history is technically true. What's false is the accompanying notion that life in the nineties must have been intractably intertwined with the internet. It was not (or at least not for the vast majority of the populace, for the vast majority of the period). In 1997, for the first (and only) time, U.S. revenues from fax machine sales exceeded $1 billion. Small businesses needed a fax machine more than they needed an online connection. It was essential technology for all of the 1990s. But fax machines can't create or sustain their own version of history, so the memory of the fax machine remains as it is remembered by the internet—as an archaic oddity of the 1980s whose sole historical significance was its replacement by technology that was superior.

In *The Sun Also Rises*, a character is asked how he went bankrupt. "Two ways," the man replies. "Gradually, then suddenly." For almost a century, this insight has been referenced so often that it has become its own kind of cliché, in part because it applies to almost everything. Ernest Hemingway's description of change is the way most things change. It is, however, an especially apt encapsulation of how the internet became the inescapable whirlpool of cultural life. The internet was an amorphous concept constantly described as encroaching, yet always two years away. It was both an unavoidable future and an unworkable playground, controlled by strangers you didn't know and didn't want to meet. "I don't understand this whole thing about computers and the superhighway," sci-fi novelist Ray Bradbury told an audience of college students in 1995. "Who wants to be in touch with all of those people?"

The system was free, so the product was you. Maybe you set up an email account in 1993 and used it twice. Maybe you watched the Sandra Bullock thriller *The Net* in 1995. Maybe you rifled through your mailbox in 1997 and realized you'd been sent a free CD with the software for America Online, only to mysteriously receive six more of those free discs over the next eighteen months. The internet was coming. The internet was coming. The internet was coming. When was it coming? Soon. How soon? Not today, and maybe not tomorrow. But definitely soon. It was always never quite there. And then, one day, there it was—impossible to avoid and impossible to recognize until the update was complete and all alternatives had been eliminated.

There's no date for when the transfer of power occurred. The record of the transfer has edited itself.

○ ○ ○

What has happened here is a telescoping of memory, where contemporary understandings are projected upon distant time frames, generating the delusion that those ideas have always been around. There's wholesale acceptance about when the modern version of the internet began—it emerged during the 1990s. There are entrenched ideas (both positive and negative) about what the internet is, conceded even by those who disagree with the veracity of the assertions: the way it refigures politics and social organization, the degree to which it alters the experience of adolescence, its contradictory ability to connect and estrange simultaneously, and its overall acceleration of the news cycle. These are the complicated qualities that make the internet what it is. The disconnect is that those entrenched perceptions are almost entirely extensions of social media, which was not part of the nineties at all. Facebook didn't start until 2004. Twitter wasn't founded until 2006. Instagram didn't launch until 2010. The earliest equivalent to the social media experience was the "chat rooms" integrated into the desktops of AOL and CompuServe, where people (mostly teenagers) of the late nineties exchanged anonymous public messages about random subjects, some cultural and some personal. Whenever people describe the strengths and weaknesses of "the internet," they are usually describing experiences that never happened during the internet's first decade of assimilation. Yet it *feels* like these complexities were *always* there, and that even the earliest conversations about how the internet was reinventing society were fixated on scenarios that couldn't possibly be understood until the twenty-first century. The authority of the internet is so immersive and absolute that it now seems to have existed for longer than it has, and that its present-tense incarnation is the way it always was.

In September of 1995, *The Washington Post* and *The New York Times* both published an essay titled "Industrial Society and Its Future," authored by a writer they did not know. The manifesto was mailed to these publications by the Unabomber, an anti-technology terrorist who'd been sending self-made bombs through the U.S. mail since 1978. The Unabomber claimed he would continue his attacks if his manifesto was not published in full. The anonymous bomber had already been infamous for a decade. He was dubbed "the UNAbomber" due to the institutions he initially targeted (the letters "UN" stood for "universities" and the letter "A" stood for "airlines"). He'd already killed three people and injured twenty-three others. The bombs were tagged with false clues and the selection of his victims exhibited no pattern. An extensive multiyear manhunt by the FBI and the ATF never came close to establishing his profile or whereabouts. Composed on a manual typewriter, this thirty-five-thousand-word manifesto represented the only viable lead. The newspapers complied with the Unabomber's demands, partially out of fear but also as a means for figuring out who this person was: The hope was that someone might read the screed and recognize its syntax and prose style, leading to the bomber's identification.

"Industrial Society and Its Future" is a byzantine exploration of a basic philosophical idea. Its premise is that advances in technology have damaged and destabilized all of civilization, starting around the year 1760. Reliance on machines, the Unabomber argues, limits human freedom by changing the very understanding of personhood. "Technology," he writes, "is a more powerful social force than the aspiration for freedom." The pervasiveness of the industrial system, so inescapable that it's unquestioned, pushes people toward artificial goals and irrational pursuits. It robs individuals of the ability to think and feel autonomously, convincing them to willfully adopt whatever irrational rules society claims to require. There is no separation, the Unabomber insists, between "good" and "bad" technology: It's all part of the same symbiotic structure, asserting control over consumers who thoughtlessly seek to be controlled.

What this manifesto hyperbolically depicts, in the most negative context possible, is the internet. It describes the internet more accurately than it describes anything else. That, however, is either a total coincidence or a discomfiting confirmation of the document's thesis. "Industrial Society and Its Future" was written by a person who had lived without electricity since 1971. It was written by a person who likely never sent an email, who'd never seen Sandra Bullock, and who'd never been annoyed by a free copy of AOL software inside his mailbox. "Industrial Society and Its Future" is not about the internet. It just seems like it.

The Unabomber, a man named Ted Kaczynski, currently resides in a Colorado supermax prison. Born in Chicago in 1942, he was a mathematical prodigy, admitted into Harvard at the age of sixteen. By the time he turned twenty-five, he was teaching math at the University of California. But Kaczynski was a troubled person with dangerous ideas. He was verbally combative and incapable of compromise. He resigned from Cal in 1969, eventually moving to an off-the-grid cabin in rural Montana. Living in solitude without electrical power or running water, he traveled by bicycle and raised his own food. His hobbies were reading classic books in their original language and constructing homemade bombs from wood and metal, most of which were mailed to college professors he'd never met. When finally captured in 1996, Kaczynski looked like a bearded wild man, the unwashed caricature of a brilliant, misanthropic ecoterrorist. His attorneys wanted to plead insanity, but Kaczynski refused—he knew classifying himself as mentally ill would invalidate the credibility of his manifesto, which is all that he cared about. He elected to serve as his own attorney and accepted a life sentence in prison, dodging the death penalty but never retracting his all-encompassing hatred of technology.

In light of how the world has evolved, it's hard to think about Kaczynski without thinking about the internet, even though the word "internet" appears only once in the thirty-five-thousand-word text of "Industrial Society and Its Future" (and only in passing). The content of Kaczynski's ideology and the conditions of the Internet Age feel as though they *must* be connected, despite the impossibility of a man living without electricity having any real understanding of what network computing was. And in the end, a connection did come to exist—or more precisely, two connections. The first connection is that Kaczynski has become a folk hero among the most radical arm of anti-tech environmentalists, and these groups and individuals would never be able to find each other without the aid of the internet. Somewhat incongruously, technology is an essential component to anti-technology organization. Because of the web, the digitized text of "Industrial Society and Its Future" will never disappear.

The second connection is that, were it not for the internet, it's possible Kaczynski would still be living in Montana as a free man.

Kaczynski's terrorism was so meticulous and disorienting that there was almost no way the FBI would have ever figured out who he was. The only reason he was captured was that his younger brother, David Kaczynski, read "Industrial Society and Its Future" and recognized glimpses of his estranged sibling's personality. Some of the thoughts and phrases were reminiscent of handwritten letters Ted had sent David in the past. The only reason David read "Industrial Society and Its Future" was that his wife forced him to do so. David did not believe his brother could possibly be a murderer; his wife, however, was not so sure (she'd always had a weird feeling about Ted). She made David promise to give the manifesto a look, just in case. The couple went to a nearby magazine shop and tried to buy a copy the week after it was published in the *Times* and the *Post*. Every edition of both newspapers had already been purchased. They then went to the local college library to find a copy, but the section of the newspaper containing the manifesto had been removed. David was ready to give up and go home, but the librarian mentioned another option: the internet. It was something David had heard of but never before used. "Here I am," David explained years later, "on this newfangled technology, trying to figure out if my brother is this anti-technology terrorist." One can imagine David Kaczynski logging on for the first time, hearing all those little sounds of the nineties: a dial tone, the eleven rapid beeps, the high-octave whistles, and the stereophonic white noise. David Kaczynski entered the digital world his brother intuitively despised. What he saw within this network of networks confirmed his greatest fear. He had no choice but to go to the police. He had to stop his brother from killing strangers.

Kaczynski had been correct. Technology was a more powerful force than his aspiration for freedom.

[alive in the superunknown]

IT WAS A STORY THAT HAPPENED SO MANY TIMES TO SO MANY PEOPLE
that the retelling of the anecdote became a little boring, even though no two
versions of the story were ever the same. The structure was identical, but the
details were always different.

The story went like this: A person would be driving at night, usually
alone. There was no good music on the radio, or perhaps the trip was passing
through a desolate stretch of highway where FM stations couldn't reach. In
hopes of staying awake, the driver flipped over to the AM frequency, where
the signals carried farther. And what they inevitably found was a voice—the
calm, rational voice of a (seemingly) normal man talking about things that
were unhinged and irrational. "Were you or any of your friends bitten by the
chupacabra?" the man might ask a listener who called into the show. Such
queries were posed without a hint of condescension. If the next caller claimed
the government had built a paramilitary society underneath the Arizona
desert, the calm voice might ask, "So what do you think they're doing down
there?" If the third caller claimed to be Satan and insisted that many Catho-
lic priests were zombified followers of his regime, the calm voice would rhetorically remark, "Well, that may or may not be true."

The show would go on like this for five hours, an unrelenting litany of unscreened radio callers insisting that everything understood about the world was not necessarily the way that it was, and that the edges of reality were darker and more remote than the government or the media would accept or admit. The calm voice responding to these claims was a bespectacled middle-aged man named Art Bell, the neutral receptacle for every negative integer on the continuum of possibility.

Born in 1945, Bell was a former air force medic who hosted radio shows out of his home in Pahrump, Nevada. His best-known program was *Coast to Coast AM*, carried live by 145 stations and once estimated to have around 10 million listeners a week (Bell also prerecorded a syndicated show, *Dreamland*, similarly focused on aliens and paranormal activity). The beating heart of *Coast to Coast* was the bizarro callers, but its backbone was Bell's openness: Though he might express skepticism, he was never judgmental (and though he long insisted the show was only a form of entertaining journalism, he did claim to have seen a UFO himself in 1991).

The primacy of Bell's presence was a product of the period: While it was easy to be crazy in the early nineties, it was difficult for like-minded crazy people to organize. In the pre-internet age, holding conspiratorial beliefs usually meant holding those beliefs in isolation—you read discredited books, you wrote letters to fringe magazines, and you listened to *Coast to Coast AM* alone in the garage. The thought of an unsubstantiated conspiracy theory crossing into real politics (or even being quasi-validated by a mainstream newspaper) was absurd. Only the internet could make that possible. Before social media, there was no way to gauge the size of a conspiracy population, and individuals promoting unconventional concepts surrendered their credibility within the straight world. When Oliver Stone released the film *JFK* in 1991, it trafficked in a conspiracy a majority of Americans accepted—that the assassination of John F. Kennedy had involved more than one gunman. But *JFK* was still ridiculed in most serious publications, sometimes before the movie was even released. Stone was marginalized as a loon for promoting a possibility most people already believed.*

Bell's radio program was a midnight beacon for the professionally goofy, but it did not normalize the antisocial underground. More often, *Coast to Coast* perpetuated the supposition that conspiratorial people were unreliable narrators and amusing weirdos. What normalized conspiracy theorists far more was *The X-Files*. Debuting on Fox in 1993, *The X-Files* was a sci-fi drama about two FBI agents who investigated criminal cases involving monsters and unexplained phenomena. The agents were named Fox Mulder and Dana Scully. Mulder, played by David Duchovny, believed every conspiracy was possible, in part because his sister had been abducted by aliens when he was twelve. Scully, played by Gillian Anderson, was a physician who did not accept anything unsupported by science. Much of the show's creative tension came from Mulder and Scully's interaction, a platonic relationship that felt extra sexual because the pair was *not* having sex (and when they finally did, fans were disappointed). The program was also noteworthy for its inversion of traditional gender stereotypes—it was the man who was intuitive and emotional, and it was the woman who was objective and detached. That dynamic made *The X-Files* popular and beloved. And that, perhaps inadvertently, did the same for conspiratorial thinking.

Television is a character-driven medium, and viewers tend to experience TV shows through whatever on-screen character they care about the most. For roughly half *The X-Files'* audience, that character was Fox Mulder—a handsome, sarcastic psychoneurotic defined by a phrase that eventually became a meme and the subtitle of an *X-Files* film: "I want to believe." It was

---

*A CBS News poll from 1998 found that 74 percent of the country still assumed there was a cover-up in the Warren Commission Report, the official government document on the 1963 assassination of the thirty-fifth president. What's somewhat surprising is that belief in a JFK conspiracy has marginally decreased during the twenty-first century, while the belief in countless other conspiracies has steadily climbed.

not just that Mulder was convinced that conspiracies were real—he *wanted* them to be real, as both an explanation for how the world worked and a confirmation of his own sense of self. He was an acceptable, desirable kind of paranormal theorist: a smart, independent person who asked a lot of questions but still listened to reason. If someone saw themselves as Fox Mulder, they did not see themselves as the type of hysterical outsider who called into Art Bell's radio show. They saw themselves as curious, open-minded, and *normal.*

This was a normal that was new.

7 Three True Outcomes

WHEN STRANGE NEWS HAPPENS IN A HIGH-STATUS WAY, COVERAGE OF
the strangeness tends to get hit with one of three criticisms. The first (and
most common) accusation is that the media fixates too much on the weirdness and overhypes its actual significance. The second accusation counter-
intuitively suggests the media isn't recognizing the weirdness *enough* and
underplays the true depth of its novelty. But the third criticism is a contradictory combination of the first two: The weirdness is covered so exhaus-
tively, but so robotically and uncritically, that the weirdness gets normalized
and stops feeling weird.

Michael Jordan's attempt at professional baseball falls into category three.

"It is easy to be wise after the event," claimed Sherlock Holmes in the
1922 story "The Problem of Thor Bridge"—an aphorism whose profundity
derives from its obviousness. Yet this seemingly unassailable axiom does not
apply to Jordan's baseball career, a scenario that still defies clear-cut compre-
hension. Because of how history would eventually uncoil, the thirteen
months Jordan spent as an outfielder in the Chicago White Sox farm system
has become a charming, curious anecdote within the larger story of his leg-
end. Jordan, when he first retired from basketball in 1993, was already the
most famous athlete in the United States, having won three Most Valuable

Player awards and three consecutive NBA titles. When he reentered the league in 1995, he immediately reestablished himself as the singular star, won another three titles, and retired (again, temporarily) as the greatest basketball player the world had ever seen. His tenure as a baseball player is the intermission in between, often analyzed but never truly explained.

Selected third overall by the Chicago Bulls in the 1984 NBA draft, Jordan spent the last half of the eighties as an electrifying scoring machine with unforeseen marketing potential and an inclination toward selfishness. He was consumed with winning but only satisfied if he was also the main reason his team won. For a time, the shooting guard was probably best known for introducing the most famous leather sneaker in the history of shoes, the Nike Air Jordan (first sold in 1985, at a retail price of $65). Chicago didn't reach the NBA Finals until 1991 and lost the opening game of the seven-game series to the less talented, more experienced Los Angeles Lakers. Down 0–1 at home, the overnight consensus was that Jordan was still not ready to win. The Bulls proceeded to pound the Lakers over the next four games and dominated the league for the next twenty-four months. It would be years before Jordan was ever underestimated again.

Jordan's supremacy was unquestioned, and not just on the court. Outside of NBA commissioner David Stern, he was the single most powerful individual in the sport. When the International Basketball Federation decided to let professional basketball players compete in the 1992 Olympics, Jordan privately said he would only agree to play if the U.S. roster did not include Isiah Thomas, Jordan's most hated opponent from the Detroit Pistons. When the much-publicized "Dream Team" of pro players was finally put together, Thomas—certainly among the twelve best players of his generation—was not-so-mysteriously excluded. Though a handful of other players on the squad had issues with Thomas's personality, Jordan's opinion was the only one that mattered. He had many enemies but no real rival. Charles Barkley of the Phoenix Suns was awarded the league MVP in 1993, and the award was seen as a defensible measure of the statistical season he'd just delivered—but even as Barkley accepted the trophy, no one seriously thought he was actually *better* than Jordan (and when the Suns lost to the Bulls in that June's championship series, Jordan averaged 41 points a game). By the end of his ninth campaign, the gap between Jordan and everyone else was as staggering as it was accepted. His '93 retirement was unexpected but explicable: Jordan was tired, a little bored, and mourning the death of his father (who had been murdered that July).

His decision to play baseball was harder to reconcile.

The most conventional take on Jordan's decision was tied to his dad's death: "It began as my father's idea," Jordan said in '94. His father's favorite sport had always been baseball, and Jordan idolized his father (MJ was notorious for sticking out his tongue whenever he played anything, a tic he'd come to mimic by watching his dad, a mechanic, stick out his tongue while working on car engines). The least conventional take was also tied to his father's death: A (somewhat cruel) conspiracy theory emerged that Jordan only attempted baseball because he was serving a secret suspension from the NBA, enforced as a consequence of his gambling addiction and his alleged ties to organized crime, and that the murder of James R. Jordan Sr. had not been random, but retribution for unpaid gambling debts.

The least complicated explanation is that Jordan simply liked baseball, though that requires a suspension of disbelief from almost everyone involved. It's hard to imagine how Jordan could rationally believe he'd be able to seamlessly transition to a different sport. Bo Jackson and Deion Sanders had managed to play football and baseball simultaneously, but they'd excelled at both sports in college and presented unusual combinations of raw athleticism, even among pro athletes. Jordan was now thirty-one years old, had not played baseball since high school, and possessed a wiry six-foot-six frame that was only ideal for the game of basketball. Still, Jordan was so metaphysically gifted at one sport that it seemed shortsighted to deny him a shot at another. The owner of the Chicago Bulls, Jerry Reinsdorf, also owned the Chicago White Sox. Jordan was still under contract with the Bulls, and Reinsdorf agreed to continue paying Jordan his annual salary of $4 million a year. Jordan was assigned to the White Sox's AA minor league affiliate in Birmingham, Alabama. Coverage of his new career was endless, focused on the assumed unlikelihood of his success. The cover of *Sports Illustrated* featured a photo of Jordan swinging wildly at a bad pitch, with the cover line "Bag It, Michael!" The argument from *SI* was that Jordan was a dilettante disrespecting the game. It was a condemnation of his ego and his skills. But what it failed to contextualize was just how strange baseball became during the 1990s, and that Jordan's ill-fated desire to try was perhaps the last moment when baseball could still be justifiably viewed as the centerpiece of American sports.

The concept of baseball's exceptionalism—that the sport held a unique place in U.S. life and would always be recognized as the national pastime—managed to subsist long after the plausibility of that designation had been statistically obliterated. In 1990, more than twice as many people preferred watching football to watching baseball, and this had been true since the middle seventies. But the social experience of baseball was still rooted in the years just following World War II, when it was more popular in America than all other team sports combined. Granted, polling people about their favorite sport is an inexact science. Opinions can be twisted by the temporary success of the local franchise or the outsized celebrity of one individual (interest in the NBA decreased when Jordan retired and rebounded immediately upon his return). But the ingrained notion of baseball's singularity was unchallenged for the first half of the twentieth century and still anecdotally present in the decades that followed. Baseball movies of the 1980s (1984's *The Natural*, 1988's *Bull Durham*, 1989's *Field of Dreams*) did not merely use baseball as the backdrop for the story—the sport was framed as a magical, quasi-religious experience that transcended hitting or pitching. In 1988, TV ratings for Major League Baseball were slipping precipitously, but the New

York Yankees were still able to sell their local broadcast rights for $483 million, the most lucrative sports deal of the era.

There was a tenacious impression that baseball was somehow more important than other sports. It was taken more seriously, by people alleged to be serious. There was still a generational memory of 1941, when Ted Williams hit .406 and Joe DiMaggio had a 56-game hitting streak. The prologue of novelist Don DeLillo's masterwork *Underworld*, published in 1997, opens at a Giants-Dodgers pennant playoff game from 1951. The peak of baseball had coincided with the peaking of white middle-class society, and baseball's displacement by football was sometimes viewed as a symptom of national decline. "Football combines two of the worst features of American life," wrote conservative baseball scholar George Will. "It is violence punctuated by committee meetings." In 1994, PBS debuted the Ken Burns documentary miniseries *Baseball*, chronicling the history of the sport as a shadow history of the twentieth century. It did not seem coincidental that Burns's previous nine-episode PBS series had examined the Civil War. Thinking about baseball as only a game was reductionist. It was (supposedly) bigger than that. It was a way to understand the American experience.

Jordan joined the Birmingham Barons within a paradigm where this was still true, or at least still accepted as a viable assertion.

Spring training in '94 was captivated by his presence. Jordan was, by a wide margin, a bigger celebrity than anyone involved with Major League Baseball, even if he had no real chance of competing at the Major League level. He was, at best, an unpolished prospect. Once the season started, the emphasis shifted back to the regular players. Tony Gwynn of the San Diego Padres was on the cusp of hitting .400, something that hadn't happened in five decades. Atlanta pitcher Greg Maddux's ERA was 1.56, exhibiting a control of the strike zone not seen since Ferguson Jenkins in 1971. The best team was the Montreal Expos. But all this would be wiped away by a work stoppage that ended the season in August and canceled the World Series. Pessimists thought this shutdown would kill baseball entirely. It did not. But it does represent the point where baseball's past became more desirable than base-ball's future, an inversion that would never really reverse itself.

The possibility of pro athletes striking (and its management counter-part, the lockout) was not innovative. There had been a fifty-day baseball strike in 1981 that eliminated 713 games from the schedule. There were two NFL strikes in the eighties that temporarily suspended the seasons of 1982 and 1987. At the end of the nineties, NBA owners would lock out the players and delay the start of basketball by three months. The baseball strike of 1994, however, was the strike that left a residue. There was widespread belief that neither the players nor the owners cared about the consequences for the sport or its fans, and that the long-standing cliché of baseball being sacred was suddenly a bit preposterous.

It was the rare example of an athletic work stoppage where both sides of the dispute were blamed equally.

Whenever a sports league experiences a strike or a lockout, it's popular to frame the conflict as millionaires (the players) arguing with billionaires (the owners). What's strange, though understandable, is that for almost all of the twentieth century, the public usually sided with the billionaires. Own-ers are often faceless middle-aged businessmen who might not be recogniz-able in their own community; their wealth is colossal but conceptual. Players are visible, young, and often minorities. Their salaries are regularly printed in the newspaper, and they make a lot of money for an unessential activity many people would do for free. When pro athletes strike, it tends to be for greater professional freedom (in the form of free agency) or a greater share of the revenue they generate for the league. Since players are relatively rich and abundantly famous, it has traditionally been easy to paint them as greedy and ungrateful. There's also a naive belief that pro athletes should *want* to play, almost for altruistic reasons, whereas owners are seen as transposable businesspeople, expected (and therefore allowed) to act selfishly in the best interest of their business.

Those opinions were still around in 1994. There was, however, a new component: a higher awareness that the owners were negotiating in bad faith. What the owners wanted, more than anything else, was a way to control player salaries. The problem was that they'd already proven untrustworthy in their recent attempts to do this. In the 1980s, team owners were directly instructed by MLB commissioner Peter Ueberroth to collude. Ueberroth's private advisement was for owners to communally agree not to offer any free agent a contract that reflected the player's actual market value, killing any possibility of a bidding war that could escalate salaries. The most infamous example was Andre Dawson, an all-star free agent who signed a $500,000 contract with the Chicago Cubs in order to get away from the Montreal Expos. Dawson wanted to leave the Expos because the hard artificial turf in Montreal's Olympic Stadium was destroying his knees, and the Cubs played on natural grass. The annual $500K he accepted from Chicago was half as much as the Expos were willing to pay and perhaps a third of what he was actually worth, but no other team made an offer. Dawson took the pay cut and won the National League MVP award the following season. Ueberroth was forced out of the commissioner's chair in 1989, replaced by NL president Bart Giamatti (who died a few months later). In 1991, arbitrators ruled that Major League Baseball owed the players a combined $280 million for three separate collusion grievances. The secret strategy of collusion was dead. The new transparent strategy was a salary cap.

The owners started pushing for a hard salary cap in 1992. They also wanted to decrease the players' share of MLB revenue from 56 percent to 50 percent and end the practice of salary arbitration.* The players believed the threat of a strike was the only way to stop these changes from being forcibly

---

*Salary arbitration in baseball is a way to set the salary for a player who is not yet eligible for full free agency but has accumulated several years of service time. If the two sides can't compromise on a new deal, the player and the team exchange offers, and a panel of arbitrators listen to arguments from both parties. The panel then accepts one of the two salary figures, but never an amount in between. The thinking is that by forcing an all-or-nothing decision, both sides are motivated to make the most reasonable, realistic offer (since any offer too high or too low would be discarded out of hand).

implemented when the collective bargaining agreement expired on the last day of 1994. They set a strike deadline of August 12, 1994, working from the premise that the owners would cave in order to stop the cancellation of the postseason. The players misjudged the owners' resolve. The owners were completely willing to cancel the World Series, arguing that 19 of the 28 MLB franchises were already losing money. White Sox owner Reinsdorf claimed he was even willing to miss all of the following season, if that's what it took. He claimed a year without baseball would lose less money than the alternative.

The league's new commissioner, Bud Selig, officially killed the season on September 14. For the first time in ninety years, there was no World Series. That December, the owners implemented a salary cap. That cap was later revoked and replaced with a luxury tax.* In January of the following year, President Bill Clinton demanded that the owners and the union reopen negotiations and hammer out an agreement. Nothing happened. The owners decided they'd play the 1995 season with replacement players, much like the NFL had done during the football strike of '87. Beyond being unpopular, the plan proved legally unworkable. The players finally agreed to return to the game at the end of March, truncating the 1995 season by eighteen games. When the sport resumed, attendance was down and TV ratings had fallen even farther. More significant, the social standing of baseball had diminished in unexpected ways. The Burns *Baseball* documentary had premiered around the same time the World Series was canceled and became one of the most watched series in the history of PBS. But the sport Burns lionized as foundational American history did not synchronize with the sport that was still being played.

The '94 strike was a scenario where something everyone supposedly understood was proven irrefutably. The cynical assertion that professional

---

*A luxury tax imposes a financial penalty on any team that spends more on player salaries than the team budget that's dictated by the league (a budget that's the same for every club). In other words, teams can pay players as much as they want, and players aren't limited in how much they can make. But if a franchise goes over that budgeted amount, it has to pay a tax, motivating teams to stay under the budget threshold (and theoretically keeping the league in competitive balance).

sports was only concerned with money had existed for decades, but now it seemed like no one involved with baseball was even trying to pretend that this wasn't the case. Canceling the World Series appeared to bother fans and writers considerably more than the owners and the players. The owners kept insisting they were going broke, but ticket prices were increasing and more than 50 million people had attended baseball games in 1994, despite the elimination of 948 games. Bobby Bonilla was making $6.3 million a year for the New York Mets and Cecil Fielder would make $9.2 million with the Detroit Tigers, all while the median household income in the U.S. was less than $35,000. Any complaint from either side of the dispute felt like sarcasm.

"There's still a significant percentage of the American people, probably you and I among them, who really believe baseball is something special," President Clinton told NBC anchorman Tom Brokaw early in 1995, when the strike was still in effect. "And you know, there's a few hundred owners and a few hundred more players, and baseball generates two billion dollars' worth of revenues every year. About a thousand people ought to be able to figure out how to divide that up and give baseball back to the American people." The message was reasonable, but it had the opposite effect. Clinton's description of the greed contradicted the fantasy that baseball, in any way, belonged to the American people, and it seemed silly that a modern politician would still try to argue that it was.

What happened in 1994 hurt the ethos of baseball, and the consensus was that this had been a strike where absolutely everyone lost. Yet, on paper, both sides won. The players stopped the salary cap and saw their salaries grow faster than ever before (a decade after the strike, the highest-paid player in the league made almost four times what Bonilla was earning in 1995). The value of franchises dramatically increased: A club like the Cleveland Indians, valued at $103 million in 1994, was worth $292 million ten years later. The owners had banked on the fact that no matter what they did, sports fans had no other summer option and would inevitably return, and the owners were right. In fact, three seasons later, the game experienced a miniature renaissance.

For a few months in 1998, baseball was—again—a national fascination. But the explanation behind that fleeting recovery ultimately backfired, and—again—something everyone supposedly knew was proven irrefutably.

○ ○ ○

In the wake of the '94 strike, the image of baseball had shifted. The tone was more derisive and less romantic. To an extent, that progression was happening within all sports (and within all of American life). But unlike football and basketball, the way baseball was played had changed less than the way people thought about it.

A football game in 1995 bore no resemblance to a football game from 1945. The greatest pro basketball player from the fifties, George Mikan, could not have made an NBA roster in the eighties. The physical and technical evolution of football and basketball had been so dramatic that the past wasn't comparable with the present. That wasn't true with baseball. Baseball had evolved less. The aesthetics and physiology were more similar than different, and it was not remotely unreasonable to suggest that the greatest player of all time was still an overweight alcoholic who'd retired in 1935. Part of what made baseball historically compelling was its ability to transcend time. The skills of hitting and pitching were static, frozen in amber. It was the rare game where statistics from the past were comparable with statistics from the present.

And then Brady Anderson hit 50 home runs in one season.

Brady Anderson was a center fielder who spent his best years with the Baltimore Orioles. He entered the league in 1988 as a scrappy, fleet-footed leadoff hitter; had he played in the fifties, they would have called him a "Punch and Judy." During the first eight years of his career, he appeared in 945 games and hit a total of 72 home runs. His first great year was '92, when he hit 21 home runs, stole 53 bases, and made the All-Star Game. But then, as a thirty-two-year-old in 1996, something distorted. Anderson became a power-hitting machine. Throughout all of the 1980s, not one player hit 50 home runs in a season. Now a low-profile spray hitter—a guy weighing less than 200 pounds, who'd hit only 16 homers the year before—was amassing numbers that crushed the accomplishments of the previous generation's best sluggers. A *Sports Illustrated* article from the summer of '96 focused on the inordinate number of baseball players inexplicably enjoying career years. Brady, the article noted, was "a fitness fanatic" who'd built a 1,500-square-foot gym in his Lake Tahoe home and prepared for the season with "his usual grueling training sessions, including running sprints up a local mountain." Another *SI* article about Anderson was published the following season, attempting to explain how all this had happened:

> At 6'1" and 190 pounds, he has the build of a light heavyweight boxer, with a narrow waist, broad shoulders, thick neck and thighs. . . . His upper arms are immense, with veins that look like swollen rivers running across them in every direction. . . . So how did he do it? How did Anderson, in 1996, more than triple his average home run total from the previous four years . . . neither he nor his teammates, coaches and manager can settle on a single theory, except to say that his mental game caught up with his physical attributes.

Brady Anderson appeared in *Muscle & Fitness* magazine, but he never tested positive for steroids or any other performance-enhancing drugs. This might be because he never used them, though the more plausible explanation is that he was never tested. Baseball didn't start testing for performance-enhancing drugs until 2003. In the 1997 season, Anderson regressed to his former self, hitting only 18 homers. This, somewhat paradoxically, has become the best argument *against* the assumption that Brady was using PEDs: If baseball wasn't testing for steroids, why would he have stopped using them? Why did this anomaly only happen in 1996? It's a valid question, only undercut by absolutely everything else now known about baseball from this time.

The late nineties will forever be defined as baseball's Steroid Era, to the exclusion of all other events that transpired within that same window of time. Anderson's inconceivable '96 season isn't even among the most remembered details of the period, when batting numbers irrationally mushroomed and almost every top player was later questioned about drug use (Ken Griffey Jr., who hit 56 home runs two years in a row with the Seattle Mariners, is one of the era's rare superstars above suspicion). This scandal proved even more damaging than the '94 strike. The most depressing episode emerged from what was temporarily seen as the apogee of late-twentieth-century baseball: In 1998, the country was captivated by the most astounding home run race in the history of the sport. Mark McGwire, a stoic hulk with a compact swing, clubbed 70 home runs for the St. Louis Cardinals. He was chased (and sometimes passed) all summer by Sammy Sosa, a magnetic Chicago Cub hailing from the Dominican Republic. Sosa unexpectedly hit 66 home runs and boyishly hopped out of the batter's box whenever he smashed a ball deep. The two adversaries appeared to genuinely like each other, amplifying the feel-good nature of the competition. Bob Ley, the most credible of ESPN broadcasters, argued that the last time sports had made Americans feel this good was when the 1980 U.S. Olympic hockey team defeated the Soviet Union. McGwire and Sosa had redeemed baseball. When it was later proven that both had used PEDs (despite their years of denials), it was more deflating than unfathomable. Some fans felt betrayed, but most just felt stupid. McGwire was the most physically imposing hitter of all time, who'd somehow grown stronger as he got older. Sosa was a thirty-year-old adult with acne. It seemed so retrospectively obvious—and, *in retrospect*, it was. In this scenario, it really is easy to be wise after the event. But that revisionism overlooks the complexity of trying to recognize a problem when the source of that problem was still impossible to quantify or understand.

There's a tendency to export the memory of the Steroid Era into two sequestered camps. The first camp argues that this was something everyone knew was happening and willfully ignored (because everyone liked the results). The second camp claims this was something no one knew was happening (and that fans were innocent and immature). But the cognitive reality was much less straightforward.

There was, certainly, an awareness that steroids were something that existed in the world, and that steroids made athletes bigger and faster. Hypermuscular Canadian sprinter Ben Johnson had destroyed Carl Lewis at the 1988 Olympics, only to test positive for stanozolol and have his gold medal stripped. But there was still confusion about how these chemicals worked and why they were effective. What's now widely understood about performance-enhancing drugs is the *totality* of their value.

Anabolic steroids are synthetic derivatives of testosterone, and testosterone makes muscle grow. But that's only part of the advantage, and arguably not even the critical one: Steroids allow athletes to train harder and recover faster. There's also a two-sided psychological impact: A hitter using steroids knows he has a physical advantage, and a pitcher who suspects an opposing hitter is using PEDs will be less confident in his own ability to challenge him. These details are no longer mysterious. But in the nineties, the knowledge around steroids was less sophisticated. There was a fantasy that an athlete injected these drugs and instantly became stronger, almost as if steroids were a magic bullet. Since rational people are conditioned to believe magic isn't real, it felt illogical to think steroids could turn a bad player into a good player or a good player into a great one. The escalating size and speed of athletes was readily apparent, but that had been happening for decades. Every new generation was bigger and faster than the previous generation. There was also anecdotal disagreement over how much PEDs would aid an athlete attempting a complicated skill. It made sense that steroids could help Ben Johnson run faster in a straight line for a short distance, but baseball was all craft. Hand-eye coordination was everything, and a 500-foot home run wasn't worth more than a 450-foot home run.

More than anything else, there was discomfort with a skepticism based solely on conjecture. Baseball didn't test for steroids and players never talked about steroids. That passage from the *Sports Illustrated* story on Brady Anderson now seems comically credulous, but there was no other way to professionally report on such a situation: You couldn't accuse someone of an untraceable infraction that was impossible to verify and denied by everyone involved. And the refutations were not casual. The PED denials from athletes of this period were so adamant and uncompromising that taking an adversarial position adopted the tenor of a conspiracy theory. The nineties were a cynical age, but some optimistic social contracts were still in place. If a person insisted on something that couldn't be disproven, that person was generally believed.

Commissioner Selig was concerned enough about the explosion in numbers to hire a former *Chicago Tribune* baseball writer, Jerome Holtzman, to file a report examining the incongruity between the statistical history of baseball and the surge in home runs. But Holtzman, who'd covered the sport since the 1940s, immediately assured the commissioner that he was confident nothing was amiss, even before he started his research. "I asked him for a report on the spike in offensive numbers—what did they say about the integrity of the game and, specifically, did they indicate steroid use," Selig later wrote in his memoir. "He knew how worried I was, but he didn't think anything was happening that was out of whack with the history of baseball. . . . He said he knew it would show that anyone pointing toward steroids was 'making too much of it.'"

The players were not innocent, but they were seen as innocent until irrefutably proven guilty. An even more egregious illustration of this trust was experienced not in baseball, but in cycling. Lance Armstrong was a national hero, miraculously recovering from testicular cancer in 1997 before becoming the greatest American rider in the history of the sport. Born and raised in Texas, he won the Tour de France seven years in a row. Throughout his career, Armstrong was continuously accused of doping, most aggressively by French journalists. He denied this constantly, suing those who claimed otherwise and ruining the lives of teammates and acquaintances who contradicted his purity. Armstrong used his political influence to beat the testing system and risked his reputation by suing people for expressing falsehoods he knew to be true. When he finally admitted his transgressions in 2013, it was common to redraft any misguided faith in his previous defiance as a collective case of childish gullibility, especially since drug use* has always been intertwined with cycling. But it wasn't that simple in 1999. Armstrong was a philanthropic superman who'd almost died from a disease, staring into the eyes of the public and saying, "I have never taken performance-enhancing drugs." His righteousness was too extreme to reject. There was a humanistic obligation to believe what he said.

The nineties' ambivalence regarding steroids was not a case of the public rejecting what was perceptibly impossible. It was the public accepting the implausible, based on the best evidence available. It was crazy, but not as crazy as it's remembered.

○ ○ ○

The disenchantment with baseball's false glory of 1998 would not be fully felt for years. At the time, it was simply part of an exceptionally memorable summer of sports. In June, Jordan and the Bulls defeated the Utah Jazz for their second three-peat as NBA champions. Jordan hit the final shot of the series, was named Finals MVP for the sixth time, and retired again (but again, only temporarily). Now thirty-five, Jordan was disgusted with Chicago general manager Jerry Krause, who'd vowed to break up the team after the season and dismiss head coach Phil Jackson (whom Jordan liked and respected). Jordan also had nothing left to prove, having dominated the league in two separate intervals.

Jordan's first return to basketball was in the spring of 1995. He'd quit baseball earlier that year, the moment he realized Selig was seriously considering

---

*Armstrong experimented with the entire spectrum of performance enhancers, but his drug of choice was erythropoietin, commonly abbreviated as EPO. It's normally a treatment for anemia that increases the blood's ability to carry oxygen. One of the psychological side effects of EPO is that it also spurs motivation.

using minor league replacements to fill the rosters vacated by the players still on strike. Jordan expressed solidarity with the striking players and did not want to be exploited as a celebrity scab. He'd hit a paltry .202 with the AA Barons, along with 3 home runs and 114 strikeouts. His attempt to cross over had failed. What is conspicuous, however, is the way this failure was reappraised over time. Jordan's manager with the Barons was Terry Francona, who'd later win the World Series twice as manager of the Boston Red Sox. In 2020, Francona claimed Jordan would have made an MLB roster if he'd committed to the sport for three years. Michael Jordan was such an amazing basketball player that people slowly convinced themselves he was also pretty good at baseball.

In 2001, Jordan came out of retirement a second time, this time to play with the Washington Wizards, a franchise he partly owned. He was also president of basketball operations, meaning he essentially signed himself. He then hired as head coach Doug Collins, who'd served as Jordan's coach with the Bulls early in his career (and was, fairly or unfairly, perceived as someone Jordan could control). Jordan was still more famous than any other player in the league. *The Washington Post* assigned a beat reporter* to exclusively cover MJ throughout his second return, separate from the rest of the team. The Wizards never made the playoffs during Jordan's two years on the roster, and he dealt with injuries both seasons. This final comeback was ultimately perceived as an egocentric overstep that sullied the memory of his nineties greatness; it's sometimes lumped in with his attempt at baseball as an example of self-confidence spiraling into narcissism. Yet this negative projection ignores how Jordan actually performed as a Wizard. He averaged 22.9 points a game in his first Washington season and 20 in his second. As a forty-year-old man, he scored 43 points in a game against the New Jersey Nets. Was his second comeback a mistake? Perhaps. But it wasn't a disaster. It was crazy, but not as crazy as it's remembered.

---

*The reporter, Michael Leahy, later wrote a book about the experience titled *When Nothing Else Matters*. It was critical of Jordan's tenure with the Wizards.

[vodka on the chessboard]

THERE ARE THINGS FORGOTTEN BY CHANCE, AND THERE ARE THINGS forgotten on purpose. But then there are things that aren't really *forgotten* as much as they are deliberately ignored, usually because the memory has come to necessitate an elephantine level of discomfiting rationalization. America's involvement with the 1996 Russian democratic election falls into this third category. Boris Yeltsin, the boozehound incumbent, overcame mass unpopularity to win reelection as Russian president, significantly due to assistance from clandestine United States operatives and the support of Bill Clinton.

When the news of this subversion first surfaced, it was hailed as a masterstroke of U.S. statecraft. The July 15 cover of *Time* magazine pulled no punches: "Yanks to the Rescue: The Secret Story of How American Advisers Helped Yeltsin Win." Decades later, the concept of interfering with another country's election (and particularly an election in Russia) has adopted a more sinister overtone, and there's a revisionist temptation to claim the role America played in the affair was exaggerated. But it did happen, and it's almost inconceivable to imagine Yeltsin winning reelection had it not.

As leader of the Russian Soviet Federative Socialist Republic, Yeltsin had won big in Russia's inaugural democratic election in '91, but his nation was experiencing the quagmire of chaos one would expect from a geographically gigantic landmass rapidly converting from state-controlled communism to capitalistic sovereign democracy. The Russian parliament tried to impeach Yeltsin in '93, but Yeltsin deployed the military to remain in control. Some half-jokingly claimed Yeltsin's approval rating was lower than that of Stalin, a tyrannical dictator who'd been dead for forty years. It appeared Gennady Zyuganov, leader of the Russian Communist Party, would win the '96 election, perhaps easily.

From the U.S. perspective, any halfhearted return to communism was a step backward. Yeltsin (who'd sunk to the bottom of preelection polls) was the opposite of perfect, but he was the best option available and Clinton liked him personally.* Clinton helped him get a $10.2 billion loan from the International Monetary Fund. But the more intriguing (and less verifiable) aspect to Yeltsin's comeback was the work of three American consultants secretly living in Moscow's President Hotel and "Americanizing" the Yeltsin campaign strategy.

The U.S. operatives—Richard Dresner, George Gorton, and Joe Shumate—presented themselves as harmless sales representatives, transferred to Moscow with the aim of selling flat-screen TVs. What they were really doing was assisting Tatiana Dyachenko, Yeltsin's thirty-six-year-old daughter, who ran his campaign despite having no political experience. The three consultants were paid $250,000 for four months of work. What they realized was that Russian politicians raised with a Soviet mind-set had never needed to consider what voters wanted or how voters thought. There was no way Yeltsin could win by claiming he'd done a good job in his first term (because he hadn't), nor could he ingratiate himself by making grand promises about the future (because the Russian people were conditioned to disbelieve any-

---

*Though not much of a drinker himself, Clinton expressed amusement over Yeltsin's alcoholism and noted that Boris was always an affable drunkard. Once, while presumably wasted, Yeltsin randomly called Clinton on the telephone and proposed they meet up for a secret summit on a submarine.

thing he said). His political approach required a wholesale Western reinvention. Yeltsin needed to go negative.

The consultants had a twofold plan. Part of it was to study everything George Bush had done during his 1992 U.S. presidential campaign and always do the exact opposite (Bush, like Yeltsin, had refused to accept that he was an unpopular incumbent). The more nuanced half of the strategy was to focus not on what the Russian people wanted, but on what they feared: a return to breadlines, a potential civil war, and the possibility of social unrest that would never go away.

"Stick with Yeltsin and at least you'll have calm—that was the line we wanted to convey," Dresner later explained. "So the drumbeat about unrest kept pounding right till the end of the [election cycle], when the final TV spots were all about the Soviets' repressive rule."

Here again, it's difficult to discern precisely how vital American involvement with the '96 Russian election was. We do know that Yeltsin was way behind in 1995 and somehow won easily in '96, and that most historians classify the entire race as either mildly or heavily corrupt. The expressed U.S. position on the meddling was that America had a stake in the outcome, Yeltsin was the best hope for the expansion of democracy, and bloodlessly shaping international policy is the definition of what diplomacy is. It wasn't a conspiracy. It was a plan, and the plan worked. It's just not a plan we prefer to remember.

8 Yesterday's Concepts of Tomorrow

THERE'S A QUESTION WITHIN ALL NONESSENTIAL TRANSACTIONS THAT'S hard to avoid and harder to answer: Do consumers demand what they want, or are consumers convinced to want whatever they're offered? Part of the problem is semantic (what does it really mean to "want" something you don't "need"?). Another part is economic (a rich person might demand what a poor person wouldn't even consider, and vice versa). The real complexity, however, is that both contradictory possibilities are always plausible, and sometimes at the same time. It happens constantly, although rarely with as much clarity as with the beverage industry in 1993.

There's no evidence that people of the nineties wanted clear versions of beverages that were readily available in non-clear form. It wasn't something that was possible to want, because it's not something people imagined. There are many reasons not to drink Pepsi, but "It's too dark" has never been among them. There's always been a demand for lighter beer, but nobody ever asked for a beer so light that it would be possible to look through the bottle and read a newspaper. So why were such beverages invented? Why, from roughly 1992 to 1995, did the beverage industry operate from the position that there was an underserved sector of the populace who desperately wanted transparent drinks? When forced to construct an explanation, the conventional wisdom is always *purity*: Clear beverages were erroneously viewed as healthier, since they didn't have artificial coloring and ostensibly resembled water. And it's possible this was true, for somebody, somewhere. But that's not why this happened, nor does it explain why the trend collapsed. A concept like Zima—a citrusy version of Coors beer, scrubbed into translucence by charcoal filters—was the liquid manifestation of a cultural phase in which informed insincerity was the only way to understand anything. Zima was ridiculous . . . but did that actually mean it was brilliant? The only viable conclusion was "sort of."

Coors Brewing Company announced the invention of Zima in 1992, describing it as a "malt-based spritzer." The word *Zima*, displayed on the packaging in a futuristic font, translated as "winter" in Russian. Zima had roughly the same alcohol content as normal beer (4.7 percent by volume) and was intended for consumption in the same venues, by the same type of beer-obsessed people (Coors specifically instructed liquor stores to never place Zima next to the wine coolers). The flavor was nothing like beer. It was closer to cheap champagne mixed with Sprite, and—unlike beer—it was the opposite of an acquired taste. Every new Zima went down slightly worse than the previous Zima. There was, however, something perversely enticing about a drink that seemed to come from a post-apocalyptic wasteland in which color did not exist. There was an ingrained assumption that Zima must be expressly targeted at *somebody*, but nobody knew who that was. Was Zima supposed to be for women? Was it secretly directed at minors, or maybe toward the gay community? Was there a demographic of insecure consumers who didn't like beer but still identified as macho beer drinkers? Could you get drunk on Zima and pass a Breathalyzer test? Was it actually for stealth alcoholics who wanted to drink at the office? At first, Zima's inscrutability was its greatest advantage: In 1994, Coors sold a mind-boggling 1.3 million barrels of a beverage nobody understood.

"I had 15 the other night, and the thing is, you can drive with it. Your breath doesn't smell like alcohol," a thirty-six-year-old furniture mover told

The Village Voice. "The only thing that irritates me is why don't they stop the bullshit and tell us what's in it."

This reaction was common. People did not look at Zima and assume it was a purer, healthier version of regular beer. People looked at Zima and assumed it was bizarre and possibly insidious. What secret ingredient made beer invisible? What was going on here? In reality, Zima was just the cheapest version of regular Coors, stripped of all identifiable characteristics and injected with a blast of citrus flavoring. It wasn't anything, really. But that's why it (temporarily) worked: It was an unexplained idea.

Crystal Pepsi employed the same philosophy, although with $40 million worth of marketing and even less technical innovation. After a soft launch in '92, PepsiCo went for the jugular during the 1993 Bills-Cowboys Super Bowl with a commercial scored by Van Halen, made to look identical to the band's video for "Right Now," MTV's 1992 winner for Video of the Year. The relationship between the music and the drink became unbreakable. "Right Now" was a mature, piano-driven rock track with a message about embracing the present moment, imbuing Crystal Pepsi with a forced sense of modernity. The advertisement was so reminiscent of the music video that the original video started to feel like an advertisement. The drink itself was unadulterated illusion: It was regular Pepsi, minus the food coloring and twenty-seven calories (but the amounts of high-fructose corn syrup and caffeine were identical). The fact that many consumers perceived Crystal Pepsi as having a different flavor from the original cola was a consequence of psychology, which also led to its doom.

When first released, Crystal Pepsi performed remarkably well. It immediately captured 1 percent of the total soda market, equating to almost half a billion dollars a year. As with Zima, people were curious. Its newness was inarguable. But there were flaws. Crystal Pepsi was presented as a visual product. It looked like 7Up, so that's what people anticipated it would taste like. Yet despite its clarity, it tasted like regular cola, and the human mind does not respond positively to familiar products that contradict expectations.

It generates physiological anxiety.* Pepsi was (a) telling people to drink something that unconsciously disturbed them, while (b) latently suggesting this new, disturbing product was a healthier alterative to regular Pepsi, the foundation of their entire business model. Making matters worse was Coca-Cola's 1993 introduction of Tab Clear, another translucent beverage with an overtly sinister purpose: It was terrible on purpose.

Tab Clear was a diet cola with no caffeine and a heavy aftertaste. Almost no one wanted regular Tab, much less a colorless version of what it already was.† But visually, Tab Clear *seemed* like competition for Crystal Pepsi, so the two products were predictably placed next to each other in retail stores and intertwined in the minds of the public. Crystal Pepsi was just a gimmicky version of regular Pepsi, but Coca-Cola persuaded people to incorrectly view it as a caffeine-free diet drink that resembled their worst product.

"We would launch a Tab Clear product and position it right next to Crystal Pepsi, and we'd kill both in the process," Coca-Cola marketing strategist Sergio Zyman explained in the 2011 book *Killing Giants*. "It was a suicidal mission from day one. Pepsi spent an enormous amount of money on the brand and, regardless, we killed it. Both of them were dead within six months."

The prospect of a terrible beverage created to kamikaze a moronic beverage is an apt metaphor for this entire period of marketing. The so-called Clear Craze of the early nineties involved the production of many unnecessary things: clear Ivory soap, clear mouthwash, clear gasoline. It was a novelty based on a logic that was based on conjecture: "There is a lot of fear these days about what's in the water, what's in the food," Ash

---

*This is from the abstract of a 2014 academic paper titled "The Role of Arousal in Congruity-Based Product Evaluation": "New products are often incongruent with consumer expectations. Researchers have shown that consumers prefer moderately incongruent products, while being adverse [sic] to extremely incongruent products. . . . This suggests that creating excitement around a product launch may be good for incremental innovation, but it may not be a good idea for something truly innovative."

†Tab, the first diet drink Coca-Cola ever created, was finally discontinued in 2020.

DeLorenzo* told *The Philadelphia Inquirer* in 1993. "The idea of something being clear is that if you can't see any impurities, there aren't any." Here again, the key word is *idea*. It was (briefly) popular to consume something familiar that looked alien, even if doing so unconsciously made you nervous. But that seemed like a dumb thing to admit, so the fake explanation became quasi-empirical. The explanation needed to be scientific, or—if that was impassable—it needed to be "science adjacent."

In 1975, it was possible for an advertising executive to place a smooth Mexican stone inside a box, call it a Pet Rock, price that rock at $4, and become a multimillionaire in less than a year. In the seventies, the joy of straightforward dumbness had been enough. In the nineties, you had to pretend dumbness was smart. Zima and Crystal Pepsi were miniature examples. But there were big ones, too.

MTV launched *The Real World* in the summer of 1992, a wonderful time for watching people do nothing. The concept was to place seven young strangers in a New York loft apartment and film what happens when "people stop being polite" (which happened right away) and "start getting real" (which barely happened at all). The series was a generational success, continuing through thirty-three iterations and essentially defining the genre of reality television. Over time, it has become common to classify *The Real World* as a social experiment, broadcast in public. It was not, of course, an actual experiment. It was a soap opera that was supposed to write itself. This (among other things) makes it diametrically opposed to Biosphere 2, a 1991 endeavor that placed eight people inside a three-acre simulation of reality in order to see if they could stay alive. Biosphere 2 *was* an experiment, technically speaking. It *was* science. But it operated more like an unscripted soap opera, imbued with a tension MTV could never have fabricated.

---

*DeLorenzo was described by the publication as a "trend analyst and forecaster."

The Biosphere 2 facility still exists, rising from the Arizona desert like a two-car garage for Optimus Prime. The nearest town is Oracle, with a population just over 3,500. From most vantage points, Biosphere 2 resembles a larger version of the Cleveland-based Rock & Roll Hall of Fame; from other angles, it looks a little like the Hall of Justice from the Hanna-Barbera cartoon *Super Friends*. The five-story greenhouse is now owned by the University of Arizona. Children can attend weeklong science camps inside its walls, assuming their parents are aware that the structure still exists. There aren't many things in North America this gargantuan and complicated that have been so widely dismissed, though the handful of people who remember it at all will likely remember it forever.

First, the name: Biosphere 2 was called "Biosphere 2" because there was already a Biosphere 1, which was Earth. The goal of Biosphere 2 was to re-create the world of Biosphere 1, but under glass. What's slightly confusing is that, years before Biosphere 2, there was a project called BIOS-3,* constructed in Siberia by the Russians in the 1970s. BIOS-3 was a much smaller closed system, constructed underground. That facility was part of the Soviet space program. Decades later, when Biosphere 2 was designed and built north of Tucson, the media message was similar: It, too, was a simulation of what might eventually become a human colony in outer space. That was the espoused goal. But this, as it turns out, was never a realistic possibility. Biosphere 2 is a pressurized structure with a glass roof. It would be impossible to build such a structure on the airless surface of the moon (or on the mostly airless surface of Mars). In practice, Biosphere 2 was primarily an ecology project, better suited for understanding the regular Earth we were all currently using. Still, it's easy to understand why the premise of a mammoth laboratory preparing for life in space became the publicity hook. There was

---

*The Russians had been working on this sort of thing for a while. BIOS-1 was constructed in 1965. BIOS-1 was revamped in 1968 and renamed BIOS-2. The underground BIOS-3 facility was finished in 1972 and remained operational for years.

an ever-growing consensus that Earth was changing, and that this was some-how both the fault of humans and beyond human control.

Throughout the late twentieth century, the term "global warming" was more common than the more encompassing "climate change." The year 1998 would be the hottest year on record, up to that point, and scientists had been warning of atmospheric increases in carbon dioxide since 1956.* What this scientific data meant to the average person, however, remained fluid and open to interpretation. A 1992 poll† found that 68 percent of Americans believed global warning was real. That number declined to 57 percent in 1994. By 2000, it was back up to 70 percent. It was an existential problem people kept ignoring and denying and reconsidering, in hopes it would be solved by magic. Biosphere 2 had the qualities of magical realism. It started to seem like a terrestrial space station might solve the existential problem, even though a space station was never what it was.

So what was it? The objective description is impressive: It was a series of domes and chambers that encompassed seven different biomes—a rain forest, a savannah, a small ocean, a fog desert, some wetlands, an agricultural realm, and a "residential" habitat for the eight humans living and working inside. The various climate zones were intended to harbor 3,800 species of plant and animal life. It took over four years to build and cost between $150 and $200 million, mostly financed by one of the richest people in the country, a Texas billionaire named Ed Bass. The subjective description of Biosphere 2 is trickier to quantify. In 1974, Bass had spent some time at Synergia Ranch in New Mexico, a so-called ecovillage. The still-operational ranch (some call it a commune) was run by a Harvard-educated geological engineer named John P. Allen. Together, Bass and Allen would found a company

---

*In '56, Canadian physicist Gilbert Plass published a study he titled "The Carbon Dioxide Theory of Climate Change." The intensity of the problem, however, has escalated. In 1994, the concentration of carbon dioxide in the Earth's atmosphere was 358 parts per million. It's now well over 400 parts per million.

†These polls were conducted by the Massachusetts-based Cambridge Reports/Research International.

called Space Biospheres Ventures, eventually turning the theory of Biosphere 2 into a hard reality. But the motives for doing this remain a bit confusing.

When explaining why Biosphere 2 was constructed, Allen notes that it was the fusion of three things. One was "ecotechnology" (the science of fulfilling social needs without disrupting the environment). That made sense. The second was "the enterprise for developing potentiality," a collection of corporate buzzwords that could mean almost anything. But it was Allen's third component, "the Theater of All Possibilities," that was unabashedly bizarre. What did a massive ecological dome in the Arizona desert have to do with theater arts? Why was a research project of this magnitude connected with an experimental traveling theater troupe founded by San Francisco hippies in 1967? What could be the connection between biological science and avant-garde theater? From the beginning, there were questions about how seriously this venture was supposed to be taken. In 1987, when construction had just begun, the mainstream science magazine *Discover* called Biosphere 2 the most exciting U.S. venture since the Apollo moon landing. But this take was not universal. *The Village Voice* ran a three-part series on the project in 1991 that tore it to shreds, questioning its scientific rigor and comparing Allen to maniacal death-cult leader Jim Jones. The Biosphere brain trust disagreed with that assessment, although not as vigorously as one might expect.

"There was a NASA cult that got us to the Moon in the sixties," Bass argued in a rare 1991 interview. "If what's at work is mindless conformity, manipulation and so forth, that would be frightening, that would be shocking. But as far as dedication to a project, discipline, hard work and so forth, I would say NASA's effort that got us on the Moon and Biosphere 2 have a lot in common."

Allen was not exaggerating when he used the phrase "the Theater of All Possibilities." Yes, this was a theater group, but it was applied to *all* possible ideas. Everything in life, Allen believed, was a form of theater. In the seventies, the synergist collective had built a large ocean vessel from scratch, having no previous experience with shipbuilding. It worked, and they sailed the vessel around the world multiple times. What Bass and Allen were truly trying to accomplish is hard to define. They did, however, accomplish the assembly of Biosphere 2. It was operational by September of 1991. The first mission involved four men and four women (five Americans, two people from Britain, and one from Belgium). They entered the facility wearing matching full-body jumpsuits, a sartorial decision that increased the positive perception that Biosphere 2 was a space station and the negative perception that it was a cult. The so-called Biospherians would stay inside the dome for two years. If it worked, they would never have to leave the facility for anything. Biospherian Mark Nelson, a then forty-four-year-old ecological researcher in charge of the wastewater system, remembers the daily schedule in mathematical terms:

> On September 26, 1991, we entered Biosphere 2 to begin our experiment. Like astronauts, we had plenty of tasks to fill our days. Farming took up 25 percent of our waking time, research and maintenance 20 percent, writing reports 19 percent, cooking 12 percent, biome management 11 percent, animal husbandry 9 percent. We spent the rest of our time doing media interviews and handling miscellaneous matters. We built in off days for rest and to observe changes in our growing biosphere.

> We grew our food and raised and slaughtered livestock. We worked in labs, maintained equipment, and spent time in our living quarters. Growing good nutritious food was a top priority, requiring everyone to work three to four hours a day for five days a week. None of us had come from a farming background. Hunger became a new experience—and our constant companion. We existed the way humans had from time immemorial. Did our farming improve as we went along?

You bet. Hunger is a great motivator. If you don't grow it, you can't eat it.

The absence of food was a greater problem than Nelson's diary suggests. The crops were supposed to be pollinated by honeybees and hummingbirds, but the birds and bees all died. Nelson lost 25 pounds, and at least one other crew member lost twice that much. Yet this medically supervised "healthy starvation" would have likely ranked only third on the laundry list of Biospheric problems. The most pressing issue was that the facility was running out of breathable air. Microbes in the soil were producing carbon dioxide faster than photosynthesis was creating oxygen. After sixteen months, the oxygen level had dropped from 20.9 percent to 14.2 percent, the equivalent of living at the summit of the Swiss Alps. There was no way to fix the problem, so outside oxygen had to be pumped into the facility, creating a momentary period of oxidized euphoria for the eight Biospherians.

This necessary O_2 injection slaughtered the premise of the experiment. It was supposed to be an entirely closed system, sealed from within. Whatever life the crew was able to construct inside the structure's walls would be irrelevant if the inhabitants couldn't survive without help from the outside. That conflict led to the second pressing problem: social disorder. Half of the Biospherians wanted to scrap the goal of proving that a simulation of Earth could be accomplished without any help from the outside; they wanted to focus instead on the unique opportunity to pursue science in a huge laboratory *almost* disconnected from the rest of the world. The other half wanted to keep the original objective intact, even though that would require most of the daily work to focus on troubleshooting facility flaws and doing whatever was most necessary to stay alive. The eight crew members split into adversarial factions. The two groups, trapped within the same finite space for two years, wouldn't even talk to each other (there were no punches thrown, but a few allegations of spitting).

Nonetheless, the first Biosphere mission was completed in '93—not exactly as planned, but not without some measure of mild success. The public understanding, however, was that the mission had failed. The day-to-day problems encountered by the crew received far more attention than any of their subtle achievements. This escalated when the second Biosphere mission was launched in March of 1994, and a new person was hired to manage Space Biospheres Ventures: Steve Bannon.

Bannon, who'd eventually become famous and infamous for spearheading the populist strategy behind Donald Trump's presidential victory in 2016, was (at the time) a former investment banker with Goldman Sachs. He was immediately concerned with the overhead costs of the project, prompting some members of the Biosphere inner circle to worry that Bannon's cost-cutting measures would put the lives of crew members at risk. Five days after Bannon was hired, two crew members from the first Biosphere mission crept up to the facility at three a.m. and opened up one of the main airlocks and a few of the emergency exits, citing fear that the people inside were in physical jeopardy. They also broke some windows. Four days after that, the captain of the second mission walked out of the facility and quit. The incomplete mission was over by September, followed by a handful of lawsuits* and a takeover of the facility by New York's Columbia University. Columbia managed the structure for the next eight years, mainly using the ocean biome as a means for studying the impact of global warming on coral reefs.

The legacy of Biosphere 2 remains open to interpretation. It often seems like the most stunning triumph was the architecture of the building itself (its chief engineer, William Dempster, invented huge lung-like expansion chambers that kept the structure airtight). But what's most historically instructive is that this project was attempted at all. It was a collision of multiple worldviews that could have only intersected at the specific time that they did.

---

*The detail most repeated about the post-Biosphere legal entanglements is that Bannon referred to marine biologist Abigail Alling, one of the original Biosphere crew members who later vandalized the dome during the second mission, as a "self-centered, deluded young woman" who was also a "bimbo."

Biosphere 2 was seen as a potential solution to two overlapping extinction fears—climate change and nuclear holocaust (still a common concern when the concept was hatched in the 1980s). "Western civilization isn't simply dying," Allen said during the construction phase. "It's dead. We are probing into its ruins to take whatever is useful for the building of the new civilization to replace it." Another factor was a growing belief that super-rich private citizens might have better solutions to problems once considered responsibilities of the state (the political enthusiasm for H. Ross Perot during this same period is not coincidental). But a third, stranger worldview was also in play: the maturation and normalization of New Age bullshit.

The aforementioned "Theater of All Possibilities" was not merely a sideshow to Biosphere 2. It was a driving philosophical force. Allen was a metallurgical-mining engineer, but he was also a playwright and author who sometimes published under the pseudonym "Johnny Dolphin." His sensibilities* pushed seemingly unlike disciplines—stage performance, ecology, and biotechnology—into what could be described as an optimistic doomsday religion, if such a paradox is possible (Marc Cooper, the *Village Voice* writer who savaged the project, basically framed the organization in those terms). This is why Biosphere 2 could have only happened when it did.

In the early seventies, when New Age thinking was emerging as a movement, it was a fringe ideology practiced by people purposefully living outside conventional society. The most troubling example was a separatist group like Heaven's Gate, a New Age sect that started in 1974 and evolved into a Christian, monastic super-cult that believed a coming UFO would take them to a new level of existence. It concluded with the March 1997 mass suicide of thirty-nine Heaven's Gate members (the suicidal cultists wore Nikes, put exactly $5.75 in their pockets, willfully swallowed applesauce mixed with barbiturates, placed plastic bags over their heads, and waited for the starship to

---

*Though not connected, there are aspects to the Theater of All Possibilities that feel vaguely reminiscent of some of the theater workshops described in the 1981 film *My Dinner with Andre*.

arrive). By the dawn of the twenty-first century, New Age thinking had become a quaint remnant of the pre-Reagan past, the wackmobile ideology behind Erhard Seminars Training and *Hair* and vegan Deadheads selling crystals at Joshua Tree. But there was also an era between those periods, when some of those early New Age pioneers had matured into entrepreneurial adults. It was during this fleeting stretch—roughly 1985 to 1995—when someone like Allen (sixty-two years old at the time of Biosphere 2's launch) could reasonably convince a billionaire like Bass (who was forty-six) to invest so much money into a scientific project that was not necessarily scientific. The fact that it seemed outlandish was not a disadvantage. It needed to be outlandish to matter.

What society classifies as "credible" is almost always a product of whichever social demographic happens to be economically dominant at the time of the classification. The early nineties were the closest New Age dogma ever came to real credibility, simply because it was the only time when those who cared about it most had enough cultural and economic power to force it into being.* The belief was that anything was now possible, and that the limitations humans had accepted in the past were not necessarily real.

The people who thought those things were correct, although not for the· reasons they assumed.

◡ ◡ ◡

The news broke in February of 1997, but the breakthrough itself was already seven months old. The story came from Scotland, devoid of forewarning, and it prompted a lot of people to have unusually dramatic conversations that started like this: "Have you heard about that sheep?"

---

*This was an era when a pro basketball coach like Phil Jackson could win multiple titles and be viewed as the best coach in the sport while incessantly espousing principles of Zen Buddhism and Native American cosmology. Jackson applied these concepts to the Chicago Bulls (and, later, the Los Angeles Lakers) in practical ways, not far removed from conventional motivation and mindfulness techniques coaches had used for decades—but never with such direct willingness to use New Age language and never with such widespread levels of respect and admiration. In 1995, Jackson published a self-help book called *Sacred Hoops: Spiritual Lessons of a Hardwood Warrior.*

It was a high-water mark for misinformed arguments about genetics and semi-informed jokes about Dolly Parton.

"It's unbelievable," Princeton molecular biology professor Lee Silver told *The New York Times*. "It basically means that there are no limits. It means all of science fiction is true."

What had happened was this: The previous July, a team of UK genetic researchers at the Roslin Institute in Edinburgh had cloned an adult female sheep. It had taken 277 tries, but a fifty-two-year-old embryologist named Ian Wilmut had successfully combined the DNA from the cell of one sheep with the unfertilized ovarian egg cell of another sheep. The ovarian cell had been stripped of its nucleus, making it a vessel for duplication. The original cell had come from a female sheep's mammary gland, which is why the eventual offspring was named "Dolly" (in tribute to buxom country singer Parton). The institute had kept the information secret for half a year, in part because scientific journals were reluctant to publish research that had already been covered by mainstream media (and the attention this achievement would receive was immediately obvious). They also wanted to make sure the new mammal lived. She did. Dolly seemed wholly normal, no different from any other Finnish Dorset sheep in any other barn.

The hyperbolic nature of Silver's response in the *Times* might have been slightly personal: The news about Dolly broke just as he was about to coincidentally publish a book explaining why mammalian cloning was impossible. But this type of reaction became the standard public takeaway. There were always two responses inherent to any consideration of the cloning. The first was that this act was remarkable, game-changing, and proof of science's potentiality for the reinvention of life. The second was that cloning must be feared and controlled, and that some kind of tragic scenario was inevitable. Because how could something this incredible *not* be dangerous?

The nineties anxiety over cloning was, almost exclusively, a mass media creation. In the wake of Dolly's subsistence, President Bill Clinton was compelled to announce his desire for legislation that would ban human cloning, arguing that the concept "has the potential to threaten the sacred family bonds at the very core of our ideals and our society." This declaration wasn't altogether different from announcing a bill outlawing invisible vampires. The existence of Dolly only meant that cloning a human was theoretically possible, which it theoretically always had been. There was no evidence anyone with the rarefied scientific acumen and limitless funding required for such a pursuit had any interest in cloning a person.* There was also a collective lack of understanding of what the mechanics and intent of mammalian cloning actually were.

Society never had any qualms with the concept of selective breeding in agriculture, where two plants or animals were purposefully bred in hopes of producing an offspring that would possess specific desirable traits from both. This had been going on for thousands of years. The problem with selective breeding is that the process is inefficient (it hinges on the mere *probability* that the desired traits will be passed from one organism to the next). Mammalian cloning, if perfected, would guarantee that the desired traits could always be precisely replicated in the new animal. Moreover, there seemed to be a myopic unwillingness to accept that human clones were already present in the world: Identical twins share almost 100 percent of the same DNA. Cloning happens in nature. Yet the cultural connotation of the word *cloning* was (and is) almost universally negative. This was true before Dolly was created and after she was famous. Her laboratory birth simply served as the hinge point for how those anxieties evolved and accelerated.

Prior to Dolly, the fear around cloning had adopted a backward-facing posture. Its sci-fi depiction was typically akin to a modernized take on Mary Shelley's *Frankenstein*—cloning would allow scientists to reanimate what

---

*One not-very-significant exception to this was a Chicago physicist named Richard Seed, who immediately declared he would start cloning humans before a governmental ban could be put in place. "We are going to become gods," Seed insisted. "If you don't like it, get off. You don't have to contribute. You don't have to participate. But if you're going to interfere with *me* becoming god, we're going to have big trouble." Seed planned to start a commercial business where he would replicate people at a cost of $1 million per clone. He never came close.

had long been dead, and fiction writers raced to see who could come up with the worst possible thing to bring back to life. From a creative standpoint, the winner of that contest was novelist Allan Folsom, author of the 1994 thriller *The Day After Tomorrow*. The novel was about a conspiracy to clone Adolf Hitler from his cryogenically frozen head. Ten years later, an unrelated disaster movie titled *The Day After Tomorrow* was released in multiplex theaters, and the profile of that 2004 film would effectively erase the existence of the 1994 book. The novel, however, was briefly a pretty big deal. It was Folsom's debut, yet publisher Little, Brown paid $2 million for the rights. It debuted at number 3 on the *New York Times* bestseller list, proving that there's no greater value stock than any story that brings back Hitler.

A far more lasting version of cloning fiction was *Jurassic Park*. Nothing mainstreamed the nuts-and-bolts fluency of cloning more successfully. Written by prolific techno-novelist Michael Crichton, the 1990 *Jurassic Park* novel was partially based on the work of a team of entomologists who had managed to remove the DNA from ancient insects trapped in amber. If insect DNA could be trapped in suspended animation, Crichton presumably imagined, why not T. rex DNA? The subsequent 448-page book invents an island zoo filled with living dinosaurs, cloned from blood found inside prehistoric insects preserved in fossilized resin. The dinosaurs, somewhat predictably, escape from captivity during a security breach and go on a rampage. The well-paced, user-friendly novel was hugely popular and adapted into a 1993 Steven Spielberg film that was, for several years, the highest-grossing picture in cinema history. Spielberg's movie, though entertaining, is now primarily defined as a technical achievement: The dinosaurs, built through computer-generated imagery, were lifelike to a degree never before seen. It was also the first film to utilize fully digital sound.

Beyond spawning a generationally momentous film, Crichton's novel is important for at least two other reasons: It introduced chaos theory into the public consciousness and popularized a handful of enlightened paleontological theories that were not widely known to casual consumers (the notion of dinosaurs as warm-blooded creatures that evolved into birds, the concept of sauropods as non-aquatic herd animals, etc.). Neither the book nor the film could be classified as anti-science, but in both versions, the role of cloning is depicted as an example of mankind's egocentric overreach, much like atomic testing in the early Godzilla movies. The ominous theme is voiced by a character named Ian Malcolm, a sardonic mathematician portrayed in the film by Jeff Goldblum: "Your scientists were so preoccupied with whether they could, they didn't stop to think if they should." Any relationship between cloning and any functional purpose (particularly the future field of stem cell research) was not really part of the civilian discourse. The focus was always on the worst-case possibility—a secular desire to re-create something that was not supposed to exist.

Over and over, fictional representations of genetic manipulation fixated on the metaphysical tragedy that would accompany its success. The 1992 British TV movie *The Cloning of Joanna May* was about a controlling husband who'd secretly created three clones of his ex-wife (the problem being a lack of consent from both the original woman and her replicants). The 1996 Michael Keaton comedy *Multiplicity* was about an overworked husband who cloned himself multiple times to make his life easier (the problem being that every new copy was inferior to the previous copy, like a Xerox of a Xerox). The 1997 dystopian film *Gattaca*, while not strictly about cloning, worked from the premise of infants being genetically engineered at birth, thereby making them biologically and socially superior to those born in the traditional way (the problem being, as described by the film's tagline, that "there is no gene for the human spirit"). This trope was so widespread that Italian-born academic Giovanni Maio outlined four messages he saw as inherent to virtually all movies about cloning:

1. The clone is evil (while the original is good)

2. The creator of the clone is punished for breaking a taboo

3. The creation of the artificial human occurs within a civilization of decay

4. Order is only restored upon the destruction of the clone

It's not exactly surprising that films about cloning dwelled on the problems cloning might create. Drama is about conflict, so a movie where clones are cloned and everything is fine is not much of a movie. Cinematic scientists tend to be more diabolical than scientists in reality. Still, the dissonance between the public sensitivity to genetic engineering and the actual progress being made can be seen as a signpost for the modern anti-science movement in Western culture. The creation of Dolly the Sheep was the single biggest intellectual jump of the nineties. Some assumed it could never be achieved. It was. Some assumed Dolly would have numerous internal weaknesses and deformities. She did not. Others assumed Dolly would only survive for a few months. She lived over six years, dying of a respiratory cancer common to sheep raised indoors. By every possible metric, this experiment worked. Yet that success only served to fuel another assumption—that whatever eventually came of this could only be awful, and that the coming awfulness was arriving faster than previously expected.

In 2000, the British rock band Radiohead released an album titled *Kid A*. Anticipation for the record was unusually fervent. The band's previous album (1997's *OK Computer*) had been acclaimed as a minor masterpiece, and Radiohead was widely considered the most commercially popular band still making artistically important music.

Kid A was shrouded in pre-release secrecy. No advance copies were available to critics.* When it finally came out in October, the reception was complicated: The music was a departure from the group's previous work, sonically

---

*A week before it came out, the television network MTV2 attained a vinyl copy of *Kid A* and broadcast the album in its entirety, simply by playing it on a turntable and pointing a camera at the record player. Interest in hearing *Kid A* was so intense that people were willing to stare at the static image of a record player spinning a black circle for forty-seven minutes. Some of us recorded it.

closer to electronica or post-rock. It was less melodic and lyrically esoteric. *Kid A* became the number 1 album in both the U.S. and the UK, but the standard modifier to describe it was "difficult." It had been a while since a rock album was given such serious contemplation, and part of that analysis focused on the meaning of the title. The trendy theory, spurred by a minor mention in the British music publication *New Musical Express*, asserted that "Kid A" was a reference to the first cloned baby, which Radiohead vocalist Thom Yorke believed to already exist. Such a connection made sense to the group's fan base. Radiohead (and Yorke in particular) had built a nonmusical ethos around alienation, social anxiety, and the escalating oppression from an expanding corporate dystopia. Obsessing over the menace of genetic engineering felt like a predictably Yorkean move. But like so many other things related to clones and cloning, this was a false calamity people wanted to accept. Yorke finally explained this in a *Rolling Stone* interview that December:

Is *Kid A* really about cloning humans?

That was entirely my fault [*laughs*]. Early on, Stanley Donwood, who does our artwork, and I started doing this thing, *Test Specimen*, a cartoon about giving birth to a monster, the Frankenstein thing . . . The idea was loosely based on stuff we were reading about genetically modified food. We got obsessed with the idea of mutation entering the DNA of the human species. One episode was about these teddy bears that mutate and start eating children. . . . It was this running joke, which wasn't really funny. But in our usual way, it addressed a lot of our paranoia and anxieties. "Kid A" was just a name flying around— it was a name of one of the sequencers.

The world, as always, was changing. But it seemed increasingly possible that it was changing faster than its inhabitants could understand, so they just had to pretend that they did.

[the importance of being earnest]

IT'S HARD TO OFFEND PEOPLE BY WRITING ABOUT EVENTS FROM NINE
hundred years ago, but William Manchester found a way. The Wesleyan University professor's twentieth book, the 1992 popular history *A World Lit Only by Fire: The Medieval Mind and the Renaissance*, was a highly engaging bestseller harshly criticized by just about every serious academic who read it. Part of Manchester's mistake, according to his detractors, could be seen in the book's subtitle. The author was preoccupied with crawling inside the skulls of people who'd been dead for centuries, usually concluding that they were disgusting idiots. The book's skeleton key is found at the end of its very first paragraph, where Manchester delivers his overall take on the Dark Ages: "After the extant fragments have been fitted together, the portrait which emerges is a mélange of incessant warfare, corruption, lawlessness, obsession with strange myths, and an almost impenetrable mindlessness."

This sentence is noteworthy for many reasons, one of which is that it might be totally wrong. But its more illuminating feature is something that often happens with popular history: An attempt at analyzing the distant past ends up being more astute about the living present. Manchester's description of the Dark Ages accidentally serves as an almost perfect photo negative of the decade when *A World Lit Only by Fire* was released, beloved, and criticized.

The nineties, at least in North America, were not a time of incessant warfare: The Cold War ended, the Gulf War was brief, and the War in Afghanistan was a speck on the horizon. There was (of course) some corruption in the nineties, as there always is and always shall be. But the Iran-Contra affair was in the past, while Enron and Bernie Madoff were still unseen problems of the future. It was not a period of lawlessness (crime went down and prison populations went up, mostly with nonviolent offenders). It was not a period obsessed with strange myths (the populace grew more secular and increasingly skeptical of the American Dream). And it absolutely was not, to any degree, a period of "impenetrable mindlessness." This was a decade of full-on metacognition, when people spent an inordinate amount of time thinking about why they were thinking whatever it was they were thinking. Every thought was assumed to have a deeper meaning, and the meaning of those thoughts had to be dissected in order to justify the original intellectual process. Which is why thoughtful people kept reintroducing the New Sincerity, over and over and over again.

There have been many versions of the New Sincerity, always unified by the same motive: the belief that people should be honest about what they feel, and that consumers of art should not reward artists who use emotional estrangement as an intellectual crutch. In the late eighties, there was a New Sincerity music scene in East Texas, although the musicians were all too sincere to succeed nationally. In September of 1991, *Esquire* ran a long story on the New Sincerity that mostly mocked the idea, claiming that habits like cocaine were part of the Old Sincerity ("it made you improvise, lie, and cheat for amusement") while ecstasy was a drug for the New Sincerity ("it kills irony"). *Esquire* used two different covers for the issue: one with David Letterman smiling and one with David Letterman scowling. The theory was that people who supported the New Sincerity would want the copy where Letterman looked nice. New Sincerity logic was (very briefly) applied to movies, and particularly movies made by Kevin Costner. But the zenith of its influence occurred in the late nineties, when it temporarily became the dominant way to think about literature. The movement was driven (as was so often the case) by a David Foster Wallace essay, but the term was most incessantly applied to writers like Dave Eggers and Zadie Smith, eventually leading to pro-earnestness polemics like *For Common Things: Irony, Trust, and Commitment in America Today*, a 1999 nonfiction book from a twenty-five-year-old home-schooled Harvard graduate named Jedediah Purdy.

"I'm not arguing in favor of the restoration of naïve to a place of honor," said Purdy. "But I do think there's something corrosive in all-pervasive, reflective skepticism. It's laziness disguised as sophistication."

The New Sincerity was a psychological double bind, akin to asking if God could create a rock God couldn't lift. On one hand, it was hard to be "against" the New Sincerity on principle, because only a jerk would be "against" the notion of being sincere. But it was also a categorization no one would ever apply to themselves, nor was it a publishing genre anyone wanted to be pushed into. To openly claim you were offering some new kind of sincerity latently implied everyone else was lying ("The new sincerity doesn't sound very far from the new smugness," noted Purdy). It was confusing. An author like Eggers wrote about grim human experiences (his parents' deaths from cancer) with total vulnerability, but his memoir's sardonic title was *A Heartbreaking Work of Staggering Genius* and its humor seemed like the savviest version of post-modern cleverness (one long section focused on Eggers's failed audition to become a cast member on *The Real World*).

The New Sincerity offered no gray area—either you cared about it too much or you didn't care at all. To those who saw ironic distance as a creeping cultural affliction, there was no creative crisis more damaging; to almost everyone else, it seemed liked an imaginary problem that could not matter any less than it appeared. But what the New Sincerity was, and what it always is, was anxiety over the comfort of emotional uninvestment, magnified by the luxury of introspection.

Emotional uninvestment made so many contradictions fun and enriching. It was simultaneously possible to view Pavement as the finest band of the decade while also seeing them as five guys who weren't even trying (and who ridiculed any rival who did). A movie like Todd Solondz's *Happiness* was an acute examination of loneliness and a disturbing depiction of pedophilia, but it was also very funny (particularly in moments that should have felt, in any authentic context, unspeakably sad). The impeachment of President Bill Clinton was both serious (due to the implications) and comedic (due to the circumstances). If you did not really care, any experience could be entertaining. And this made pensive people uncomfortable, even within moments of unadulterated joy. Shouldn't the best things in life also be the most important things? Shouldn't fiction be imbued with the same morality as reality? What is the purpose of art if not to connect with the deepest part of other people, and isn't the whole notion of classifying something as "so bad that it's good" just a way of avoiding the beautiful incongruity of thoughts and feelings?

This was the crux of the psychosomatic problem: *I think I should feel guilty for enjoying something I don't actually care about.* The solution was to be less cynical, and one way to be less cynical was to elevate the expression of sincerity. But trying to be sincere on purpose is like trying to be spontaneous on command—it ends up having the opposite effect. If the goal was to kill irony, the old version of sincerity wouldn't work. So we had to invent a new one, again and again and again.

9   Sauropods

THIS BOOK IS BEING WRITTEN WITHIN AN UNPRECEDENTED HISTORICAL moment. However, that would be true no matter when it was written. I'm typing this sentence during a global pandemic, but I'd probably consider the current historical moment *unprecedented* even if COVID-19 had never come into existence. Every time period that's ever transpired has seemed unprecedented to the people who happened to live through it; no one has ever believed the Chinese aphorism "May you live in interesting times" did not apply to the life they were coincidentally living. So here's something interesting about the times happening right now, since "right now" is the only place we can ever be: If you ask a semi-educated young person to identify the root cause of most American problems, there's a strong possibility they will say, "Capitalism."

Polls taken throughout the presidential tenures of Donald Trump and Joe Biden persistently show that people between the ages of eighteen and twenty-nine view socialism more positively than capitalism, especially if they're Democrats (the once-promising 2020 presidential campaign of Elizabeth Warren was derailed by her unwillingness to identify as a socialist, torpedoing her vocal support among the so-called extremely online). Capitalism is connected to every extension of American life, so it can be cited as the source for almost any social ill: wealth disparity, the legacy of slavery, housing shortages, monopsony, clinical depression, the tyranny of choice, superhero movie franchises. Its alleged insidiousness is ubiquitous, and that places the present moment at odds with the 1990s. In the nineties, when a semi-educated young person was asked to identify the root cause of most American problems, the probable answer would not have been *capitalism*. The more likely response would have been *commercialism*.

That shift prompts a loaded question—what's the core ideological difference between those two generational complaints?

On the surface, both seem like strains of cynicism. But that's not accurate. A hatred of commercialism is unconsciously optimistic. It operates from the (possibly naive) premise that—in and of themselves—things have merit, regardless of what those things are. Social sickness only emerges from how those things are presented: Art is intrinsically good, but attempts to make it palatable to those who don't understand art make it bad. It's cool to wear flannel, but not if someone is convinced to wear flannel as a way to be cool. Christmas is wonderful, but hearing "Jingle Bells" in a mall two weeks before Thanksgiving is perverse. The problem of commercialism is the motive, and that can be recognized in how the thing is packaged. This differs from a hatred of capitalism, where the problem *is* the thing. Anything produced through capitalism is a tool of capitalism, so the things people most desire become the obstacles upholding capitalism most effectively. The notion of intrinsic merit is superfluous, since the only quality capitalism values is the perpetuation of itself. A hatred of capitalism is consciously pessimistic. It works from the premise that—if you are American—the very structure of your workaday reality is pernicious.

If one is trying to understand the idealistic difference between people who lived through the nineties and people born into the nineties, this is a good place to start. It was certainly possible to be against capitalism in the nineties, but much harder to have your opinion taken seriously (particularly since all the noncapitalist societies seemed to be collapsing or surrendering). It's still possible to take a modern stand against commercialism, but that argument runs counter to the creative aspiration of almost everything produced (the idea of a commercial product becoming "more commercial" is not a compromise but the self-evident goal). Part of this is fashion. The twenty-three-year-old activated personality railing against commercialism in 1993 might be emotionally identical to the twenty-three-year-old activated personality railing against capitalism in 2023. But even if that's true, the transitory worldviews they adopt get hammered into the transitory structures of society and interpreted by people who have no investment in the underlying conflict. In the same way that every historical era feels extraordinary within the moment it happens, the present-tense status of culture exists in a constant state of crisis, with the tenor of the crisis shaped by whatever people assume to be the cause. The assumption in the nineties was commercialism. The assumption this morning is capitalism. Philosophically, it's a meaningful disconnect. Yet both positions do share one common enemy: the psychological dominance of mass success.

When staring into the shallow mirror of time, there's an intellectual inclination to de-emphasize the significance of everything super-popular and prioritize off-kilter artifacts that emerged from the counterculture (often based on the paradoxical premise that the fringe invents the ideas that will become normative in the future, when they will no longer be viewed as significant). There's logic to that methodology, assuming the goal is graphing the path of a society over decades. But when you're still trapped inside a specific window of time, the prevailing forces are the forces that run the show. Anything that gets invented on the fringe is a reaction to whatever (or whoever) has aesthetic control.

There was a sense, coming out of the 1980s, that the difference between something that grew colossal and something that stayed local was a reflection of how commercial that thing *allowed* itself to become. Looking back, there's now a sense that the elevation of specific entities was the predictable result of a market controlled by the mundane appetites of whoever had the most disposable income. Both possibilities are impossible to disprove. Mass popularity is a zero-sum game that will always confirm whatever is offered as the explanation, so any espoused theory behind why certain things got huge is not that illuminating. But what's revelatory are the *values* that hugeness expressed, on purpose or by chance. Those values illustrate what the mass culture wanted, and those values represent what the counterculture wanted to reject.

There's no way to engage with a song like "Achy Breaky Heart" without fixating on the incongruity between the magnitude of its popularity and the overwhelming consensus that it was terrible. This was not a case of backlash, where people started making fun of a song as a result of its omnipresence—people ridiculed "Achy Breaky Heart" the first time they heard it, as it was climbing the charts, while they were dancing to it. Written by a Nashville songwriter named Don Von Tress in 1990, the title of the song was changed to "Don't Tell My Heart" when recorded by a country group called the Marcy Brothers in 1991. The Marcy Brothers altered the chorus, changing the words "achy" and "breaky" to the more formal "aching" and "breaking." Their version tanked. A year after that, an unknown singer in California named Billy Ray Cyrus released his own cover of the track, arranged almost identically to the Marcy Brothers' version but with the folksy syntax of the original composition. Its success was seismic.

"Achy Breaky Heart" became the first country single in almost ten years to sell a million copies. It hit not only number 1 on the country charts but number 4 on the *Billboard* pop charts, higher than the zenith of "Smells Like Teen Spirit." It reintroduced the phenomenon of line dancing, where people in bars would align in parallel rows on the dance floor and simultaneously mimic the same steps. The song itself was a chemical compound of sonic guile: It was musically and lyrically repetitive, with every chord change and verse laser-focused on catchiness and immediacy. Its singer was often classified as a one-hit wonder, although that's not true (Cyrus would ultimately have over thirty songs that cracked the charts). "Achy Breaky Heart" is sometimes considered a novelty tune, though that ignores its homogeneity (the song's themes and construction were rote interpretations of most mainstream country music from the period). The only novelty was its hugeness. And what it was, really, was an example of what happens when culture moves in two opposing directions at the same time.

Rock, despite its supremacy, was ideologically moving away from itself. The idea of chasing fame and trying to look sexy was suddenly embarrassing. Grunge musicians openly disdained the posturing of longhaired arena rock, most notably its relationship to masculinity. Kurt Cobain appeared on MTV's *Headbangers Ball* in 1991 wearing a yellow dress. The band Mudhoney made of fun of singers they saw "shirtless and flexing" like "a macho freak." But the public appetite for those qualities was still there, and country artists increasingly encroached upon the classic tropes of classic rock. Cyrus was a caricature of that migration: He wore his hair in a mullet, often performed in sleeveless shirts, and appeared to be more influenced by polished eighties power rock than the roots of country music. There was a level of calculated redness to his neck: It was erroneously publicized that he'd tried to cash a $1.6 million royalty check at his local bank's drive-through window. When he spoke, he talked like a rural Southerner: His Kentucky drawl defined him as country, and his vocal delivery was genre specific. But the packaging of "Achy Breaky Heart" translated to people who normally associated themselves as non-country fans.

"It's just a song that everybody can rock to," Cyrus would say. Traditionalists found his persona peculiar (during a '92 appearance on *Good Morning America*, Waylon Jennings cryptically speculated, "I think maybe his shoes are too tight"). But the landscape was shifting. The things casual consumers liked about "new country" were the same things casual consumers had liked about "old rock." The music itself was important, but secondary to the experience it offered and the lifestyle it valued. It proudly embraced what was no longer progressive. Cobain had grown up loving groups like Aerosmith and Led Zeppelin, made music in the same genre, and named one of his own songs "Aero Zeppelin." Yet someone like Cobain still came to believe that Aerosmith and Led Zeppelin were degrading.* Cyrus did not. His music sounded nothing like Led Zeppelin, but it had the same goal: universality, devoid of any reflection about what that meant or symbolized. Rock artists were becoming less willing to provide that sensibility, so country artists took it over.

The crossover of "Achy Breaky Heart" was a micro example. The macro example was Garth Brooks.

Garth Brooks was, by a broad margin, the biggest musical act of the decade. He would have been the biggest act of whatever decade he lived through, because Brooks is the biggest solo artist of all time. He released twelve albums during the nineties, and eight would eventually sell more than 10 million copies. His worst-selling release was a second attempt at a Christmas album that still went platinum. These statistics are both world-shattering and predictable: No musical act from any period was ever as unapologetically interested in raw numbers. Garth cared about money, but not as much as he cared about his reach. Citing his belief in "the Wal-Mart school of business," Brooks would slash the retail price of his late-nineties albums in order to generate mind-numbing opening-week sales. His emphasis was always on volume. When Brooks toured the world for 220 concerts in the middle of the decade, he capped the price of every ticket at $20. Though he almost certainly lost some short-term revenue by doing this, it guaranteed that every show was a 100 percent capacity sellout. The traditionally regional draw of country music was disconnected from his popularity: When he put on a free show in

---

*"Although I listened to Aerosmith and Led Zeppelin, and I really did enjoy some of the melodies they'd written, it took me so many years to realize that a lot of it had to do with sexism," Cobain said in 1993. "The way that they just wrote about their dicks and having sex."

Manhattan's Central Park, 980,000 people showed up.* It's challenging to come up with any two other nineties artists (from any musical genre) whose combined commercial impact equates to that of Brooks by himself.

What's curious, however, is how rarely Brooks is identified as an iconic nineties figure. His first album came out in spring of 1989, and he announced his (temporary, five-year) retirement in the fall of 2000. The nucleus of his career falls precisely within the decade's parameters. There's no misunderstanding about his dominance throughout this period (it sometimes seems like the main thing people know about him), and there's no better illustration of country's evolution into a surrogate for a worldview once defined by stadium rock: Though Garth's modernized version of honky-tonk was most musically reminiscent of George Strait, his live show was influenced by Kiss and his songcraft aspired to Billy Joel (two artists Brooks covered and often referenced). Brooks's relative lack of historical clout does not compute. Yet it's possible that this future disregard was already presupposed at the height of his success, which illogically propelled him further.

There's a long tradition of celebrities who are beloved for seeming "ordinary." Brooks is part of that lineage, and perhaps its apex predator. It started with the abject whiteness of his name: Garth. It seemed like a fictional name someone would select† for the explicit purpose of not seeming hip. He was enthusiastic and jovial, with the body of a former athlete who still played a little slow-pitch softball on the weekend (as a high school quarterback in rural Oklahoma, Brooks went 0-5 as a starter, but his right arm was still lively enough to throw the javelin for Oklahoma State). He always wore a hat because he was always going bald. But the quality that made Brooks most relatable was a kind of unforced, benevolent populism. His signature song,

---

*Or at least that's what Garth's publicity department claimed at the time. In actuality, you probably can't physically fit 980,000 fans into a concert at Central Park. But Simon & Garfunkel drew 600,000 people there in 1981, and Brooks seemingly pulled a bigger number than that.

†Brooks's first name is actually "Troyal," which was his dad's name. "Garth" is his middle name. In orchestra with the popularity of Dana Carvey's character from *Wayne's World*, there will likely never be another time period when the name "Garth" is so present in the mass culture.

the 1990 single "Friends in Low Places," was about a blue-collar jackass who shows up at his ex-girlfriend's black-tie wedding and makes a drunken toast about the failure of their relationship. It's absolutely a song about class. But what's unusual is the way it does not frame the affluent characters as fake or immoral, nor does it paint the narrator as sympathetic or extra-real. It's possible to impose those meanings onto the lyrics, but only if the listener wants those sentiments to be true. The literal message of "Friends in Low Places" is an *acceptance* of class difference, fortified by the suggestion that living in an "ivory tower" is not necessarily better than living in a dive bar. The payoff phrase is repeated in the chorus: "I'll be okay." Garth's version of populism did not pit the poor against the elite. Instead, it implied that the difference was immaterial, and that all people ultimately want the same ordinary things. He could somehow represent multiple personas at the same time. To his base, Brooks was an apolitical figure. There was no secondary meaning to loving an album like *No Fences* or *The Chase*. It didn't seem to matter that Brooks was more openly political than almost any major country artist of the period, or that his views did not represent the assumed conservatism of country listeners: His lyrics addressed domestic violence and gay rights, and the song "We Shall Be Free" was inspired by (and sympathetic to) the 1992 Los Angeles riots. He received no criticism for these opinions, nor did he receive credit.

There was, unsurprisingly, media confusion over how to contextualize what Brooks was doing (and the success he was experiencing). He appeared on the cover of *Rolling Stone*, but only once, in 1993. When citing the relationship between nineties country and seventies rock, Brooks offhandedly drew a comparison between himself and the Eagles. His point was about similarities in the music, but the upshot focused more on the discernment of his ambition. The fact that Brooks had graduated from college with a degree in advertising increased the skepticism.

"For years," pop critic Eric Weisbard wrote in *Spin*, "fans have been trying to explain to their 'urbane' friends how impressive Garth's music is." But later, in the same (mostly positive) album review, the writer admits he's "never been sure if Brooks is a complete sham or not" and questions the semiotic implications of Garth's CD covers. There was always a desire to analyze the bigness of Brooks as some kind of cultural unicorn, strategically capitalizing on anti-intellectual forces only Garth could see.

The real explanation was less complicated.

It was, in essence, a combination of three things. The first was taste: Unlike most creative people, Garth's personal taste in music naturally gravitated toward artists who were commercially huge. As a consequence, he never had to *construct* a hit—all he had to do was write songs that sounded the way he liked songs to sound. His most unabashedly radio-centric singles still felt like organic extensions of his own agency. That naturalism was amplified by his productivity: Throughout the nineties, the only year Brooks did not release an album was 1996. He was a workaholic who never allowed a glimmer of opportunity for another artist* to usurp his dominion. What mattered most, though, was his singularity of purpose: His only goal was to provide maximum entertainment to the largest possible audience at all possible times. Brooks was immune to the prevailing attitudes of the era; he did not view total commitment to the consumer as a compromise of his artistic credibility. Garth operated in a separate silo, disassociated from all other conceptual abstractions and cultural intersections. He appeared to have no interest in the signifiers of credibility, which made him difficult to criticize in any damaging way. It was easier for journalists to simply not take him seriously, despite his observable position as the most popular artist on Earth. The illogic of that response validated his approach. He didn't need anyone to certify what everyone already knew.

---

*The only performer to rival Garth during this time was Shania Twain, a Canadian artist whose synthesis of country and rock was completely unsubtle. Her albums *The Woman in Me* (from 1995) and *Come On Over* (1997) were cowritten and produced by Robert John "Mutt" Lange, a mercurial, high-gloss perfectionist best known for producing hard-rock acts like AC/DC and Def Leppard. Those two Twain albums would sell a combined 32 million copies. Twain and Lang married in 1993 and later divorced.

"A genius," jazz pianist Thelonious Monk once said, "is the one most like himself." By that definition, Brooks was the Wonder Bread genius of his generation. No musician so famous had ever seemed so comfortable with who he was. There was no tension between the art he wanted to provide and the art his audience expected.

But then, for reasons that will likely never be explained, he tried to go the other way.

The Garth empire finally took a hit in 1999, when Brooks became something other than himself in the goofiest way possible. For much of that year, Brooks dedicated himself to an alter ego named Chris Gaines, a fictional Australian alt-rock musician intended to serve as the main character in a never-released movie titled *The Lamb*. Brooks wore a wig and grew a soul patch. He recorded a soundtrack for the nonexistent movie and promoted it on *Saturday Night Live* (schizophrenically hosting the show as himself while performing musically as Gaines). The album of mid-tempo rock tracks went double platinum, a testament to Brooks's popularity. It was also the defining misstep of his career. Every possible analysis was negative. Was he trying to separate himself from country music? Was he trying to separate himself from country music, but without the integrity of real artistic risk? Was this proof of his previously invisible insecurity? Was it proof that his ego had extended beyond his skill? Was he so desperate to sell albums that he even wanted to sell them to people who didn't like his music? Whatever the true explanation was, it didn't matter. Brooks looked ridiculous. Which hadn't mattered before, but it mattered now, because now he looked ridiculous as someone who wasn't Garth Brooks.

The distinction between television at the end of the 1980s and television at the start of the new century was not about the way it looked or the way it was watched or the financial incentives behind why it was there. All those things did change, but the changes were secondary and incremental. High definition was introduced to the U.S. in 1998, but almost no one had an HDTV (ESPN didn't broadcast a game in hi-def until 2003). The earliest digital recording system, TiVo, wasn't readily available until 1999. People spent the nineties sitting through commercials, and streaming live programming on any device that wasn't a conventional television was pretty much off the table. For the viewer, the bodily experience of consuming TV stayed pretty much the same. What changed existentially was what TV was supposed to mean (and, in a few cases, what it actually meant).

The most noteworthy TV drama of the eighties* was *Dallas*, in part for the way it reflected the zeitgeist but mostly due to its sheer popularity. The 1980 episode of *Dallas* revealing who shot the program's main character was simultaneously watched by an estimated 83 million Americans at a time when there were only 226 million people in the entire country. *Dallas* finally went off the air in May of 1991. *The Sopranos* debuted on HBO in January of 1999 and became the model for what came to be called "prestige television," a designation that simply didn't exist when *Dallas* was cock of the walk. *Dallas* was important, but it wasn't prestigious at all.

Dallas was a CBS Friday night soap opera about Texas oil barons. It was considered a fun, juicy distraction and not all that different from *Dynasty*, the rival ABC drama about Denver-based oil barons airing on Wednesdays. The final episode of *Dallas* experienced a mild uptick in viewership but was generally ignored (many of the 83 million who'd watched in 1980 didn't even know the show was still being made in 1991). *The Sopranos* was also a fun distraction, though it was never described in those terms. A mob drama about family dynamics and psychotherapy, *The Sopranos* was taken seriously

---

*It should be noted that the most critically acclaimed TV show of the 1980s was probably *Hill Street Blues*, a cop show that was viewed as a quantum leap in terms of realism. Yet even the most positive reviews of *Hill Street Blues* were expressions of bewilderment over the fact that it wasn't idiotic. Writing a 1985 cover story for *TV Guide* (!), Joyce Carol Oates (!!) mentioned how *Hill Street Blues* was one of the only programs watched by her colleagues at Princeton (!!!) and that it was an exception to the baseline rule of television, which was that TV was "entertaining, often highly diverting, but not intellectually or emotionally stimulating."

in a manner previously reserved only for theatrical film, ushering in the (previously unfathomable) notion that the medium of TV might now be superior to the medium of cinema. After the finale of *The Sopranos* aired in 2007, viewers and critics analyzed the episode's final ten seconds for the next ten years.

So what changed from 1991 to 1999?

The long answer is complicated. But there's also a short answer, although that's even more convoluted than the long one: the validity of emotionally investing in the unreal.

Almost everything about how television was perceived in the early nineties can be encapsulated within one three-second clip from the fourth season of *Seinfeld*. The premise of the two-part episode, titled "The Pitch," is built around its two main characters, Jerry and George, pitching a sitcom to NBC based on the banality of their day-to-day lives. The brilliance of the concept was the depth of its meta-commentary: *Seinfeld* was an NBC sitcom based on the day-to-day banality of Jerry Seinfeld and Larry David, who were now concocting a story line where the fictional versions of themselves were trying to concoct a fictional version of their already fictional life. This level of self-awareness was virtually nonexistent in the television topography of the time. It was legitimately innovative. But the episode's make-or-break moment comes from an exchange between George (whose character was based on David) and Russell Dalrymple, the fictional NBC president (based on the real-life NBC executive Warren Littlefield). George is explaining the potential show to NBC and adamantly insisting the program will be "about nothing." There will be no stories and no conflicts. At one point, he suggests the show may feature characters silently reading. The point, according to George, is that this will be a TV show where nothing happens, ever.

"Well, why am I watching it?" asks Dalrymple.

"Because it's on TV," replies George.

While it seems like George is being obtuse, he's deftly describing the reasonable way to think about television throughout the nineties. It had the potential to be almost anything, and many of the previous creative restrictions were evaporating. But how that freedom was used was almost immaterial. The quality of the content was irrelevant.

"Remember, it's just TV," future podcaster Marc Maron wrote in a 1993 essay about the expansion of cable systems. "It was created to sell stuff, to distract." The living room television was still, in the words of former FCC commissioner Mark Fowler, "just another appliance. It's a toaster with pictures." You turned it on and watched whatever it gave you. The level of exposure was very high and the expectations were very low. It was a source of entertainment when no better entertainment was available, which was most of the time.

○ ○ ○

The past is a mental junkyard, filled with memories no one remembers. If someone glances at the *Billboard* singles chart from any random week of the nineties, they will always find a handful of songs that were extremely popular before being wholly erased from the historical record. That process makes sense: The *Billboard* song chart contains one hundred "hot" songs that change every week, so a music fan who dislikes Top 40 radio might not hear a noteworthy single even once. Movie theaters shuffle the decks every weekend. Sales for a high-profile novel might stall at ten thousand copies before the book goes out of print five years after it was published. Most popular entertainment is designed to be niche and disposable. What separated nineties TV from this junkyard was the scale—the massive number of people who regularly watched insignificant programs before involuntarily erasing them from their own brain.

During the 1991–92 ratings season, just before *Seinfeld* aired "The Pitch," the sitcom *Room for Two* was the tenth-highest-rated show on television. *Room for Two* starred Patricia Heaton (who'd later costar on *Everybody Loves Raymond*) and Linda Lavin (previously starring in the long-running sitcom *Alice*). *Room for Two* was on ABC for two seasons, and its first season was

seven episodes. Its Nielsen rating during that year was 16.7, with every ratings point representing 1 percent of American TV households. There were
just over 95 million U.S. households in 1992, and roughly 98 percent had at
least one television. This means every episode of *Room for Two* averaged a
bare minimum of 15.5 million viewers. It ranked just behind the CBS sitcom
Major Dad, which pulled an even larger audience over the span of a full
twenty-four-week schedule. Yet if a five-hundred-page encyclopedia about
the history of television were written today, neither of these shows would be
mentioned, even in passing. Their historical weight is less than zero. So what
does it mean that—every week—these immaterial shows were experienced
by more people than that aforementioned finale of *The Sopranos*?

It means George Costanza was correct.

Television in this period was still dictated by the constraints of time and
the boundaries of available space. Its main utility was just being around.
There was an accepted passivity to its consumption. The most critical factor
within the introduction of any TV pilot was whatever show immediately preceded it, based on the principle that people would be too lazy to change the
channel. An extremely popular show like *Seinfeld*, airing on the same night
as the equally popular *Friends*, was used in this capacity constantly. The
Kirstie Alley vehicle *Veronica's Closet*, when packaged in NBC's Thursday
night lineup, could sustain a weekly audience of 24 million viewers. When it
was moved to Monday, its viewership dropped to 8 million. *The Naked Truth*,
a comedy about a tabloid newspaper starring Téa Leoni, was a middling success at ABC before moving to NBC in 1997 and getting slotted directly after
Seinfeld. It instantly became the country's fourth most popular program
but was canceled the following year. The reason for its cancellation didn't
matter, since virtually anything that was placed in that specific time slot
would succeed at roughly the same level. If NBC actually had created a show
that was just people quietly reading magazines and inserted it after *Seinfeld*,
it absolutely would have been watched by 20 million people (at least for one
episode).

In the post-*Sopranos* universe, television became a space for creative singularity. The goal from showrunners was to create something that had never been seen on TV before. In the seventies and eighties, network television had been structured around *types* of shows ("This is our Western, this is our hospital drama, this is our family sitcom, this is our ribald sitcom to air an hour after the family sitcom," etc.). The early nineties were an evolved extension of the eighties. It wasn't just the type of show that mattered. It was the *feel* of the show. It was a little like FM radio from the late seventies, where the goal was to program music that was superficially distinctive, yet recorded and produced with the same taste and composition, generating the sensation of one endless song (in hopes that the listener would never change the station). The force driving this trend was a newfound recognition among advertisers: Not all television viewers were equal. The size of the audience mattered, but not as much as who that audience was. One twenty-five-year-old living in a city was worth two rural sixty-five-year-olds. In 1995, a thirty-second commercial on the Angela Lansbury mystery show *Murder, She Wrote* cost $115,000. *Murder, She Wrote* was in its eleventh season and still ranked among the ten most popular programs in America. But airing the same thirty-second commercial on *The Single Guy*, an affable *Seinfeld* knockoff that lasted just two seasons, cost $310,000. *The Single Guy* was worth more because it aired directly after *Seinfeld*, and NBC had placed it there because it had the right feel for Thursday night. Which, somewhat confusingly, does not mean it felt like *Seinfeld*. It means it felt like *Friends*.

Though tried many times, attempts at replicating the "feel" of *Seinfeld* always proved unworkable. Its comedic perspective was too eccentric and too personal to reproduce on purpose. *Seinfeld* managed to thread an incongruous needle—its characters were misanthropic without being unlikable. Shows that hoped to mirror the tone (such as ABC's *It's Like, You Know . . .*) inexorably skewed too much in either direction. As *Seinfeld* progressed, there was also an increased emphasis on absurdist scenarios that only paid off if the viewer had already accepted that these fake characters were real people.

To anyone outside of that bubble, the humor would seem impenetrable. The mid-nineties British sketch show *Mash and Peas* once made a parody of *Seinfeld* that was retitled *I'm Bland . . . Yet All My Friends Are Krazy*. The premise of the sketch was that "Jerry" repeated boring references to losing his keys while the rest of the ensemble shouted nonsensical catchphrases and behaved psychotically. It bore no resemblance to what the real program was like, yet perfectly captured how tedious and bewildering its comedic sophistication might look to anyone who didn't already know what they were supposed to be seeing. The tone of *Seinfeld* only worked on *Seinfeld*. Copies did not resemble the original.

But with *Friends*, tonal replication was plausible.

Because *Seinfeld* and *Friends* were both hugely popular series that aired on the same network on the same night, they will always be connected. If viewed cursorily, the similarities appear to outweigh the differences: Both were about white people preoccupied with dating, set in New York but filmed in Los Angeles. *Friends* would never have been made if *Seinfeld* weren't already around. The "feel," however, was different. The feel of *Friends* became the template for what advertisers wanted. It checked all the necessary boxes, and some of those boxes were incredibly specific.

Friends was about six friends, three male and three female, who lived in the West Village. It lasted ten years. When it debuted in 1994, the characters were all supposedly between the ages of twenty-four and twenty-seven, although they seemed slightly older. When the show concluded, they were all supposedly between the ages of thirty-four and thirty-seven but behaved like people slightly younger. In spirit, they were all eternally twenty-nine. The ethos of the series was the "in between" intricacy of early adulthood, when your friends are more important than your family and you've yet to start a family of your own. It was, in some obvious ways, a manifestation of social trends—Americans were marrying later in life and rejecting the onset of traditional adult responsibilities. But this wasn't as straightforward as attracting twentysomething viewers by making a show about twentysomething people.

Friends became the model for how to pinpoint generational concerns without directly recognizing that generations exist. The feel of *Friends* was a depiction of the present moment, filtered through the prism of a timeless reality.

The year before *Friends* came into being, a sitcom called *Living Single* had debuted on Fox. It was about six young adults, two male and four female (all of whom were Black), living in Brooklyn. In subsequent years, it has become fashionable to argue that *Friends* was merely the gentrified, Caucasian rip-off of *Living Single*, designed for a more coveted advertising demo (in 1996, when *Friends* was the country's third most popular show overall, it ranked only ninety-ninth within Black households). Some of the parallels are hard to discount. One of the less obvious ones was the way both programs aggressively embraced modernity, but only as an abstraction. A key line from the *Living Single* opening theme song was "In a nineties kind of world / I'm glad I got my girls." What is meant by "a nineties kind of world" is never explained, by the song or by the show. The implication is that the characters are having experiences that could only be happening *right now*, despite the fact that those experiences were not necessarily tied to anything that was happening in the nonfictional universe.

Friends worked the same way. Outside of a running gag about the gratuitous TV series *Baywatch*, one memorable 1995 episode about a Hootie and the Blowfish concert, and an odd 1998 plotline referencing the Angela Bassett film *How Stella Got Her Groove Back*, it tended to reside in a generic universe that did not intersect with the cultural moment. The character of Joey was a soap actor whose idol was Susan Lucci, a daytime actress on *All My Children* who'd already been famous for twenty years. The cast did not purposefully dress in a way that tied them to the time period, although sometimes that happened by accident (oversized shirts were the norm). They pushed culture more than they pulled at it (when Jennifer Aniston cut her hair in a layered bob, the style was dubbed "the Rachel" after the name of her character and became the hottest haircut in the country). It's rare for any episode of *Friends* to inform the viewer of when the events are supposedly unfolding. Yet the series' overall trajectory is a catalog of what would now be seen as a collection of cliché Gen X concerns, mainstreamed through avatars who didn't look or sound like cliché Gen Xers. Almost every episode involves the friends sitting around a coffee shop* in the middle of the day. Only one character (Chandler, played by Matthew Perry) consistently holds a conventional office job, and it's depicted as a robotic prison sentence. Their expressed anxieties don't match the condition of their lives—everyone is always struggling, despite their physical attractiveness and their ability to live in upscale Manhattan apartments no struggling person could afford. Most critically, *Friends* was continually about *longing*: the longing for love, the longing for success, and the longing for meaningful relationships that aren't based on previous definitions of meaning. *Friends* trafficked in the very nineties belief that the only difference between friendship and romance is a physical barrier, and that the best person to sleep with is probably your best friend (and by the series finale, four of the six single friends had morphed into two sets of couples).

This dissonance was the *Friends* "feel" that other shows desperately wanted to copy: the ability to immerse itself in emerging generational dilemmas, performed by characters who did not readily identify as members of that generation. Granted, the specific enormity of *Friends* was a product of the chemistry between the actors and the depth with which those personalities resonated (in 2002, the six were able to negotiate a deal that paid each of them $1 million per episode, a concession by NBC that the show wouldn't work without every individual component intact). But the separation of real

---

*The fictional *Friends* coffee shop, an establishment called Central Perk, is an example of how the semiotics of the present moment rarely align with the way that moment will be reanimated in the future. If a contemporary TV show was retroactively designing a "mid-1990s coffee shop," it would make the place either much cooler or much more corporate than the Central Perk of *Friends*. The shop would need to say something about the people who patronized it. But the shop on *Friends* is exactly in between: an uninteresting, comfortable place to get a muffin in the middle of the afternoon, but not a Starbucks-like chain or a comedic signifier of wealth or class or soullessness. Central Perk was created to be the most neutral establishment possible. It represents nothing. It could exist at any time, in almost any city.

time from cultural timeliness mattered. These were thoroughly modern people, but they shopped at Pottery Barn. None of the characters were supposed to be cool, so the audience didn't need to be cool in order to understand why they were appealing. They were not products of their time; they were products within time. *Friends* directly addressed the insecure ideologies of the nineties without acknowledging that the nineties had a meaning, or even that "the nineties" were a thing that was happening. It was casual modernity.

○ ○ ○

Friends, *Seinfeld*, and a revolving door of texturally similar sitcoms all aired on Thursday, an authoritarian night of entertainment NBC branded as "Must See TV." Thursday was considered an especially attractive evening to advertisers, based on the assumption that upwardly mobile young people would stay home on a Thursday but go out on the weekend. These were the most valuable shows occupying the most valuable space. At its high point, 75 million people watched some portion of NBC's Thursday night programming almost every week.

The cleanup hitter in the "Must See" lineup was *ER*, an intense medical drama based on a twenty-year-old screenplay by Michael Crichton (written when he was still a medical student) and backed by Steven Spielberg. It was popular and formally unorthodox—one episode was broadcast live, another was presented in reverse, and the penultimate episode of the first season was directed by Quentin Tarantino. Thursday night was also the original launching pad for *Frasier*, a spin-off from *Cheers*. Starring Kelsey Grammer and rooted around the life of a psychiatrist hosting a Seattle-based radio show, *Frasier* is (technically) the most critically lauded sitcom of the late twentieth century, winning the Emmy for Outstanding Comedy Series in five consecutive years. If a modern TV series with the viewership and acclaim of *ER* or *Frasier* emerged in the twenty-first century, it would automatically be placed in the "prestige" category of television. But the principal memories of these two shows prove how indifferently TV was taken in the nineties, even by those most invested in it.

The cast of *ER*, when considered in total, is a remarkable collection of acting talent. Yet it's mostly a list of people who used *ER* to become movie stars (most obviously George Clooney), journeyman film actors who could be lead performers only if they switched to TV (most notably Anthony Edwards), and a host of individuals trying to raise their profile in the hope of becoming character actors in midlevel theatrical movies. Despite its reach and respect, *ER* was either the place you were going to leave or the place you ended up. When Tarantino agreed to direct his episode, there was bemused confusion over his willingness to work in a second-rate medium (he'd won an Oscar for *Pulp Fiction* just two months before). The legacy of *Frasier* is even more baffling. It was, relative to just about every other extension of ultra-mass media, unabashedly highbrow. It had little relationship to *Cheers*, a blue-collar show latently obsessed with comedic erudition; *Frasier* was a white-collar show openly obsessed with intellectual sophistication. Characters casually joked about Jungian philosophy, Sergei Rachmaninoff, and Alfred, Lord Tennyson. The driving conceit was almost a comedy of manners, where uptight snootiness collided with the coarseness of middle-class life. It was cleverly written and smartly cast. But its dynastic grip on critics and Emmy voters galvanized a paradox: *Frasier* was seen as brilliant television because it focused on characters who would never watch television. Its self-loathing elitism was proof of its intelligence.

In 1997, the alt-rock band Harvey Danger had a minor hit with the song "Flagpole Sitta." One of the lines from the song was, "And I don't even own a TV," which was a phrase a certain kind of person used to say a lot during this era. It was a sign of pretension, but also code for brainpower and maturity—a person without a television was not a slave to passivity, since passivity was the only possible outcome from interacting with a medium whose job was to fill time. Though accepted as true by virtually every knee-jerk intellectual of the time, it's increasingly difficult to understand why TV was considered so inferior to not just film, but to almost every other variety of entertainment from this era. The prevalence of that dismissive view clearly had no relationship to its popularity—statistically speaking, television was more popular than everything. But here again: In the nineties, that was its own kind of problem. If everyone enjoyed something, how good could it possibly be?

○ ○ ○

The economic story of the movie *Titanic*, like the historical event the movie was based upon, is a story almost everyone knows, assuming we pretend "knowing the story" means "knowing how it ends." It's hard to imagine a person aware of *Titanic* (the film) without some awareness of how popular and pervasive it almost instantly became. It would be no different from knowing that *Titanic* (the boat) had been a luxury British passenger ship without any knowledge that it also hit an iceberg. *Titanic* earned $1.8 billion at the box office, making it the highest-grossing movie ever produced. Theatrical re-releases eventually pushed the final gross closer to $2.2 billion. Even without the factor of inflation, those numbers feel unreal. What's even kookier is that fiscal statistics slightly underrate the film's social footprint. There was a movie culture pre-*Titanic* and a different kind of movie culture post-*Titanic*. It had looked like the world of cinema was moving one way, but then it moved back.

Titanic was released in 1997, twenty years after *Star Wars*. Beyond the ability to generate revenue, the two pictures share a creative commonality: If one's only exposure to either film were the pages of the script, the only conclusion one could draw is that this movie must be terrible. And in both cases, such a conclusion would miss the point. Movies that succeed on this scale work through a three-step process, where dialogue is an inessential part of the equation. Step one is the expectation the moviegoer brings into the theater (i.e., an aspiration that the movie will transcend regular life and generate a heavy emotional resonance). Step two is the movie itself, which must be wholly experiential (i.e., visually arresting and morally clear). Step three is the ecstatic, cultic response to step two's success at fulfilling the expectations outlined in step one. It's an inverted equation. It requires a lot of unconscious mental work before and after the film is viewed, while demanding a conscious rejection of critical thinking while the movie is on the screen.

When this process works, it blows people away. It prompts a certain type of consumer to pay for the same movie dozens and dozens of times. *Star Wars* did this so effectively that it changed the calculus of the entire entertainment industry, and lots of eighties mass culture (cinematic and otherwise) was launched through some tweaked version of the *Star Wars* model. There was, however, a growing attitude in the nineties that this philosophy had extended beyond reason, and not just for the deadening effect it was having on art. It had become fiscally unwise. The cost of producing a standalone blockbuster was escalating faster than any across-the-board increases in box office receipts. Investing $100 million into one film was a risk. Investing $50 to $70 million in multiple films was a safer hedge.

The budget for *Titanic* was $200 million.

It seemed like such a terrible idea.

Knowing what we know now, it's difficult to think about *Titanic* as a mistake, even though that was the consensus up until it opened that December. Part of the suspicion was over the inflexible inevitability of the plot—how do you make a story dramatic if absolutely everyone knows how the story will end? Its potential success seemed to require an unrealistic level of public interest in an event from 1912. The other alleged deathblow was the film's relationship to water. In 1995, Kevin Costner had starred in (and essentially controlled) *Waterworld*, a dystopian portrait of Earth after the melting of the polar ice caps. Prior to *Titanic*, it was the most expensive film ever made. And though *Waterworld* eventually turned a profit internationally, it was seen as a humiliating failure, blamed in part on the logistics of making a movie dependent on seawater. That concern was compounded by the single-minded oceanic obsession of *Titanic* director James Cameron. Cameron's artistic commitment to water cannot be overstated. In order to get footage of the actual *Titanic* shipwreck, he and a film crew dove 12,500 feet to the floor of the Atlantic Ocean—and not just once, but twelve times. He did this in 1995, before he'd even started writing the *Titanic* screenplay. Cameron was well established as a major action director, best known for the first two *Terminator* films and a previous underwater epic from 1989, *The Abyss*. He had a reputation as a control freak, a real-life embodiment of the self-absorbed Hollywood director who refuses to compromise on anything impinging upon his vision. He also had a serial tendency to fall in love with his female collaborators, only to lose romantic interest when he changed projects. "*Titanic* was the mistress he left me for," said actress Linda Hamilton, a woman who'd had the good fortune of starring in both *Terminator* films and the misfortune of serving as Cameron's fourth wife. Decades later, these qualities are sometimes used as evidence of Cameron's drive and perfectionism; in retrospect, it does seem obvious that Cameron was the only tyrant who could have brought *Titanic* to life. But at the time, his arrogance did not instill trust. He appeared to be wasting money on purpose (in scenes where characters on the ship ate caviar, Cameron served the actors actual beluga caviar). It was assumed the future memory of *Titanic* would be closer to *Heaven's Gate* than *Star Wars*.

The film was scheduled for release in July of '97. That didn't happen. The production was always behind schedule. It finally appeared in U.S. theaters just before Christmas, with a theatrical running time of three hours and fourteen minutes. The movie's interminable length was understood to be the final spine-snapping straw—with that running time, most movie houses could only show *Titanic* once an evening (as opposed to the usual twice), automatically slicing the maximum size of its nightly audience in half. Cameron privately believed the movie would lose around $100 million. But then it came out. The reviews were good, the word of mouth was fantastic, and people just kept seeing it, over and over again. It was the most popular movie in America for fifteen consecutive weeks and stayed in the top ten for another three months after that. The song played over the closing credits, Celine Dion's "My Heart Will Go On," was the number 1 single in twenty different countries. *Titanic* was nominated for fourteen Academy Awards and won eleven. While accepting the award for Best Director, Cameron quoted the most embarrassing line of dialogue from his own script: "I'm the king of the world!" Had this come from almost any other nineties figure, that would have seemed like self-deprecating irony. Coming from Cameron, it was not.

○ ○ ○

The magnitude of *Titanic*'s success confirms that much of how the nineties are explained in retrospect can only be applied intermittently. The traits that made *Titanic* colossal contradict the broad characterizations of the era. This doesn't mean those broad characterizations were wrong. It just means they were always possible to ignore, and that certain desires are immune to transformation.

The mechanical narrative of *Titanic* is about the sinking of an unsinkable ship. The human narrative is about a rich girl who falls in love with a poor boy, chronicled through the McGuffin of a blue diamond necklace lost at sea. The female lead was twenty-two-year-old Kate Winslet, and the performance made her a star. She would become the most decorated actresses of her generation. It is, however, still possible to imagine *Titanic*'s trajectory with someone else as the lead actress. It's not possible to imagine such a trajectory without the presence of Leonardo DiCaprio. The mania surrounding DiCaprio in the wake of *Titanic* was astronomical, bordering on unsettling. His unprecedented ascendance was the product of two divergent phenomena: He was the last actor to achieve superstardom as a vestige of the monolithic Hollywood system and the first actor to become a megastar within the emerging paradigm of postmodern celebrity. He will always be the only person to have both of those experiences at the same time.

Prior to *Titanic*, DiCaprio was just a good, young actor. He had an ectomorphic body, an unthreatening demeanor, and a playful intensity that translated as confidence. He'd received positive attention for portraying a mentally impaired teenager in 1993's *What's Eating Gilbert Grape*. In 1996, he starred with Claire Danes in the stylized Shakespearean adaptation *Romeo + Juliet*, which officially pushed him into the category of "heartthrob." He was a logical choice for the male lead in *Titanic* (Matthew McConaughey was the only other significant contender), and his subsequent performance was fine (although, unlike Winslet, he wasn't nominated for an acting Oscar). But the response from audiences was so overwhelming that part of covering *Titanic* inevitably became an exercise in trying to explain why people were so obsessed with Leonardo DiCaprio. Article after article emphasized how teenage girls were seeing the movie multiple times, a box office phenomenon previously associated with adolescent boys. DiCaprio was twenty-three, but he looked younger and acted older. There was also this idea—impossible to prove or disprove—that the perception of the character DiCaprio played and the perception of the person he actually was had morphed into a singular entity, and that the consumption of *Titanic* was simply the means for consuming its main actor. Instead of buying a ticket to *Titanic* and seeing DiCaprio, it was as if kids were buying a ticket to DiCaprio, who happened to be inside a movie called *Titanic*. He was bigger than the biggest movie of all time. And what's noteworthy about this was not that it happened, but what DiCaprio did to sustain and expand this hyperbolic level of popularity: almost nothing.

DiCaprio was not a recluse. He participated in all the perfunctory functions expected of someone promoting a movie, he showed up at the various award shows, and he led an active social life.* But he did very little in terms of self-marketing. He rarely gave interviews and appeared in only five movies in the six years following *Titanic* (one of which was a small role in Woody Allen's *Celebrity*). He carried himself like a star from the distant past—an enigmatic, larger-than-life chimera who revealed little about himself or his ambitions. What had changed was the amount of people who now did that work for him. In a 1998 story headlined "Loving Leo," *The Boston Globe* described a new metric for measuring popularity:

> Meanwhile, on the teen message boards of America Online, there are more than 30,000 postings from young subscribers pertaining to DiCaprio. The next highest number for any star, teenage actor Jonathan Taylor Thomas, is 15.

That second statistic is obviously (and absurdly) incorrect. It's mostly evidence of how new and confusing the internet still was in 1998, when a mistake so egregious could go unnoticed by a major metro newspaper and all the smaller papers that reprinted it in syndication (the story hit the AP wire and ran uncorrected all over the country). It's entirely possible the newspaper copy editors proofreading the article had never heard of AOL chat rooms and had little idea what "postings" even referred to. Yet if we assume the actual number of posts for *Home Improvement* star Thomas was 15,000 (instead of 15), it would still mean DiCaprio was twice as popular among this nascent variety of adolescent who saw fandom as a responsibility. It wasn't enough to cut out a photo of DiCaprio from *Tiger Beat* and tape it to your

---

*Throughout this period, adult gossip about DiCaprio focused on his leadership of the "Pussy Posse," a pack of young performers (including Leo's best friend Tobey Maguire, magician David Blaine, and future *Entourage* star Kevin Connolly) who spent their evenings carousing in the nightclubs and bars of New York and Los Angeles. An improvisational, black-and-white, *Clerks*-like film titled *Don's Plum* involved several of these people, all playing fictionalized versions of themselves. Set in a diner, it was mostly shot in one night, but the movie was legally blocked from North American release by DiCaprio and Maguire (who found the final product embarrassing and problematic).

bedroom wall—you also needed to discuss him in a public forum, promote him to like-minded strangers, and argue for his cultural supremacy. Every day, DiCaprio was analyzed online with a rigor and enthusiasm conventional journalists would have never afforded any performer who predominantly appealed to kids. No detail about his life was irrelevant. The *Globe* story notes that one of the hot issues of contention on AOL message boards was nebulous concern over DiCaprio's sexual orientation, a debate based on no information whatsoever. "I think he might be bisexual," said one of the teens interviewed for the story, "because, like, in this one picture of him I saw, he had his shirt open in the middle. It just didn't look right."

DiCaprio's follow-up film to *Titanic* was the seventeenth-century costume drama *The Man in the Iron Mask*. The budget was $35 million. Widely perceived as awful, its box office revenue was still a staggering $183 million. Unlike most teen icons, DiCaprio's leverage as a cinematic powerbroker decreased only negligibly over the next twenty years. He appeared in fewer movies than most of his peers, but any appearance by DiCaprio automatically qualified a picture as substantial. *Titanic* made him the kind of perpetual movie star that was supposedly a remnant of a different age—the untouchable, unknowable playboy who can only be understood through the scant movie roles he elects to accept. His career is both a contradiction of what is assumed about modern stardom and a living example of how many of those assumptions are created by a media complex that willfully misunderstands what consumers actually want. Which, in all probability, is the easiest way to comprehend why *Titanic* was the most successful movie of the century.

What now seems most "interesting" about nineties movie culture is all the movies that explicitly *tried to be interesting*, along with an arbitrary collection of high-concept popcorn films that have been recontextualized *to seem interesting* when viewed in a scholarly way. The former category encompasses the upsurge of independent cinema and the exploration of previously ignored perspectives (these are films like 1999's *Boys Don't Cry* and 1998's *Smoke*

Signals). The latter category comprises ostensibly dumb movies that developed camp followings (1991's *Point Break*, 1995's *Showgirls*) and over-the-top political allegories (such as 1997's *Starship Troopers*). Yet the single most interesting thing about *Titanic* is its total commitment to expressing nothing that could be construed as interesting, now or then. Convention is never broken. The class dynamics are primitive and devoid of insight. The characters are (at best) two-dimensional templates. The deepest moments of emotion could have been sequenced by a computer. *Titanic* is an example of what British academic Sean Cubitt calls "neobaroque cinema," an escapist style of filmmaking prioritizing technical execution over everything else. The on-screen characters behave predictably, placed within a universe where their behavior is predetermined (*Titanic* is essentially a three-hour flashback). They exist to support the completion of their inescapable doom. Their only job is to go down with the ship. What's impressive about *Titanic* is the architecture—a compliment that feels like denigration. But it isn't. *Titanic* tapped into the reservoir of industry realities everyone always claims to concede while continually refusing to fully accept: Some people want entertainment to challenge them, but most people don't. Some people care about acting, but more people care about actors. Some people see computerized visual spectacle as a distraction from cinematic art, but most people consider visual spectacle to be the art form's central purpose.

Titanic took these truths farther than any film of its era. Cameron's hubris was validated in totality. It was never a terrible idea. It was just an uninteresting one, which is what was necessary for *Titanic* to become what it became.

[giving the people what they want, except that they don't]

MEET JOE BLACK WAS RELEASED IN THEATERS IN NOVEMBER OF 1998. Starring Brad Pitt as Death and lasting more than three hours, it was a lackluster romance with elements of supernatural realism. The only memorable scene involves Pitt being struck by both a minivan and a taxicab within the span of twenty-four frames. It cost $90 million to make and earned $44 million domestically, which would normally define it as a forgettable flop. But *Meet Joe Black* holds a strange cinematic distinction: It is almost certainly the all-time highest-grossing movie among ticket buyers who did not watch one minute of the film.

Before screenings of *Meet Joe Black*, movie houses across the country debuted the 131-second trailer for *The Phantom Menace*, the first prequel to the original *Star Wars* trilogy, slated for the summer of 1999. The result was a phenomenon that had never happened before and hadn't even been imagined as a prospect: There were numerous reports of people buying full-priced tickets for *Meet Joe Black*,* watching the *Phantom Menace* trailer, and then immediately exiting the theater.

---

*The *Phantom Menace* trailer was also shown before two other 1998 movies, *The Waterboy* and *The Siege*. But *Meet Joe Black* is the only film really connected to this specific phenomenon. *The Waterboy* was an Adam Sandler teen movie that was hugely successful on its own "merit," whatever that term is supposed to signify in this instance. *The Siege* was a lackluster action movie that's most remembered for being offensive to Arab people, although it seems plausible that a *Star Wars* fan might have wanted to see what it was before getting up and going home. *Meet Joe Black* is the outlier, as it was a high-profile production that was long, slow, and not geared toward the type of person who cares about Wookiees.

"We've never heard of a trailer packing people into a theater," Paul Dergarabedian told *The New York Times*. Dergarabedian was president of Exhibitor Relations, a company analyzing box office performance. "It's a precedent-setting event."

It's unknown how many ticket buyers actually did this, or whether all the articles claiming the practice was widespread were exaggerations (in '98, any trend story in *The New York Times* was challenging for readers to contradict, so it was automatically assumed to be accurate). But it certainly *felt* like a reasonable possibility, pretty much everywhere in North America. Nobody questioned it. Pre-release anticipation for *The Phantom Menace* was so unlike every previous version of expectation that no response was beyond the pale. In Hollywood, *Star Wars* superfans started living in tents on the sidewalk outside of movie theaters, lining up for the chance to buy tickets six weeks before opening night. This was even stupider than it sounds: At the time, no theater chain in the country had definitively secured the rights to show *The Phantom Menace*. It was possible—and somehow unsurprising—that people were living on the street in order to buy tickets for a movie that might not even be available.

The fervor surrounding *The Phantom Menace* was an amalgamation of several obvious factors: Here was a canonical extension of the late twentieth century's most popular entity, written and directed by the same man (George Lucas) who'd come up with the original idea, delivered to a willfully unhinged fan base that had waited fifteen years for a movie they'd long assumed would never happen. The fact that it eventually earned over $1 billion is an afterthought that barely warrants mention (anything less would qualify as fiscally disappointing). What matters more is what *The Phantom Menace* has come to represent: the saddest repudiation—and the harshest confirmation—of the entire Generation X ethos.

The pop culture lionized by young adults of the nineties was often based on a myth: the dogmatic belief that things they'd loved as children had always been appreciated with adult minds. There was a misguided notion that the populist esoterica of the seventies that had come to signify kitschy subversion—the daredevil Evel Knievel, the sitcom *Good Times*, the pop band ABBA—had *always* been seen and experienced in the same way they were now being recalled in retrospect. To classify this as simple "nostalgia" isn't quite accurate, because the process was proactive and methodical; the goal, it seemed, was to increase the intellectual value of bygone consumer art in order to make it match the emotional resonance that had been there all along. There is no better example of this than the original 1977 *Star Wars*. So much time and effort had been invested in the *Star Wars* obsession that the film was mentally reimagined as something it never was: a movie about human emotion, made for adult humans. When *The Phantom Menace* finally arrived, people who'd been ten years old in 1977 were now thirty-two. And what those thirty-two-year-olds saw was a slow retread of the original film, loaded with computerized special effects that were more sophisticated but less revelatory. The movie was not good. That, however, was not the problem. The problem was that *The Phantom Menace* forced people to realize they'd been betrayed by the falseness of their own constructed memories.

Movie critics disliked *The Phantom Menace*, but diehards hated it more. The easiest, laziest detail to blame was the introduction of a character named Jar Jar Binks. A semi-aquatic humanoid Trachodon with bunny ears, Jar Jar Binks was the first exclusively CGI character in movie history and unilaterally perceived as annoying, except by those more concerned with the possibility that he was racist. To some, Jar Jar epitomized the coldest view of George Lucas as an auteur—a technical taskmaster who preferred designing actors on a computer so that he'd never have to confront living people with actual feelings.

It was an intriguing personality critique, albeit highly unfair. Lucas had tried pretty goddamn hard to satisfy an entire generation of strangers who likely wouldn't have been satisfied by anything he delivered. Did such a mean-spirited categorization bother him?

Maybe. But not really.

"I'm sorry if they don't like it," said Lucas. "They should go back and see *The Matrix*."

10 A Two-Dimensional Fourth Dimension

TITANIC **WAS THE ECONOMIC CHAMPION OF NINETIES HOLLYWOOD, VERIFIED** through box office statistics. The most consistently successful star was Tom Hanks, though cases could be made for Mel Gibson, Tom Cruise, Denzel Washington, or Julia Roberts. Quentin Tarantino was the signature director, a skewed designation that's more debatable; either *Slacker* or *Fight Club* could be justifiably tagged as the decade's most generationally edifying film, though that kind of classification is obviously subjective. There are many ways to get different answers by looking at the same things. But when considered through the prism of *all* possible contexts, both within the year of its release and all the years that followed, it's hard to claim any movie from this period had as much wide-ranging significance as *The Matrix*. It dominates the category so decisively that it can be appreciated without even being watched.

The Matrix was a sci-fi action film about a computer-simulated world constructed during a war between humans and self-aware computers. The movie is a series of interlocking contradictions that should not equate to the blockbuster it became. It was written and directed by Lilly and Lana Wachowski, who were still living in 1999 as men. Their eventual gender transition is now the most glaring subtext to *The Matrix*, directly illustrated when the story's main character has to choose between swallowing a blue pill (which would allow him to continue living a false, fabricated life) and swallowing a red pill (allowing him to experience physical existence as it actually is). The metaphoric meaning of this decision has been projected back upon the Wachowski siblings, prompting Lilly to eventually admit that this was, in fact, the original thematic intention (there was even a transgender character in the original script, but the story arc was killed by the studio during preproduction). The vision of *The Matrix* as an elaborate transgender allegory is now the ruling framework when considering the film's historical significance, leapfrogging the initial frenzy over its technical achievements (most notably the introduction of "bullet time," where intense on-screen action was frozen while a virtual camera shifted the angle of observation). But gender identification is only one piece of the *Matrix* puzzle. It morphed multiple ideas in unexpected ways.

The Matrix opened on the last day of March in 1999. It was neither a summer movie nor a holiday movie (unless you count Easter, which the movie industry does not). It earned $37 million in its first five days, an unheard-of sum for an R-rated film released at such a low-traffic time of year. Part of the reason it was pushed into theaters that spring was to avoid competing against *The Phantom Menace* in the summer, a decision that proved wise. But the larger lesson was that a movie's relationship to the calendar mattered less than previously believed. *The Matrix* confirmed that a major film could now be positioned anywhere, at any time. The commercial power of cinema was no longer dictated by the habits of society; those habits could be shaped. *The Matrix* also reinvented the reading of Keanu Reeves, both as an actor and as a person. Reeves had spent much of the decade as a celebrity goober—a great-looking guy best known for being a bland actor (at least by traditional acting standards). In 1993, the ArtCenter College of Design in Pasadena offered a class called "The Films of Keanu Reeves," a scholastic examination of overheated postmodernism. "This really isn't about being a good actor," explained the professor. "It's not about applauding quality. I haven't even seen all of Keanu's films. That's my way of eroding authority in the class, so I can be closer to the students." Building a collegiate class around Keanu was shorthand for academic sarcasm. Reeves had played a time-traveling moron in the 1989 comedy *Bill & Ted's Excellent Adventure*, and the traits of that movie were applied to Reeves as a human: He fell somewhere between a smart person's interpretation of a meathead and a meathead's projection of an intellectual.

Keanu was a star, but often for movies hinging on self-conscious irrationality (the 1994 hit *Speed* was about a city bus wired to explode if its speedometer dipped below fifty miles per hour). He had funny hobbies. Reeves played bass for the nondescript alt-rock band Dogstar and unsuccessfully tried to convince audiences not to notice he was there, even though his presence was the only thing anyone cared about. His version of cool was not the nineties version of cool: Keanu was a masculine airhead. But then he was cast in *The Matrix*, and everything reversed. All the things that were once seen as vapid or devoid of affect became charming. A blankness that previously suggested naiveté now suggested wisdom. The sublime experience of the movie was injected into the actor's real-life identity. *The Matrix* was deeper than it appeared and insightful about concepts that were more felt than understood. Over the next twenty years, those same qualities would be poured into Keanu. In the film, his character is absorbed into the "the matrix." As a persona, *The Matrix* was absorbed into Reeves.*

So what, exactly, made this film smart enough to turn a hipster doofus

---

*The desire to classify Reeves as brilliant peaked in late 2020, when *The New York Times* published a list of the twenty-five greatest actors of the twenty-first century and somehow placed Keanu at number 4 overall. Now, granted, almost every discriminating reader knows that this kind of list is desultory, and the *Times* understands that any subjective list has to be a little idiotic in order to get attention. The twenty-five actors were selected for representational motives as much as for their actual talent, and the list was compiled by only two writers. Meryl Streep was ignored entirely. But the fact that Keanu Reeves was one of the people they placed in the top five illustrates just how much goodwill the critical community now feels toward a person they once ridiculed with regularity.

into a hipster Copernicus? It's not as if no one had ever made an intelligent sci-fi movie before. "We were interested in a lot of things," Lilly Wachowski told *The New York Times*. "Making mythology relevant in a modern context, relating quantum physics to Zen Buddhism, investigating your own life."

These statements are all true, though none are as essential as the screenplay's most basic conceit. About twenty minutes into the story, the protagonist (Keanu as the computer hacker Neo) swallows the red pill and has the nature of unreality explained by his mentor (Morpheus, portrayed by Laurence Fishburne). Neo learns that what has always been assumed to be life is a sophisticated simulation. He's transported inside a computer program that is indistinguishable from the sensation of being alive.

"This isn't real?" asks Neo.

"What is real?" he is rhetorically told in response. "How do you define *real*?"

The question itself was not groundbreaking. René Descartes wrote about the same ideas in the seventeenth century, and much of the movie's language was taken directly from Jean Baudrillard (the same Frenchman* who'd published *The Gulf War Did Not Take Place* eight years prior). What made this specific interpretation so seismic was the set and the setting: A philosophical concept traditionally requiring a semester of explanation was illustrated in the span of ninety seconds, inside a mainstream movie seen by more than a million people in its opening weekend. More critically, it was delivered in the year 1999, a moment in modernity when the mass public was finally ready to consider a process they'd intuitively (and relentlessly) experienced for decades.

The Matrix seemed like it was about computers. It was actually about TV.

There are a handful of news events from the nineties that are now used as historical data points. The Clarence Thomas hearings of 1991. The chasing

---

*Considering his contrarian take on almost everything, it is unsurprising that Baudrillard vehemently criticized *The Matrix* for misrepresenting his ideas and declined opportunities to consult on the film's sequels.

of O. J. Simpson in a Ford Bronco in 1994. The shootings at Columbine High School in 1999. These events destroyed lives and altered the future, and they happened the way that they happened. Yet the collective experiences of all those events were real-time televised constructions, confidently broadcast with almost no understanding of what was actually happening or what was being seen. The false meaning of those data points was the product of three factors, instantaneously combined into a matrix of our own making: the images presented on the screen, the speculative interpretations of what those images meant, and the internal projection of the viewer.

What is real? How do you define real?

The Matrix resonated not because it was fantastical fiction, but because it was not.

The bombing of the Alfred P. Murrah Federal Building was a worst-case scenario in every way imaginable. On the morning of April 19, 1995, a wiry, inconspicuous twenty-six-year-old man drove a rented Ryder van into downtown Oklahoma City. The van contained 5,000 pounds of explosive material. He parked the vehicle near the entrance of the nine-story federal building, ignited a two-minute fuse, and walked away. The explosion would obliterate the government building's front façade and cause half of the mid-rise structure to instantly collapse. It killed 168 people (including 19 children, most of whom were in the facility's day care center). It occurred without any warning, in a city assumed to have no political significance (a detail that amplified the universality of the fear). The perpetrator, Timothy McVeigh, was an American citizen and a decorated military veteran. He'd served in the Gulf War and hated the government. His actions might have been easier to comprehend had he been visibly psychotic, but he was not: Up until his execution in 2001, he spoke of his attack with cogent, clinical language, sometimes writing essays that compared his act of domestic terrorism to memorable military assaults by sovereign nations. He expressed no remorse, once telling a journalist that his coming execution only meant the final score was "168 to 1." He remained calm and composed while awaiting lethal injection, eating two pints of mint chocolate chip ice cream as a final meal. The profile of the attack brought greater attention to the propaganda that influenced McVeigh, like the white supremacist novel *The Turner Diaries*, as well as making McVeigh a folk hero to anti-American theorists for decades to come. The bombing could not have played out any worse than it did.

There is, however, an unusual stability to how the Oklahoma City bombing came to be understood—the unexpected benefit of the initial coverage being so straightforwardly wrong.

The night of the explosion, CNN reported that the bombing had all the signifiers of an attack from the Middle East. Network anchorwoman Connie Chung said, "A U.S. government source has told CBS News that it has Middle East terrorism written all over it." *The Wall Street Journal* compared the event to the kind of car bombs normally seen in Beirut. There was, for roughly forty-eight hours, a shared incorrect assumption about why the Murrah building had been destroyed. Once McVeigh was apprehended, the explanation was reversed and the complexity evaporated. This wasn't someone from Syria. This was someone from upstate New York. It wasn't an international network of terrorists. It was one guy, helped by two other guys (Terry Nichols and Michael Fortier, and Fortier's involvement was so minor he spent less than nine years in prison). There was also no confusion over McVeigh's purpose: When arrested, he was wearing a T-shirt that said, *"Sic semper tyrannis,"* the Latin phrase supposedly exclaimed by John Wilkes Booth after he'd assassinated Abraham Lincoln. McVeigh was candid about his reasons for blowing up the federal building, directly pointing to the 1992 government standoff at Ruby Ridge and the 1993 siege on the Branch Davidian compound in Waco, Texas. Because the media had been so wrong in their preliminary analysis, this wholesale correction somehow seemed extra reliable. McVeigh is the worst domestic terrorist in U.S. history, self-motivated by personal animosity toward the government. The shared under-standing of that is remarkably clear and generally undisputed. There are conspiracy theories about the Oklahoma City bombing, but fewer than one has come to expect from any tragedy of this magnitude. Even his most confused sympathizers see McVeigh as a singular dissident acting alone. Why? Because the Oklahoma City bombing is the exception that proves the rule: Con-spiracy theories arise from *gradations* of information, delivered indecisively. McVeigh's case was more like a toggle switch: We were first told one version of reality, and then we were told the opposite, confirmed by the criminal himself.

The scenarios that activated McVeigh were more open to interpretation. The incident at Ruby Ridge had involved a separatist family living in a cabin in rural Idaho. The family exchanged gunfire with federal marshals for 11 days, leading to the killing of three people and resulting in a wrongful death suit against the U.S. government that eventually paid over $3 million to the family. The situation in Waco was even more intense: A cult (or cultlike) organization was surrounded by federal authorities for 51 days in the spring of 1993, ending when the compound's buildings caught fire and 76 people died inside. Six other Davidians had already been killed by federal agents during a mostly unsuccessful raid in February.

In both of those cases, the meaning and conditions of the confrontations are still disputed by almost everyone who knows anything about them. The patriarch of the family at Ruby Ridge, Randy Weaver, was possibly a racist and definitely involved with illegal gun sales, yet most concede his wife and fourteen-year-old son should not have been killed. The entire siege was con-fusing and probably unnecessary. The leader of the Branch Davidians, David Koresh, claimed to be the messiah and was accused of pedophilia. The Davidians were stockpiling automatic weapons and believed the world was ending. But they weren't endangering the local community, skeptics insist the blaze was intentionally started by the government,* and some of the survivors still support and defend Koresh (who shot himself during the incineration).

For someone like McVeigh—and everyone else, really—the experience of following the events in Waco was a creative process. It was like a TV series scripted by writers who'd run out of plotlines. For most of the 51-day encounter, nothing in Waco was happening: There were unseen people inside the compound and there were militarized ATF authorities stationed at the perimeter of the encampment. We watched people watching people. Local and national media were expected to cover the standoff on a daily (and sometimes hourly) basis with no access to anything, corralled as far as possible from the scene and only fed information from officials who (according to many involved journalists) blatantly lied about what was really going on. Almost out of necessity, the ever-expanding news hole was filled with auxiliary information intended to show the "complete picture" of who was inside the compound (Koresh's ability to memorize Scripture and his acumen as a singer-songwriter were mentioned incessantly). There's no one to blame for this, because the additional information was engrossing and reporters had nothing else to explain. But the result was a pastiche of speculative and contradictory data that allowed the public to manufacture whatever meaning they wanted.† There was evidence that Koresh was a raving madman and there

---

*Equally common is the belief that Koresh and the Davidians started the fire themselves as a mass suicide.

†This seemingly backward concept—that giving people more information makes them understand things less—is well described in the book *The Black Swan* by Nassim Nicholas Taleb. In the 1960s, an experiment was conducted in which two focus groups were shown unclear images of a fire hydrant that was brought into focus at different rates: "Show two groups of people a blurry image of a fire hydrant, blurry enough for them not to recognize what it is. For one group, increase the resolution slowly, in ten steps. For the second, do it faster, in five steps. Stop at a point where both groups have been presented an identical image and ask each of them to identify what they see. The members of the group that saw fewer intermediate steps are likely to recognize the hydrant much faster. . . . The more information you give someone, the more hypotheses they will formulate along the way, and the worse off they will be."

was evidence that he was merely eccentric. There was strong evidence that the compound was a dystopia, but some weak evidence that it was a utopia. There was justification for believing what the federal agents said and justification for questioning their account. By constantly providing people with more and more conflicting data within an essentially static situation, it was possible for the audience to invent whatever narrative they desired. For someone like McVeigh, a radicalized loner naturally sympathetic to the Branch Davidians' outlook, the ATF's April 19 attack on the compound was video proof of a political actuality he'd already internalized: He watched tanks being driven through the walls of compound residences while a loudspeaker repeatedly broadcast the phrase "This is not an assault. This is not an assault." Even in 1993, that level of ironic cognitive dissonance was too much.

McVeigh watched the buildings in Waco burn, live on his television, operating from the position that the people inside were innocent. It perpetuated his belief that the loss of innocent lives was acceptable collateral damage in a war he was fighting alone, inside his own mind. It was possible for him to believe this, because it had become possible for anyone to believe anything.

It had been this way for a while.

○ ○ ○

The compulsion to reconsider the past through the ideals and beliefs of the present is constant and overwhelming. It allows for a sense of moral clarity and feels more enlightened. But it's actually just easier than trying to understand how things felt when they originally occurred. The 1991 confirmation hearing of Supreme Court justice Clarence Thomas is a particularly unwieldy example. When reexamined by those who missed the original affair, the conflict is comically straightforward. The accusations levied against Thomas no longer seem eligible for debate. But Thomas's confirmation hearings coincided with the onset of reality TV, and that is how they were discussed at the time. And because it was 1991, the issues raised were so new that seemingly self-evident points of fact were tribulations much of the country had never previously considered.

Thomas, then forty-three, was nominated by George H. W. Bush to succeed Thurgood Marshall on the court. The nomination wasn't thrilling to progressives (who saw Thomas as an anti–affirmative action reactionary) or hard-right conservatives (who viewed his nomination as a kind of tokenism, since the only Black justice in history was being replaced by a candidate whose lone similarity was the color of his skin). Things got wild when the FBI interviewed University of Oklahoma law professor Anita Hill, a woman who had worked for Thomas during the early 1980s. Hill said Thomas had sexually harassed her. The anecdotes she provided were impossible to verify but highly detailed and too atypical to be total fabrications. When eventually described and broadcast on live television, those details morphed into a kind of prurient litmus test that was less about Thomas's qualifications and more about how people wanted the world of work to be.

The process lasted almost one hundred days. The day that mattered most was Friday, October 11. "Nothing like what happened today has ever happened before," PBS newsman Jim Lehrer said that evening. His analysis was correct. Hill and Thomas both testified before fourteen senators to express and deny the accusations of harassment. The committee chairman was Delaware senator Joe Biden. Thomas spoke first, Hill spoke second, and then Thomas spoke again. The content of these testimonials—and especially Thomas's repudiation of what Hill had said—now seems outrageous. But in 1991, the most outrageous aspect was that these things were being talked about at all.

Thomas was more emotional than Hill. He denied everything and referred to himself as "a victim of this process," explaining how his life and reputation had been destroyed by Hill's accusations (which he said were especially hurtful because Hill "was a person I considered a friend" who had "never raised any hint that she was uncomfortable with me"). Throughout his testimony, he used the awkward phrase "sex harassment" instead of "sexual harassment," which (either intentionally or accidentally) reiterated the fact that the relationship between Hill and Thomas was never physical. He also proposed a clever and persuasive gambit: Thomas said he would no longer put up with the humiliation of having his life dissected in public, and that the Senate should just confirm him or not confirm him, almost as if he no longer cared about the job itself.

"I never asked to be nominated," he said. "It was an honor. Little did I know the price, but it was too high."

The crux of Hill's statement was that Thomas had pursued her romantically against her wishes and regularly made her uncomfortable. The Senate committee pushed for specifics, in part because certain aspects of the story had already leaked to the press. Those salacious specifics are what captivated America. Hill said Thomas liked to talk about the size of his penis and the clothes Hill wore to work. One of her anecdotes involved Thomas's interest in pornography and name-checked the porn star Long Dong Silver. The most memorable of her allegations was that Thomas once looked at a can of Coca-Cola on his desk and asked, "Who has put pubic hair on my Coke?"

Thomas exited the room after his initial appearance and did not return until Hill was finished. He then denied everything Hill had said, but also added that he hadn't listened to one word of her testimony. He then dropped the rhetorical equivalent of an atomic bomb.

"This is a circus," Thomas said. "This is a national disgrace. And from my standpoint, as a Black American, as far as I am concerned, it is a high-tech lynching for uppity Blacks who in any way deign to think for themselves, to do for themselves, to have different ideas, and is a message that, unless you kowtow to an old order, this is what will happen to you. You will be lynched, destroyed, caricatured by a committee of the U.S. Senate, rather than hung from a tree."

The Thomas-Hill battle continued through the weekend, but the war basically ended with the "high-tech lynching" line. Thomas was confirmed by the Senate on October 15 and has served his tenure as a conservative, laconic, habitually criticized member of the court. What remains compelling about his 1991 nomination is the way it forced people to take entrenched positions on issues that had always existed but could previously be ignored.

Television is what made that happen.

If the accusations about Thomas had involved some humdrum ethics violation, it's likely the proceedings would have only mattered to news-hounds (prior to 1981, Supreme Court nominations weren't televised at all). But due to the sexual nature of the allegations, the October 11 testimonies were aired live on both ABC and NBC and watched by around 27 million people (a number three times larger than the audience for that night's American League playoff game on CBS between the Minnesota Twins and the Toronto Blue Jays). It captivated people who had little interest in current events and might have been otherwise unable to name a single member of the Supreme Court. It was also broadcast raw, in real time, like a sporting event without announcers. This allowed viewers to guide themselves through the experience *before* journalists and pundits tried to explain what was supposed to be meaningful. It reduced the disagreement to uncut emotional reaction. What people deemed as important became unusually personal.

Had Anita Hill been white, the proceedings would have adopted a classic racial tension (and that would have almost certainly hurt Thomas). But because both parties were Black (and because Thomas had used phrases like "high-tech lynching" in his defense), it presented a *Sophie's Choice* for sympathetic liberals: Was this mostly about racism or was this mostly about sexism? Even more perplexing was the view of Hill's baseline credibility, perhaps the hardest schism between the world of today and the world of 1991. Thomas was nominated on July 1. A Gallup poll suggested 52 percent of the country was in favor of his appointment, with only 17 percent against it (31 percent had no opinion). Hill's allegations came to light in September, first through hazy media reports and later through her direct testimony. The way people respond to the testimony of a stranger is always subjective. Still, it's difficult to imagine how someone watching Hill talk to the Senate committee would not see her as, at the very least, reasonable. She is measured and consistent. Her visual presentation is conformist and conservative. When asked by Alabama senator Howell Heflin if she has a "martyr complex," she chuckles and does not appear offended. Above all, Hill makes it clear that she only came forward after the committee contacted her and that she has nothing to gain from making these charges. Which is why it's so confusing (and to some, maddening) that another Gallup poll, this one from October 14, showed that public support for Thomas's affirmation had risen to 58 percent in the wake of Hill's testimony. And this uptick was not merely an interesting reflection of what the average person thought—Bob Dole, the Senate minority leader from Kansas, admitted that Thomas would have likely been rejected if polling had moved in the other direction.

The contemporary explanation for why this happened is always simple: Society is a sexist patriarchy. But that response works from a modern mindset, where it's unthinkable to imagine a professional man making unwanted jokes about pubic hair without being seen as a sexual harasser. Such thinking was not always universal. The very first sexual harassment case in U.S. history (under Title VII of the Civil Rights Act) had happened just fifteen years before this hearing. For many Americans, the Anita Hill allegations were the first time they had considered the possibility that sexual harassment could exist without a direct demand for sexual activity (which is why Thomas's use of the specific phrase "sex harassment" was so willfully misleading). In 1991, it was still possible for someone to believe Hill's account without believing that what she described qualified as harassment. When Hill had applied for a position at Oral Roberts University in 1983, Thomas had provided her with a recommendation. The (now common) understanding that a subordinate might ask for help from a superior despite his unwanted behavior was still a baffling contradiction to many people. And this was true for both genders. A poll in USA Today showed Hill's support among women was only around 26 percent.

Which is not to suggest *no one* believed Hill: Both *The New York Times* and the *Los Angeles Times* took editorial stands against Thomas's confirmation. There was an entire episode of the CBS sitcom *Designing Women* about the hearings that generally sided with Hill (though one female character did side with Thomas). The 1992 song "Youth Against Fascism" by Sonic Youth includes the line "I believe Anita Hill," which is not exactly a subtle expression of support. But most adults in the country did not fully believe her (or they did, but didn't care). Was that sexism? Yes. Was it an early example of that perplexing nineties paradox where institutions were viewed cynically while institutional figures were believed? Probably. But it was also the power of television to shape rationality through irrational means. Anything experienced through the screen of a television becomes a TV show. Forty years of network programming had trained people to associate the performance of emotion with the essentialism of truth, and Thomas had been much more emotional than Hill. He seemed angry, sad, confused, and uncompromising. She just made a good argument, which—on television—is never enough.

To suggest the saga surrounding the O. J. Simpson murder trial was "experienced like a television show" is a little like suggesting interest in the rivalry between Tonya Harding and Nancy Kerrigan was not necessarily a reflection of the popularity of Olympic figure skating. It's such a self-evident insight that it can't be called insightful. There's almost no way to consider any aspect of the O.J. debacle without imagining a televised moment memorized from real life, from the recontextualized analysis of those moments in the seven-and-a-half-hour ESPN documentary *O.J.: Made in America*, or from the fictional reenactment of those moments in the FX limited series *American Crime Story: The People v. O. J. Simpson*. It was irrefutably the biggest crime story of the decade, arguably the biggest crime story of the century, and a news event that sustained international interest for (a now unthinkable) sixteen consecutive months. It is a hinge moment in U.S. media history, ostensibly for its effect on race and celebrity but mostly for the way it combined tragedy and stupidity on a scope and scale that would foretell America's deterioration into a superpower that was also a failed state. It was the TV show that proved everything that had always been feared and suspected about the medium of TV.

The most mind-melting aspect of the O. J. Simpson story is that the story no longer seems like what it was: the story of a guy who murdered two people and got away with it. That "detail" has become the media version of a McGuffin, in the same way the murder of Laura Palmer has little to do with the way people remember *Twin Peaks*.

Simpson was a former Heisman Trophy winner and the best NFL running back of the 1970s. He later became an actor and a broadcaster. He allegedly killed his ex-wife, Nicole Brown Simpson, along with a waiter, Ronald Goldman, who happened to be at Brown's town house on the night of the homicides. I employ the word "allegedly" only out of journalistic habit and professional sarcasm. It's pretty much impossible to find people who are still of mixed mind about what happened on the night of June 12, 1994, including members of the jury who declared Simpson not guilty in 1995. "I'm probably pretty sure that [Simpson] probably is the person that went over there and killed Nicole Brown Simpson," admitted jury member Lon Cryer in 2017.

The case against O.J. was exhaustive: DNA evidence proves he was at the scene of the crime on the night that it happened. There was a long history of Simpson's physically abusing Nicole, once prompting her to directly tell police, "He's going to kill me!" Simpson had no alibi as to where he was on the night of the slayings, which wouldn't seem so troubling had he not later published a book titled *If I Did It*, where Simpson painstakingly described his obsession with Brown and inexplicably detailed how he would have "hypothetically" murdered Brown and Goldman, if that had been his desire. His hypothetical was remarkably similar to how the murders actually occurred. O. J. Simpson is perhaps the only person who has ever written a memoir about how he would have killed people he incessantly claimed not to have killed. There are almost no scenarios that could make Simpson appear guiltier than he actually does, outside of O.J. wearing a body camera while performing the decapitation. The obviousness of Simpson's guilt was key to the postmodern drama. There was a game show quality to watching the trial: Could Simpson's "dream team" of defense lawyers win an argument that seemed impossible to take seriously?

Just before the "not guilty" verdict was announced, polling indicated that over 70 percent of white Americans thought Simpson was a murderer, while over 70 percent of Black Americans thought he was innocent. But those stats were fleeting and deceptive—twenty years after the trial, a similar poll found that a majority of Black people now classified Simpson as guilty (and the percentage of whites who agreed had climbed over 80). What had changed? The main difference was that this TV show was no longer on the air. Any misplaced passions dissolved into logic. Looking at the case retroactively, purely as a collection of facts, only one conclusion can be drawn. But *while it was happening*, the trial provided an almost limitless spectrum of possibilities as to what this televised conflict was actually about, most of which had nothing to do with what happened at Brown's condominium in the upscale neighborhood of Brentwood, California.

Within the nonfictional fiction of this narrative, Simpson was the antihero in an extended metaphor about the meaning of justice. It was a math equation: The fact that he stabbed two people to death had to be weighed against the history of racism in America. O.J. often appeared to be a very guilty man who had nonetheless been framed by the Los Angeles Police Department. He was a Black superstar who'd spent most of his career marketing himself as a man who transcended race, only to have race become the foundation of his defense. From across the courtroom, he looked like an unsmiling version of the same guy who'd been in commercials for Hertz rental cars and slapstick movies like *The Naked Gun*. Those innocuous media appearances now felt like sinister illusions that masked the real O.J. But who was "the real O.J."? Was he still a person, or was he now just a character? There were so many other characters within the daily televised melodrama, all of whom temporarily became the most famous person in America: the racist L.A. cop who played by his own rules (Mark Fuhrman), the handsome bozo who lived in the pool house (Kato Kaelin), the provocative defense attorney (Johnnie Cochran) who'd be parodied on *Seinfeld* just two days after Simpson's acquittal. It was possible to discuss the Simpson trial without talking about Simpson at all: There was rabid interest in the relationship between prosecuting attorneys Marcia Clark and Christopher Darden, and about Clark's assortment of haircuts. Like a Russian novel where the subtext dwarfed the plot, one could extrapolate highbrow concepts that were only tangentially connected to the case: the economics of justice, the deep-rooted prejudice against interracial relationships, an assertion that the high-profile exoneration of a guilty Black celebrity could serve as symbolic reparation for three hundred years of oppression. Yet there were also embarrassing moments of manufactured theatrics: When the prosecution (stupidly) forced Simpson to try on a glove found at the scene of the murder, Simpson histrionically behaved as if the glove were several sizes too small. "If it doesn't fit, you must acquit," argued his attorney. The fate of a man accused of two homicides was salvaged by a catchphrase. The world had become *RoboCop*.

In the years since 1995, much of society has developed a false memory of the Simpson trial, where the eventual outcome is recalled as a foregone inevitability everyone saw coming. Partially due to the (extraordinary) ESPN documentary and the (better-than-expected) Fox fictionalization, there's a sense that tactical mistakes made by the prosecution were obvious and that the jurors didn't understand the new science of DNA. This is not how it was at the time. At the time, most people either had no idea what the verdict would be, or they were fairly certain Simpson would be convicted. Much of that certainty came not from the trial, but from an event that preceded it, simultaneously experienced by most of the country.

Five days after the murders, on the Friday morning of June 17, 1994, Simpson was asked to surrender to authorities. Instead, he disappeared. That afternoon, his attorney, Robert Kardashian, read a letter the still-missing Simpson had left behind. Written in the past tense, it had all the signifiers of a suicide note ("I've had a great life," Simpson wrote. "Please think of the real O.J. and not this lost person"). For almost an hour, people wondered whether it was only a matter of time before his corpse would be found. But then he reappeared, very much alive, holding a gun to his head in the back-seat of a white Ford Bronco on I-405, chauffeured by a former teammate named Al Cowlings (later identified as O.J.'s closest friend). The freeway was cleared of westbound traffic as a fleet of police cruisers and multiple news helicopters followed the Bronco in a low-speed chase (Cowlings rarely pushed beyond forty miles per hour). After ninety minutes on the road, the vehicle finally returned to Simpson's residence just before eight p.m. Pacific Time. Less than an hour after that, Simpson gave himself up to the police. Items found inside the Bronco included $9,000 in cash and a fake mustache and goatee.

Now, the two things most remembered about this spectacle are (a) the seemingly insane people standing along the highway who witnessed the chase in person, and (b) the insane number of television viewers who watched the chase from the comfort of their own living rooms. It is the defining night of the nineties and a phenomenon that is somehow both difficult to understand and entirely unsurprising. The number of people who watched the chase is estimated to be around 95 million, many of whom were watching the NBA Finals before NBC interrupted coverage of a basketball game with coverage of a slow-moving SUV. It has become a totemistic experience in American cultural lore—one of those rare events for which virtually everyone who was alive can recall where they were and who they were with while the drama unfolded.

What makes it so evocative of the nineties is how devoid of drama it actually was.

Watching the original TV feeds of the O.J. chase is the ultimate illustration of *liveness* and its insidious projection of false intensity. Once you know the outcome of the chase, the actions leading up to that finale become not just boring but borderline painful. One cannot reconnect with the feeling that this event was ever captivating. The newscasters compulsively repeat the same phrases (some version of "What you are seeing right now is unbelievable"), speculate on minor details (such as what off-ramp the vehicle *might* take), and occasionally say nothing at all for long stretches of time. Knowing what is now known, it's hard to overlook how limited the potential outcomes really were—the Bronco could stop or the Bronco could keep going. There is nothing singularly powerful about any of the on-screen images. But this was a truly unscripted event, and not in the way the Rockets-Knicks title game was unscripted. A basketball game can only be a basketball game. This was a nexus of serious things that had never happened before, unified by a wavering consensus that the stakes were still low and that this was still (mostly) entertainment.

Two people had been brutally killed by a familiar celebrity. The celebrity killer was fleeing law enforcement in the most public way possible. There was a real chance he might kill himself in front of 95 million people. None of this, however, was terrifying. It was merely "disturbing," and mostly because the most interested parties did not seem disturbed at all. The detail always noted in remembrances of the Bronco chase is the throngs of bystanders cheering for Simpson as the car rolled down the freeway, congregating on overpasses and holding makeshift cardboard signs proclaiming, "The Juice Is Loose." It seemed perverse then and still seems perverse now. Yet this can also be understood as the primordial impulse of what would eventually drive the mechanism of social media: the desire of uninformed people to be *involved* with the news, broadcasting their support for a homicidal maniac not because they liked him, but because it was exhilarating to participate in an experience all of society was experiencing at once.

○ ○ ○

Twelve months after the Simpson verdict was broadcast live to 150 million viewers, Fox News launched as a network alternative to "regular" news, though it positioned itself as not altogether different from the news it was competing against. Its similarities to CNN far outweighed its divergence. The same can be said for MSNBC, which went on the air a few months before Fox News in the summer of 1996.

There was, unquestionably, an assumption that Fox News, created by Australian tycoon Rupert Murdoch and directed by American political operative Roger Ailes, would lean its political coverage toward the right (Murdoch's empire was built on populism and Ailes had worked with Reagan and Bush). But Fox News started operations with a shoestring budget, and it wasn't even available in New York or Los Angeles.* MSNBC, a union of NBC and Microsoft, was considered credible almost instantly. It presented no fixed perspective or ideology, outside of trying to meld the emerging internet with traditional broadcast news (in the earliest days of MSNBC, one of the on-air personalities was Ann Coulter). Print journalists covering the MSNBC launch took it seriously and applauded its ability to break news (most notably an airline crash that happened just two days after the network went on air). In an Associated Press story by media reporter Frazier Moore, the only problem with MSNBC was that its talent seemed too self-consciously hip: "Why do these pundits—diverse in gender, ethnicity and politics—all seem to be so young? Don't people over 50† have insights and opinions?" The channel appeared poised to compete immediately. But MSNBC struggled. Despite a

---

*Murdoch immediately filed a $2 billion antitrust lawsuit that alleged cable provider Time Warner had conspired with Ted Turner, the creator of CNN, to freeze Fox News out of major U.S. markets.

†Jodi Applegate, the first anchorperson to appear on-screen for MSNBC, was thirty-two.

massive influx of cash from Microsoft, MSNBC was forced to downsize 20 percent of its staff within the first year.

By January of 1999, prime-time viewership for cable news was still following an expected orbit. CNN, almost twenty years old at this point, averaged just over 1 million viewers a night. Fox News had about 281,000, and MSNBC was around 256,000. Fox and MSNBC were ancillary news organizations—if you preferred either channel to CNN, it was mostly a manifestation of personal taste. CNN was the twenty-four-hour news equivalent of Coca-Cola, while Fox and MSNBC were battling to see who could become Pepsi. There was very little *meaning* to watching any of these channels. That would change dramatically in the next century, when MSNBC evolved into a mouthpiece for Democratic talking points and Fox News became indistinguishable from the GOP itself. By 2020, CNN had declined into RC Cola.

What Fox realized on election night in 2000 (when its ratings spiked upward) and what MSNBC came to accept a few years later was something increasingly visible throughout the nineties, but too journalistically depressing to openly embrace: People watch cable news as a form of entertainment, and they don't want to learn anything that contradicts what they already believe. What they want is information that confirms their preexisting biases, falsely presented through the structure of traditional broadcasting. It had to *look* like objective journalism, but only if the volume was muted. Moreover, the bias expressed cannot be subtle or unpredictable; partisan audiences want to know what they're getting before they actually get it. Unless cataclysmic events are actively breaking, the purpose of cable news is emotional reassurance.

Because of what Fox News eventually became, there's a belief that it has dictated American conservative thought since the day it debuted. This is not true. A study conducted by the University of California at Berkeley examined the impact of Fox on the 2000 election, exclusively focusing on communities where Fox News was available. The study found "no significant effect" on voter share, ultimately concluding that Fox News convinced "between 0 and 2.1 percent of its viewers to vote Republican." The scholars went on to say that audiences understood that the outlet had a built-in bias and that its viewers "rationally use that knowledge when watching the Fox news programming."

The past is not merely a foreign country. The past is an alternative cosmos.

○ ○ ○

There are few words misused by broadcasters as habitually as *surreal*. Something is not "surreal" just because it's weird or unexpected. *Surreal* means "beyond the real," so it can't describe anything that exists in reality. A tiger walking through a shopping mall would be frightening and fantastic, but it wouldn't be surreal unless the tiger melted into the floor. When a child in *The Matrix* bends a spoon with his mind, the child has done something surreal; when a child walks into a school cafeteria and shoots his classmates, he is doing something utterly and unspeakably genuine. The 1999 massacre at Columbine High School in Littleton, Colorado, was not a surreal event. But it was, when viewed through the cameras of the school's security system, the closest we'd ever come to moving beyond the real.

Columbine High was nowhere near to being the first American school shooting. Less than a year before Columbine, a mentally ill fifteen-year-old killed two of his classmates and wounded twenty-five others at Thurston High School in Springfield, Oregon. The history of such acts is disturbingly long, dating back to the dawn of public education in the New World. But Columbine High represents the baseline for a different level of school shooting—the full incarnation of a nightmare that had previously seemed like a theoretical possibility too extreme to actually occur. It's also a mega-depressing example of manufactured meta-history, where the slaughter of thirteen people was obscured by the need to impose a cogent narrative upon a scenario that had no cogent explanation. It was the epitome of that three-phase creative process: the disorder and guesswork of the live event, the subsequent seventy-two hours of random speculation and false explanation, and ten years of debunking all the incorrect conjecture about what had motivated the killers to do what they did.

The assault took place on April 20, the anniversary of Adolf Hitler's birth and a date that can be numerically abbreviated as 4/20, a slang term for smoking marijuana. These factoids were often mentioned in connection to Columbine, the only problem being that neither had any relationship to anything that happened. Initial TV footage of the shooting was nothing but extended exterior shots of the nondescript school building, the type of characterless educational facility common in suburban communities. It was impossible to know what was happening inside, though it was obviously something terrible. Phone calls coming from inside the school caught the ambient echo of gunshots. Sometimes a group of kids would be seen fleeing from the building, and sometimes they would all have their hands on their heads, as if they were all somehow criminals. The most chilling images would come later, from the security camera inside the cafeteria: Two students, armed to the teeth with semiautomatic weapons, appeared to be methodically hunting their classmates, many of whom were desperately hiding under tables and chairs. A few minutes past noon, the two assailants, eighteen-year-old Eric Harris and seventeen-year-old Dylan Klebold, finally killed themselves in the school library.

What happened next was a tutorial in how the first draft of history is not just incorrect but usually more tenacious than all the improved drafts that come later. Even though it's widely accepted that most instantaneous journalism about the massacre was partially wrong, those misguided myths continue to be the most universally remembered aspects (even among those who know the myths are false). The most enduring narrative is that Harris and Klebold were part of an antisocial school clique called "the Trench Coat Mafia." This was entirely untrue. It was constantly stated that Harris and Klebold were unpopular, a categorization that remains imperfect (Klebold had recently gone to prom, and both teens had other friends, some of whom they allowed to escape). There was a pervasive (and incorrect) rumor that the two murderers had been "Goth kids," leading to a national panic over what it meant to be Goth.* It was reported that Harris and Klebold were targeting jocks and cheerleaders. There is no evidence of this. It was reported that Harris specifically asked one victim if she believed in God and killed her after she said yes. It's now believed that this question was actually posed to an altogether different student whom they arbitrarily decided to spare.

The persistence of these fabrications can be mainly attributed to a communal unwillingness to admit that there was no rational explanation behind this attack. Harris was a full-on psychopath who aspired to replicate the work of Timothy McVeigh. Klebold was (at a minimum) depressed and suicidal. Despite the jaw-dropping body count, the plan they concocted technically failed: Their true hope had been to blow up the school with propane explosives and collapse the roof. Harris kept a diary that outlined the depth of his depravity: He bragged about his racism, claimed that mentally ill people should be executed as part of "natural selection," and wrote that the Nazi Holocaust had been too limited in scope ("I say KILL MANKIND. No one should survive"). He casually wondered whether someone would write his biography after he died. The final entry in the Harris diary, dated April 3, does indicate how insecurity and loneliness played a role in his desire to

---

*Goth subculture is among the most creative extensions of twentieth-century teenage life. It started in the 1980s as an outgrowth of death-obsessed post-punk bands from the UK. Over time, it became more of a fashion aesthetic and a lifestyle signifier, categorized by an interest in anything morose, depressing, historically antiquated, and/or childlike (typically infused with an injection of knowing boredom). Teenagers interested in "being Goth" did not *want* to be popular, and the rare cultural depictions of Gothness in mass media (the Johnny Depp film *Edward Scissorhands*, a *Saturday Night Live* sketch called "Goth Talk," one episode of the short-lived MTV sitcom *Austin Stories*) always focused on their self-conscious weirdness and self-induced paleness. Goths were seen as harmlessly strange and strangely harmless. The day after Columbine, that observation radically changed. By incorrectly labeling Harris and Klebold as "Goth," adults who didn't know any better suddenly assumed that Goth kids were dangerous and violent. This singular moment of misinformation damaged the subculture so severely that—going forward—the type of teens who might have previously identified as "Goth" gravitated toward the less problematic subculture of "emo," another self-applied stereotype that exhibited many of the same qualities as Gothness, except with less compelling music, brighter clothing, and less interest in the seventeenth century.

destroy ("I hate you people for leaving me out of so many fun things . . . you had my phone #"). But the alchemy of fact and fiction within the post-calamity analysis—combined with the mores and norms of the era—prompted a fragile form of cognitive dissonance: While it was wholly acceptable to view Harris and Klebold as irredeemable monsters, it was equally essential to sympathize with the plight of nameless straw-man teenagers who were theoretically being pushed toward mass violence. In 1999, bullying could be blamed for almost anything.

"Nobody's really looking at the damage that the social hierarchy of high school does to kids on a psychic level. It alienates and humiliates kids," sociologist Donna Gaines told *The Charlotte Observer* just after the Columbine shooting. Gaines's 1991 book *Teenage Wasteland* had chronicled the lives of marginalized New Jersey metalheads dealing with the deaths of four peers in a teen suicide pact. Though Gaines's empathetic perspective was valid, it was not exactly rare. Most teen culture from the previous twenty-five years had worked from the premise that popular kids were inherently shallow and unpopular kids were inherently good: *The Outsiders*, the 1982 Rush song "Subdivisions," any John Hughes movie that wasn't *Ferris Bueller's Day Off*, the X-Men, *Heathers*, Daniel Clowes's graphic novel *Ghost World*, *My So-Called Life*, Todd Solondz's *Welcome to the Dollhouse*, the 1996 song "Popular" by Nada Surf, and almost every other fictional depiction of high school pitting one sect of students against another sect of students.* The trope was so pervasive that it was reflexively applied to Columbine. Because it was (incorrectly) believed that Harris and Klebold had targeted popular kids, it was (incorrectly) assumed that this must have been a response to merciless

---

*The notable exception to this was *Beverly Hills, 90210*. The Fox teen drama launched in 1990, originally premised around the friction created by two "normal" teenagers from Minnesota who move into one of the richest communities in California. But any class tension evaporated as the cast became friends and (quite often) romantic pairs. The hugely successful, culturally influential show ran for ten years and is among the most morally positive depictions of elite society in TV history. These were very privileged characters with no real responsibilities, but all of them were framed as fundamentally good people.

bullying. This became the only sophisticated way to think about the Columbine shooting. It was not to be seen as an isolated example of two unusually disturbed kids with almost limitless access to guns; it was to be seen as an extremist manifestation of teenage angst, endemic to society as a whole, allegedly fueled by toxic video games and nihilistic pop metal.

The artist most directly blamed for the shooting was Marilyn Manson, a knowingly controversial shock rocker surging in popularity (his most recent album, *Mechanical Animals*, had debuted at number 1 on the *Billboard* charts). The fact that Harris and Klebold were not fans of Marilyn Manson did not seem to matter (they preferred the German industrial group Rammstein). A group of ten U.S. senators unsuccessfully tried to convince Interscope Records to cease distribution of Manson's music, claiming the work "glorified violence." Manson, interviewed in the Michael Moore documentary *Bowling for Columbine*, responded to accusations that he'd contributed to the tragedy with a compassion similar to that of Gaines: When asked what he would say to the kids at Columbine High, Manson replied, "I wouldn't say a single word to them. I would listen to what *they* have to say. That's what no one did." It was, to Manson's credit, a generous reaction to an event he had nothing to do with (and that could have ended his career). Yet his words also felt a little like the last scene from the worst real-life *After School Special* the country had ever experienced: "What about the children? What are the children feeling?"

When something as terrible as Columbine occurs, there's a wish to have it explain something crucial about how the world is. Learning the truth is supposed to help. In this case, it did not. The truth proved there was no meaning at all, which was more terrifying than the myth. So the truth was rejected, even after it was accepted.

◡ ◡ ◡

The importance of television throughout the nineties was easy to feel but hard to explain. The art it offered mattered less than the nature of how it worked and the centrality of its dominance. Television had become the way to understand everything, ruling from a position of one-way control that future generations would never consent to or understand. TV programs were not available when the viewer wanted to see them, but only on the day and time they were scheduled. If you needed to go to the bathroom, you waited for the commercial break and did whatever you needed to do in less than three minutes. If you didn't like what was currently on, the only options were to watch nothing, watch something you didn't like, or leave the room. Sitcoms were filmed with three cameras (they all looked the same). Dramas had an "A story" and a less important "B story" (they all worked the same). The news was the news: A person behind a desk told you one version of what was happening, and the clips that accompanied the exposition proved that whatever you were told was (more or less) what had happened. It was the internet before the internet, but it wasn't like the internet at all. You did not search for what you wanted. You were told what you wanted, within the same moment it was received. Television was not the same as life, but the relationship was closer than it had ever been before and would ever be again.

In that most critical scene from *The Matrix*, Morpheus and Neo are having their revelatory conversation inside a computer network. They are inside the network so that Morpheus can show Neo the difference between the false reality he once believed and the hard reality he must now accept. But to demonstrate that difference, Morpheus does not use a computer monitor or a hologram or an astral projection. He uses a television. And it's not some futuristic flat-screen television—it's a Radiola console model from the 1950s, produced in Australia. This is a small detail with no importance to the plot, but it's telling. Neo is a cybercriminal who lives on the internet. Computers are his life. Yet his knee-jerk mental conception of human existence is still an analog box connected to nothing, broadcasting two-dimensional images he cannot manipulate. The esoteric philosophy of *The Matrix* made sense to people not because audiences were starting to understand the newness of the internet. It made sense to people because it was an exaggerated depiction of a televised hyperreality that had been building upon itself for the previous fifty years.

A van explodes and a building collapses. A man and a woman disagree about events that happened to them both. A killer in a white vehicle drives to nowhere, as a form of entertainment. Teenagers murder teenagers and no one knows why. What is real? How do you define real? There was a spoon, and there was no spoon, and the only difference was how much you cared.

[the spin doctors]

WHEN TRYING TO UNDERSTAND WHAT A PERSON (OR AN ENTIRE GROUP OF
people) is like, the normal procedure is to identify and analyze their feelings.
But what's just as vital, and perhaps more instructive, is not *what* they feel,
but *how much* they feel. Two individuals with opposing viewpoints can seem
almost identical if both have measured, understated personalities; two individuals in fundamental agreement become adversaries if the emotional intensity of their mind-sets doesn't match up. It's a perpetual divergence that's
rarely addressed directly but informs every worldview: Should people be
more (or less) sensitive? Should people be less (or more) preoccupied with
their own sense of self, and should rationality matter more (or less) than
passion and moral conviction? It's a dissonance seen in almost every social
conflict, most perceptibly in the personas of two nineties people who had as
much impact on American life as one can have without becoming president.

Alan Greenspan told you to feel less. He never said those exact words,
but that was the tip of his intellectual spear. Greenspan was something that
had never existed before and will likely never exist again: a rock star Federal
Reserve chairman. He oversaw the U.S. banking system for four consecutive administrations, appointed by Reagan in 1987 and continuing through
Bush, Clinton, and Bush II. In the span of those nineteen years, the economy

would spike upward and spike downward, but the overall trackway was persistently positive. Since Greenspan was the only constant through this stretch—a bipartisan favorite who self-identified as a Republican but considered Clinton the best president of his tenure—he was portrayed as a one-man brain trust and the reason the United States often felt like an economic spacecraft cruising on autopilot. In the future, this opinion would be reversed and Greenspan would become a public piñata, pointedly hammered for the financial collapse that happened within a year of his leaving his post in 2006. During his reign, however, Greenspan was untouchable, fortified by a detached philosophy that people didn't always like but couldn't justifiably criticize.

Greenspan was a quirky man who looked like the least quirky human who ever lived (his physical appearance when he took over the Fed at age sixty-one was not all that different from his appearance when he left at the age of eighty). He had owlish eyeglasses and a dour expression, but was also a good dancer and a Juilliard-trained jazz saxophonist who liked to date newswomen (Barbara Walters and Andrea Mitchell among them, the latter of whom he married). He was a persuasive person who did not talk much, so it counted when he did. Greenspan pointedly dropped the phrase "irrational exuberance" into a 1996 speech and the worldwide stock market immediately tumbled.

The trust people instilled in Greenspan derived from the belief that emotion played no role in his data-driven decision-making. The foundation of his ideology was initially grounded in two philosophies: (a) the notion that only verifiable facts are worthy of consideration, and (b) Ayn Rand's Objectivist theory, promoting the idea that society would be better served if everyone always acted in their own self-interest. To say these theories are unpopular with progressives is a little like saying nuclear power is unpopular with people who owned hotels outside Chernobyl. When public opinion turned on Greenspan, these views would be used against him, particularly his personal association with Rand.* But in the nineties (and especially during the decade's last half), cold calculation was white majik. Greenspan wasn't a normal person with a normal job. He controlled numbers, and numbers were devoid of emotion. He was the serious-minded father who did not concern himself with the feelings of anyone, including himself (or so it seemed).

Oprah Winfrey was the antithesis of Greenspan. Oprah told you to feel more. A national matriarch who *did* seem to care about the feelings of everyone, she sometimes tried to present herself as a taskmaster who demanded personal responsibility. "I cannot listen to other people blaming their mothers," the talk show host said in 1994. "I have to move on. We're not gonna book a show where someone is talking about their victimization." But this outward expression of toughness belied the reassurance isolated suburbanites took from her daily TV program. More than any other celebrity, Winfrey normalized the belief that how a person felt mattered just as much as the circumstances that propelled that feeling into being.

Winfrey's rise to prominence was rapid and astonishing. It starts in 1984, when Winfrey becomes a local news host in Chicago. By 1986, she has her own show, originally seen as an alternative to *The Phil Donahue Show* (the long-running chat program that essentially created the format). Oprah overtakes Donahue's ratings in a matter of months. By 1993, she's the genre's powerbroker, asking Michael Jackson if he's a virgin in front of a television audience of 90 million (his response: "I'm a gentleman"). By 1995, her net worth is $340 million and she's surrounded by imitators, none of whom can compete. In 1996, she does an episode about mad cow disease and single-handedly craters the price of beef. That same year, Winfrey starts a book club, and her selections shape the literary landscape for a decade (novelist Jonathan Franzen is thrown into controversy simply by declining to go on

---

*Sebastian Mallaby, author of the Greenspan biography *The Man Who Knew*, has said that passages of Rand's opus *Atlas Shrugged* were likely edited or even written by Greenspan after the pair became acquainted in the 1950s.

her TV show, a decision his detractors view as ungrateful and condescending). In 2000, she creates her own monthly magazine and appears on every
cover for twenty consecutive years.

Oprah was the first Black female billionaire in the history of the planet.
Her footprint on the culture, however, was even greater than her business
acumen.

An editorial in *The Wall Street Journal* created a buzzword in August of
1996: While describing that summer's Democratic convention, the *WSJ* editorial board bemoaned the "Oprahfication" of American politics. What they
were specifically criticizing was the concept of public confession as a kind of
all-inclusive therapy, and there were certainly examples of this in Winfrey's
messaging: Oprah often talked about her own body issues and her history of
sexual abuse, and even admitted she'd smoked crack in her twenties (at a
time when the perceived difference between crack and granular cocaine was
diametric). But the term came to mean something much more encompassing. When anything in the zeitgeist was cited as an example of "Oprahfication," it was a way to signal the primacy of emotion and the feminization of
society. A 1997 story about Oprah in *U.S. News & World Report* was literally
headlined "A Woman's Woman."

"With America's general prosperity, with relative calm in the rest of the
world, has come the option of self-concern," wrote Debra Dickerson. "Women
love Oprah because she provides the outlet. Mean people hurt her feelings,
as they do others'. Like other women, she hates being fat. The difference
between Oprah and many others is that she says so—and validates ordinary
women who are quietly angry and unhappy for the same reasons. She validates them, scolds them, worries about them, and shares her love with them,
and they don't begrudge her the millions she makes off them."

The passage of time makes it difficult to accurately recall outsized personalities, mostly by demanding that we always accept the tyranny of the
present. When Dickerson noted "America's general prosperity" in 1997, the
unspoken explanation would have credited that prosperity to Greenspan;

today, even his strongest advocates feel an obligation to call him *complicated*. Earlier in that same *U.S. News* piece, the writer notes that "perhaps the only phenomenon more striking than the sway [Winfrey] holds over millions of ordinary people is the vitriol she inspires in many critics." Decades later, Oprah is above reproach and often pushed to run for the presidency. It has become risky to criticize her at all, in any way. In the undeclared war between feeling and unfeeling, there's no question about which side won. That war is over. But there was a time when those battles were still being waged, every day and in every way, on the ground and in the mind of everyone who mattered, including the man who lived in the White House.

11 I Feel the Pain of Everyone, Then I Feel Nothing

PART OF THE COMPLEXITY OF LIVING THROUGH HISTORY IS THE PROCESS of explaining things about the past that you never explained to yourself. So many temporary realties, distantly viewed in the rearview mirror, will appear ridiculous to any person who wasn't there. "How could this have happened?" they ask, and the skepticism is reasonable. Their questions are impossible to answer, outside of the non-expository truth: What seems weird now didn't seem weird then. In fact, what seems weird now once seemed predictable.

It did not feel outrageous, for example, that Pauly Shore spent much of the nineties as a bankable movie star, regardless of how baffling that notion strikes anyone who missed it entirely. In 1990, Shore was a strange-looking, five-foot-seven, twenty-two-year-old Jewish jokester. He was the son of Mitzi Shore, the owner of a popular and influential club on the Sunset Strip called the Comedy Store.* That upbringing jump-started his career, as did his

---

*Mitzi Shore played an outsized role in what would become the dominant style of stand-up comedy most associated with the eighties and nineties. Her personal taste dictated who performed at the Comedy Store, and the Comedy Store launched national personalities. Mitzi preferred dark, personal pathos and hated the detached, observational material of performers like Jerry Seinfeld. "She disliked me instantly," Seinfeld would say years later. "You needed to be a wounded, broken-wing bird, or you're not funny and you're not her kind of person . . . we immediately disliked each other. She was very outspoken about it, to my face."

close relationship with established stand-up star Sam Kinison. But the core of Shore's success was a product of his own creativity. He was committed to a character of his own design: "the Weasel," which he pronounced as "the WEEEEZ-allll."

The Weasel persona was a lowbrow combination of traits that did not naturally intersect: A non-surfing surfer who was also a lecherous nerd. A rich kid who was always broke. A charming loser who partied with rock stars but wasn't dangerous or messianic. He presented himself as much younger than he actually was and invented his own lexicon, a halting synthesis of 1980s Valley Girl slang and sexist West Coast stoner speak (women were "nugs," breasts were "cones," food was "grindage"). His national breakthrough was as an MTV on-air personality, first as a spring break correspondent and then as the host of his own MTV show, *Totally Pauly*. Shore's 1991 comedy album was called *The Future of America*, and the title was the hook—this overconfident high school dropout, with his indecipherable vocabulary and vacant worldview, was the self-generated parody of everything MTV had allegedly injected into the minds of American young people. He was his own worst-case scenario, so the only logical move was to put him in movies. The first was 1992's *Encino Man*, the story of two teens who find an unfrozen caveman in suburban Los Angeles. It made $40 million at the box office. *Son in Law*, from 1993, dumped Shore onto a farm in South Dakota and made another $36 million. The 1994 vehicle *In the Army Now* was a lazy rip-off of the Bill Murray film *Stripes*, followed by another starring role in *Jury Duty* (which was about a guy serving jury duty). *Bio-Dome*, from 1996, was a scatological satire of the Biosphere 2 project. In all five films, Shore played varying versions of the Weasel, which means he played varying versions of himself.

Consumed in the present day, all five films are astoundingly insipid,* even compared to how stupid they seemed when first released in theaters.

Encino Man was actually okay.

The prospect of multiple studios building feature-length comedies around a non-actor with a niche MTV following does not translate as a workable strategy. Yet . . . at the time . . . it did not seem strange. It did not seem strange, at all, to anyone. There was a sense of inevitability to the Weasel's ascension, as if this thing no one had asked for was obviously the culmination of what pop culture had been careening toward for half a generation. *Of course* Pauly Shore should star in a bunch of mainstream movies. *Of course* that was going to happen.

To those living in the true future of America, it would make no sense at all. But the future can't exist until the present is the past.

The president of the United States is a celebrity. There's an impulse not to view presidents in this way, because the term *celebrity* feels like a pejorative denigration. It cheapens the status of America's most important job and implies that the selection process is superficial and capricious. But that reaction is semantic: *Celebrity* simply connotes a person who is famous, and it's not really possible for any other American to be more famous than the sitting president for a sustained period of time. It's the ultimate form of celebrity, since it's the only version of that designation that automatically interlocks with history. It's exceedingly rare for other celebrity icons to last more than sixty years in the collective consciousness.* There will be a time, in the not-too-distant future, when almost no one will remember that Robert Redford was the biggest box office star of 1975, or that 1975 saw the release of *Born to Run*. But there will always be a rough awareness that Gerald Ford was

---

*Documentarian Ken Burns once made this point when discussing the Beatles: In terms of public consciousness, there tends to be a large drop-off in the casual awareness of any cultural artifact between its fortieth and fiftieth anniversary, and then a dramatic and exponential drop-off between the fiftieth and sixtieth anniversary. Almost nothing that's sixty years old remains relevant to large numbers of people. Burns cited the Beatles as the rare example of something to which this phenomenon does not seem to apply.

president in 1975, even though he was never elected and achieved almost nothing. A president is the only celebrity remembered out of civic obligation. And that, usually, works to a president's advantage.

Every active president is polarizing. Every active president is simultaneously adored and despised. The job description demands it, and the office can't be attained without making a sizable segment of the population angry. But anger fades. The memory of a president is, traditionally, a memory that ages well, often for illogical reasons. Bad policies and political betrayals stay tethered to the past while the man who made them continues to live, humanized by the rudimentary act of staying alive. Holding on to anger toward a former president is like remaining angry with someone who wronged you in high school. It seems a little pathetic and a little deranged. Which is why the legacy of Bill Clinton is so difficult to elucidate to those who missed his tenure: He's the rare example of a polarizing ex-president who saw the anger against him fade, only to have it resurface and spike upward within his own lifetime, often for the same reasons that made people like him originally.

It would be wrong to classify Bill Clinton as some kind of victim. It's easier to argue he was the opposite. But he was, in practice, victimized by something no person could possibly anticipate. Clinton was the last transcendent political figure of an era no one realized was ending. The result is a biographical distortion that somehow feels recent and ancient at the same time. Clinton's own self-descriptions make him sound like a presidential primordial: In a 2011 speech, he claimed to have sent only two emails during the eight years he lived in the White House (one to John Glenn and one to military troops in the Adriatic). It was his way of illustrating just how different things were in the very recent past. But that sort of casual claim could no longer be made in 2011. The year 2011 existed within the new paradigm, where a publication like *The Atlantic* would assign a reporter to investigate whether this harmless anecdote was false, four years after the speech was delivered (and as it turns out, Clinton had an AOL account in 1993). Over and over, Clinton acted like the man he was: a brilliant, craven, self-interested pragmatist born in 1946. It made him the defining figure of the nineties and a charismatic personality who will never be classified as truly good.

If, like so many people, Clinton is remembered for only one thing, it will be for his affair with Monica Lewinsky, a twenty-two-year-old White House intern. If, like so many other people, Clinton is remembered for a collection of choices that aggregate into one overall portrait, it will be for his relationship with Lewinsky and the numerous other women who accused him of pursuing unwanted (or consensual-but-extramarital) sexual encounters, a number stretching into the double digits. Either prospect makes him an irreconcilable villain among young people (and particularly young women) who have little or no memory of Clinton's time in office. It's an impossible thing to explain, way beyond the cinematic stardom of Pauly Shore: How could a married forty-nine-year-old "liberal" president (a) chronically seduce an unpaid subordinate less than half his age, (b) receive nonreciprocal oral sex inside the Oval Office, (c) get caught, (d) lie about it, (e) never directly apologize to the involved woman, and (f) still experience his highest presidential approval rating *immediately after* being impeached for lying under oath about the nature of that sexual relationship? Every component of the scandal is so averse to the post-#MeToo worldview that any neutral attempt at contextualizing or rationalizing the action is viewed as a crime unto itself. This, without question, is the reason Clinton will never be embraced by those who barely remember his presence. But there's also a secondary reason, and that reason is more byzantine.

Clinton, more than any other national political force, adopted neoliberalism as his central governing principle. His version of neoliberalism—the application of market-driven solutions to traditional Democratic concerns, like poverty and job creation—can be traced to Charles Peters, author of a 1982 essay titled "A Neoliberal's Manifesto." The essay's opening sentence is a concise description of Clinton's worldview: "If neoconservatives are liberals who took a critical look at liberalism and decided to become conservatives, we are liberals who took the same look and decided to retain our goals but to abandon some of our prejudices."

It's a centrist approach, though it didn't seem that way to center-right observers in 1992: "Neo"-liberalism still meant liberalism, and any outlook advocated by a draft-dodging, pro-abortion Democrat had to be leftist. It was not until late in his second term (when he repealed the Glass-Steagall Act* and deregulated the derivatives market†) that Clinton's centrism became overt. He latently supported free trade more than he latently supported labor unions. But here again—none of this was a detriment, at the time. It tended to validate the political image he'd worked to cultivate in the face of constant right-wing cynicism. Clinton was a realist who could always find the necessary compromise. He saw the subjective world through economic metrics. He was, in fact, the kind of open-minded political architect who could (as Charles Peters instructed) abandon his prejudices. What Clinton could not (and did not) anticipate was a future where leftists would see ideological prejudice as sacred.

"What began as a new form of intellectual authority, rooted in a devoutly apolitical worldview," critic (and former Hillary Clinton speechwriter) Stephen Metcalf wrote in 2017, "nudged easily into an ultra-reactionary politics." To partisan thinkers of this sect, neoliberalism is the root of all the world's problems, thus framing Bill Clinton as the catalyst for pretty much every dilemma of the twenty-first century (including the eventual election of Donald Trump). For this, Clinton is disparaged, and the fact that he embraced centrism by design pushes that dislike toward hatred.

○ ○ ○

Clinton's presidential ascension began at the 1992 Iowa caucuses, where he was a nonfactor who received 2.81 percent of the vote. That September, the

---

*This 1999 repeal deregulated investment banking, which some believe led to the financial crisis of 2007.

†This is a complicated concept that has to do with a contract between two or more parties, where the value of the contract is "derived" from an underlying financial asset. Derivatives can (apparently) be used to mitigate or reward risk, although I'd be lying if I claimed to understand how. But the one thing everyone seems to concede about the derivatives market is that its deregulation *definitely* led to the financial crisis of 2007.

Dallas Cowboys opened their NFL season by beating the Washington Redskins 23–10 on *Monday Night Football*, the start of a 13-3 campaign that would culminate with the first of three Super Bowl victories they'd amass in a dynastic four-year window. These events seem completely unrelated. They are not.

The Cowboys' success in the nineties was built on a trio of superstar skill players,* a dominating offensive line, and a defense that emphasized team speed. The engineer was head coach Jimmy Johnson, who'd been hired by his old college buddy Jerry Jones. The pair had played football together for the University of Arkansas in the sixties.

Jones purchased the Cowboys in 1989 for $140 million. Jones had first made big money in oil during the seventies but got even richer in the natural gas industry, starting around 1980. His company, Arkoma, quickly entered an exclusive relationship with the utility that supplied natural gas to all of Arkansas. That utility was Arkansas-Louisiana Gas Inc., better known as Arkla. The CEO of Arkla was a guy named Sheffield Nelson, a longtime acquaintance of Jones (they'd previously partnered on a variety of rich-guy ventures—real estate, a TV station, racehorses). It was a real sweetheart deal: Even when natural gas prices dropped to 50 cents per thousand cubic feet, Arkla was committed to paying Arkoma $4.50 for the same quantity. The excess cost was dumped onto consumers. Sheffield resigned from Arkla in 1984 to pursue political opportunities. The only way for Arkla's new CEO to get out of the terrible Arkoma deal was to buy Jones's company outright for $174 million. Later, the Arkansas Public Service Commission charged Arkla with fraud, based on the one-sided deal with Jones and Arkoma. When Sheffield Nelson ran for governor of Arkansas in 1990, that old Arkoma corruption became a wedge issue in the campaign, contributing to a landslide for the incumbent governor: Bill Clinton, a rising Democratic star who'd managed to win his fifth gubernatorial term before his forty-fifth birthday.

This connection is not revealing or gobsmacking. It's arguably not even

---

*Quarterback Troy Aikman, running back Emmitt Smith, and wide receiver Michael Irvin.

a coincidence, and perhaps not a significant one if it is. But it shows something about the imposed interconnectivity of living a public life: So often, the formative experiences of historically notable people seem to glancingly intersect with the lives of other notable people, almost like there's a magnetic attraction among all individuals destined for greatness. Yet the more likely explanation is that these haphazard collisions spur both parties to pursue goals that eventually make their early interactions quasi-meaningful. It's always framed as surprising, for example, that Hillary Clinton (then Hillary Rodham) was a staff attorney during the Watergate impeachment hearings in 1974, and then married a man the following year who himself would be impeached roughly twenty-five years later. "You can't make my life up," Hillary would later joke. The connection seems like amazing trivia. But perhaps it explains the attraction between a woman academically intrigued by high-stakes political chess and a man who intuitively understood the dangerous contradiction between his growing political ambition and his own human weakness.

Here is Bill Clinton writing about himself:

I am a living paradox—deeply religious yet not as convinced of my exact beliefs as I ought to be; wanting responsibility yet shirking it; loving the truth but often times giving way to falsity. . . . I detest selfishness, but see it in the mirror every day. . . . I view those, some of whom are very dear to me, who have never learned how to live. I desire and struggle to be different from them, but often am almost an exact likeness. . . . I, in my attempts to be honest, will not be the hypocrite I hate, and will own up to their ominous presence in this boy, endeavoring in such earnest to be a man.

This passage can be found in Clinton's 2004 autobiography *My Life*, but that's not when he wrote it. He wrote it as a high school junior as an assignment for English class, later admitting he did not fully understand what he was writing or what he was trying to convey. It's obviously unreasonable to hold any person to the portrait they paint of themselves at the age of sixteen. Still, there's a level of straightforward awareness to these thoughts that is hard to find elsewhere in *My Life*, a 1,008-page book that often reads with purposeful monotony. Like the journal of many precocious teenagers, it exhibits a fixation on the realization that one's interior life is always contradictory. But what's different with Clinton is his preternatural ability to compartmentalize those contradictions into a worldview that's perfectly balanced. He is emotionally troubled by this paradox, but not in a way that stops him from doing whatever he desires intellectually. His teenage self-portrait remained remarkably stable for the rest of his life. The people Clinton would always understand best were those most like him—people who existed in a state of moral and psychological ambivalence.

The most transparent illustration of this quality comes not from the beginning or end of his presidential tenure, but from the middle. Statistically, Clinton's 1996 reelection victory was authoritative: He received a higher percentage of the popular vote than he did in '92 and more than doubled the electoral total of his Republican opponent, Bob Dole. Dole, an admirable seventy-three-year-old senator from Kansas, was not exactly a robust rival: He was much older than Clinton and had suffered an injury during World War II that effectively paralyzed his right arm (he tried to mitigate the problem by sticking a pen into the fingers of his immobilized limb, though that tended to showcase the injury more). On a campaign stop in California, Dole fell off the stage. He had been Gerald Ford's running mate when Ford lost in 1976, and became the GOP candidate in '96 by default. An old-school balance-the-budget fanatic, Dole had put in his time and deserved his shot, but the deck was stacked against him in almost every way (Clinton's campaign spending almost doubled what Dole spent). In retrospect, the whole '96 election cycle feels like an afterthought—the rare modern election where voters weren't constantly told that this was the most important decision they would ever make. Voter turnout dipped below 50 percent for the first time since 1924. It's hard to imagine Clinton losing to this particular man at that particular time. Yet less than two years before election night, Clinton's goose seemed cooked, and his strategic response suggests even he assumed he was on the precipice of defeat.

The off-year election of 1994 hit the Democrats like a jackhammer to the jowls. The Republicans took control of both houses of Congress in what was feverishly labeled the Republican Revolution, although a more accurate description would have been the Predictable Revolution. Clinton had won in '92 as the youthful, liberal colt in a three-horse race, but his core message was classically moderate—middle-class families would get a tax cut and welfare would be reformed. That never happened. Georgia's Newt Gingrich, the idea-obsessed, mongoose-like Speaker of the House, had marshaled his power as the face of "the Contract with America," a collection of specific and abstract conservative talking points that outlined the Republican agenda. The details of the contract mattered less than the tone with which it was pitched. Clinton was concurrently cast as every kind of possible failure: immature and unqualified to lead, but also a lying leftist, but also a McDonald's-gorged good ol' boy who gave his wife the job of nationalizing health care against the will of the people (which was untrue for at least two reasons*). "What was unsettling about the overwhelming rejection of Clinton in the 1994 Congressional elections," wrote Steve Erickson in his book *American Nomad*, "was the extent to which it was personal." Gingrich's savvy was making an off-year election more national than local, forwarding the vision that this state-by-state landslide was proof that voters now realized the 1992 election had been a mistake. The stature of Clinton in '94 adopted the doomed, ineffectual posture of Jimmy Carter in '78. He seemed destined to be a one-term president.

---

*The Clinton health care vision was not really liberal or conservative, but a middle strategy between the two (it rejected a single-payer system but forced employers to either fully cover all their employees or pay a tax that would expand coverage for anyone who didn't have insurance). It was also not something that Americans unilaterally opposed—by 1990, support for health care reinvention was the highest it had been in forty years.

The strategic solution was emblematic of his entire career. Clinton quietly (some would say secretly) reached out to Dick Morris,* the stridently amoral political consultant who always served as Clinton's most trusted adviser in moments of peril. At the time, Morris was mostly working for Republicans, but he was a free agent who switched alliances easily. The Morris plan was unlike any other political approach in U.S. history. The emphasis was on polling, but that wasn't the innovative part. Clinton had relied heavily on polling when he won in 1992. The innovation was to look at voters as pure consumers and to exclusively focus on voters who didn't have a defined political ideology.

"The most important thing for him to do was to bring to the political system the same consumer rules and philosophy that the business community has," Morris would explain in 2002. "I think all of this involves a changed view of the voters, so that instead of treating them as targets, you treat them as owners. Instead of treating them as something you can manipulate, you treat them as something you can learn from."

Described in those terms, it sounds like benevolent common sense. But the underlying goal was more ruthless.

What Morris spearheaded was a kind of political polling that did not have an overt relationship to politics. The polling firm PSB Insights† was enlisted to conduct what they called a "neuropersonality poll" on potential voters. The intent was to create a psychological profile based not on a respondent's ideology, but on their metaphysical desires. What TV shows did they watch? What did they worry about? Did they like to dance? What day-to-day problems felt beyond their control? The whole idea was to isolate *exactly* what an individual wanted, regardless of the magnitude or societal import. That

---

*Morris remembers the first reconnection with Clinton as an unexpected twenty-minute phone call where the president asked Morris's opinion on the political ramifications of the United States invading Haiti.

†PSB is an abbreviation of Penn, Schoen & Berland Associates, operated by Mark Penn, Douglas Schoen, and Michael Berland. Penn and Schoen were prep school classmates in the seventies who later attended Harvard together.

was step one. The second step was to disregard the wants and desires of any poll respondent who exhibited a preexisting opinion on who they would vote for. There was no value in considering the thoughts of anyone who was already for them or already against them. The only voters who mattered were undecided swing voters.

The result was a new kind of "small ball" platform that confounded Clinton's cabinet. Instead of structural transformations, Clinton promoted a string of specific measures appealing to secular, middle-class, values-oriented parents who were perched on the partisan fence: support for school uniform policies, restrictions on tobacco, and the insertion of V-chip technology into televisions to stop kids from accessing pornography. Nothing was left to chance. The phrase "Building a Bridge to the 21st Century" became the new campaign motto when it polled at 61 percent, outpacing "Building a Bridge to the Year 2000" (54 percent) and "Building a Bridge to a Second Term" (39 percent). No detail was too arcane to calculate. Clinton's 1996 State of the Union address was capped at forty minutes when polling data indicated casual voters would dislike a speech that droned on for too long.

"I think the key to understanding Morris—his hold on the President and his success at helping Clinton assert himself—is that he was not bound to what passed for reality in Washington," Michael Waldman wrote in his 2000 book *POTUS Speaks*. Waldman had been a policy aide for Clinton and later served as his director of speechwriting. What kept happening, Waldman noted, was that Clinton would want to come out in favor of (for example) a balanced budget. The traditional operatives on Clinton's staff, like George Stephanopoulos and Leon Panetta, would view such a desire as intricate and potentially unworkable. They would see nothing except obstructions. But "Morris would simply look at the polls, tap a question on his handheld computer and announce, *'The President should come out for a balanced budget.'"* Morris saw no problem with advertising a product that didn't yet exist. If the plan didn't work as intended, the malfunction could be fixed later, in the exact same style. The key was keeping Clinton near the political center, where he could comfortably drift either left or right, depending on what was required in the moment.

Morris's tenure on the '96 campaign was cantankerous and brief. It concluded during the Democratic convention in August. Morris constantly clashed with the same consulting team he'd hired and was ultimately forced to exit after the tabloid *Star* magazine exposed a lengthy relationship he'd conducted with a prostitute. It was an awkward, if not necessarily stunning, conclusion. But the Morris gambit had worked: Once it became a head-to-head race versus Dole, Clinton never trailed. The grimness of '94 proved overblown, rapidly relegated to the memory cave. What was galvanized, however, was the nature and intelligence of Bill Clinton. His nature was to continually migrate toward the moving center of wherever the populace happened to be; his intelligence was an ability to understand how that populace had been conditioned to see the world through an inflexibly consumerist lens.

The 1980s had been the penultimate step in an evolution happening throughout the twentieth century, increasing in speed after the Second World War. There was now complete integration between the notion of living a normal life and the ubiquity of how the larger culture was packaged and presented by the media. This, in many ways, was the crux of the Generation X conundrum—how (for example) was it possible for a person to reject the illusion of advertising if their only concept of authenticity had been constructed by advertising? How was it possible to see politics as separate from entertainment if the defining president of their adolescence had started his career as an actor? In the same way twenty-first-century adults would grow comfortable with classifying their own personalities as "brands," late-twentieth-century adults nonchalantly accepted the possibility that their principal social function was to serve as consumers. Dick Morris helped Clinton realize this intellectually. But Clinton's natural inclination needed no instruction. He understood what people wanted, and not just in a material sense. His enemies labeled him Slick Willy, as if Clinton were constantly trying to unload a used Buick. What he was really selling was a less tangible commodity: the signifiers of empathy. Yes, he was a kind of salesman, because that's what postmodernity required.

○ ○ ○

When impressionists (and especially lazy impressionists) delivered their comedic interpretation of Clinton, the phrase they always used was "I feel your pain," expressed with a sympathetic Southern drawl. It became the Clintonian trademark, even though the origin of the phrase is unrelated to how it came to define him. It appears that Clinton literally said "I feel your pain" only once, at a fundraiser in the spring of 1992, angrily responding to an AIDS activist named Bob Rafsky* who accused Clinton of not caring enough about the AIDS crisis. Clinton says these four words loudly and emphatically, a little mad at the guy for questioning the sincerity of his sentiments. It's strange that people would later see this phrase as Clinton feigning sympathy he never feigned, but that's the nature of memory. Somehow, the version of this quote people erroneously remember has been mentally inserted into both (a) a moment from a 1992 town hall presidential debate when Clinton expressed real understanding of the recession, and (b) his speech following the 1995 Oklahoma City bombing, which was Clinton at his apex.

It was four days after the OKC tragedy when Clinton unleashed the best nine minutes of his presidency. The word-for-word content of the address he gave at the memorial prayer service is pretty good, but that's not the important part; on the page, the speech he delivered was not that different from the speech that was expected. The 914 words were a collaboration composed by multiple writers, much of which was drafted and fine-tuned on the helicop-

---

*It should be noted that after this confrontation, Rafsky was asked by Clinton to help draft an agenda for how his administration should deal with the crisis. Rafsky died from AIDS-related complications less than a year after the original incident at the fundraiser.

ter ride from DC to Oklahoma City. A phrase like "One thing we owe those who have sacrificed is the duty to purge ourselves of the dark forces which gave rise to this evil" does not scan as unscripted material. But the brilliance was in the way the words were said. Here was a guy reading carefully crafted sentences off a piece of paper, yet pausing and changing tempo and behaving as though the speech were being invented as he went along. And he was not doing this to trick anyone—it's not like he was trying to create the false impression of someone speaking extemporaneously. He was not. He was in no way hiding the fact that the speech was directly in front of him or that this was a public performance. The audience knew exactly what was happening. Yet Clinton managed to make that audience—both in the room and across the country—suspend their inherent understanding of how politics are manufactured.

John Kennedy was the first television president, and Ronald Reagan's background in Hollywood allowed him to understand the power of TV in a way his predecessors had not. But Bill Clinton was the president who recognized that television was a medium intimately understood by everyone who had never experienced life without it. Citizens in other countries do not view the American people as particularly bright, and Americans themselves sometimes use words like *sophisticated* and *elite* as pejoratives.* But by the early nineties, Americans had developed a sophisticated, elite understanding of how television works. Without even trying, they could dissect a broadcast like Clinton's Oklahoma City address with the acuteness of self-taught media analysts. And within those conditions—within the context of *grading* a speech's sincerity as much as *feeling* that sincerity—Clinton was unstoppable.

---

*"The strain of anti-intellectualism has been a constant thread winding its way through our political and cultural life, nurtured by the false notion that democracy means that *my ignorance is just as good as your knowledge.*" Prolific science fiction author Isaac Asimov wrote that sentence in 1980, and it had become a widely accepted view by the time he died in 1992. Though it was hidden from the public at the time, Asimov died from complications due to HIV, contracted via a blood transfusion in 1983. The Asimov family did not reveal this until 2002, in justifiable fear of anti-AIDS prejudice.

Throughout the summer of 1992, MTV made the institutional decision to become heavily involved with the presidential campaign, allegedly to increase voter turnout (the campaign was called "Choose or Lose") but really as an unabashed advocate for Clinton's candidacy. In June, Clinton appeared in front of an MTV audience of young adults and took their questions. The show was moderated by Tabitha Soren, a wonkish twenty-four-year-old journalist who'd also appeared in a 1987 Beastie Boys video. George H. W. Bush was dismissive of MTV, granting Soren only a brief interview on a moving train (and only after receiving criticism for ignoring younger voters so openly). Clinton, however, loved it. As a sitting president, he returned to MTV in 1994 for another town hall event, this time called "Enough Is Enough." The main topic was gang violence, but the exchange people remember is when an audience member asked Clinton about his underwear and whether he preferred boxers or briefs (he said "usually briefs," which somehow came across as surprising). There was an eye-roll quality to much of this publicity, not unlike his 1992 appearance on *The Arsenio Hall Show*, where Clinton wore sunglasses and played the saxophone. There was a desire to portray it as pandering and unserious. The results, however, were almost always good for Clinton. Unlike most politicians of his era, he did not appear to be fighting popular culture. He appeared to simply view it as the culture that was popular, and he'd engage with it on its own terms.

In 1994, MTV aired season three of the reality show *The Real World*, this time set in San Francisco. Though the series would run for decades, season three was its sociocultural high point, punctuated by a gay Cuban-American house member, Pedro Zamora, suffering from HIV. Zamora dramatically died just a few hours after the airing of the season's finale. To the surprise of almost everyone who watched *The Real World*, Clinton publicly addressed Zamora's death, praising his activism and stating, "Now no one in America can say they've never known someone who's living with AIDS." This, of course, is both technically and figuratively wrong. You only knew of Zamora if you watched a specific reality show on a specific youth-oriented cable network, and—even if you did—it was impossible to "know" someone by watching him on a heavily edited program for twenty-two minutes a week. The central criticism of *The Real World* was that it wasn't real at all. But Clinton understood what everyone watching him understood: Claiming to know someone as a TV personality has a different meaning from knowing someone in daily life, and anything that happens on television is happening to society at large, including those people who don't realize it's happening at all. He understood that people wanted to believe watching a show on MTV was a legitimate life experience, even if they themselves were dubious about what they were seeing as they were seeing it. He understood that young people did not actually expect him to feel their pain. What they wanted was someone who seemed to be *trying* to feel their pain, through the language and medium they had inherited. It was a reality of diminished expectations: Clinton was a paragon of empathy not necessarily because of what he felt, but because he understood how empathy was supposed to look on television. Which is not to say he was lying or pretending, because that's not the point. It merely means that the degree to which his feelings were genuine was secondary to the degree to which he was trying to take something impossible and make it plausible.

Clinton was raised in Hot Springs, Arkansas, a resort community already calling itself "Sin City" when Las Vegas was still an outpost for Mormon pioneers migrating to California. But Clinton was born in the much smaller Arkansas town of Hope, allowing him to forever present himself as the Man Who Came from a Place Called Hope. This is a meaningless distinction that doesn't reflect anything about what Clinton was actually like. It only matters as support for the unending accusation that who Clinton was and how he presented himself were not the same. It's a dumb contradiction to focus on, since such incongruities exist for every public figure who ever lived. But it mattered more with Clinton, if only because he kept forcing people to deal with it. The conflict over who he was did not emerge over time. It was always there, before anything else.

The first time a mass audience of disparate Americans experienced Clinton was a TV interview where he sat next to his wife and admitted that he'd cheated on her. It aired on the January 26, 1992, episode of *60 Minutes*, following a Super Bowl that had been watched by almost 120 million people. Like so many of his sexual misadventures, the confession damaged a woman more than it damaged him. That *60 Minutes* interview is now mostly remembered for something Hillary said:

"You know, I'm not sitting here, some little woman standing by my man like Tammy Wynette," she said. "I'm sitting here because I love him, and I respect him, and I honor what he's been through and what we've been through together. And you know, if that's not enough for people, then heck—don't vote for him."

When Hillary ran for president in 2008 and 2016, these words haunted her. They seemed to disappoint the people who believed in her and further repel the people who did not. In '92, however, those words were excellent for Bill. He was still such a presidential long shot that having an enormous TV audience for any reason—including his own infidelity—was a net positive. It was even possible that admitting their marriage was imperfect may have positioned Clinton as a normal adult with relatable weaknesses. A 1991 study by sexological feminist Shere Hite claimed that 70 percent of married women had cheated on their spouses. A similar 1993 study said the same thing about 72 percent of married men. The nineties were not a puritanical era. Still, the ability to sidestep the specific problem in front of him exacerbated the larger problem that would never go away. Though he admitted he'd "caused pain" in his marriage, Clinton directly denied that he'd had an affair with an Arkansas singer named Gennifer Flowers, a woman who said they'd been sexually involved for twelve years during the 1970s and '80s (and who eventually got a state government job with Clinton's assistance). It was an illustration of Clinton's compulsion to intertwine fact and fiction in the most perilous ways imaginable: He conceded he'd had an affair (true), possibly multiple affairs (true), but not the particular affair that was forcing him to discuss his other affairs (false). If he was willing to admit he'd cheated on his wife, why did he insist that it hadn't happened with the one woman who had the most irrefutable evidence that it had?

"There is a difference between reputation and character," Clinton said in 1995, "and I have increasingly less control over my reputation but still full control over my character." That sounds like an insightful realization that should apply to everyone, but it didn't apply to Clinton himself. He was, relative to the circumstances, amazingly adroit at rehabilitating his reputation in the face of adversity, including accusations of murder.* What he was unable to control was who he was. For twenty-five years, he never discussed why he risked his entire presidential career on a relationship with an intern he never took seriously. When he finally addressed this, in a documentary series about his wife, the closest he came to an explanation was to say he did not know how to properly "manage" his "anxieties." Throughout the documentary, he appears contrite and regretful, although it's hard to imagine how appearing any other way would not have been seen as diabolical. Pursuing a relationship with Monica Lewinsky was probably the dumbest personal decision any normal president has ever made—not the *worst* decision, but the dumbest. So dumb, in fact, that a reasonable person is forced to conclude Bill Clinton must have needed the excitement that came with the risk of what he was doing. He did not, in any way, have full control over his character.

A vivid regurgitation of the Lewinsky affair is both tawdry and unnecessary. The facts of the case can be studied in detail by reading *The Starr*

---

*In 1993, deputy White House counsel Vincent W. Foster committed suicide in his car with a .38 revolver. For the rest of Clinton's presidency, a theory was forwarded that Foster had been murdered by the Clintons as part of the cover-up surrounding the Whitewater real estate scandal. Televangelist Jerry Falwell Sr. even financed a documentary about the accusation titled *The Clinton Chronicles*.

Report, the official investigation compiled by attorney Kenneth Starr.* The atmosphere and human toll is best explained by Lewinsky herself, who has spoken of this at length. The most basic facts are these: During a temporary federal government shutdown in 1995, unpaid interns were forced to play a bigger role in White House operations. While working on a Saturday (as he often did), Clinton began a flirtation with intern Lewinsky that became more serious after Lewinsky playfully showed Clinton the strap of her thong underwear. The pair eventually had nine sexual encounters inside the White House, although never full intercourse. Lewinsky was subsequently transferred to a job in the Pentagon and was befriended by an older coworker named Linda Tripp, who recorded many of their conversations and convinced Lewinsky to keep any physical evidence that proved she'd been intimate with Clinton (most notably a semen-stained blue dress). Tripp's recordings were given to Starr in exchange for immunity.† The impeachment Clinton faced in 1998 was not because the affair occurred, but because Clinton had lied under oath about the relationship with Lewinsky during a deposition given in response to a sexual harassment lawsuit brought forth by a woman named Paula Jones. Jones had worked for the state of Arkansas in 1991 and said Clinton exposed his penis to her in a hotel room.

Reduced to twenty-five words, the president's behavior seems even worse than it was: He lied about a consensual sexual affair with a subordinate in hopes of dodging a lawsuit over a nonconsensual sexual interaction with a relative stranger. But what's even harder to reconcile is the diametric

---

*Issued on September 9, 1998, *The Starr Report* first came across the AP wire during the afternoon. It was a little like the modern experience of following breaking news on Twitter, although the takes were longer and the reader had to be working inside a newsroom in order to see them as they appeared. The level of detail is granular: On page 64, for example, there is a dispute over the notion that one could argue that a person performing oral sex was involved in "sexual relations" but the person receiving oral sex was not, technically, involved in a sexual relationship.

†Tripp's deal for immunity remains a perplexing detail in all this, as it seems unlikely she would have faced any personal risk at all if she'd just kept quiet and done nothing. The idea of recording her conversations with Lewinsky actually came from Lucianne Goldberg, a literary agent. Tripp died from pancreatic cancer in 2020. In what can only be classified as an uncommonly classy move, Lewinsky expressed sadness over Tripp's illness and sympathy for Tripp's family.

difference between how the event was viewed in the nineties and how it's viewed now. In the nineties, Lewinsky was publicly crucified, mocked for her physical appearance, and considered culpable for what had happened; today, she is seen as having almost no agency whatsoever, almost as if she were an inebriated minor.* Jones was taken even less seriously and categorized as a redneck bimbo; today, most people accept her version of the events and see her as savvy. But perhaps the biggest difference is how the average person was socialized to judge this affair. Around Christmas of 1998, just after his impeachment trial, Clinton's approval rating famously went up to its highest point ever (73 percent). This was perceived as proof that the public had a more mature, more levelheaded view of his infidelity than members of the media, who remained obsessed with the soap opera. Though Clinton did lie under oath and (technically) obstructed justice, removing him from office for these offenses was never a real possibility. The progressive view was to see these sanctions as histrionic political theater.

Most people wanted Clinton to remain president. They just didn't trust him as a person.

The trade-off was acceptable.

It's hard to think about this period of U.S. history without concluding that certain generational stereotypes were more true than false. Baby Boomers are often branded as hypocritical on issues involving sex and gender, and the way that demographic assigned blame for the Lewinsky fiasco supports that accusation. Gen Xers were cast as a group of detached slackers who didn't care about things that didn't involve them directly. In regard to Clinton's sex life, that categorization is difficult to deny. Just before the Lewinsky scandal broke wide open, a movie called *Wag the Dog* was released in theaters. Starring Dustin Hoffman and Robert De Niro, it was a satire about a fake war in Albania that was invented to distract the public from a fictional

---

*In 2020, Lewinsky used Twitter to request that her name not even be used by members of the media when referencing the scandal.

president's sexual impropriety. The movie was bad, but its timing was impeccable. Throughout the Lewinsky scandal, whenever Clinton bombed a foreign country (which he did three times*), *Wag the Dog* was certain to be referenced at every turn. Still, that implied relationship was seen as more bemusing than tragic. The concept of anonymous people being killed as a method of political cover was rarely bemoaned as a horrific, unimaginable act. Instead, it was seen as disenchanting evidence that this was how the world worked, and that nothing was too outrageous to be implausible, and that such dark motives couldn't be proven even if they were true, and that the theory of life imitating art was now so entrenched in American psychology that it was banal to express surprise.

"This is our first black president," it was written of Bill Clinton. "Blacker than any actual black person who could ever be elected in our children's lifetime. After all, Clinton displays almost every trope of blackness: single-parent household, born poor, working class, saxophone-playing, McDonald's-and-junk-food loving boy from Arkansas."

It now seems unfathomable that such sentiments were ever expressed nonsarcastically about any white person, Clinton or otherwise. But they were indeed expressed, in 1998, only one decade before an actual Black president was elected in a landslide. And they were expressed by Black Nobel Prize winner Toni Morrison, and they were published in *The New Yorker*, and they were not perceived as controversial or particularly contrarian. Things of this nature were often written about Clinton, and they cannot be unwritten. The only way to escape this, it seems, is to write over these things and hope no once notices.

Twenty-five years after the '92 election, an essay was published in *Globe*

---

*Most memorably a 1998 bombing campaign against Iraq that took place during the impeach-ment trial, but also a 1999 military action against Yugoslavia and the ill-advised destruction of a pharmaceutical factory in Sudan that happened immediately after the scandal first surfaced.

Magazine that defines the concept of revisionism. The headline was as straightforward as a shark attack: "How Democrats Would Be Better Off If Bill Clinton Had Never Been President." The article proposed a perception of history where Clinton's sexual impropriety was just one error within a host of fatal mistakes—inadvertently destroying the safety net for millions of people by signing a bad welfare bill, packaging a positive gun law with a racist crime bill, fueling the concept of Fox News and mortally wounding the future prospects of Al Gore. "Listen to today's critiques from the leaders of the left," argues the essay's author, Neil Swidey. "If you trace their indictment back to its roots, you'll see they're really talking about Clinton." The essay starts from the position that Clinton's presidential failure is now a given, and that the only real debate is the degree to which that failure was inevitable or avoidable.

But you know, it didn't seem that way at the time.

It really did not.

Clinton made mistakes. As years have passed and society has shifted, those mistakes seem worse and worse. There's growing evidence that his overall legacy will be closer to the portrait painted by Gingrich, radio host Rush Limbaugh, and other conservative critics widely viewed as obsessive and unfair for most of the nineties. One can imagine a not-so-distant future when an indoctrinated young progressive will learn about Clinton and wonder how and why this man was twice elected president. Yet when Clinton *was* the president, the country seemed good, economically and otherwise. He was clever and competent. He loved the job and the responsibilities that came with it. Clinton instinctually reflected the ambivalence of the era in an optimistic way. Relative to the rest of the twentieth century, the nineties were a good time to be president, and he was a good president for good times.

"There was this interesting thing that was happening during the Clinton administration," recalls Zack de la Rocha, the radical Chicano frontman for the band Rage Against the Machine. "People were looking inward and not outward." Coming from de la Rocha, such a categorization is intended as an evisceration. It's supposed to suggest a kind of dreamlike negligence. What it fails to recognize is that the luxury of looking inward is not always a conscious extension of selfishness. It's sometimes the unconscious manifestation of a satisfying life, which is what government is supposed to offer its people.

That won't matter, of course.

The process of revisionism is constant. It happens so regularly that it often seems like the only reason to appraise any present-tense cultural artifact is to help future critics explain why the original appraisers were wrong. Near the end of the Clinton administration, seven months after he'd been found not guilty by the U.S. Senate, a movie titled *American Beauty* was released to tremendous acclaim. It was, by most measurable standards, the premier film of 1999: It won the Oscar for Best Picture, Best Director, and Best Original Screenplay. It dominated the Golden Globes and the British Academy Film Awards. It made $350 million at the box office and was praised by every kind of critic, including Bill Clinton (who found it slightly "disturbing" but mostly "amazing"). Those accolades are startling for two reasons. The first is that 1999 was one of the most competitive years in the history of cinema. The second is that *American Beauty* is now regularly cited as a despicable, embarrassing, problematic movie.

"Because of its blissful ignorance, *American Beauty* is a movie our culture can no longer afford to lionize," Sarah Fonder wrote in 2014, a criticism speciously operating from the premise that such lionization was still occurring. This is not a situation like 1998's *Shakespeare in Love* or 2005's *Crash*, where a film is merely seen as overrated or undeserving of its prestige. This is a situation where the movie's cast and technical prowess amplify people's outrage. *American Beauty* is hated for what it is now assumed to symbolize and justify, which only matters because it was well-made and well-acted. Had it simply been boring, no one would care. Its technical achievements make it worse, and it's now exceedingly rare to find new considerations of the film that aren't mostly (or exclusively) negative.

American Beauty centers on the life of Lester Burnham, a man who hates that life. Burnham is portrayed by Kevin Spacey, whose performance won the Oscar for Best Actor. Spacey was considered the finest "serious" actor among mainstream male stars, having already won an Academy Award for his supporting role in 1995's *The Usual Suspects*. Two decades later, Spacey would be accused of sexual assault by multiple parties. Those accusations would further denigrate the status of *American Beauty*, particularly since the Burnham character was sexually obsessed with a sixteen-year-old girl and one of Spacey's real-life accusers, actor Anthony Rapp, alleged that the assault took place when Rapp was fourteen. But by the time that scandal surfaced, the critical damage to *American Beauty* had already occurred. The issue is not with Spacey's ability or performance. The issue is that the movie sympathizes with the problems of a horny, self-interested, middle-aged predator who has come to be seen as having no problems whatsoever.

Lester Burnham lives in a beautiful suburban home and holds a high-paying magazine job he doesn't enjoy, so he gets fired on purpose. He spends his newfound free time in the garage, smoking weed purchased from the teenage boy living across the street. The boy is the son of a closeted homosexual who's also a Nazi. Burnham has a terrible relationship with his wife (Annette Bening, also nominated for an Oscar) and an equally terrible relationship with his daughter (Thora Birch), mostly because he constantly fantasizes about having sex with her best friend (Mena Suvari). "I'm just an ordinary guy with nothing to lose," Burnham says in the middle of the film, but in the final scene he gets murdered by the gay Nazi and truly loses whatever is left of whatever he's already lost. His death is supposed to redeem him, although there's an inclination to believe he deserved it.

The retroactive rejection of *American Beauty* has nothing to do with art. It's a rejection of what could reasonably be classified as a problem in 1999. This, somewhat hilariously, is also why it was so acclaimed. When it was new, *American Beauty* seemed to address uncomfortable domestic conflicts other movies were unwilling to confront. Lester's midlife crisis was viewed as a multifaceted existential concern. There was a sense his character pursued a dream many men silently desired. The modern reading is that Burnham's behavior is the juvenile manifestation of unearned privilege. Bening's career-driven character has an extramarital affair and is portrayed as shrewish and cold. The modern reading is that this depiction is sexist and that her character is heroic. Lester's infatuation with the teenager is presented in the film as uncomfortable and tragically comic. It now seems criminal, disgusting, and ineligible for use as a comedic plot point. The fact that Burnham quits a lucrative white-collar job to happily work the drive-through window at a fast-food restaurant seems oblivious and insulting to the realities of class struggle. Almost every key point in *American Beauty*—dissatisfaction with a traditional livelihood, the invisible loneliness of a sexless marriage, the shame of homosexuality, the longing for one's past, even the difficulty of buying pot—have come to represent pathetic dilemmas younger audiences consider opulent micro-concerns. Modern people hate *American Beauty* for the same reason people in 1999 loved *American Beauty*: It examines the interior problems of upper-middle-class white people living in the late twentieth century—the kind of people who voted for Bill Clinton twice and (perhaps) saw fragments of their own lives within the problems he created for himself. And it was, in all probability, the last time in history such problems would be considered worthy of contemplation.

[just try it and see what happens]

THERE WAS AN OFT-REPEATED QUOTE FROM AUTUMN OF 2000, GENERALLY attributed to ex–NBA power forward Charles Barkley in the *New York Post* (but occasionally credited to comedian Chris Rock, who may have said it first): "You know the world is going to hell when the best rapper out there is a white guy and the best golfer is a Black guy." It was a harmless, topical joke that encapsulated something deep—the creeping sense that everything commonly understood about society was inverting itself. But twenty-plus years later, the meaning of that quote feels different. For one thing, the juxtaposition of those roles does not seem to indicate a world that was going to hell, but a world that was evolving. And more significant, it captures a discombobulating societal feeling that had started percolating throughout the last half of the nineties: the electrifying possibility that previous impossibilities were now entirely possible.

This specific version of youthful optimism—the conviction that everything is suddenly different and the old rules no longer apply—is an evergreen sensation. It's believed by every person newly engaged with politics or sports or popular culture, regardless of when they were born. There was, however, slightly more justification for believing this at the end of the twentieth century. Part of that was due to the growth of the internet and the ambiguity over what that growth might entail; while it was widely assumed the internet was changing the landscape, it still wasn't clear how that change would manifest itself, which meant it could be projected as a way to reinvent anything. The other part was the realization that labeling entities as "alternative" was now a viable way to sell any otherwise unsellable product, prompting a genuine motivation to find and produce content that was once considered too off-kilter to make real money.*

Alternative rock had morphed into the dominant definition of mainstream music by the decade's midpoint. The multi-act summer touring festival Lollapalooza became the vortex of youth consumer identity, spurring a new kind of thinking within the entertainment industry: What if we convinced strange, uncompromising artists to commoditize their least strange, most compromised material? The Butthole Surfers, an avant-garde noise band from Texas whose name was too obscene to publish in newspapers, had a hot radio single with the song "Pepper" in 1996 (and when the song was written about in conservative outlets, the band would usually be referred to as "the BH Surfers"). Another drug-fueled psychedelic outfit, the Flaming Lips, found similar success in 1993 with the novelty tune "She Don't Use Jelly." Chumbawamba, a British pop group who promoted Marxist pacifist anarchy, had a massive Top 10 single about getting drunk and falling down. There was a preponderance of minor hits where the lead vocalist did not sing or rap, but instead monotonously and nonsensically talked over atmospheric backing music: "Detachable Penis" by King Missile, "Mmm Mmm Mmm Mmm" by the Crash Test Dummies, "Standing Outside a Broken Phone Booth with Money in My Hand" by Primitive Radio Gods, the campy and danceable "I'm Too Sexy" by Right Said Fred. Blues Traveler, a jam band fronted by a

---

*This happened so regularly that it stopped seeming surprising. In 1996, a well-written comedy about underemployed actors titled *Swingers* was released to moderate success. A few scenes in the film were staged in bars around the L.A. neighborhood of Los Feliz, where patrons danced to swing music by the group Big Bad Voodoo Daddy. This set off a national swing-dancing craze that lasted several years.

380-pound harmonica player, sold 6 million copies of their album *Four* and toured with the Rolling Stones. Wesley Willis, an outsider artist with schizophrenia performing cheaply produced non sequitur "songs" about whipping the ass of a llama, was exploited as a national sensation for half the decade. MTV created a show called *Amp* that tried to pitch electronica as a new incarnation of rock, and a typical video might show two Asian adolescents playing Ping-Pong or a man in a dog suit buying pulp novels off the street (though the most arresting clip was the 1997 video for the Prodigy's "Smack My Bitch Up," promoted by the network despite its nudity, its cocaine use, and its title).

Alternative music expanded into the umbrella of alternative culture, meaning the prefix "alt" could now be applied to almost anything for an instant jolt of reconsideration. There had always been structurally indefinable comedy, but now there was a definable alt-comedy scene, a thematic extension of the HBO sketch series *Mr. Show* that centered around clubs like Manhattan's Luna Lounge and Luna Park in West Hollywood. These so-called "alt comedians" were all doing different things, but they were unified by a sensibility their audience understood—this was meta comedy, based on critiquing the limitations and semiotics of traditional comedy. Sometimes a joke's punch line was that there was no punch line.

There was growing evidence that the trait drawing people to art was an artist's ability to succeed without appearing professional or studied. The 1999 horror film *The Blair Witch Project* had no recognizable stars and was predicated on the false conceit that the entire movie was unedited footage from a failed 1994 documentary. The dialogue was improvised and the camera work was distracting, but it ended up making $250 million. It was now feasible to create a major movie by making it look as if it had been made accidentally.

Here's the important thing, though: It wasn't *all* marketing. It wasn't *all* constructed. The videos on *Amp* were hypnotic. *The Blair Witch Project* was effective and original. Some of these previously impossible possibilities were superior to all models that had come before. Barkley's aforementioned reference to a white rapper and a Black golfer—Eminem and Tiger Woods—had little to do with cynical public relations or the changing taste of audiences. These were advanced versions of things that were already there, who just happened to look unlike every old version the world had ever known.

Eminem was not the first white rapper, nor was he the first talented white rapper. But he was the first white rapper to change the aesthetic parameters of the genre, and his linguistic virtuosity was the one (and only) quality that transcended the reality of his skin color. Eminem did not try to make people forget he was white. His whiteness informed everything about him. But unlike the Beastie Boys (who were credible but raised affluent) or Vanilla Ice (raised middle-class but never viewed as credible), Eminem was a Caucasian rap star who did not appear to be adopting hip-hop as an unorthodox performance style or an artistic choice. He appeared to have few other options and no other interests. He was alienated and poor, and his family life was terrible. Had he been born in 1962 (as opposed to 1972), one might have imagined him gravitating toward thrash metal or hardcore punk, or maybe just crime. But Eminem grew up in the late eighties, when hip-hop was something a white kid in Detroit could not only hear, but live in totality. That experience coalesced with his technical ability at writing, rhyming, and (above all) enunciating controversial, self-deprecating language with supernatural speed and clarity. The (often juvenile) lyrics were violent and homophobic, but plugged into current events with unexpected relevance and immediacy. For better or worse, Eminem levied his assault from the absolute dead center of mass celebrity culture. His first album was released in 1996. Within a span of five years, he was the most successful rap artist of all time.

Eminem's biggest record, *The Marshall Mathers LP*, came out in May of 2000. A month later, Tiger Woods won the British Open. Two months after that, Woods won the PGA Championship, his fifth major title. He was twenty-four years old. It appeared that nothing could stop Woods from becoming the greatest golfer who'd ever lived. Some argued he already was.

What we know now, of course, is that the passage of time has made Woods's status less clear. Woods might be the best golfer in the history of the sport, but that designation is not irrefutable. Injuries ravaged his body and a sex scandal derailed his mental focus. The memory of his career will always be mixed. But the memory of Woods at age twenty-four will always be flawless. In 2000, Tiger Woods was still *only* a golfer. Nothing else about him mattered more than that. Yes, he was Black, and golfers were rarely Black. That was huge, and certainly not invisible.* His most important sponsor, Nike, made race a central part of their promotional campaign. But he was also Asian and Native American, and he'd gone to Stanford, and he was so good at hitting a golf ball. And he wore red shirts, and his name was cool, and he was a perfectionist, and he was *just so goddamn good* at hitting a golf ball. Had anyone ever been this good at anything? There was a commercial, from 1999, where Woods wordlessly bounced a golf ball on the head of a pitching wedge for 28 seconds before whacking it in midair, like it was a baseball. It was so effortless and uncanny that people wondered if it was fake. His personality was ideal, because it did not exist. He never said anything unexpected or salacious or outrageously arrogant—pumping his fist after a clutch putt was the comprehensive portrait of his emotional output. In 1997, he'd granted an extended interview to *GQ* magazine where he made a few sophomoric jokes. After the article was published, he never said anything interesting again, at least not in public. Years later, after his life had imploded, this reticence would hound him. He would come to be seen as damaged and robotic and uncomfortable in his own body. He didn't have normal friendships. The intensity of his relationship with his father (a man

---

*The most egregious proof of Tiger's otherness was a joke made by fellow golfer Fuzzy Zoeller just before Woods won the Masters in 1997. The winner of the Masters gets to select the meal for the "Champions Dinner," a tournament banquet held the following year: "He's doing quite well, pretty impressive," said Zoeller. "That little boy is driving well and he's putting well. He's doing everything it takes to win. So, you know what you guys do when he gets in here? You pat him on the back and say congratulations and enjoy it and tell him not to serve fried chicken next year. Or collard greens or whatever the hell they serve." Woods ultimately selected cheeseburgers, chicken sandwiches, french fries, and milkshakes.

who'd maniacally trained him from infancy), once viewed as questionable, was reclassified as borderline abusive. His life story, despite its countless achievements and unimaginable wealth, would end up disenchanting, and perhaps even a little heartbreaking.

But that is only as it is now. That is not how it was then.

There was a time, not so very long ago, when he was still the human representation of neutral perfect. You cared about Tiger Woods or you didn't care about golf. There was no third option. To say he was as big as the sport itself is an insult, but not to the sport.

12 The End of the Decade, the End of Decades

CERTAIN EVENTS ARE IMPOSSIBLE TO UNDERSTAND THE FIRST TIME THEY are explained. Sometimes this is because the information is too complex to comprehend. But just as often, they're impossible to understand because the information, despite being basic and unambiguous, does not cohere into a circumstance that's rational enough to accept. The cognitive tendency is to reject the information and ask for clarification, even if the original anecdote was as straightforward as any anecdote can be. That tendency is why every person informed about what happened in the 1997 boxing rematch between Mike Tyson and Evander Holyfield inevitably responded with some version of the same question: "But what exactly do you mean when you say he *bit* him?"

What had happened, as it turns out, was exactly that. The description was not a metaphor. In the third round of the decade's most anticipated heavyweight fight, Mike Tyson—desperate, infuriated, and realizing he was going to lose—leaned into Evander Holyfield during a clinch and bit off a chunk of Holyfield's right ear. Holyfield hopped around in anguish as blood poured down his neck, the remnants of his detached cartilage still lying on the canvas.

The action was not clouded in mystery: Millions of people, including fight referee Mills Lane, had plainly seen Holyfield's ear mutilated by Tyson's teeth. But the attempt to gnaw an opponent's flesh was so outside what could reasonably be expected from a professional boxing match that there was a temporary attempt to treat the attack like an accidental infraction. Tyson was penalized two points and the fight resumed. Almost immediately, Tyson tried to chomp Holyfield again, and this time the referee did not intercede at all. At the end of the round, it was concluded that Tyson was now (quite obviously) trying to bite Holyfield on purpose, and Tyson was disqualified. Chaos erupted as the disqualified Tyson tried to rush across the ring and attack Holyfield and/or anyone who happened to be standing in the general vicinity of his corner. Police stormed the ring, and the disqualification was not officially announced to the audience for almost half an hour. For fans who hadn't watched the fight live, the explanation of what had transpired defied the most cursory understanding of how sports were supposed to work. There was awareness that Tyson was capable of almost anything imaginable, but the limitations of imagination excluded the possibility that he'd try to maim an opponent with his teeth.

The nineties were a terrible time for Mike Tyson, which is an odd thing to say about someone whose hobby was purchasing Bengal tigers. His media perception in 1989 was akin to that of Tiger Woods in 1999: It seemed indisputable that this person would eventually become the greatest practitioner in the history of his sport. He was a physically intimidating fighter, but also technically skilled and meticulously trained, in an era when great heavyweights were rare. Comedian Arsenio Hall had a stand-up bit where he argued it would be more equitable if Tyson stopped fighting humans and started fighting elephants. His charisma was sui generis—a hyperviolent Brownsville Brooklyn berserker who spoke with a lisp, loved and collected pigeons, and referred to himself as a Renaissance man. He easily won his first 37 professional fights, 33 by knockout. But then, in February of '90, an unfocused Tyson traveled to Japan and lost a title defense to James "Buster"

Douglas, an unknown challenger who had entered the ring as a 42-1 under-dog. Things only got worse from there. Tyson was convicted of rape in 1992, ultimately serving three years of a ten-year prison sentence in Indiana.* He regained the world heavyweight title upon his release, but this older, softer Tyson was a shadow of his former self. He first fought Holyfield in November of 1996, with Tyson opening as a 25-1 favorite. The smaller Holyfield was afflicted with a serious heart condition and thought to be past his prime, but he defeated Tyson in 11 rounds. The rematch (and the gnawing) happened the following summer. It's both sad and unsurprising that Holyfield—a champion in multiple weight classes who spent his entire career overcoming adversity—is mainly remembered as the guy Tyson bit. Here again, Tyson was a little like Tiger Woods. The totality of his sport felt smaller than his celebrity.

Tyson epitomizes a kind of contradictory public figure that emerged in the nineties and would dominate the encroaching epoch of reality TV and social media: an undeniably tragic figure who did not engender (or deserve) sympathy. There was a dichotomous fascination with both the external sociology of his bleak backstory and the internal psychology of his own terrible decision making. "My style is impetuous," he once said of himself, seconds after winning a fight. "My defense is impregnable. And I'm just ferocious." In the wake of the Holyfield fiasco, newspapers seemed unsure whether what had happened was mostly horrific or mostly hilarious (various headlines included "Requiem for a Chompion" in the *Philadelphia Daily News* and "Lobe Blow for Boxing" in *The Tennessean*). That summer, the incident was considered proof that Tyson had finally snapped. But now, as a very weird data point on an increasingly ominous timeline, it seems to signify the beginning of something different, for Tyson and everyone else.

---

*One of the many now unfathomable things about the nineties was the level of high-profile support for Tyson after his rape conviction. At the 1994 MTV Video Music Awards, Chuck D of Public Enemy cited Tyson as a political prisoner. That same year, an industrial group calling themselves Holy Gang released an EP titled *Free Tyson Free!* and referred to Tyson's accuser, Desiree Washington, as a "bitch." Upon his parole from prison, Tyson's first fight was purchased by over 1.5 million people on pay-per-view. The bout was over in 89 seconds.

The early nineties had been shaped by a litany of shifts that, in immediate retrospect, appeared predictable. The fall of communism, the reinventions in music and film, the rise of genetic engineering and network computing, the centrality of neoliberalism—all of these things had antecedents that explained their materialization. There was an unspoken sense that whatever was happening in the present was an understandable reaction to the past. This event was not like that. If "dog bites man" is normal and "man bites dog" is news, this was a recalibration of the former and an imploded expectation of the latter. For so many years, it had been easy to be underwhelmed. The most reliable response to everything had been a roll of the eyes and the phrase "of course." But now, suddenly and inexplicably, men were biting the earlobes off other men, on television, for money. It was too hyperbolic to dismiss. The present and the past were starting to unhook.

○ ○ ○

Y2K was a catastrophe that never happened, prompting many to conclude it was a catastrophe that had never been possible to begin with. It does, in hindsight, seem like the manifestation of a perpetual hysteria machine—a digital doomsday with a specific date and time, perfectly designed for those who longed for an apocalypse they could mark on the calendar. The knee-jerk memory of the Y2K problem tends to place it somewhere between a media hoax and a technological boondoggle, and the conventional wisdom is that the estimated $300 billion spent fixing the glitch was the economic equivalent of throwing cash into a fireplace. All of those thoughts are wrong. But how wrong? That question is harder.

Throughout 1999, the understanding of Y2K was a little like the understanding of where babies come from: Everyone knew the basic principle, but almost no one seemed to grasp how that principle translated into process. As far as the internet is concerned, the first public reference to the crisis came from a person at Reed College in Oregon named Spencer Bolles, who posted the following query on a digital tech bulletin board on January 18, 1985:

> I have a friend that raised an interesting question that I immediately
> tried to prove wrong. He is a programmer and has this notion that
> when we reach the year 2000, computers will not accept the new
> date. Will the computers assume that it is 1900, or will it even cause
> a problem?

Bolles's description of his friend's theory is the only thing about Y2K
everyone would come to understand. When computers and microchips were
engineered in the mid-twentieth century, the amount of computing space
was limited. One solution to the space shortage was to code four-digit dates
as two-digit numbers—instead of writing "1953," the coders would use "53."*
This had no bearing on anything, up and into 1999. But when the new millennium arrived, the coding would render the year 2000 as "00," which
would make computers think it was 1900. And this, apparently, would be a
technological disaster.

I include the word "apparently" not because I doubt that this was true. I
include it because even ardent believers in the Y2K cataclysm didn't fully
understand why this event would cause all the world's computers to fail at
the same time. Why did a computer chip need to know what year it was in
order to work? If an Apple computer thought it was 1900, would it somehow
believe it had not yet been invented? The mechanical explanation for how
this would obliterate the grid was too complicated to explain, so journalists
focused instead on the theoretical consequences: Power outrages would be
rampant, terminating the lives of hospital patients on life support. Gas
pumps and ATM cards wouldn't work, eliciting panic. Airline navigation
systems might go haywire. Nuclear missiles could accidentally launch. A
1997 *Newsweek* story, "The Day the World Shuts Down," quoted a data expert
who feared "on Jan. 1, 2000, a lot of elevators could be dropping to the bottom

---

*Part of the reasoning among the coders was that they (incorrectly) assumed the codes they were
writing would never be operational so far in the future.

of buildings." A *Vanity Fair* article from January of 1999 was headlined "The Y2K Nightmare" and described "a looming disaster with an immovable deadline that will touch the entire world." President Clinton signed an executive order to create the Council on Year 2000 Conversion, a group tasked with updating the federal government's bank of 7,336 computers at a cost of $8.5 billion. The Fed had to print more money because people started hoarding cash. The essence of the problem had the qualities of 1950s science fiction: The smallest possible detail, overlooked by technologists unaware of their godlike power, would instantaneously return a futuristic society to the Stone Age.

What's essential to note, of course, is that the majority of people never truly believed this would happen. A poll conducted for *CBS News Sunday Morning* in the summer of 1999 suggested 56 percent of Americans were doing absolutely nothing to prepare for Y2K. Around 36 percent of responders believed the event would cause no problems for anyone, anywhere, in any way. The wall-to-wall media coverage did not ramp up concern: A Gallup poll conducted in December of '99 found that Y2K fears were paradoxically decreasing as the doomsday date grew closer. Bill Gates declared the glitch would only be an inconvenience, and that became the prevalent forecast. Most Y2K journalism, however, emphasized the handful of people who really, *really* believed the consequences would be devastating. An Associated Press story out of Detroit indicated that gun sales were surging. A company called Crown Point, which sold premade military-style meals for survivalists, claimed a 500 percent uptick in business. There was supposedly a spike in the sale of honey, a food that doesn't require refrigeration and can be consumed in creative ways.* A Canadian named Bruce Beach, who'd built a nuclear fallout shelter north of Toronto by burying forty-two school buses underground in the early 1980s,

---

*This bizarre anecdote is from a July 1999 story in the UK newspaper *The Independent*: Richard Adee, a honey producer from South Dakota, toured across America and found demand heaviest in the Rocky Mountains. "Some places they bought cases," he said, with people carrying away sixty-pound boxes. "For a family, that's quite a bit of honey." Perhaps most worryingly, "a lot of them were computer people."

announced that fifty people could join him in subterranean safety if everything collapsed into chaos. A common profile in countless regional newspapers would tell the story of some local citizen who'd built a backyard bunker, purchased a generator, and awaited the day when Earth would stand still. These alarmists were the fringe exceptions, but they were not exaggerations: In Tara Westover's 2018 memoir *Educated*, the author describes her separatist father's rapturous preparations for the impending secular apocalypse.

The veracity of the non-calamity was recognized well before the New Year's Eve ball dropped in midtown Manhattan. London is five hours ahead of New York, and initial UK reports described nothing out of the ordinary. There were, it turns out, a few problems here and there, most notably 150 pregnant women in Yorkshire who were sent incorrect data about their pregnancies. But the lights stayed on and airplanes didn't fall from the skies. There were no elevator-related fatalities. The kinks in the U.S. were even fewer than the kinks in England (one of the only reported problems involved a few slot machines in a Delaware casino). Almost instantly, the easy reaction was that the Y2K threat had been exaggerated. But that response overlooked the time, money, and effort that had been invested in fixing the problem before it occurred.

"You never get credit for the disasters you avert," technology forecaster Paul Saffo told *The New York Times* in 2013.

"The millennium bug was real," British tech professor Martyn Thomas wrote in 2019, "and the internationally coordinated effort [to fix it] was a great success." As years have passed, the growing academic sentiment regarding Y2K is that it *was* going to wreak some level of pandemonium, and the ultimate absence of any disorder is an example of preemptive science at its absolute best.* The counterargument is that it's impossible to prove what would

---

*It has also become common for both advocates and skeptics of climate change to use Y2K as an instructive example, although for contradictory reasons. Climate change deniers cite the millennium bug as a prime example of a nonexistent disaster incorrectly guaranteed by alleged experts. Those pushing for environmental legislation cite the millennium bug as an example of a seemingly irrevocable disaster that was avoided by experts who worked to change the existing system.

have happened had the issue been entirely ignored, particularly since countries that did nothing (like South Korea) had roughly the same experience as the nations who made fixing the bug a national priority. It was also hard to ignore all the isolated, unfixed household items containing embedded microchips (such as washing machines and high-end toasters) that continued to work exactly as before.

Y2K came and went, and nothing changed at all.

And that, in its own peculiar way, became a different kind of disappointment.

When Stanley Kubrick released *2001: A Space Odyssey* in 1968—and even when Prince recorded the song "1999" in 1982—the twenty-first century felt farther away than it actually was. Viewed from a distance, it promised a future in which everything would be different, and probably better. But as that distance decreased to nil, the year 2000 began to resemble what it actually was—just another year, negligibly different from the year preceding it. Our psychedelic future had been reached, but it was merely an updated version of the previous present. Normal life was still life as normal, and that made the impotent passing of the Y2K problem oddly deflating. Nobody had *wanted* jets to crash or nuclear warheads to detonate, but it was suddenly fun (and suddenly harmless) to speculate on what it would have been like to return to the nineteenth century, if only for a few hours or days or weeks. Once it became clear that nothing tragic had transpired, it was acceptable to express sardonic nostalgia for a disaster that never occurred.

In 2000, the emotional relationship to the internet was reversed from the way it is now: Those who viewed the internet as positive were the people using it the most, while those who hated the internet tended to be people using it the least. It was still very possible for a blue-collar adult to live and work without the internet in his or her life—though research results varied, around half the U.S. population in 2000 didn't use the internet *at all*, and a sizable chunk who did were only sending and receiving email. Most essential day-to-day activities were still analog, so the concept of a world temporarily without technology was not terrifying (and maybe even preferable). And even though the problem was fixed and the consequences were minor, the psychological run-up to Y2K imbued a growing trepidation: Our ever-accelerating reliance on computers had inadvertently made society more fragile. The infiltration of technology was so immersive that two misplaced digits on a computer chip could supposedly alter everything else, in ways the average citizen would never anticipate.

Y2K was the maturation of a criticism whose echo would become normative and unyielding: We've lost control of what we have built, and we need to go back. But the road at our heels was already gone. Forward was the only way out.

○ ○ ○

The 2000 presidential election is a broken memory. It's a linear jigsaw puzzle where the pieces don't always fit, prompting many to just give up and stick the entire box back into a closet.

For all of the summer and most of the fall, the 2000 race felt stupefyingly dull: It was two conventional candidates who were somehow both familiar and unknown. Neither exhibited any quality that could pass as dynamic or transformative. They were more similar than different, or at least that's what became the analysis everybody wanted to express. A Pew Research poll found 44 percent of registered voters from both parties believed "things will be pretty much the same regardless of who wins." The race tightened in the weeks before election night, marginally stoking the attention of half-interested news consumers compelled by the prospect of a horse race coming down the stretch. The voting numbers were expected to be close. But the numbers were closer than anyone anticipated. The evening of November 7 was among the most thrilling nonpartisan nights in the history of presidential political coverage: an improbable (yet never inconceivable) scenario where the outcome of the election was truly too close to call. For thirty-six days, no one knew who would become the forty-third president. When that question was finally answered, half the country viewed the results as an institutional scam, and the two men who had once appeared identical were now diametrically different.

For the next ten months, the 2000 election represented the least stable political moment ever experienced by most American adults. It seemed like nothing crazier could ever possibly happen. But then something did, and a night that had once felt unforgettable became something acceptable to forget. The events of 9/11/2001 now dwarf the events of 11/7/2000. The memory of September 11 is deeper and the emotional toll was greater, and it temporarily made much of the previous ten years feel superficial (including the squabble over that electoral outcome). Yet the machinations of the 2000 election probably changed day-to-day life more, in ways that are less visible and trickier to elucidate. It was the beginning of absolutist binary thinking on every issue even vaguely related to politics, based on the assumption that any attempt at real compromise was either hopeless or fake. It was the end of small differences. Moving forward, all differences would be ideological. And this was partially because the two men at the center of the 2000 dispute had seemed similar in a lot of uninteresting ways. A new antagonism had to be manufactured. This reality is not a view people want to hold. Every year since the election, it has become more and more verboten to view George W. Bush and Al Gore interchangeably. But that's only because the end result of the 2000 vote conditioned society to analyze everything in the same inflexible way, even when recalling events from the past.

The headline to a May 8, 2000, article from Gallup News summarized public opinion: "Little Difference Between Gore and Bush on Important Dimensions in Election." The poll that accompanied the story suggested two things, neither of which was surprising. The first was that most voters were making their decision based on party affiliation. The second was that Bush was seen as a slightly more decisive leader who was tougher on crime, but not decisive enough to make the average Democrat break from their party. The perceived resemblance was more personal than political: These were two white guys in their early fifties who seemed to be running for president because no one else had a better idea. Gore, the son of a three-term senator, had been vice president for eight prosperous years. He was the obligatory extension of the Clinton administration. Bush was the son of a president and the governor of Texas, the most electorally significant state to support the GOP nominee in both '92 and '96. Gore was a graduate of Harvard and Bush was a graduate of Yale.* Gore's main threat during primary season had been former NBA player Bill Bradley, a senator from New Jersey who positioned himself as the more liberal option, making Gore the de facto centrist. Bush, in contrast to how his presidency would actually operate, promoted himself as a center-right alternative to hard-line Republicans.

"There's a lot of Hispanic-Americans in this state," Bush said to an audience of Arizonans in a December '99 debate. "There's a lot who live in my state as well, which is a reminder that our party must broaden our base. I've tried to use my compassionate conservative message to do just that." He preceded these words by speaking in Spanish.

This was seen as significant: Bush's ability (and his willingness) to speak Spanish made him very unlike Bob Dole, Newt Gingrich, or Pat Buchanan. His dialect was flawed, but he was trying. He was trying to reach people who weren't like him. That shifted his momentum back toward the political center, where Gore already was. The lasting memory of Al Gore tends to focus on the end of his public life, especially his indefatigable obsession with climate change. He won the Nobel Peace Prize in 2007 and was the focus of the 2006 documentary *An Inconvenient Truth*, which received two Academy Awards. But those progressive views on the environment played almost no role in his 2000 campaign.† Instead, he promised to cut taxes and to protect

---

*The 2000 election would mark the fourth consecutive presidential election involving at least one candidate with a degree from either Harvard or Yale. This trend would continue in 2004, 2008, 2012, and 2016.

†This can't really be blamed on Gore, however: In 2000, climate change was not viewed as a critical issue. In the aforementioned Gallup poll from May, responders were asked to judge the two candidates on sixteen relevant issues. Environmental policy was not even listed among the sixteen.

Medicare by placing it in "an ironclad lockbox," an awkward analogy that detracted from the message. His chosen running mate, Joe Lieberman, was as conservative as any Democrat could be and would ultimately reclassify himself as an independent in 2006. Gore's wife, Tipper, had spent much of the 1980s campaigning against rock musicians as the cofounder of the Parents Music Resource Center (PMRC). A disinterested contrarian could justifiably see Gore as the more reactionary choice.

Now, did *everyone* think like this? Of course not. In *The Nation*, a late September essay by columnist Eric Alterman was titled "Bush or Gore: Does It Matter?" Alterman's answer was yes, based on the core argument that "the Republican Party, at this moment in history, is politically and ideologically dedicated to the destruction of the very foundations of social solidarity in this country." But even in this emphatically pro-Gore essay, published in a shrilly liberal publication, every attempt at casting the candidates as different was littered with reminders that most people thought they were alike. "Gore . . . is first and foremost a pragmatic politician who will betray progressive hopes whenever it suits his larger purposes. The corporate-friendly Vice President has been nowhere near as strong as he claims on environmental issues. . . . Like Clinton, Gore will continue to back wasteful increases in military spending and the expansion of the failed bipartisan drug war in Colombia. On civil liberties, he will most likely prove just as insensitive, sacrificing important privacy rights to fight exaggerated threats from terrorism and drug trafficking. On trade and globalization issues, a Democratic President can turn out to be even worse than a Republican one."

In 2000, this qualified as an endorsement.

The race was an amicable quagmire with few provocations and an absence of passion. The Bush-Gore debates were among the least-watched in modern presidential history (Fox didn't even air the third debate live, opting instead for a new episode of the Jessica Alba cyberpunk drama *Dark Angel*). Two of the three broadcasts were watched by fewer than 38 million viewers.* Bush was bad in all three debates, rarely able to express cogent thoughts on policy. But the lowbrow consensus was that the debates played to Bush's advantage, mostly because Gore sighed too much. His ostentatious sighing and histrionic grimaces, intended to puncture Bush's inanity, mostly made Gore seem like a prick. His demeanor was condescending, his body language was inelegant, and it was (apparently) better to be uninformed than annoying. This conclusion invented a political perspective that's become omnipresent in any two-person race but still felt original in 2000: Again and again, Bush was described as the candidate voters "would rather have a beer with."

It was a very nineties way to think about a problem.

The logic here is weak and arguably nonexistent: Bush had quit drinking in 1986. He'd actually been charged with driving under the influence as a thirty-year-old—he was stopped by police after a hard night of boozing with an Australian tennis pro in a Kennebunkport bar. But that happened in 1976, so the penalty was a paltry $150 fine. The story of his old arrest did not leak until the election was one week away, and some thought the timing of the story might damage his reputation and hurt his chances. It did not.† It may, in fact, have validated the assessment that getting drunk with George Bush would be more fun than getting drunk with Al Gore. The beer company Sam Adams even commissioned the Roper Starch research firm to conduct a national poll to see which candidate Americans preferred to drink with. The results were actually closer than the general assumption—Bush won 40 to 37 (with 23 percent undecided‡). But the raw numbers were not

---

*As a means of comparison, the first 2016 debate between Donald Trump and Hillary Clinton was watched by 84 million people. In 1960, all four Nixon-Kennedy debates were watched on television by more than 60 million people, along with a robust radio audience.

†According to a poll conducted on November 3 and 4 of that year, 88 percent of respondents who classified themselves as "following the story" did not consider it a serious voting consideration.

‡It's hard to understand what kind of person would be (a) willing to participate in a poll this superfluous while also being (b) unwilling to pick a side.

what mattered. What mattered was the validation of the question itself. Why *not* vote on the basis of low-impact likability? What would be the consequences of accidentally picking the wrong guy? There were problems in America, but they were the regular problems. They were the problems that would always be problems, regardless of who lived in the White House. Some people were unemployed, but overall unemployment was at a thirty-year low. People complained about crime, but violent crime and property crime were down from the year before. It almost felt childish to place too much importance on the presidency. The president was just a person, no better or worse than anyone else. It was embarrassing to care about this stuff too much. It was a little melodramatic. That was for self-righteous people who took things too seriously. That was for people who liked Ralph Nader.

It has become common—almost compulsory—to blame Al Gore's loss in the 2000 election on third-party candidate Ralph Nader and the people who voted for him (and who would have almost certainly supported Gore if there had been only two options). The math on this is simple: Bush won the election while losing the popular vote by approximately half a million ballots. His electoral margin of victory was 271 to 266, and the entire race came down to Florida, where the margin of victory was a minuscule 537 votes. Almost 6 million Floridians voted in 2000. Nader, representing the Green Party, received 97,488 of those votes. So if just 1 percent of Florida-based Nader voters had made the practical decision of voting for Gore, Gore would have become president (and all of the post-election chaos would never have happened). There is just no way around this. Nader's damage to Gore in 2000 was irrefutably greater than Perot's damage to Bush in 1992, if only because the 2000 race was so much tighter.

But this accusation, though rational, is also incomplete. It ignores two critical realities. The first is that Florida should never have decided this election, anyway. Gore was a former Tennessee senator, yet he could not carry Tennessee, even though Clinton had won there in 1992 and 1996. Those 11 electoral votes* would have put him over the top, even without Florida. The second reality is that proponents of this theory always assert a blatantly undemocratic argument: People should not necessarily vote for the person they want, as there are only two realistic outcomes within every political dispute. Which has, since 2000, become the overriding way to think about almost everything.

Prior to 1999, Nader's reputation was about as positive as any left-leaning national figure could hope for. Defining his worldview as "moral empiricism," he spent most of his public life as the nation's highest-profile consumer activist, particularly focused on government transparency, the environment, and automobile safety. His 1965 book, *Unsafe at Any Speed*, was the catalyst for the widespread adoption of seat belt laws. Nader's expressed view on almost everything was heartfelt, intransigent, and nonsymbolic. "Every time I see something terrible," he said as a forty-nine-year-old in 1983, "I see it at age nineteen." He seemingly never had a romantic relationship,† and he claimed to live off $25,000 a year. For Nader, and especially for the people who loved him, self-righteousness was an admirable quality.

In 1996, Nader saw Bill Clinton as a corrupt pragmatist, so he ran against him for president and received less than 1 percent of the popular vote. Nobody cared. He ran again in 2000, directing almost all of his vitriol and disillusionment toward Gore. This time he received almost 3 million votes, including

---

*The explanation as to why people would not support a candidate from their own state is always complicated. Critics will insist it's usually because local citizens better understand who that person is, but that answer is too easy. A post-election article in *The New York Times* claimed Gore had spent too much time in battleground states like Michigan and Wisconsin and allowed Tennessee to slip out from under him.

†One of the classic Nader anecdotes is that General Motors, in an attempt to discredit Nader's anti-auto arguments and sully his Goody Two-shoes reputation, hired prostitutes to solicit him in a grocery store. Nader did not take the bait, and GM later apologized.

the 97,000 from Florida that forever obliterated his standing among moderate and conventional Democrats.

Why Nader ran in the 2000 election will always be a little unclear. His harshest detractors believe his only goal was to stop Gore from winning—an egocentric means for gaining political leverage. This is certainly possible, although it demands a rethinking of everything else that's known about Nader's life. A more plausible explanation is that Nader's single-minded motive was to garner 5 percent of the popular vote on behalf of the Green Party. If he'd received a 5 percent voter share, the federal government would have been required to match whatever money was raised by the Green Party for the next election in 2004.* What can be assumed, however, is that those who voted for Nader took his expressed "people before profits" viewpoint at face value. He seemed to be the only option for those who wanted to move the country dramatically left, even if there was no real chance of Nader's winning the election. Moreover, there was a rising belief that classifying any candidate as having "no real chance" of winning was an unsound prediction: In 1998, former pro wrestler Jesse "the Body" Ventura ran for governor of Minnesota, representing the Reform Party. For much of the campaign, he polled at around 10 percent. But Ventura won that election and became the hieroglyph of political unpredictability. He supported Nader and assaulted the concept of not voting for someone based on a low likelihood of success. "To me," said Ventura, "a wasted vote is not voting your heart and conscience."

In theory, this is true. In practice, Ventura was wrong. The 2.9 million people who voted for Nader from a "heart and conscience" perspective not

---

*This theory is doggedly examined by Harvard professor Barry C. Burden in his 2005 paper "Ralph Nader's Campaign Strategy in the 2000 U.S. Presidential Election." Burden's conclusion is that Nader's various campaign decisions strongly indicate he was simply trying to amass the most popular votes in order to hit the 5 percent threshold, regardless of how that impacted Gore. "Unfortunately for Nader," Burden writes, "his strategy to earn 5% of the vote failed. It is an ironic quirk of an unusual election that Ralph Nader succeeded in the goal he was not pursuing and failed at the one he cared about the most."

only wasted their vote but actively crushed their own desires: During his eight years as president, Bush moved the country to the right and didn't confront (or even recognize) most of Nader's central concerns (campaign finance reform, the minimum wage, or the environment). That said, it's not difficult to understand why a Nader fan would make the decision they did. This scenario was not like 1992, when Ross Perot offered the vision of a third presidential option; in 2000, Nader was a third-party candidate often seen as the *second* option, opposing two conglomerate candidates who were fundamentally the same. Though history has continually painted Bush and Gore as more and more dissimilar, the accepted view was that they were only different to the wonkiest of partisan wonks.* It also didn't seem like wasting a vote was that much of a waste. The possibility of someone winning the Electoral College without winning the popular vote was a factoid every high school senior understood, and such a circumstance had happened three times before. But the last instance had been in 1888, when the country's entire population was 60 million and only 11 million males participated in the election. Since 1980, the margin of victory in U.S. presidential elections had always been greater than 5 million votes. There appeared to be a hard ceiling on how much any lone individual's action could change anything outside of their own life. The world was going to happen the way it was going to happen—but here was an opportunity to criticize the system while still engaging with the process. Voting for Nader was an expression of self.

Prior to the night of November 7, Nader supporters desperately wanted you to know who they were and what they were doing. After performing on *Saturday Night Live* in October, Radiohead's Thom Yorke† held up a green

---

*A minor but telling example: In the summer of 2000, the rap-rock group Rage Against the Machine made a video for the song "Testify," directed by leftist documentarian Michael Moore. The video includes a montage of Bush and Gore expressing identical views on free trade and capital punishment before ultimately morphing their two faces into one composite human. The video's final image was Nader saying, "If you're not turned on to politics, politics will turn on you."

†Yorke, of course, was not (and is not) a U.S. citizen.

sign that read, "LET RALPH DEBATE." Nader voters were proud of the moral decision they were about to make. But by the afternoon of November 8, that moral high ground had become a mudslide, and those 2.9 million moralists were suddenly impossible to find.

○ ○ ○

The outcome of the Bush-Gore-Nader election spurred a predictable uptick in public conversation about the elimination of the Electoral College. This was incongruous, since the conditions surrounding the 2000 election were among the principal reasons the Electoral College was originally created. One of the espoused fears of the Founding Fathers was that large population centers would create a geographic imbalance during national elections.* This is exactly what happened. Gore won the popular vote by winning only twenty states. Two of them were California and New York. Florida was a tie. Over the next two months, surveys were conducted by *The Washington Post* and *The Palm Beach Post*, focused on voters whose ballots had been discounted due to mechanical malfunctions. Both surveys concluded that Gore may have actually won Florida, and that Bush's 537-vote margin of victory was inaccurate. Another study by the *Miami Herald* and *USA Today* concluded that Bush's margin of victory in the state was actually larger than originally believed, at around 1,665 votes. But—really—any neutral interpretation of the 2000 Florida results must conclude that this was a dead heat. Conducting 100 recounts would have generated 100 different outcomes. The difference was unimaginably small and exacerbated by low participation. Over 6 million Floridians cast votes, but Florida's population was 15.3 million. Even if the final "official" difference had been 1,530 votes, there's no way

---

*It must be noted that this system was created in 1787, and the real problem was that much of the Southern population was enslaved (and enslaved people couldn't vote). They had to find a way to work around this fact. There were also no real political parties at the time, and only about four million people in the whole country, and it was assumed that most voters would have no idea who they were voting for, anyway.

anyone can conclude who most citizens of Florida actually wanted to be president. It was a mathematical anomaly that may never happen again.

In the early evening hours of November 7, NBC, ABC, and CBS all declared that Gore had won Florida, based on misleading information from exit polls. That declaration was later retracted and Bush was awarded Florida about fifteen minutes after two a.m., pushing him over the top for the overall victory. Gore called Bush and conceded the race, but then called back and retracted his concession. This temporary confusion seems like a major problem. It wasn't. The problem was the resolution. If (like many historians) you consider G. W. Bush a historically bad leader who allowed his vice president to spearhead an unnecessary war, the *outcome* of the 2000 election remains problematic. But the actions of Bush's administration were dictated by the 2001 events of September 11, and nobody knows if Gore would have handled that situation any differently. The rabid nationalistic pandemonium immediately following the 9/11 attacks remains an underexamined period in American history, willfully forgotten by most people who lived through it (at the time, the fact that Bush waited twenty-six days before invading Afghanistan was viewed as an exhibition of remarkable restraint). Due to the strange way U.S. presidential elections are conducted, the closeness and commotion of the Bush-Gore race was almost a structural inevitability: At some point, the margin between two candidates in a critical state was going to be unclear. It was always something that *could* happen, and in 2000 it finally did. But the way the conflict was solved damaged the country psychologically more than the conflict itself. The surgery was successful, but the patient died.

The resolution process took thirty-six days. The technical complexities are better left to legal scholars. Some of the issues involved the quirks of physical voting methods (the dates on overseas absentee ballots, the irregular placement of hole punches on so-called butterfly ballots, etc.). The central takeaway, however, was this: Gore, quite justifiably, wanted a manual recount, and he almost got it. On December 9, a recount was started. But the U.S. Supreme Court interceded and stopped the recount, reasoning (or at least claiming) that a recount was unconstitutional and would illegitimatize the Bush presidency, since Katherine Harris, the Florida* secretary of state, had already certified Bush as the victor on November 26.

What matters most here is the breakdown of the Supreme Court's decision. It was 5–4. The five who sided with Bush were the five conservative judges—Chief Justice William H. Rehnquist, Antonin Scalia, Anthony M. Kennedy, Clarence Thomas, and Sandra Day O'Connor (O'Connor was viewed as the "swing vote," even though she was a Republican†). The four dissenting judges were all liberal. In his dissenting opinion, Justice John Paul Stevens wrote, "Although we may never know with complete certainty the identity of the winner of this year's Presidential election, the identity of the loser is perfectly clear. It is the nation's confidence in the judge as an impartial guardian of the rule of law."

His sentiment was correct, but did not go far enough.

Prior to election night, the race between Bush and Gore was a cosplay of how people thought about political culture in general: The candidates are different (but not really), the outcome matters (but not that much), and the winner will be either the affable guy we want to have a beer with or the uptight guy who seems to know what he's talking about (and it will work either way, probably). At the time, polling suggested 40 percent of Democrats and Republicans had a "favorable and warm" opinion about members of the *opposing* party. It was easy to think about politics as something that could be argued over without much risk, because the final outcome would always be some version of a compromise. Government was contentious, but also secure; it was unpredictable, but the volatility always drifted toward equilibrium. If it was impossible to know who won the presidential election (which was the case), and if there was no national panic over the dispute (which there was

---

*At the time of the election, the governor of Florida was George W. Bush's younger brother Jeb.

†O'Connor said on multiple occasions that she would not retire from the court unless a Republican was in the White House, as she wanted her replacement to be conservative. She retired in 2006, during Bush's second term in office.

not), and if a recount was possible (which it always is), it seemed senseless that the judicial branch would stop that recount from happening. And if the Supreme Court *did* stop a recount from happening, it was assumed the court's explanations would be academic and contradictory and certainly not based on partisanship. Knowing who's the president is a core component of American democracy. Had the Supreme Court's reasoning emerged from some kind of shared constitutional interpretation, the vote would have been 9–0 or 0–9. A vote of 8–1 or 7–2 would have suggested philosophical debate. Any unexpected, personalized dissonance among the nine judges would have been reassuring.

But there wasn't any, and there wasn't even an attempt to hide that. The five conservative judges accepted their criticism and moved on.

What much of the public had considered a milquetoast competition between uncharismatic clones was understood by the court as a straightforward war for control of the future. Every other aspect of political thought became irrelevant—the conservatives had a one-judge majority, and that was enough to decide who ran the world. Why pretend like this was even a question to interrogate? They made the call, everyone knew why the call was made, and there was no going back. On the biggest possible stage, it was established that every sociopolitical act of the twenty-first century would now be a numbers game on a binary spectrum. My undefined, uncommitted Gen X worldview was instantaneously worthless. That was over. Now there were only two sides to everything.

○ ○ ○

A presidential election so close that the winner would never be known felt like the postmodern endcap to an era of postmodern psychosis. Things couldn't get any wilder than that, or so we thought. Bush II settled into the Oval Office roughly ten years after his father had started the Gulf War (though his dad's old nemesis, Saddam Hussein, remained in control of Iraq). There was cerebral discomfort over how things had played out: It became popular to claim Bush should not be treated as a rightful president, or to portray Bush as a figurehead whose real job was letting Vice President Dick Cheney run the country from behind a curtain. There were protests during Bush's inauguration, although fewer than if such an electoral event had occurred twenty years earlier or twenty years later. Many of the protesters expressed continuing support for Nader, which meant they were protesting the election of a president they'd helped to elect.

It's eerie how fast the discontent evaporated. The election was a big deal, and it was treated like a big deal. It's not like the significance was ignored. Yet there was still a conviction that this would work itself out, that the differences between the two alternative realities were smaller than the similarities, and that—more than anything else—this was just how things were going to be now. The possibility of storming the House of Representatives and stopping the electoral confirmation wasn't even discussed as a radical fantasy (and if someone had tried to forward such an idea, that person would have been mocked). There was a superficial symmetry to the operation of power: George Bush had been president, and now another George Bush was president. There was another Bush in the lineage, Jeb, who was the governor of Florida. He'd probably run for president, too. Perhaps he'd face Hillary Clinton, now a New York senator unabashedly preparing for her own run at the White House. Maybe the president would just always be a Bush or a Clinton.

There's no such thing as an average American, outside of an assembly of median statistics that apply to nobody in particular. No one is explicitly everyone. At the inception of the twenty-first century, there were just over 282 million people living in the United States. It can't be argued that 282 million people believed the same things or felt the same feelings at the same time. And even if that had been the case, it's impossible to accurately reconstruct the views of the past: The part of the brain that processes semantic memory (the left temporal pole) and the part of the brain that processes emotional memory (the right temporal pole) are physiologically connected.

People inject their current worldviews into whatever they imagine to be the previous version of themselves. There is no objective way to prove that This Is How Life Was. It can only be subjectively argued that This Is How Life Seemed. And this is how life seemed: ecstatically complacent.

There had been so much hype over the impending doom of Y2K, and nothing happened. It didn't matter if the disaster had been avoided or if the disaster had never been there at all—the takeaway was that the anxiety had been exaggerated. The skeptics were proven correct. A presidential election happened and no one knew who had won, and half the country believed we'd installed the wrong guy. But so much cultural energy had been invested in arguing that Bush and Gore were identical that it was hypocritical to act like this outcome was beyond the pale. Resistance was futile, and also annoying.

It had been so long since anything terrible had happened to America that wasn't (at least partially) America's own fault. Every fear felt theoretical. Could there be a global pandemic? Yes. There was an outbreak of the Ebola virus in 1995, and it killed 81 percent of the infected. But that happened in Zaire, and it involved only around three hundred total victims (and when it happened again, five years later in Uganda, the fatality rate fell to 53 percent). Had the fall of the Soviet Union destabilized the global ecosystem? Perhaps. In 1997, *60 Minutes* interviewed former Russian Security Council secretary Aleksandr Lebed', who admitted that Russia could not account for eighty of its Cold War "suitcase bombs" (small nuclear weapons that could be deployed by one person, potentially acting alone). But the Russian government had dismissed his claims, and that report was now more than three years old, and every day that a suitcase bomb didn't detonate made the possibility of such a crisis a little less plausible. Did much of the world hate America's outsized influence on every other country? Absolutely. In October of 2000, two suicide bombers attacked the Navy destroyer USS *Cole*, killing seventeen soldiers while the ship refueled in Yemen. A terrorist organization called al-Qaeda was credited for the attack, punctuated by a recruitment videotape that surfaced the following summer. The tape showed al-Qaeda members celebrating the bombing of the *Cole*, including footage of al-Qaeda leader Osama bin Laden reading a poem that appeared to praise the suicide mission. But this, it seemed, was the price of being the last remaining superpower: a random attack on military personnel, financed by a third-world country and occurring seven thousand miles east of Washington, DC.

These things were problems, but the problems were abstractions. They were *New Yorker* stories you didn't need to finish. The domestic concerns of 2001 were even softer. They were still the concerns of a nineties mentality. Two particular stories became default examples for what Americans were supposedly obsessed with throughout the summer. The first fixated on the fear of shark attacks: The July 30 cover of *Time* magazine classified 2001 as the "Summer of the Shark," an editorial decision significant for both its sensationalistic unseriousness and technical inaccuracy (the number of 2001 shark attacks had actually decreased from the year before). The other story was another intern sexcapade, this time with a darker twist: On May 1, a twenty-four-year-old Washington, DC, woman named Chandra Levy inexplicably vanished (she'd been interning with the Federal Bureau of Prisons). Her neighbors claimed to have heard a scream coming from her apartment building at four thirty a.m. Levy's father told police he believed Chandra had been having an affair with Gary Condit, a fifty-three-year-old married congressman who happened to represent the region of California where Levy's parents lived. Condit unconvincingly denied the affair and was never officially connected to the disappearance, but their secret relationship was the center of the story. Certain qualities were reminiscent of the Clinton-Lewinsky scandal, though this was more of a classic true-crime scenario. Two days before her disappearance, Levy had called her aunt, a woman who served as her private confidante about Condit and knew all the details of their affair. Levy left a phone message that said she had "big news" to tell the aunt when she next saw her. What was the news? What did it imply?

The retrospective emphasis on these two specific stories—even their mention here, in the previous paragraph—has become a contrivance. They're supposed to illustrate how Americans were consumed by non-stories while ignoring the foreboding signs of impending danger. There's a propensity to paint the entire summer of 2001 as "the Before Time," a naive period of easy innocence and lazy stupidity. It is the kind of projection that can only happen through revisionism. The *Time* story about sharks would have received less attention if it had been understated and accurate (the notoriety came from everyone's realizing it was dippy and wrong). The Levy story involved a woman who was murdered, hypothetically due to her involvement with a national political figure (the news was salacious, but by no means superfluous). What was happening, really, was the media version of what physicist and philosopher Thomas Kuhn had classified as "normal science" in his controversial 1962 book *The Structure of Scientific Revolutions*. Kuhn categorized "normal science" as the day-to-day work scientists do while operating within the framework of a preexisting, universally accepted paradigm. Kuhn's assertion was that, most of the time, scientific work mostly entails refining little details within a larger umbrella concept that everyone accepts as obviously true. This process continues until the paradigm transforms. The summer of 2001 can be viewed similarly. These were the final months of "normal journalism," before the transformation.

All of the twenty-first century is lumped into the Internet Age, but most of 2001 was still the twentieth century in spirit. Daily newspaper circulation that year was 55.6 million, a statistic similar to the circulation figures from forty years prior. That number would be cut in half over the next twenty years. In 2001, the nightly world news on the three major networks still combined for a rating of 23.4, equating to 33 million viewers (a perpetual viewership greater than the audience for the 2020 Academy Awards). The structure of journalism wasn't that different from how it had worked in the 1960s, and it shaped a much different model for the delivery of information. Time was not elastic. Data was delivered in autonomous chunks. The news cycle was rigid and predictable. The size and content of a newspaper was dictated by the number of advertisements that newspaper had sold in advance. The amount of information in an episode of *World News Tonight* was regimented and prioritized by what could be placed inside a thirty-minute window strategically interrupted by commercial breaks. The contemporary media landscape of today—where most things are incrementally reported as they occur and instantly slotted into a singular, intersectional political narrative shared by both sides—was only just beginning, and only on cable. Minor news items seemed minor because they weren't automatically interbred with all other news.

Whenever the world rapidly and dramatically changes, the gut response is that society must be disintegrating. There's a long-standing belief that national trauma shatters the existing status quo and splinters the interconnectivity that creates a phantasm of security. What happened to North America after the eleventh of September was the inverse of that. Society did not, in any way, disintegrate. Instead, it was irrevocably jammed together. Every conversation became the same conversation. Ideological differences were inflamed, but not because of intellectual separation. It was the narcissism of small differences, amplified into differences that were no longer small. The phantasm that got shattered was the possibility of living an autonomous life, separate from the lives of others.

To look at the front pages of random newspapers published on September 10 of 2001 is to look at manifold realities, a multiverse of disconnected experiences all happening less than five hours apart. It was not just the local stories that were dissimilar. It was the full view of what mattered. The *Los Angeles Times* led with a forthcoming attack by Senator Joe Biden on the Bush administration's missile defense system, though there was also an above-the-fold story about KFC's strategy for selling chicken in China. The *Star-Telegram* in Fort Worth analyzed indications of a coming recession and the solvency of Social Security. The banner headline of *The Tennessean* focused on the inordinate amount of federal aid directed to the farming industry, while the *St. Louis Post-Dispatch* reported on how rural Americans were less healthy than those living in the suburbs. The front of the *Chicago*

Tribune addressed Mexican border control. The *Honolulu Star-Bulletin* prioritized a study suggesting as many as 1 in 100 U.S. children might be involved in the sex trade. *The Des Moines Register* expressed concern over a possible flu vaccine shortage. The lead story of the *Detroit Free Press* was about the ongoing investigation surrounding the 1975 disappearance of Jimmy Hoffa, while the top of the *Reno Gazette-Journal* noted that Barry Bonds was on pace to hit 70 home runs. There was some overlap in coverage—a shooting in Sacramento, a suicide bomber in Israel, the previous afternoon's slate of NFL games—but nothing close to a unifying fixation everyone was discussing at the same time. No stories were viral. No celebrity was trending. The world was still big. The country was still vast. You could just be a little person, with your own little life and your own little thoughts. You didn't have to have an opinion, and nobody cared if you did or did not. You could be alone on purpose, even in a crowd.

The New York Times was chucked on doorsteps the following morning. There were disparate stories on page A1—the supply of stem cells, a controversy over school dress codes, the competitive morning TV market, and five others. The physical newspapers arrived to subscribers around the same time nineteen men with box cutters passed through low-security checkpoints in four different airports and boarded four cross-country domestic flights. The flights were hijacked, the planes crashed into buildings, 2,977 people died, and the nineties collapsed with the skyscrapers.

Acknowledgments

This book was written under usual circumstances. The writing process presented unique complexities, at least in comparison to the previous books I've published. I am appreciative for everyone who helped me complete this inessential project.

I must first thank my editor at Penguin Press, Scott Moyers. I feel like Scott willed this book into existence, especially during the period before I'd even written a single word. His associate editor, Mia Council, was equally integral to the manuscript's construction. The copy edits from Aja Pollock were critical, as was the dogged fact-checking of Ben Phelan.

I owe a huge debt of gratitude to Nona Ethington. She is a human library.

Daniel Greenberg has now been my literary agent for twenty years. He will remain my agent for the next twenty years, unless one of us (or both of us) dies.

The following people read early versions of this manuscript and made arguments or suggestions that prompted me to rewrite or rethink at least one sentence: Rob Sheffield, Jennifer Williams Raftery, Patrick Condon, Jon Blixt, Bob Ethington, Brian Raftery, Rex Sorgatz, David Giffels, Ben Heller, John Backer, Phoebe Reilly, Jon Dolan, and Steve Kandell.

The following people had intangible impacts on what became the book's final draft, perhaps without even knowing that such impacts had been made: Michael Weinreb, Greg Milner, Eli Saslow, Sean Howe, Alex Pappademas, Chris Ryan, Sean Fennessey, Ross Raihala, Dennis Sperle, Michael Schauer, Rick and Kerry Sparks, Matthew Ericksen, Bill Simmons, Andy Greenwald, Chad Hansen, David Beck, Caryn Ganz, Robert Huschka, Luke Shockman, Mark Pfeifle, Amy Everhart, Jon Miller, Denise Bower, Nick Chase, Ellen Shafer, Eric Peterson, Greg Korte, Steve Marsh, Wesley Morris, Mathew Sletten, Jennifer Maerz, Mike and Chrissy Maerz, Douglas Coupland, and (of course) Brant Rumble.

I must continually thank Florence Klosterman, all of my brothers and sisters, and all of the sons and daughters of all of my brothers and sisters.

It would have been impossible for me to write any of this (or do anything, really) without Melissa Maerz, the author of *Alright, Alright, Alright*, the amazing mother of my children, and the person who gave me the idea for the epigraph to this book. I could not love you any more than I do. "Am old horse."

Part of me thinks I should individually thank every single person I experienced the nineties with, since they all shaped how that decade seemed at the time and what I remember about that decade now. This, however, would be thousands and thousands of people, many of whom might be somewhat freaked out to realize I remembered them at all. It also occurs to me that—if I tried to credit every influential person I knew during the nineties—I would also need to cite all the mass media I consumed during those years, and that just feels insane. It does not seem reasonable to thank (for example) the members of Drivin N Cryin just because I listened to *Fly Me Courageous* for four months in 1991. Then again, by specifically mentioning I'm *not* going to acknowledge Drivin N Cryin, I suppose I inadvertently have done exactly that. There's just no way to do this in a manner that accurately reflects my reality. But I will say this: If I knew you in the nineties (or you knew me), part of you might be inside this book, somewhere or somehow. So . . . thanks for that. It could have been worse.

Sources

This is a book of popular criticism, and my assumption is that it would not meet the rigorous standards of an academic publication. Still, I have done my best to make any straightforward statement of fact as accurate as possible. My journalistic impulse is to credit sources in the same sentence that contains the information itself. I typically did not, however, note the source for data that is widely available and seemingly obvious (Pearl Jam was a rock band, the O. J. Simpson trial could be watched on television, etc.). I sometimes worked in reverse, searching for source material that verified what I thought I remembered. This process worked roughly half the time.

An extended list of sources can be found below. There is also a handful of books fleetingly (or unconsciously) referenced in multiple chapters: Colin Harrison's *American Culture in the 1990s*; W. Joseph Campbell's *1995: The Year the Future Began*; Brian Raftery's book on the films of 1999, *Best. Movie. Year. Ever.*; *The Spin Alternative Record Guide*; Tom Roston's *I Lost It at the Video Store*; and several others. However, I have still included those books in the bibliography of chapters where they had a direct influence on the content.

1. Fighting the Battle of Who Could Care Less

Rex Sorgatz, *The Encyclopedia of Misinformation*. Abrams Image, 2018.

Peter Wonacott, "The Mystery of Mandela's Arrest." *The Wall Street Journal*, Dec. 21, 2012.

Esteban Ortiz-Ospina and Max Roser, "Happiness and Life Satisfaction." Our World in Data, 2013, revised May 2017. ourworldindata.org/happiness-and-life-satisfaction.

Baby Boomer Headquarters: Prices—Then and Now. http://www.bbhq.com/prices.htm. [Inactive.]

Sarah Kessler, "The Incredible Story of Marion Stokes." *Fast Company*, Nov. 21, 2013.

"Millennials Projected to Overtake Baby Boomers as America's Largest Generation." Pew Research Center, March 1, 2018.

Amitai Etzioni, "The Fast-Food Factories: McJobs Are Bad for Kids." *The Washington Post*, Aug. 24, 1986.

Douglas Coupland interview, Nov. 2019.

Jim Fitzgerald, *SlamNation* interview. YouTube clip, posted July 10, 2013. https://www.youtube.com/watch?v=d2YfJdmVQHU.

Board of Governors of the Federal Reserve System, "Distribution of Household Wealth in the U.S. since 1989." https://www.federalreserve.gov/releases/z1/dataviz/dfa/distribute/table/.

David M. Gross and Sophfronia Scott, "Living: Proceeding with Caution." *Time*, July 16, 1990.

Steven Daly and Nathaniel Wice, *Alt.Culture: An A-to-Z Guide to the '90s—Underground, Online, and Over-the-Counter.* HarperPerennial, 1995.

Drew Jubera, "Twentysomething: No Image in the Mirror—The 'Lost Generation' Attempts to Find Its Way in the Boomers' Wake." *The Atlanta Journal-Constitution*, June 10, 1991.

Anne Gowen and Sean Piccoli, "A Generation Lost in Time—Rebellion? Twentysomethings Find It's Too Much Trouble." *The Washington Times*, Oct. 15, 1991.

Franz Nicolay, "The Rise and Decline of 'Sellout.'" *Slate*, July 28, 2017.

Gustavo Turner, "Reality Bites: The Ultimate Sellout?" *LA Weekly*, Jan. 5, 2012.

Jen Chaney, "Friends Is a Gen X Show. Why Don't We Ever Call It That?" *New York*, Sept. 17, 2019.

Jon Wurster email interview, Nov. 25, 2019.

Colin Harrison, *American Culture in the 1990s.* Edinburgh University Press, 2010.

[projections of the distortion]

William Grimes, "The Ridiculous Vision of Mark Leyner." *The New York Times Magazine*, Sept. 13, 1992.

"The Liars Club." *The New York Observer*, March 6, 2006.

Elizabeth Wurtzel, *Prozac Nation.* Riverhead Books, 1994.

Mark Leyner, *Et Tu, Babe.* Vintage, 1993.

2. The Structure of Feeling (Swingin' on the Flippity-Flop)

Bradley J. Birzer, "The Optimism of Ronald Reagan." *The Imaginative Conservative*, Feb. 6, 2015.

Mark Yarm, *Everybody Loves Our Town: An Oral History of Grunge.* Crown Archetype, 2011.

Michael Azerrad, *Come As You Are: The Story of Nirvana.* Main Street Books, 1993.

Charles R. Cross, *Heavier Than Heaven: A Biography of Kurt Cobain.* Hyperion, 2001.

Randall Rothenberg, *Where the Suckers Moon: The Life and Death of an Advertising Campaign.* Alfred A. Knopf, 1994.

Craig Marks, "Let's Get Lost." *Spin*, Jan. 1995.

Clay Tarver, "The Rock 'n' Roll Casualty Who Became a War Hero." *The New York Times Magazine*, July 2, 2013.

Rock Is Dead?, documentary directed by Daniel Sarkissian, 2020.

Chris Harris, "Filter's Richard Patrick Reflects . . ." *Billboard*, May 8, 2020.

[i see death around the corner]

Ian Katz, "Death Wish." *The Guardian*, Sept. 20, 1996.

Wesley Case, "Tupac Shakur in Baltimore: Friends, Teachers, Remember the Birth of an Artist." *The Baltimore Sun*, March 31, 2017.

"Tupac Interview at 17 Years Old—1998." YouTube clip, posted Feb. 3, 2017.

"Tupac's Police Records—Arrests & Charges." 2PacLegacy, June 16, 2019.

Rob Kenner and Eliva Aguilar, "Rappers Talking about Kurt Cobain." *Complex*, April 4, 2014.

Chuck Phillips, "Who Killed Tupac Shakur?" *Los Angeles Times*, Sept. 6, 2002.

Eric Malnic and Chuck Phillips, "Possible Suspect in Tupac Shakur Death Killed in Shootout." *Los Angeles Times*, May 30, 1998.

3. Nineteen Percent

Albert Menendez, *The Perot Voters and the Future of American Politics*. Prometheus Books, 1996.

Gulf War from Iraq's Perspective. Animated documentary by the Armchair Historian, YouTube, posted July 19, 2019. https://www.youtube.com/watch?v=Wxj-xCiiay0.

Adam Clymer, "War in the Gulf: Public Opinion; Poll Finds Deep Backing While Optimism Fades." *The New York Times*, Jan. 22, 1991.

"Excerpts from Iraqi Document on Meeting with U.S. Envoy." *The New York Times International*, Sept. 23, 1990.

HyperNormalization, BBC documentary directed by Adam Curtis, 2016.

John F. Hale, "The Making of the New Democrats." *Political Science Quarterly* 110, no. 2 (Summer 1995), 207–32.

John Harris, "Ross Perot—the Father of Trump." *Politico*, July 9, 2019.

Elizabeth Kolbert, "The 1992 Campaign: Media; For Perot, What TV Gives It Can Also Take Away." *The New York Times*, May 9, 1992.

Elizabeth Kolbert, "The 1992 Campaign: The Media; Perot's 30-Minute TV Ads Defy the Experts, Again." *The New York Times*, Oct. 27, 1992.

Steve Daley, "Perot's Dig at Persian Gulf War Exposes Soft Underbelly of Bush's Victory." *Chicago Tribune*, June 14, 1992.

Jonathan Martin, "Ross Perot and Donald Trump: Presidential Candidates and Outsiders, Looking In." *The New York Times*, July 9, 2019.

Galen Druke, "Long Before Trump, There Was Ross Perot." FiveThirtyEight.com, Oct. 24, 2016.

The Perot Myth. Documentary short, FiveThirtyEight.com.

"Ross Perot: On the Issues." OntheIssues.org. www.ontheissues.org/ross_perot.htm.

Zach Helfand, "The Economist Who Believes the Government Should Just Print More Money." *The New Yorker*, Aug. 20, 2019.

"How Groups Voted in 1992." Roper Center for Public Opinion Research. http://ropercenter.cornell.edu/how-groups-voted-1992.

James Mann, *Rise of the Vulcans: The History of Bush's War Cabinet*. Penguin Books, 2004.

John Dillin, "Election by Equation: 2 Analysts See a Bush Win." *The Christian Science Monitor*, April 22, 1992.

Allan J. Lichtman, *The Keys to the White House*. Madison Books, 1996.

[casual determinism]

"Displaced Companies Finding Temporary Shelter." Hackensack, NJ, *Record*/Associated Press, March 1, 1993.

"World Trade Center Plagued by Fire and Safety Codes." *Los Angeles Times*, Feb. 27, 1993.

National Gypsum Heritage Archives. "Operations: Ships."

Forecasting the "Storm of the Century." National Oceanic and Atmospheric Administration, 2007.

Jared Plushnick, "25 Years Ago: Remembering the 1993 Superstorm." wkrn.com (Nashville), March 13, 2018.

Tom Moore, "The Great Superstorm of March 1993 Will Be Long Remembered." Weather Concierge, March 8, 2019.

David Gates, "White Male Paranoia." *Newsweek*, March 28, 1993.

"Publicity Falls Down on Job of Promoting Douglas Film." Odessa, TX, *American*/Associated Press, Feb. 28, 1993.

4. The Edge, as Viewed from the Middle

Steven Pinker, "The Game of the Name." *The New York Times*, April 5, 1994.

Howard Kurtz, "You Don't Say." *The Washington Post*, Nov. 29, 1993.

Robert Novack, "Political Correctness Has No Place in the Newsroom." *USA Today*, March 1995.

Paul Fischer, "2 Live Crew." *The First Amendment Encyclopedia*. mtsu.edu/first-amendment/article/1447/2-live-crew.

Nick Keppler, "The Time the Supreme Court Ruled in Favor of 2 Live Crew." Mental Floss, March 5, 2016.

Jeff Wallenfeldt, "Los Angeles Riots of 1992." *The Encyclopædia Britannica*, updated April 22, 2020.

Jessie Carney Smith, ed., *Encyclopedia of African American Popular Culture*. Greenwood, 2010.

Meg Walker, "2 Live Crew Singer Arrested after Show Deputies Cite Lyrics, Obscenity." *South Florida Sun-Sentinel*, June 11, 1990.

Brentin Mock, "What Was Lost in the Fires of the L.A. Riots." *Bloomberg CityLab*, April 25, 2017.

Frank Clifford and David Ferrell, "The Times Poll: L.A. Strongly Condemns King Verdict, Riots." *Los Angeles Times*, May 6, 1992.

"Cartoon on MTV Blamed for Fire." Associated Press, Oct. 10, 1993.

"A ROC Exclusive: Ice-T Speaks Out on Censorship . . . ," interview by Mike Heck. THE ROC, 2008. http://theroc.org/roc-mag/textarch/roc-11/roc11-09.htm.

Sheila Rule, "'Cop Killer' to Be Cut from Ice-T Album." *The New York Times*, July 29, 1992.

"Ice-T Controversy During the L.A. Riots." YouTube clip, posted Nov. 29, 2013.

Frank Newport, "In U.S., 87% Approve of Black-White Marriage, vs. 4% in 1958." Gallup, July 25, 2013.

John R. Ricker, "What Is Ebonics (African American English)." Linguistic Society of America.

Wayne O'Neil, "Ebonics in the Media." *The Radical Teacher*, Fall 1998.

Salikoko Sangol Mufwene, "African American English." *Encyclopædia Britannica*.

Queers Read This! Anonymous leaflet, June 1990.

Queer Nation, "Queer Nation NY: Our History." QueerNationNY.org, 2016.

Yusuf Tamanna, "When Did We Start Referring to Ourselves as Queer?" *Vice*, June 19, 2018.

Ben Detrick, "*Kids*, Then and Now." *The New York Times*, July 21, 2015.

Spin, April 1993.

Robert Levine and Steve Hochman, "Deal Has *Spin* in a Phair-Sized Snit." *Los Angeles Times*, Oct. 9, 1994.

Spin, Sept. 1998.

Will Hermes and Sia Michel, eds., *Spin: 20 Years of Alternative Music*. Three Rivers Press, 2005.

Rolling Stone, Nov. 1995.

Kristen Schilt, "'A Little Too Ironic': The Appropriation and Packaging of Riot Grrl Politics by Mainstream Female Musicians." *Popular Music and Society* 26, no. 1 (2003).

[the slow cancellation of the future and the fast homogenization of the past]

Melissa Maerz, *Alright, Alright, Alright: The Oral History of Richard Linklater's* Dazed and Confused. HarperCollins, 2020.

5. The Movie Was about a Movie

Tom Roston, *I Lost It at the Video Store: A Filmmakers' Oral History of a Vanished Era.* CreateSpace, 2017.

Johnnie L. Roberts, "The VCR Boom: Prices Drop as Their Popularity Continues to Grow." *Chicago Tribune,* Sept. 22, 1985.

Aljean Harmetz, "Wearing Spielberg Down to Put 'E.T.' on Cassette." *The New York Times,* May 17, 1988.

Aljean Harmetz, "Marketing 'Top Gun' Cassette." *The New York Times,* Jan. 15, 1987.

Marc Berman, "Orion, McDonald's Dance with 'Wolves' Deal." *Variety,* Nov. 16, 1992.

"How the VCR Defined Home Entertainment." The 8 Percent, July 25, 2016.

"Television Audience 2008." The Nielsen Company, 2009.

National Association of Theater Owners (2020)

Quentin Tarantino: Hollywood's Boy Wonder. BBC Television documentary, 1994.

Movie Body Counts. http://www.moviebodycounts.com/contact.htm.

Mark Seal, "Cinema Tarantino: The Making of *Pulp Fiction*." *Vanity Fair,* Feb. 13, 2013.

Roger Ebert, "Tarantino's 'Pulp Fiction' Goes Heavy on the Violence." *Chicago Sun-Times,* May 20, 1994.

Rita Kempley, "*Pulp Fiction*: A Slay Ride." *The Washington Post,* Oct. 14, 1994.

Kenneth Turan, "'Fiction': Quentin Tarantino's Gangster Rap: Sure, the Director Can Write. But Does He Deserve All the Hype?" *Los Angeles Times,* Oct. 14, 1994.

Stanley Kauffmann, "Shooting Up." *The New Republic,* Oct. 14, 1994.

Jim Delmont, "Tarantino's 'Pulp Fiction' Strikes False Note about Gangsters: Bizarre Comedy Is Too Violent and Too Long." *Omaha World-Herald,* Oct. 17, 1994.

Joe Urschel, "Playing Violence Just for Laughs." *USA Today,* Oct. 18, 1994.

Linda Chavez, "*Pulp Fiction*: Violence as Art?" *USA Today,* Jan. 18, 1995.

[the power of myth]

Tim Gayle, "Is It Time for College Playoffs?" *Prattville Progress,* Dec. 11, 1990.

David Ingold and Adam Pearce, "March Madness Makers and Takers." Bloomberg News, March 18, 2015.

6. CTRL + ALT + DELETE

Natalie Wolchover, "Why It Took So Long to Invent the Wheel." *Live Science,* March 2, 2012.

"Vint Cerf." Internet Hall of Fame. internethalloffame.org/inductees/vint-cerf.

Nicholas Negroponte, *Being Digital.* Alfred A. Knopf, 1995.

Bill Gates, *The Road Ahead.* Viking Press, 1995.

Douglas Rushkoff, *Cyberia: Life in the Trenches of Hyperspace.* HarperCollins, 1994.

"The Strange New World of the Internet." *Time,* July 25, 1994.

Knut Lundby, ed., *Mediatization of Communication.* De Gruyter Mouton, 2014.

Imagining the Internet: A History and Forecast. Elon University. https://www.elon.edu/u/imagining/.

Megan Garber, "Our Numbered Days: The Evolution of the Area Code." *The Atlantic,* Feb. 13, 2014.

Kevin Cooke and Dan Lehrer, "The Whole World Is Talking." *The Nation,* July 12, 1993.

Jonathan Luff, "The Battle for the Soul of the Internet Has Well and Truly Begun." *Wired,* June 5, 2017.

Mary Bellis, "The History of Google and How It Was Invented." ThoughtCo., Feb 11, 2020.

Richard L. Brandt, *The Google Guys*. Penguin/Portfolio, June 28, 2011.

Dean Takahashi, "Multimedia Masters." *Los Angeles Times*, Feb. 6, 1994.

Rachel Beck, "Girls Turn On to PC Games Tailored for Them." Associated Press, Nov. 7, 1997.

Gene Crider, "With Instant Access via the Net, Who Knows What You're Missing?" *The Times and Democrat*, Jan. 11, 2000.

Tyger Latham, "The Google Effect." *Psychology Today*, July 16, 2011.

Jacques Leslie, "The Cursor Cowboy." *Wired*, Feb. 2, 1993.

"Sales of Fax Machines in the United States: 1990 to 2010." Statista.com, July 31, 2009.

Keith Wagstaff, "The Good Ol' Days of AOL Chat Rooms." *Time*, July 6, 2012.

"'Caller ID' Stirs Debate on Phone Privacy." *The New York Times*, Feb. 11, 1990.

Bob Wisehart, "1 in 4 Has Unlisted Number." *The Charlotte News*, July 9, 1974.

American Dialect Society, www.americandialect.org.

W. Joseph Campbell, *1995: The Year the Future Began*. University of California Press, 2015.

John H. Richardson, "Children of Ted." *New York*, Dec. 11, 2018.

Michele Boldrin and David K. Levine, "Economic and Game Theory: Why Napster Is Right." dklevine.com/general/intellectual/napster.htm.

"Mark Fisher: The Slow Cancellation of the Future." YouTube clip, posted May 21, 2014.

John Perry Barlow, "A Declaration of the Independence of Cyberspace." Electronic Frontier Foundation, Feb. 8, 1996. eff.org/it/cyberspace-independence.

Gordon Welty, "Theodor Adorno and the Culture Industry." Presented to the annual meeting of the Popular Culture Association, March 30, 1984.

Neil Strauss, "Pennies That Add Up to $16.98: Why CD's Cost So Much." *The New York Times*, July 5, 1995.

Glenn Kessler, "A Cautionary Tale for Politicians: Al Gore and the 'Invention' of the Internet." *The Washington Post*, Nov. 4, 2013.

"1997 Long Distance Phone Rates Pricing Survey." Consumer Action, Feb. 1, 1997.

The Internet Show, directed by Phillip Byrd for PBS, 1995.

Downloaded, directed by Alex Winter, 2013.

Unabomber: In His Own Words, directed by Mick Grogan, 2018.

Ted Kaczynski, "Industrial Society and Its Future" (manifesto), 1995.

[alive in the superunknown]

Brad Kava, "Ghosts, Flying Saucers: Bell Knows Entertainment." *San Jose Mercury News*, June 2, 1995.

"Going to X-Tremes." *Los Angeles Daily News*, March 29, 1996.

Scott Dickensheets, "Art Bell's Strange Universe." *Las Vegas Sun*, March 4, 1997.

7. Three True Outcomes

"Sports" (1937–2017), Gallup. https://news.gallup.com/poll/4735/sports.aspx.

Ray Bradbury, *The Stories of Ray Bradbury*. Introduction by Christopher Buckley. Alfred A. Knopf, 2010.

Dayn Perry, "1994 MLB Strike 20th Anniversary: Who Was to Blame?" CBS Sports, Aug. 11, 2014.

Cliff Corcoran, "The Strike: Who Was Right, Who Was Wrong and How It Helped Baseball." SI.com, Aug. 12, 2014.

Cork Gaines, "Sports Chart of the Day: The Cost of Air Jordans and LeBrons Through the Years." *Business Insider*, Aug. 24, 2012.

Ira Berkow, "A Humbled Jordan Learns New Truth." *The New York Times*, April 11, 1994.

Dan O'Kane, "NBC's Longtime Baseball Spotlight Beginning to Dim." *Tulsa World*, July 7, 1989.

Zack Moser, "Andre Dawson and the Overlooked Collusion Cases of the 1980s." Wrigley-ville, Sept. 21, 2015.

Rob Neyer, *Rob Neyer's Big Book of Baseball Blunders*. Touchstone Books, 2006.

"Average Median Household Income in the United States from 1990 to 2018." Statista.com, 2020.

Mickey Lauria, ed., *Reconstructing Urban Regime Theory: Regulating Urban Politics in a Global Economy*. Sage Publications, 1997.

"Cleveland Indians Franchise Value from 2002 to 2020." Statista.com, 2020.

Tom Verducci, "The Best Years of Their Lives." *Sports Illustrated*, July 29, 1996.

Michael Bamberger, "Brady Hits 'em in Bunches: After Surpassing All Expectations with an Unworldly 50-Home-Run Season, What on Earth Can Brady Anderson Do for an Encore?" *Sports Illustrated*, April 14, 1997.

"Lance." *30 for 30*, ESPN Films, 2020.

Bud Selig, *For the Good of the Game: The Inside Story of the Surprising and Dramatic Transformation of Major League Baseball*. William Morrow, 2019.

Michael Haupert, "MLB's Annual Salary Leaders Since 1874." Society for American Baseball Research, 2019.

"Bag It, Michael: Jordan and the White Sox Are Embarrassing Baseball." *Sports Illustrated*, March 14, 1994.

The Last Dance, episode 7. ESPN, 2020.

Tyler Lauletta, "Michael Jordan's Minor League Manager Terry Francona Says He Could Have Made the Majors with a 3-Year Commitment to Baseball." *Insider*, May 13, 2020.

"Long Gone Summer." *30 for 30*, ESPN Films, 2020.

[vodka on the chessboard]

Michael Kramer, "Rescuing Boris." *Time*, July 15, 1996.

David Shimer, "Election Meddling in Russia: When Boris Yeltsin Asked Bill Clinton for Help." *The Washington Post*, July 26, 2020.

Thomas Graham interview. *Frontline*, 2014.

Sean Guillory, "Dermokratiya, USA." *Jacobin*, March 13, 2017.

Michael Crowley, "Putin's Revenge." *Politico*, Dec. 16, 2016.

8. Yesterday's Concepts of Tomorrow

Jeffret Leib, "Coors Chases Seagram with Own Malt Spritzer." *The Denver Post*, July 22, 1992.

Lorenzo Chavez, "Coors Malt Spritzer Gets Plaudits, Pans Zima." *Rocky Mountain News*, Aug. 7, 1992.

Leslie Savan, "Zecrets of Zima." *The Village Voice*, June 3, 1994.

Brendan Koerner, "The Long, Slow, Torturous Death of Zima." *Slate*, Nov. 26, 2008.

Stuart Elliott, "Tough Old-Style Campaign for Pepsi's 'New Age' Drink." *The New York Times*, June 12, 1992.

Jeffrey Scott, "Tapping a Trend: Coca-Cola to Test Clear Soft Drink." *The Atlanta Journal-Constitution*, Sept. 2, 1992.

"New Pepsi: Unclear." *USA Today*, Dec. 21, 1992.

Adam Bryant, "Coke Adds a Clear Cola to Its 'New Age' Stable." *The New York Times*, Dec. 15, 1992.

Annetta Miller and Karen Springen, "Clear, and Cashing In." *Newsweek*, Feb. 15, 1993.

SOURCES

Karen Heller, "A Clear Trend Has Emerged, Can't You See?" *The Philadelphia Inquirer*, Aug. 4, 1993.

Michael Kelley, "Colorless Drinks Are Just a Fad, Experts Clearly See." *The Commercial Appeal*, June 4, 1993.

Jorge Casuso, "Biosphere, Alternative to Earth, to Open Soon in Arizona." *Las Vegas Review-Journal*, Aug. 23, 1991.

Mark Nelson, "Biosphere 2: What Really Happened." *Dartmouth Alumni Magazine*, May/June 2018.

Biosphere 2: Story of Original Design and Building. Documentary short, Institute of Ecotechnics, Sept. 25, 2015.

"Biosphere 2: An American Odyssey." Retro Report, *The New York Times*, June 10, 2013.

Erik Conway, "What's in a Name? Global Warming vs. Climate Change." NASA, Dec. 5, 2008.

Matthew C. Nisbet and Teresa Myers, "Twenty Years of Public Opinion about Global Warming." *Public Opinion Quarterly* 71, no. 3 (Fall 2007).

Rebecca Reider, *Dreaming the Biosphere: The Theater of All Possibilities.* University of New Mexico Press, 2009.

Joel Achenbach, "Biosphere 2: Bogus New World." *The Washington Post*, Jan. 8, 1992.

Carl Zimmer, "The Lost History of Biosphere 2." *The New York Times*, March 31, 2019.

Curt Suplee, "Brave Small World." *The Washington Post*, Jan. 21, 1990.

William J. Broad, "After 10,000 Mistakes, Biosphere Is in Hot Pursuit of Credibility." *The New York Times*, Sept. 22, 1992.

Spaceship Earth, documentary directed by Matt Wolf, 2020.

William J. Broad, "As Biosphere Is Sealed, Its Patron Reflects on Life." *The New York Times*, Sept. 24, 1991.

William J. Broad, "Biosphere Gets Pure Oxygen to Combat Health Woes." *The New York Times*, Jan. 26, 1993.

William J. Broad, "Too Rich a Soil: Scientists Find the Flaw That Undid the Biosphere." *The New York Times*, Oct. 5, 1993.

Jim Erickson, "The Man Who Ran the Biosphere: Co-founder Allen Called Guru; 'A Commune Became a Cult.'" *The Arizona Daily Star*, July 17, 1994.

Eric Stern, "Manager Vowed Revenge on Alling, Her Lawyer Says." *Tucson Citizen*, May 24, 1996.

Jane Poynter interview ("Biosphere 2 crewmember & author Jane Poynter interview"), YouTube clip, posted Sept. 19, 2006. https://www.youtube.com/watch?v=bPK05evoFHw.

Heaven's Gate: The Cult of Cults. HBO/CNN miniseries, 2020.

Christine Corcos, Isabel Corcos, and Brian Stockoff, "Double-Take: A Second Look at Cloning, Science Fiction and Law." *Louisiana Law Review* 59 (Summer 1999).

Giovanni Maio, "Cloning in the Media and Popular Culture." EMBO Reports, March 7, 2006.

"The Story of Dolly the Cloned Sheep." Retro Report, *The New York Times*, Oct. 14, 2013.

Karen Weintraub, "20 years after Dolly the Sheep Led the Way—Where Is Cloning Now?" *Scientific American*, July 5, 2016.

Gina Kolata, "Scientist Reports First Cloning Ever of Adult Mammal." *The New York Times*, Feb. 23, 1997.

"President Proposes Human Cloning Ban." *Science*, June 8, 1997.

Bryan Curtis, "The Cult of Jurassic Park." *Grantland*, Nov. 7, 2011.

"So Who Exactly Is Richard Seed?" *New Scientist*, Jan. 17, 1998.

"Cloning Dolly the Sheep." AnimalResearch.Info, Nov. 3, 2014.

David Fricke, "People of the Year: Thom Yorke of Radiohead." *Rolling Stone*, Dec. 14, 2000.

[the importance of being earnest]

William Manchester, *A World Lit Only by Fire: The Medieval Mind and the Renaissance*. Little, Brown, 1992.

Andy Smith, "Shoulders to Hold Party for CD Release." *Austin American-Statesman*, Sept. 30, 1993.

David Daley, "Young Author's Call for Sincerity Strikes a Nerve." *The Hartford Courant*, Jan. 2, 2000.

"The New Sincerity?" *The Des Moines Register*, Aug. 14, 1991.

Peter W. Kaplan and Peter Stevenson, "Wipe That Smirk off Your Face." *Esquire*, Sept. 1, 1991.

James C. Collins, *Film Theory Goes to the Movies*. Psychology Press, 1993.

9. Sauropods

David Boaz, "Young People Like 'Socialism,' but Do They Know What It Is?" *National Review*, Oct. 25, 2018.

Morgan Gstalter, "7 in 10 Millennials Say They Would Vote for a Socialist: Poll." *The Hill*, Oct. 28, 2019.

Dave Paulson, "Story Behind the Song: 'Achy Breaky Heart.'" *The Tennessean*, May 3, 2019.

Robert Przybylo, "Collected Wisdom: How Milt Bassett Changed Garth Brooks' Life." *The Oklahoman*, July 24, 2010.

Billy Ray Cyrus interview, *MTV News*, 1992.

"Billy Ray's Big Check." *Set It Straight with Midland* podcast, episode 10, Nov. 27, 2019.

"Kurt Cobain on Identity." *Blank on Blank*, interview with Jon Savage, July 22, 1993.

Anthony DeCurtis, "Garth Brooks: Ropin' the Whirlwind." *Rolling Stone*, April 1, 1993.

Eric Weisbard, "Review: Garth Brooks, *Fresh Horses*." *Spin*, Feb. 1996.

Garth Brooks: The Road I'm On, Netflix documentary miniseries, 2020.

Mike Duffy, "Sitcoms' Lack of Diversity Obvious as Black and White." *Knight-Ridder Tribune*, March 6, 1996.

Jethro Nededog, "How the *Friends* Cast Nabbed Their Insane Salaries of $1 Million per Episode." *Business Insider*, Oct. 6, 2016.

Brian Eggert, review of *Titanic*. *Deep Focus Review*, Sept. 8, 2019.

Miguel Cima, "17 Behind-the-Scenes Secrets You Didn't Know about *Titanic*." *Business Insider*, April 2, 2018.

Sarah Marshall, "The Incredible True Story of How *Titanic* Got Made." *BuzzFeed*, Dec. 17, 2017.

Paul Grainge, *Brand Hollywood: Selling Entertainment in a Global Media Age*. Routledge, 2008.

James Rampton, "James Cameron: My Titanic Obsession." *The Independent*, Aug. 9, 2005.

Christopher Goodwin, "James Cameron: From Titanic to Avatar." *The Times* (London), Nov. 8, 2009.

Tom Brueggemann, "Gamechangers in Box Office History." *IndieWire*, March 29, 2020.

Sherri Winston, "Leomania." Fort Lauderdale *Sun Sentinel*, May 5, 1998.

Nathan Cobb, "Loving Leo." *The Boston Globe*, April 22, 1998.

Zeynep Yenisey, "The Untold Story of Don's Plum." *Maxim*, Aug. 13, 2019.

Colin Harrison, *American Culture in the 1990s*. Edinburgh University Press, 2010.

Sean Cubitt, *The Cinema Effect*. MIT Press, 2004.

Nielsen Media Research. 2020.

SOURCES

Anna McCarthy, *Ambient Television: Visual Culture and Public Space*. Duke University Press, 2001.

"National Television Penetration Trends." Television Bureau of Advertising, 2016.

"Television." *AdAge Encyclopedia*, Sept. 15, 2003.

Ed Bark, "30 Seconds on Seinfeld? That Will be $490,000." *Dallas Morning News*, reprinted in *Chicago Tribune*, Oct. 2, 1995.

Josef Adalian, "The Architects of NBC's Classic Must-See Lineup Reveal How *Friends* and *ER* Became Legends." *Vulture*, Sept. 18, 2019.

[giving the people what they want, except that they don't]

Kathleen Craughwell, "It's a Long Time to Go for a Movie Far, Far Away." *Los Angeles Times*, April 10, 1999.

Bernard Weinraub, "Now Playing: Two New Minutes of *Star Wars*." *The New York Times*, Nov. 23, 1998.

10. A Two-Dimensional Fourth Dimension

Stephanie Marriott, *Live Television: Time, Space and the Broadcast Event*. SAGE, 2007.

Paddy Scannell, *Television and the Meaning of "Live."* Polity Press, 2014.

W. Joseph Campbell, *1995: The Year the Future Began*. University of California Press, 2015.

Bruce Haring, "'The Matrix' Trilogy Is about Being Transgender, Says Co-Director Lilly Wachowski." *Deadline*, Aug. 8, 2020.

Susan Orlean, "Keanu Reeves (in Theory)." *The New Yorker*, March 14, 1994.

"What Did Baudrillard Think about *The Matrix*?" YouTube clip, posted Sept. 10, 2019, by Jones Ceika.

Richard Bernstein, *Dictatorship of Virtue*. Vintage Books, 1995.

Andrew Cohen, "Tyranny, from Tim McVeigh to Ginny Thomas." *The Atlantic*, March 18, 2010.

Jeremy Schwartz, "Lessons for Media Still Echo from Waco Tragedy." *Austin American-Statesman*, April 18, 2018, updated Sept. 25, 2018.

Michael Lynch, "What Happened at Waco?" *Reason*, Oct. 4, 1999.

Waco: The Rules of Engagement, documentary directed by William Gazecki, 1997.

Jon Ronson, *Them: Adventures with Extremists*. Picador Press, 2001.

"Clarence Thomas: Supreme Court Nomination Hearings from PBS *NewsHour* and EMK Institute." YouTube clip, no date.

"Other Voices." *News Herald*, Oct. 16, 1991.

"Polls Find Most Back Thomas." Associated Press, Oct. 14, 1991.

Brian Raftery, *Best. Movie. Year. Ever.: How 1999 Blew Up the Big Screen*. Simon & Schuster, 1999.

"Nomination of Judge Clarence Thomas to Be Associate Justice of the Supreme Court of the United States," hearing transcript, U.S. Committee on the Judiciary, Oct. 11, 12, and 13, 1991. U.S. Government Printing Office, 1993.

Janie Velenica, "Americans Didn't Believe Anita Hill." *FiveThirtyEight*, Sept. 17, 2018.

Barry S. Roberts and Richard A. Mann, "Sexual Harassment in the Workplace: A Primer." *Akron Law Review* 29, no. 2 (1996).

Carl Bialik, "Most Black People Now Think O.J. Was Guilty." *FiveThirtyEight*, 2016.

Jasmine Brown, Katie Muldowney, and Lauren Effron, "What OJ Simpson Juror Thinks of Simpson Now, Two Decades after Criminal Trial." ABC News, July 19, 2017.

Robyn L. Cohen, "Prisoners in 1990." U.S. Department of Justice, May 1991.

Allen J. Beck and Paige M. Harrison, "Prisoners in 2000." U.S. Department of Justice, August 2001.

Christopher B. Mueller, "Introduction: O. J. Simpson and the Criminal Justice System on Trial." *University of Colorado Law Review*, 1996.

"Turner-Murdoch Feud Escalates into Lawsuit." *Tallahassee Democrat*, Oct. 10, 1996.

Frazier Moore, "Cable's MSNBC Off to a Fast Start." Associated Press, Aug. 8, 1996.

"Cable News Prime Time Viewership." Pew Research Center, March 13, 2006.

Stefano DellaVigna and Ethan Kaplan, "The Fox News Effect: Media Bias and Voting." NBER Working Paper 12169, April 2006. nber.org/papers/w12169.

Gillian Brockell, "Bullies and Black Trench Coats: The Columbine Shooting's Most Dangerous Myths." *The Washington Post*, April 20, 2019.

Trinity Hartman, "Nationwide, Teens Who Don't Fit In Now Live in Fear." *The Charlotte Observer*, April 24, 1999.

Retrontario, Sept. 11, 2020.

[the spin doctors]

Sabastian Mallaby, *The Man Who Knew: The Life and Times of Alan Greenspan*. Penguin Press, 2016.

"Was Alan Greenspan a Hero or a Villain?" Sebastian Mallaby interview. *Conversations with Jim Zirin*. PBS, July 6, 2017.

Alex Pollack, "Alan Greenspan's 'Irrational Exuberance': Then and Now." *Real Clear Markets*, Aug. 16, 2017.

Dana Skrebneski, "Oprah, Act Two." *Entertainment Weekly*, Aug. 9, 1994.

Randy J. Taraborrelli, "How Oprah Does It All." *Redbook*, Aug. 1996.

"Bathos and Credibility." *The Wall Street Journal*, Aug. 30, 1996.

Debra Dickerson, "A Woman's Woman." *U.S. News & World Report*, Aug. 29, 1997.

Michael Jackson Talks to Oprah . . . Live. ABC TV special, Feb. 10, 1993.

11. I Feel the Pain of Everyone, Then I Feel Nothing

Jay Martel, "The Perils of Pauly." *Rolling Stone*, July 9, 1992.

WTF with Marc Maron (podcast), guest Jerry Seinfeld, June 8, 2020.

Patrick Andelic, "Unlike Most Former Presidents, Bill Clinton Is Becoming Increasingly Unpopular." *Quartz*, January 18, 2018.

Jeffrey M. Jones, "Hillary Clinton Favorable Rating at New Low." Gallup, Dec. 19, 2017.

Adrienne Lafrance, "The Truth About Bill Clinton's E-mails." *The Atlantic*, March 12, 2015.

Charles Peters, "A Neoliberal's Manifesto." *Washington Monthly*, May 1983.

Stephen Metcalf, "Neoliberalism: The Idea That Swallowed the World." *The Guardian*, Aug. 18, 2017.

Lily Geismer, "Democrats and Neoliberalism." *Vox*, July 11, 2019.

Christopher S. Wren, "McVeigh Is Executed for Oklahoma City Bombing." *The New York Times*, June 11, 2001.

Michael Collins, "Hillary Clinton's Ties to Impeachment Inquiries against Three Presidents." *USA Today*, Oct. 26, 2019.

Anthony Salvanto and Jennifer DePinto, "George H. W. Bush: The Public's View of Him During His Presidency." CBS News, Dec. 4, 2018.

Bill Clinton, luncheon address to American Society of Newspaper Editors. Transcript, April 13, 1994.

"The History of Campaign Spending." Metrocosm, August 2, 2015.

"The Rise and Resounding Demise of the Clinton Plan." *Health Affairs*, Spring 1995.

Dick Morris interview with Chris Bury, "The Clinton Years," *Frontline*, June 2000.

SOURCES

A Century of the Self. BBC documentary miniseries, 2002.

Steve Erickson, *American Nomad*. Henry Holt, 1997.

Richard Stengel and Eric Pooley, "Master of the Message." *Time*, Nov. 6, 1996.

Richard L. Berke, "Call-Girl Story Costs President a Key Strategist." *The New York Times*, Aug. 30, 1996.

Bill Clinton, Oklahoma Bombing Memorial Prayer Service Address, April 23, 1995.

Neil Swidey, "How Democrats Would Be Better Off If Bill Clinton Had Never Been President." *Globe Magazine*, July 10, 2018.

Tom Cotton, "Clinton's Politicking Is Sincere." *The Harvard Crimson*, Oct. 19, 1996.

Michael Kruse, "The TV Interview That Haunts Hillary Clinton." *Politico Magazine*, Sept. 23, 2016.

Eric Anderson, "Five Myths about Cheating." *The Washington Post*, Feb. 13, 2012.

"Declaration of Gennifer G. Flowers." *The Washington Post*, March 13, 1998.

Public Papers of the Presidents of the United States, William J. Clinton. Federal Register, National Archives and Records Administration, 1995.

Russell L. Riley, "Bill Clinton: Life before the Presidency." *U.S Presidents*. Miller Center, University of Virginia.

Jim Jerome, "A Place Called Home." *People*, Jan. 11, 1993.

Michael Waldman, *POTUS Speaks: Finding the Words That Defined the Clinton Presidency*. Simon & Schuster, 2000.

Robert S. V. Baer, "The Making of Bill Clinton." *U.S. News & World Report*, March 3, 1992.

Garry Wills, "Clinton's Forgotten Childhood." *Time*, June 8, 1992.

George Will, "When Private Behavior Becomes a Public Matter." *Austin American-Statesman*, August 15, 1991.

Interview with Bill and Hillary Rodham Clinton, *60 Minutes*, Jan. 26, 1992.

Matthew Cooper and Donald Baer, "Bill Clinton's Hidden Life: An Interview with Bill Clinton." *U.S. News & World Report*, Oct. 14, 1992.

Taylor Branch, "Clinton without Apologies." *Esquire*, Sept. 1996.

Toni Morrison, "On the First Black President." *The New Yorker*, Oct. 5, 1998.

Karen Sebold, "How the Social Context of Bill Clinton's Childhood Shaped His Personality: Using Oral History Interviews of His Childhood Peers and Relatives." Master's thesis, University of Arkansas, 2008.

David Maraniss, *First in His Class: A Biography of Bill Clinton*. Simon & Schuster, 1995.

Stephanie Li, "The Parallel Lives of Bill Clinton." *American Literary History* 24, no. 3 (Fall 2012), 509–22.

Bill Clinton, *My Life*. Alfred A. Knopf, 2004.

The Starr Report. Prima Publishing, 1998.

Joe Nick Patoski, *The Dallas Cowboys*. Little, Brown, 2012.

Jeremy D. Larson, review of *The Battle of Los Angeles*. Pitchfork, Aug. 9, 2020.

Richard Andrew Voeltz, "How Well Has *American Beauty* Aged? A Critical Review of the Suburban Film Genre." *49th Parallel* 39 (2017).

Roger Ebert, "A Seat in the Balcony with Bill Clinton." RogerEbert.com, Feb. 3, 2000.

Sarah Fonder, "Fifteen Years Later, 'American Beauty' Is Just a Bad, Pretty Movie." *Decider*, Sept. 8, 2014.

[just try it and see what happens]

Mal Florence, "Morning Briefing." *Los Angeles Times*, Oct. 25, 2000.

David T. Z. Mindich, *The Mediated World: A New Approach to Mass Communication and Culture*. Rowman & Littlefield, 2020.

Anthony Bozza, "Eminem Blows Up." *Rolling Stone*, April 29, 1999.

Charles P. Pierce, "Tiger Woods, the Man. Amen." *GQ*, April 1997.

Jeff Benedict and Arman Keteyian, *Tiger Woods*. Simon & Schuster, 2019.

Emily Sollie, "Masters Champions Meals." *The Augusta Chronicle*, 1999.

12. The End of the Decade, the End of Decades

Gwen Knapp, "Reaction Shows Boxing Industry's Hypocrisy." *San Francisco Examiner*, July 1, 1997.

"Chasing Tyson." *30 for 30*, directed by Steve Cantor, ESPN Films, 2015.

"The Y2K Bug: Much Ado About Nothing." Retro Report, *The New York Times*, May 30, 2013. youtube.com/watch?v=SoGNiHV09BU.

Ted Rose, "Who Invented Y2K and Why Did It Become So Universally Popular?" *Slate/The Baltimore Sun*, Dec. 22, 1999.

Dennis Dutton, "It's Always the End of the World as We Know It." *The New York Times*, Dec. 31, 2009.

"CBS Poll: Y2K Bug Only a Pest." CBS News, July 20, 1999.

Frank Newport, "American Concern About Y2K Continues to Drop." Gallup News Service, Dec. 22, 1999.

Robert Sam Anson, "The Y2K Nightmare." *Vanity Fair*, January 1999.

Zachary Loeb, "The Lessons of Y2K, 20 Years Later." *The Washington Post*, Dec. 30, 2019.

Andrew Marshall, "America Stocks Up on Guns and Honey for Y2K." *The Independent*, July 18, 1999.

Martyn Thomas, "The Millennium Bug Was Real—and 20 Years Later We Face the Same Threats." *The Guardian*, Dec. 31, 2019.

Rory Cellan-Jones, "Millennium Bug—Was It a Myth?" BBC News, Aug. 6, 2018.

"Minor Bug Problems Arise." BBC News, Jan. 1, 2000.

Andrew Pollack, "Chips Are Hidden in Washing Machines, Microwaves and Even Reservoirs." *The New York Times*, Jan. 4, 1999.

"Y2K Bug," updated by Adam Augustyn. *Encyclopædia Britannica*.

Andrew Perrin and Maeve Duggan, "Americans' Internet Access: 2000–2015." Pew Research Center, June 26, 2015.

David W. Moore, "Little Difference Between Gore and Bush on Important Dimensions in Election." Gallup News Service, May 8, 2000.

"More Voters Say It Really Matters . . ." Pew Research Center, Aug. 13, 2020.

Thomas E. Mann, "Reflections on the 2000 Presidential Election." Brookings Institution, Jan. 1, 2001.

Gary W. Cox and Jonathan Rodden, "Demonization." Research Group on Political Institutions and Economic Policy, Harvard University, 2019.

Bill Scher, "Nader Elected Bush: Why We Shouldn't Forget." *RealClear Politics*, May 31, 2016.

"The 2000 Presidential Election—A Mid-Year Gallup Report." Gallup News Service, June 22, 2000.

Gerald M. Pomper, "The 2000 Presidential Election: Why Gore Lost." *Political Science Quarterly* 116, no. 2 (Summer 2001).

Jim Rutenberg, "The 2000 Campaign: The Viewers—Number of Debate Viewers Rises from the First but Remains Low." *The New York Times*, Oct. 19. 2000.

Drew Desilver, "5 Facts about Presidential and Vice Presidential Debates." Pew Research: Fact Tank, Aug. 20, 2020.

Martin Kettle, "Florida 'Recounts' Make Gore Winner." *The Guardian*, Jan. 28, 2001.

Yascha Mounk, "The Inverted Likability Test." *The Atlantic*, Jan. 2, 2020.

SOURCES

"Bush Acknowledges 1976 DUI Charge." CNN, Nov. 2, 2000.

Erica J. Seifert, *The Politics of Authenticity in Presidential Campaigns, 1976–2008*. McFarland, 2012.

"Crime in the United States, 2000." Federal Bureau of Investigation press release, 2000.

Richard Pérez-Peña, "The 2000 Elections: Tennessee; Loss in Home State Leaves Gore Depending on Florida." *The New York Times*, Nov. 9, 2000.

Barry C. Burden, "Ralph Nader's Campaign Strategy in the 2000 U.S. Presidential Election." *American Politics Research* 33, no. 5 (Sept. 2005).

Jack W. Germond and Jules Witcover, "Ventura Knows of Voting for Spoilers." *The Baltimore Sun*, Nov. 8, 2000.

"Media Recount: Bush Won the 2000 Election." *PBS: Nation*, April 3, 2001.

Edward Foley, "George W. Bush vs. Al Gore, 15 Years Later: We Really Did Inaugurate the Wrong Guy." *Salon*, Dec. 19. 2015.

Erin Blakemore, "How Sandra Day O'Connor's Swing Vote Decided the 2000 Election." The History Channel, Oct. 28, 2018.

Darryl Lindsey, "Thousands Protest Bush's Inauguration." *Salon*, Jan. 21, 2000.

Dr. Tim Luijkx and Dr. Bruno Di Muzio, "Temporal Pole." *Radiopaedia*.

Scott Parrish, "Are Suitcase Nukes on the Loose?" Middlebury Institute of International Studies at Monterey, Nov. 1997.

"Ebola Virus Disease." World Health Organization, Sept. 2014.

"Video Shows bin Laden Urging Muslims to Prepare for Fighting." CNN World, June 21, 2001.

William J. Brod, "Scientists Say Frenzy over Shark Attacks Is Unwarranted." *The New York Times*, Sept. 5, 2001.

John Thrasher, "11 Things to Know About the Chandra Levy Murder." *Oxygen*, March 22, 2018.

"Newspapers Fact Sheet." Pew Research Center, July 9, 2019.

Bill Carter, "Nightly News Feels Pinch of 24-Hour News." *The New York Times*, April 14, 2003.

"Nightly Evening News Ratings." Pew Research Center, March 13, 2006.

Index

3 1170 01154 3422